KT-172-642

Entertaining at Home

Rachel Allen

Entertaining at Home

Collins

First published in 2010 by Collins

HarperCollins Publishers
77–85 Fulham Palace Road
London W6 8JB

www.harpercollins.co.uk

14 13 12 11 10
9 8 7 6 5 4 3 2 1

Text © Rachel Allen, 2010
Photographs © Kate Whitaker, 2010

Rachel Allen asserts her moral right to be
identified as the author of this work.

A catalogue record for this book is available
from the British Library.

ISBN: 978-0-00-730903-0

Design: Smith & Gilmour, London
Colour reproduction by Dot Gradations
Printed and bound in Germany by Mohn Media

All rights reserved. No parts of this publication may be
reproduced, stored in a retrieval system or transmitted,
in any form or by any means, electronic, mechanical,
photocopying, recording or otherwise, without the
prior permission of the publishers.

CONTENTS

Introduction

....

Friends, family, good food, good times – this is what entertaining is all about. It can be as relaxed as flopping down on the sofa with a few friends to share nibbles and drinks, or as formal as getting out your best china and ironing your tablecloth for a three-course meal. How you choose to share your time and your cooking creations with your loved ones is entirely up to you. What each kind of gathering has in common, however, is a happy, welcoming atmosphere, and the main ingredient for that is you.

The kind of entertaining my family tends to do at home is most often spontaneous and casual. Maybe there's a big pot of cassoulet bubbling away gently in the oven and we'll realise there's enough to share, so after a phone call or two we find ourselves with several hungry friends arriving at the door with bottles in hand. But there are also times when we'll have a larger gathering or a particularly special evening when we want to push the boat out and make more of an effort with both the food and the table decorations.

In this book I hope to give you the inspiration and tools you will need to entertain for any gathering, whether relaxed and intimate or a great big bash, while actually getting to enjoy yourself as well. It doesn't matter if you're a seasoned cook or a complete novice in the kitchen; I've tried to give you achievable recipes that take the mystery and complication out of cooking for a special occasion. And you'll find many of the recipes easy enough to cook to make *any* meal a special occasion.

Your guests

Whatever sort of entertaining you are doing, do let your friends know what kind of party it is, whether a casual plate-in-your-hand-type supper, a stand-around evening of cocktails and canapés, or a more chi-chi dressy affair. There's nothing worse than turning up in jeans only to find that everyone else is in a little black number.

Be sure to always ask about food allergies or other dietary requirements. It's often easier to make the same food for everyone, so don't plan your food until you know what your limitations are. Of course, if your plans are to have a barbecue or a big roast, you may need to prepare something special for your vegetarian guests, but for the most part, simple allergies shouldn't be such a problem that everyone has to have a limited menu. There are so many options – it's not as scary as you think.

If you're planning a very special occasion where you're either cooking a more elaborate meal or you have a large crowd, you may wish to send out proper invitations with an RSVP so that you know exactly how many you're cooking for before you do your shopping.

On the day of your party, think about having nibbles such as nuts or canapés ready to tide everyone over until all your guests have arrived – or to keep them fed if things are running late in the kitchen!

Your home

If you are doing more grown up, or 'formal' entertaining, take the time to think about atmosphere and how to create a welcoming setting so your guests feel you've made a little extra effort to make them feel special and relaxed. Little touches such as candles or fairy lights rather than harsh lighting from above can really help set the scene. Besides, who (or indeed what room) doesn't look better in the soft glow of candlelight?

Flowers make any home look more dressed up, but that doesn't necessarily mean investing in bouquets from the florist. Even just some little vases or jars of hand-picked flowers from your garden add a thoughtful touch. And you don't need to limit them to the table – put them in the kitchen, living room, even the bathroom.

Your table

If you're having a larger group of people and are feeling creative (and have the time), you may even wish to make table decorations and/or place settings for each of your guests. It also means you can control who sits next to who! It's great fun to make name tags and people love taking them home. Be as creative as you wish. Below are some of my favourite table-decorating ideas:

* Everyone loves place cards! Try old-fashioned packing labels with the guest's name written on and tied around a napkin or the base of a wine glass, or even pierced through onto a satay stick. Or if you're feeling ambitious, make cookies or biscuits for each guest with their name written in icing or chocolate.

* If you don't have napkin rings, just tie a pretty piece of ribbon around your napkins, perhaps in different colours for each napkin. To jazz it up further, you can tie on fresh rosemary and/or bread sticks.

* For a really special event, place mini wrapped presents on each place, tied up with twine or ribbon and with a name tag.

* For a seaside theme try candles in oyster or scallop shells or sand in the bottom of glass candle holders or pretty glass jars with tea lights; pebbles, slate or driftwood pieces with guest's names in chalk; shells on the table.

* For a holiday splash, place Christmas baubles in little glasses or shallow tumblers around the table; spray some holly lightly with glitter, place small branches in a flower vase with baubles hanging off (place sand in the bottom to keep the branches in place). You can write guests' names on bay, holly or ivy leaves with gold or silver pen.

* At Easter, you can try a similar trick – from small branches hang painted eggs. You can also spray the branches silver or gold. You could even do a mini version with quail's eggs! Place mini pastel-coloured Easter eggs or little chicks around the table.

* In autumn, place pumpkins and squashes in groups on the table and/or outside the front door.

* For national holidays, place little flags at each setting or down the centre of the table.

* For your floral arrangements, try not to have one enormous bouquet in the middle of your table. Instead, make smaller arrangements in lots of small glass holders of different sizes so your guests can see over them. Or try small terracotta pots of herbs or little flowering plants, or put miniature bulbs, such as bluebells or narcissus, in a pot or glass vase for a temporary display. Avoid overly scented flowers, which may overpower your food.

SETTING THE TABLE

Not everyone has an extensive range of cutlery to set a formal place setting, so don't panic about

doing this 'properly'. But I often do get asked, 'Where should the water glass go?' or 'Where should I put a side plate?', so if you want to set a fancy table, here is the general thinking on how your place setting should look:

Dessert fork and spoon   Water   Red wine   White wine

Bread plate   Starter fork Main course fork   Plate and napkin   Main course knife Starter knife Soup spoon

What to serve?

Choosing your menu is the first important step to a good party. More often than not in planning what you serve, seasonality is the key. But menu planning is also about choosing dishes that will both complement each other and be enjoyable to eat together. So avoid a repetition of ingredients from course to course, as well as ensuring you have different colours and textures of food throughout. Ensure, too, that each of the elements when added up are not too heavy.

As before, be sure to get any dietary restrictions from your guests well in advance of your planning. Don't feel you need to plan three big fancy dishes – one show stopper will be enough to create a memorable meal if you are time-starved but still want to impress. Your other courses (should you choose to serve them) can then be less complicated. You also don't need to serve fancy dishes just because you're having guests – simple food beautifully presented in your warm loving home can have just as much of an impact, if not more so.

At the end of each chapter I have grouped together my favourite recipe combinations or advice for preparation to make well-balanced menus in order to help simplify your planning.

PREPARING AHEAD

Do remember that entertaining should be about you having a good time too, so the more prepared you are, the easier and more fun it will be. Much to my husband's complete puzzlement, I find list-making and even an 'order of work' (writing out in what order and when things should be prepared and cooked) a great help.

For stress-free entertaining, choose your menu well in advance rather than on the day or the day before. Shopping ahead is always going to make things easier! Be sure to include some recipes that can be prepared in advance so you can get ahead and not be stuck at the stove while your friends are all having a great time without you. If you are making something quite ambitious for a main course, then make sure your starter or dessert is easier to prepare. I have included lots of recipes for the time-poor, sweet-toothed among you.

It sounds so obvious, but write down exactly what you need, including any suggested cookware sizes, then check it very carefully so you can be certain you have everything you need once you get to the till.

On the day itself, set plenty of time aside to get yourself ready. Even if you're still putting things in the oven when your guests arrive, you want to feel ready to entertain. Easier said than done sometimes, but this is where working out the timings in advance will come in handy.

Also don't forget to place the basics on the table ahead of your guests arriving, like bread and butter or olive oil, salt and pepper, or any sauces you may need. You don't want to have to keep jumping up and running to the kitchen.

One very important point to make is that entertaining does not have to be costly. Clever, seasonal shopping, and even a bit of foraging if you have the time and the resource (even if just for flowers), can lead to a great get-together. Why not invite your friends over for a relaxed casserole, or ask them to each bring a dish? Either tell people what you would like them to bring (a salad, a dessert) or let them bring what they want for a 'pot-luck' party – though this may not be everyone's idea of a balanced meal! You can give them a general idea of what you want them to bring (a starter or a main, for example), so you don't end up with ten desserts and no dinner…

If you want to have a more formal meal on a budget, think about simple but delicious stews, pasta or vegetarian dishes. Entertaining doesn't have to be fancy – but just a little thought, such as laying the table beforehand, can make it feel special. If you're having a special celebration but don't want to splurge on Champagne, try less expensive, but still delicious, Prosecco or Cava. Or make it go further by making Champagne cocktails such as buck's fizz or Bellinis.

You also needn't feel pressure to serve a lavish three-course meal – one lovely main and a dessert is just as special.

Drinks

Not everyone is a wine expert. In fact, most people can feel a little intimidated when it comes to serving the 'right' wine with their meals. The easiest way to get around the stress of what to serve is to go to a good wine merchant and ask them to suggest not only what to serve with your meal, but how much to serve per person – which is, of course, entirely subjective, but the experts will take this into account! If you're planning a large party, wine merchants also often offer discounts on multiple bottles, so don't be afraid to ask what deals they have going for bulk purchases. For bigger parties, they may also supply returnable wine or champagne glasses free of charge. Just ask!

If you choose to serve cocktails, try to limit these to one or two, unless you really enjoy acting as bartender and/or have a big budget.

Be sure to have soft options for those who don't drink alcohol. Even if you just posh-up a big jug of ice water by adding lemon or lime, or mint – or even coriander.

Keeping calm …

Don't be afraid to ask for help! Nobody expects you to be a superhero, so if you need help chopping, recruit a friend or family member. If you're having a big party, enlist a few people to be on standby to pass things around and pick things up as the evening progresses. You don't have to do it all single-handedly.

One handy but easily forgotten tip when preparing is to clean as you go along so that your guests don't arrive to a mess and so you have an easier clean-up afterwards. Chuck out packaging, put things in the dishwasher and wash-up bowls or utensils. It'll also help keep your head clear if your space is as clutter-free as possible.

Try to remember that part of the fun of entertaining is the preparation itself. So crank up the music, pour yourself a glass, and go for it! Remember, everyone will appreciate your hard work and probably only you will notice if something isn't quite as you expected. It doesn't have to be perfect, it's all about the having fun and sharing great times with those you love. Be prepared to have a few mishaps and you'll have a much better time!

I hope this book helps you create many memorable meals. Above all, enjoy!

BRUNCH

Baked eggs with creamy kale
Wild mushrooms on toast with chive hollandaise
Citrus honeyed fruit
Sweetcorn fritters with mango and avocado salsa
Hot buttered oysters on toast
Lazy weekend Bloody Mary
Isaac's frittata

LUNCH

Spinach soup with rosemary oil
Skirt steak with spicy potatoes
Oven-baked courgette tortilla
Stir-fried tofu with noodles
Celeriac soup with roasted hazelnuts
Tuscan beans on toast
Creamy fish pie with mushrooms, cucumber and leeks
Tagliatelle with smoked salmon and avocado
Clams marinara
Crab bisque
Salade Niçoise
Chicken and cabbage salad
Thai noodle broth
Pork rillettes
Game terrine with celeriac remoulade
Penne with asparagus and Parma ham
Venison sausages with celeriac purée
Stocks

DESSERTS

Polenta, orange and almond cake
Almond meringue with apricot purée
Orange meringue roulade
Apple snow with shortbread biscuits
Mango and raspberry Bellinis
Apple and blackberry bread and butter pudding

BRUNCHES AND LUNCHES

Getting together with friends and family doesn't always mean
'dinner'. You can have just as special a meal before the sun goes down.
Birthdays, Mother's Day, or just getting together with the girls are reason
enough to plan a nice meal together. Brunch is one of my favourite meals –
it allows you to put a little extra something into what is essentially a late
breakfast, and it means you can have a sneaky glass of something fizzy
or a Bloody Mary before noon! Here you'll find many ideas for easy
and special daytime meals.

Baked eggs with creamy kale

....

SERVES 6
VEGETARIAN

25g (1oz) butter
900g (2lb) kale with stalks
   removed before weighing
Salt and ground black pepper
350ml (12fl oz) single or
   regular cream
Pinch of freshly grated
   nutmeg
6 eggs
350g (12oz) Glebe Brethan
   or Gruyère cheese, grated

Six 100ml (3½fl oz) ramekins
   or ovenproof dishes

This is delicious for brunch. If you can't get kale, use spinach. I love to use the Irish farmhouse cheese Glebe Brethan for its delicious flavour and melting texture, but you can use Gruyère instead.

1 Preheat the oven to 180°C (350°F), Gas mark 4.

2 Add the butter to a large wide frying pan and place over a medium heat. Add the kale and season with salt and pepper. As soon as the kale wilts and becomes tender, add the cream and nutmeg, then allow to bubble for 3–5 minutes until thickened.

3 Divide the kale between the ramekins or dishes, placing it around the inside of each dish and leaving a small well in the centre.

4 Break one egg into each dish and sprinkle the grated cheese over the top. Bake in the oven for 8–10 minutes or until golden on top and bubbling around the edges. Scatter over a little pepper and serve immediately with a little toast on the side.

Wild mushrooms on toast with chive hollandaise

....

3 generous handful of
    wild mushrooms
50g (2oz) butter, plus
    extra for spreading
6 slices of bread
100ml (3½ fl oz) chive
    hollandaise (see below)

For the chive hollandaise
2 egg yolks
100g (4oz) butter, diced
Squeeze of lemon juice
1–2 tbsp chopped chives
Salt and ground black pepper

I like to use chanterelles or oyster mushrooms for this recipe. Chanterelles are one of my favourite mushrooms. They have a huge amount of flavour and their colour is like liquid gold. Here they transform what is essentially just mushrooms on toast into a luxurious breakfast treat.

1 First make the hollandaise sauce following the instructions on page 159, stirring the chopped chives into the cooked sauce just before seasoning,

2 Next carefully clean the mushrooms. The best way to do this is to brush off any soil or debris with a pastry brush. Avoid washing them as this will make them soggy during cooking.

3 Place a large frying pan on a high heat and allow it to get quite hot. Add the butter and when it has melted and starts to foam, tip in the mushrooms. Season with salt and pepper and cook for 3–5 minutes, tossing regularly.

4 Meanwhile, toast the bread and spread with butter.

5 When the mushrooms are cooked, taste for seasoning then arrange on top of the hot buttered toast, drizzle with the chive hollandaise and serve immediately.

Citrus honeyed fruit

....

Juice of 1–2 limes
1–2 tbsp runny honey
2–3 tsp chopped mint
    (optional)
750g (1lb 10oz) mixed fruit,
    such as melon, bananas,
    raspberries, pineapple

The sweet-sour combination of lime juice and honey is a lovely way to enhance the flavours of some fruit. I like to add chopped mint for a fresh taste. This is ideal for serving at breakfast.

1 In a large bowl, mix together the lime juice, honey and mint (if using). Peel any of the larger fruit (if necessary) and cut into bite-sized pieces. Add all the fruit to the bowl and stir to cover.

2 Leave to macerate for 10–15 minutes before serving.

Sweetcorn fritters with mango and avocado salsa

....

MAKES 15–20 FRITTERS
SERVES 4–6
VEGETARIAN

2 eggs, separated
3 tbsp milk
50g (2oz) plain flour
1 tsp baking powder
½ tsp salt
200g (7oz) tinned or frozen
   and defrosted sweetcorn
   (drained weight)
4–6 tbsp olive oil

For the mango and avocado salsa
1 avocado
1 small or ½ medium–large
   mango
2 spring onions
1 tbsp extra-virgin olive oil
2 tbsp roughly chopped
   coriander
Squeeze of lemon juice
Salt and ground black pepper

These gorgeous light fritters make a delicious brunch when eaten with the avocado and mango salsa, but they can be served on their own as a starter. You'll need a good ripe avocado and mango for the salsa, which shouldn't be made more than half an hour to an hour in advance or the avocado will discolour.

1 First make the salsa. Peel the avocado and mango, remove their stones and cut the flesh into 1cm (½in) cubes). Trim and finely slice the spring onions.

2 Put all the salsa ingredients into a large bowl, gently mix together and season to taste with salt and pepper, then set aside.

3 Place the egg yolks in another bowl and mix together with the milk. Sift in the flour, baking powder and salt. Mix together until smooth then stir in the sweetcorn.

4 In a separate bowl, whisk together the egg whites until they form stiff peaks, then carefully fold into the corn mixture.

5 Place a frying pan on a medium heat and add 3 tablespoons of olive oil. (If using a large frying pan, you may need to add more oil – it should completely cover the base of the pan.) When the oil is quite hot, add tablespoon-sized blobs of the mixture, very lightly flattening these with the back of the spoon if they are too lumpy. Cook for 30 seconds–1 minute or until golden and crusty underneath, then, using a fish slice or palette knife, gently turn over and cook for a further minute or so on the other side. They are cooked when they are golden in colour and have a light spring to the touch in the centre.

6 Remove from the pan and drain on kitchen paper. Repeat with the rest of the mixture. (You can do several at once, but be careful not to overload the pan or they will stick together. You will need to add more oil for each new batch.) Serve as soon as possible; kept warm in a baking tray in a low oven where they can sit for about 30 minutes, though they are best eaten straight from the pan!

Hot buttered oysters on toast

....

SERVES 6

18 oysters (3 per person)

50g (2oz) butter, plus extra
    for spreading

6 slices of bread

1 tbsp lemon juice

Salt (optional) and ground
    black pepper

For a little bit of decadence these make a fabulous starter or a light meal.

1 Open the oysters one by one. Place an oyster on a tea towel, flat side up. Wrap your non-cutting hand in another cloth so you won't get cut if the knife slips. Take an oyster knife, look for a chink in the shell at the narrow, hinged end, then insert the blade and, applying quite a bit of force, press, turn and lever upwards.

2 Put the opened oysters into a sieve set over a bowl and cut away the flesh from the shells. Discard the shells or wash them and use as salt and pepper holders. Tip the juices into a heavy-based frying pan, then, on a high heat, bring the juices to the boil. When they are boiling, whisk in the butter.

3 Add the oysters and, still on a high heat, toss for 1 minute or until the oysters are warmed through and have firmed up slightly and the sauce slightly reduced.

4 Meanwhile, toast the bread and butter it, and place on plates.

5 Just before serving, add the lemon juice and taste – it probably won't need any salt. Place the oysters on the buttered toast, pour over the juices, add a grinding of black pepper and serve.

Lazy weekend Bloody Mary

....

SERVES 10

50ml (2fl oz) Worcestershire
    sauce

1 tsp Tabasco sauce

1 tsp celery salt (optional)

5 tbsp lemon juice

1 tsp grated horseradish

1 tsp peeled and finely chopped
    shallot

1.8 litres (3 pints) tomato juice

2 tbsp dry sherry

300ml (½ pint) vodka

10 small sticks of celery, to serve

This refreshing tipple is strictly for Sunday mornings. Celery salt isn't essential, but it goes to perfection, so do get hold some if you can.

1 Whiz all the ingredients in a blender, then strain the mixture through a fine sieve. Serve in glasses over ice with a stick of celery.

Isaac's frittata

....

SERVES 4-6
VEGETARIAN
(with non-vegetarian variations)
8 eggs
50ml (2fl oz) milk
Salt and ground black pepper
2 tbsp chopped chives or
    parsley
110g (4oz) Gruyère cheese,
    grated
25g (1oz) butter

25cm (10in) diameter
    ovenproof frying pan

A frittata is a thick and almost endlessly versatile Italian omelette. It can be flavoured with just herbs and cheese or almost a whole fried breakfast!

1 Preheat the grill on a medium setting.

2 Break the eggs into a bowl and whisk together with the milk, seasoning with salt and pepper. Next gently mix in the herbs and grated cheese.

3 Place a large non-stick frying pan on a low–medium heat. Add the butter and when it has melted and starts to foam, add the egg mixture to the warm pan. Using a wooden spoon, scrape the cooked mixture from the bottom, from the outside in, filling its space with liquid egg by gently tilting the pan. Do this 5–6 times, then allow the mixture to cook for a further 2–3 minutes or until the bottom of the frittata is golden – you can tell this by lifting it slightly up at the edge using a palette knife or fish slice.

4 Take the pan off the heat and place under the grill, making sure that you leave a gap of a few centimetres between the frittata and the grill element. Continue cooking for a few minutes until the mixture has fluffed up nicely and is beginning to turn golden brown on top, by which stage the frittata will have cooked through to the centre.

5 Using a palette knife or fish slice, loosen the edges and slide onto a plate. Serve immediately or allow to cool to room temperature.

VARIATIONS
Make the recipe as above, adding the following to the basic egg mixture just before cooking:

Breakfast frittata: 150g (5oz) sliced mushrooms, fried in a little butter and seasoned with salt and pepper, and 10 rashers of streaky bacon, cut into 1cm (½in) pieces and fried until crispy.

Frittata ranchera: 150g (5oz) peeled and chopped onion, sweated in a little sunflower oil or butter, 4 small tomatoes cut into 5mm (¼in) dice, 1 tablespoon of finely chopped and deseeded red chilli (or more to taste) and 2 tablespoons of chopped coriander.

Spinach soup with rosemary oil

For the rosemary oil
1 sprig of rosemary,
  broken in half
50ml (2fl oz) olive oil

For the spinach soup
15g (½oz) butter
110g (4oz) peeled and
  chopped onions
150g (5oz) peeled and
  chopped potatoes
Salt and freshly ground
  black pepper
600ml (1 pint) vegetable stock
  (see page 50)
600ml (1 pint) milk
275g (10oz) spinach (any
  large stalks removed before
  weighing), chopped

The aromatic flavour of rosemary, drizzled as an oil over this soup, works to perfection with spinach. Instead of making the rosemary oil, you could add 1 tablespoon of chopped rosemary leaves to the soup just before blending, or a pinch of freshly ground nutmeg.

1 Put the rosemary in a small saucepan with the olive oil and heat gently on a low heat until tepid. Remove the pan from the heat and let the rosemary infuse for 10 minutes. Strain the oil through a sieve into a jug.

2 For the soup, melt the butter in a large saucepan, add the onions and potatoes, season with salt and pepper, cover with a lid and cook on a very low heat for 10 minutes, stirring every now and again.

3 Meanwhile, pour the stock and milk into another saucepan, bring to the boil and add to the vegetables. Bring the mixture back up to the boil, then tip in the spinach and cook, uncovered, over a high heat for 1–2 minutes or until the spinach is just cooked.

4 To preserve the fresh flavour, blend the soup straight away, in a blender or using a hand-held blender. Serve in individual bowls with a drizzle of rosemary oil over the top.

Skirt steak with spicy potatoes

....

SERVES 6

750g (1lb 10oz) potatoes
  (unpeeled if small), cut into
  1–2cm (½–¾in) dice
Salt and ground black pepper
75ml (3fl oz) olive oil
4 cloves of garlic, peeled and
  crushed or finely grated
1–2 red chillies, deseeded and
  finely diced
2 tbsp cumin seeds, toasted
  and ground (see tip below)
6 generous tbsp chopped
  coriander or parsley
6 thin skirt steaks (each
  weighing about 110g/4oz)

A lunchtime steak is not for the faint hearted, so this is one to save for the weekend. Skirt steak is wonderfully tender and has a great flavour, though it needs to be cooked very quickly or it can overcook and toughen.

1 Place a saucepan of water on a high heat, add 1 teaspoon of salt and bring to the boil. Add the potatoes and cook for 3–5 minutes or until they have slightly softened, then drain thoroughly before tipping onto kitchen paper to dry completely.

2 Set a large frying pan on a high heat, pour in 50ml (2fl oz) of the olive oil and, when hot, add the potatoes and cook, tossing frequently, for 3 minutes. Add the garlic, chillies and cumin and cook for a further 3–5 minutes or until the potatoes are golden and crispy, then tip in the chopped herbs.

3 While the potatoes are cooking, fry the steaks. Place a separate frying pan (cast iron if possible) on a high heat and allow it to get very hot. Season the steaks on both sides with salt and pepper, add the remaining oil to the pan and cook the steaks for about 1 minute on each side. (If you overcook them, they will toughen.)

4 Remove the steaks from the pan and serve straight away (they can be kept warm in a low oven for 5–10 minutes, if needed) with the sautéed potatoes on the side.

RACHEL'S TIP

To toast and grind nuts or seeds, place the nuts or seeds in a frying pan on a high heat and cook, tossing frequently, for about 1 minute or until the nuts/seeds are browned. They toast very quickly, so take care not to burn them. To grind them into a powder, use a pestle and mortar, a coffee grinder dedicated to the purpose, or place the nuts or seeds in a plastic bag and use a rolling pin to crush them.

Oven-baked courgette tortilla

....

SERVES 6
VEGETARIAN

150g (5oz) new potatoes
Salt and ground black pepper
300g (11oz) courgettes
2 tbsp olive oil
8 eggs
2 tbsp single or regular cream
2 tbsp chopped mint
150g (5oz) feta cheese,
   roughly crumbled

25cm (10in) diameter
   ovenproof frying pan

In Spain, a 'tortilla' describes a large omelette that usually contains fried potatoes. Add to it practically anything you like, within reason, depending on what is in season. Here there are nuggets of softened feta and moist courgette with the cooling refreshment of mint.

1 Preheat the oven to 200°C (400°F), Gas mark 6.

2 Place the potatoes in a sauccpan and cover with water. Add a good pinch of salt and bring to the boil, then cook for 20 minutes or until tender. Drain, then peel and cut into 2cm (¾in) chunks and set aside.

3 Halve the courgettes lengthways and slice into 1cm (½in) pieces. Pour the oil into a large ovenproof frying pan on a medium heat, add the courgettes, season with salt and pepper and cook for 5–7 minutes or until softened, tossing occasionally.

4 Meanwhile, in a large bowl whisk the eggs together with the cream and mint and season with salt and pepper.

5 Add the potatoes and feta to the courgettes in the frying pan and lightly mix together. Pour in the whisked eggs and cook for 5 minutes or until golden underneath, then cook in the oven for 10–15 minutes or until just set in the centre. Serve immediately with a fresh green salad.

Stir-fried tofu with noodles

SERVES 3

VEGETARIAN

2 tbsp toasted sesame oil

1 tbsp peeled (see tip below) and finely chopped root ginger

4 cloves of garlic, peeled and finely chopped

½ red chilli, deseeded and finely chopped

4 spring onions, trimmed and finely sliced

400g (14oz) firm tofu, cut into 1.5cm (⅝in) cubes

2 small pak choi, shredded into 1cm (½in) slices

250g (9oz) thin rice noodles or soba noodles

4 tbsp light soy sauce

1 tbsp Chinese rice wine or dry sherry

1 tbsp sesame seeds

2 tbsp chopped coriander

Tofu is a social butterfly, at its happiest when surrounded by lots of flavourful friends, literally soaking up anything you want to pair it with. This is an extremely quick and easy dish to make, as well as being very healthy and nutritious.

1 Set a wok or large, non-stick frying pan on a high heat and pour in the sesame oil. When it is very hot, add the ginger, garlic, chilli and spring onions and stir-fry quickly for 30 seconds or until the garlic begins to turn golden.

2 Add the tofu cubes and stir-fry for a further 4–5 minutes or until they begin to brown around the edges, then add the pak choi and stir-fry for a further 2–3 minutes or until the pak choi is wilted.

3 Meanwhile, cook the rice or soba noodles following the instructions on the packet.

4 Add the soy sauce, rice wine or dry sherry to the tofu mixture, along with half the sesame seeds and half the coriander. Cook for a further 2 minutes. Divide the cooked noodles between individual bowls, spoon over the tofu mixture and sprinkle with the remaining coriander and sesame seeds.

RACHEL'S TIP

To peel root ginger, try using the tip of a teaspoon rather than a peeler; this is not only easier, but you also remove less of the ginger flesh in the process.

Celeriac soup with roasted hazelnuts

....

SERVES 6
VEGETARIAN
25g (1oz) butter
1 onion, peeled and chopped
1 potato, peeled and chopped
1 celeriac, peeled and chopped
Salt and ground black pepper
About 900ml (1 pint 12fl oz)
   vegetable stock (see page 50)
75ml (3fl oz) single or
   regular cream
Handful of chopped mixed
   herbs

To serve
Handful of roasted, peeled
   (see Rachel's tip below) and
   roughly chopped hazelnuts
2–3 tbsp chopped parsley

Celeriac has a surprisingly subtle celery-like flavour considering its aggressively gnarled appearance. The hazelnuts in this soup provide a gorgeous crunchy contrast to the smooth creamy finish.

1 Melt the butter in a large saucepan on a low–medium heat, add the chopped onion, potato and celeriac and season with salt and pepper. Place a butter wrapper or piece of greaseproof paper on top, cover with a lid, reduce the heat to low and cook for 7–8 minutes, stirring regularly.

2 Pour in the stock, bring to the boil, then reduce the heat and simmer for a further 10 minutes or until the vegetables are completely soft. Add the cream and the chopped herbs and blend the soup in a blender or using a hand-held blender until it is smooth and velvety. Taste for seasoning.

3 To serve, ladle into warmed bowls and sprinkle with the roasted hazelnuts and parsley.

RACHEL'S TIP
To roast and peel hazelnuts, preheat the oven to 200°C (400°F), Gas mark 6. Place the hazelnuts on a baking tray and cook for about 10 minutes or until their skins have darkened, then remove from the oven. To remove the skins, wrap the nuts in a clean tea towel while they are still warm (I find this tends to slightly stain the tea towel, so don't use your favourite!) and rub together. The skins should come off easily.

Tuscan beans on toast

VEGETARIAN

400g (14oz) dried haricot or
    cannellini beans
1 bay leaf
8 large cloves of garlic, peeled
6 slices of bread
Butter, for spreading
6 tbsp chopped parsley
2 tbsp lemon juice
4 tbsp olive oil, plus extra
    for drizzling
Salt and ground black pepper
Lemon wedges, to serve

This is the best ever beans on toast that you can imagine. But there's no tomato sauce here, just lots of delicious sweet pungent garlic, fresh lemon juice and lashings of chopped parsley. Serve on your favourite kind of toast.

1 Soak the beans overnight in enough cold water to cover by several centimetres. Drain the beans and place in a large saucepan filled with fresh cold water. Add the bay leaf and garlic and bring to the boil. Reduce the heat, cover with a lid and simmer for 1–2 hours or until very soft, skimming off any foam that rises to the surface.

2 Just as the beans have finished cooking, toast the bread, spread with butter and place on individual plates.

3 Meanwhile, drain most of the liquid from the beans, leaving a few tablespoons with the beans in the pan. Take out one-third of the beans and the garlic and mash together to form a rough paste.

4 Discard the bay leaf and stir the paste into the cooked beans, along with the parsley, lemon juice and olive oil. Season with salt and pepper and serve on the slices of hot buttered toast with some extra oil drizzled over and lemon wedges.

RACHEL'S TIP

If you are being spontaneous and want to make this immediately, instead of the dried beans you could use 3 x 400g tins of cooked haricot or cannellini beans. Drain and rinse the beans, then place in the saucepan with the bay leaf and garlic, peeled and crushed, and simmer on a low–medium heat for about 5–10 minutes (or until the beans are soft enough to mash), then proceed as above.

Creamy fish pie with mushrooms, cucumber and leeks

....

8 potatoes (about 1.2kg/2lb 10oz) potatoes, unpeeled
Salt and ground black pepper
50g (2oz) butter
500g (1lb 2oz) button mushrooms, sliced
600g (1lb 5oz) round white fish, such as haddock, pollack, cod or hake, cut into 6 portions
½ cucumber (about 200g/7oz), peeled (optional) and cut into 1cm (½in) cubes
250g (9oz) trimmed and finely sliced leeks
275ml (9½fl oz) single or regular cream
250g (9oz) Gruyère cheese, grated

30 x 20cm (12 x 8in) pie dish or 6 individual dishes about 10cm (4in) in diameter

This fish pie is so easy to make. You don't need to mash the potatoes and pipe them over the top as they are layered into the pie. Leeks and mushrooms are a classic combination, but the fairly unusual inclusion of cucumber gives this pie a lovely set of textures.

1 Preheat the oven to 180°C (350°F), Gas mark 4.

2 Fill a large saucepan with enough water to cover the potatoes, add 1 teaspoon of salt and bring to the boil. Add the potatoes and cook for about 10 minutes or until half cooked (but not soft all the way through). Drain and allow to cool, then peel and cut into slices 5mm (¼in) thick.

3 Meanwhile, set a large frying pan on a high heat and add the butter. When it melts and starts to foam, add the sliced mushrooms, season with salt and pepper and cook, stirring frequently, for 3–4 minutes or until lightly golden.

4 Place half of the potatoes in a layer in the single pie dish or individual dishes, followed by a layer of the sautéed mushrooms then the fish (one portion per dish if using individual dishes). Add the cucumber and leeks, season with salt and pepper, then top with a final layer of potato slices, and season again with salt and pepper.

5 Divide the cream between each dish, or if making a large pie then pour all the cream in the one dish – it should come about halfway up the layered ingredients. Finally, sprinkle each dish (or the single large dish) with the grated cheese.

6 Bake in the oven for 15–20 minutes for individual pies or 20–30 minutes for a single large one, until the top is golden and bubbling, by which point the fish should be cooked all the way through. Serve hot and bubbling.

Tagliatelle with smoked salmon and avocado

SERVES 6
600g (1lb 5oz) dried tagliatelle
25g (1oz) butter
50ml (2fl oz) olive oil
2 cloves of garlic, peeled and
    crushed or finely grated
3 tbsp chopped herbs, such
    as chives, tarragon or basil
300g (11oz) smoked salmon,
    cut into 1cm (½in) pieces
Salt and ground black pepper
1 tbsp cream cheese
2 ripe avocados, peeled, stones
    removed and flesh diced
Juice of ½ lemon

Rich and velvety, this simple dish is easy to throw together, yet with the avocado and smoked salmon it retains a degree of luxury. It should be served immediately as the avocado will quickly brown.

1 Cook the tagliatelle following the instructions on the packet.

2 While the pasta is cooking, place a saucepan on a medium heat and add the butter and olive oil. When the butter has melted, add the garlic and cook for 2 minutes, then add the herbs and smoked salmon, season with salt and pepper and cook for a further minute.

3 Remove from the heat and stir in the cream cheese, followed by the diced avocado. Drain the pasta and toss with the smoked salmon mixture, squeeze over the lemon juice, taste for seasoning and serve immediately.

Clams marinara

....

SERVES AT LEAST 6
1.5kg (3lb 5oz) fresh clams
Salt
5 tbsp olive oil
1 onion, peeled and chopped
4 cloves of garlic, peeled and
    finely chopped
2 tbsp plain flour
2 tsp sweet smoked paprika
250ml (9fl oz) dry white wine
3 tbsp chopped parsley
    (optional)
Squeeze of lemon juice
    (optional)

This clam dish is great rustic Spanish food for casual entertaining. Serve it as a tapa or in a big bowl in the centre of the table, letting your guests help themselves. Make sure you have lots of crusty white bread to mop up all the delicious juices. You can make this with paprika (sweet or hot) or you can use chopped parsley instead. I like to use sweet smoked paprika.

1 First wash the clams by placing them in a bowl of cold water with a good pinch of salt and leaving them for 10 minutes, so that they release any remaining sand. Drain in a colander or sieve and sort through them, discarding any shells that are open and which don't close when tapped on a worktop.

2 Pour the olive oil into a large, heavy-based saucepan on a medium heat, add the onion and garlic and cook for 6–7 minutes or until nearly soft and slightly golden.

3 Add the flour and the paprika and stir for 30 seconds, mixing them in with the oil. Pour in the wine, stirring to remove any lumps from the flour, then tip in the clams, cover with a lid and cook for 3–4 minutes over a medium heat or until they have opened (discarding any that don't).

4 Stir in half the parsley (if using) and taste the sauce for seasoning, adding a little lemon juice if necessary. Serve in a big wide bowl with the remaining parsley over the top and some good crusty white bread to mop up all the delicious juices.

Crab bisque

....

A bisque is a gorgeous rich creamy soup made using fish, shellfish or meat. This crab bisque is fab – the sweetness of the crab meat is lightened ever so slightly by the tomatoes and ginger. You can either buy cooked crab meat or to cook your own (see below). Serve the soup as a starter or for lunch with crusty bread.

SERVES AT LEAST 6

50g (2oz) butter
1 onion (about 200g/7oz), peeled and chopped
Salt and ground black pepper
400g (14oz) cooked crab meat from 2 medium–large crabs (white and brown meat if possible)
100ml (3½fl oz) dry white wine
2 tsp peeled (see page 27) and finely chopped root ginger
600ml (1 pint) Crab or Prawn/ Shrimp Stock (see opposite) or fish stock
200g (7oz) chopped fresh or tinned tomatoes
100ml (3½fl oz) single or regular cream

1 Melt the butter in a large saucepan on a medium heat, then add the onion with some salt and pepper and cook for 6–8 minutes or until the onion is softened but not browned.

2 Add all the remaining ingredients apart from the cream and simmer gently for 15–20 minutes or until the tomatoes are completely soft.

3 Remove the saucepan from the heat and whiz the soup in a blender. Reheat gently if necessary and stir in the cream, season to taste and serve immediately with some crusty bread.

COOKING A CRAB

1 First place the crab in the freezer for a couple of hours so that it is unconscious before boiling. To cook it, place in a large saucepan, cover with water, add 1 tablespoon of salt for every 1.2 litres (2 pints) of water and bring to the boil.

2 Simmer on a medium heat for 20 minutes per 450g (1lb) and then pour off about two-thirds of the water, cover with a lid and continue to cook for a further 6 minutes. To check to see if the crab is cooked, gently shake it quite close to your ear and you shouldn't hear liquid splashing around. Remove the crab and allow to cool.

3 Once the crab has cooled, remove the large claws and crack these (using a heavy weight or nut crackers), then extract every bit of meat using the handle of a teaspoon. Retain the shell if making

dressed crab or stock, otherwise discard all of the shell. Turn the body of the crab upside down and pull out the centre portion.

4 Discard the gills, known as 'dead man's fingers', each about 4cm (1½in) long. Scoop out all the lovely brown meat and add it to the white meat from the claws. The meat can be used immediately or frozen for future use.

NOTE: 450g (1lb) of cooked crab in the shell yields approximately 175–225g (6–8oz) crab meat.

Crab or prawn/shrimp stock

MAKES ABOUT 1.2 LITRES (2 PINTS)
1 litre (1¾ pints) crab, prawn or shrimp shells
1 glass of dry white wine
1 large onion, peeled and roughly chopped
1 stick of celery, trimmed and roughly chopped
1 carrot, peeled and roughly chopped
2 tbsp tomato paste
A few sprigs of parsley
1 small bay leaf
6 whole black peppercorns
1 tsp salt

If you have any shells left over after preparing and eating shellfish such as crabs, prawns or shrimps, then use them to make this shellfish stock. It can be used for the Crab Bisque (opposite) as well as the Ballycotton Prawn Soup (see page 204). Stock can easily be frozen in small portions to be used whenever you need.

1 Place the shells in a saucepan, cover with 1 litre (1¾ pints) of water and bring to the boil.

2 Add the remaining ingredients, bring back up to the boil, then reduce the heat and simmer (but do not boil) for 30 minutes, skimming off any foam that appears on the surface. If you are making crab stock, it is necessary to simmer the shells in a pan covered with a lid for 20 minutes.

3 Pour through a fine sieve or through muslin and use immediately or either keep in the fridge for up to 48 hours or freeze for up to 1 month.

RACHEL'S TIP
If you are using large crab shells, first break them up slightly by placing them in a thick plastic bag and bashing them with a rolling pin or even a hammer.

Salade Niçoise

....

SERVES 6
18 small new potatoes,
   unpeeled
Salt and ground black pepper
18 French beans
3 handfuls of rocket leaves
3 chunky tuna steaks, seared
   (see page 171)
6 eggs, hard-boiled (see tip
   below), peeled and cut
   into quarters
2 tbsp chopped parsley
2 tbsp sliced or torn basil
6 very ripe tomatoes, cut
   into wedges
24 black olives with the stones
   in, or pitted if you prefer
   (see tip below)
2 tbsp capers, drained and
   rinsed
9 spring onions, trimmed and
   cut into 1cm (½in) chunks
18 tinned anchovies, drained
   and rinsed
Handful of chopped mixed
   herbs

For the dressing
3 tbsp extra-virgin olive oil
1 tbsp red wine vinegar
1 tsp runny honey
2 cloves of garlic, peeled
   and crushed

This is, of course, a classic, and when made with freshly seared tuna and delicious seasonal vegetables, lovely free-range eggs and really good olive oil, it is a perfect, fresh daytime dish.

1 Place the potatoes in a saucepan and cover with water. Add a good pinch of salt and bring to the boil, then cook for 20 minutes or until tender. Drain the potatoes and cut into 2cm (¾in) chunks and set aside.

2 Meanwhile, bring another saucepan of water to the boil, add a good pinch of salt and cook the French beans for 3–4 minutes or until just cooked but still a little 'squeaky' when bitten, then drain and set aside.

3 Next make the dressing by placing all the ingredients in a clean screw-top jam jar. Season with a little salt and pepper, then place the lid on the jar and shake vigorously. Set aside.

4 Place the rocket leaves in a serving dish, then arrange the cooked potatoes and beans randomly on top, along with the remaining ingredients. Season with salt and pepper, pour over the dressing and sprinkle with the herbs. Toss the salad so all the ingredients are evenly coated in the dressing and serve immediately.

RACHEL'S TIPS

Boiling the eggs for 8–9 minutes will leave the whites completely cooked but the yolks still ever so slightly soft, which is ideal for this dish.

Try to resist buying olives that come ready-pitted in jars as they have much less flavour. To pit them, just give them a bash with the flat side of a chopping-knife blade and remove the stones.

Chicken and cabbage salad

....

SERVES 6-8

4 large cooked chicken breasts
   or thighs, shredded
1 tsp chopped tarragon
3 tbsp extra-virgin olive oil
1 tbsp balsamic vinegar
200g (7oz) streaky bacon
   rashers
½ green leafy cabbage, such
   as Savoy
2 green eating apples, grated
3 large carrots, peeled and
   grated
2 tbsp mayonnaise
   (see page 317)
Salt and ground black pepper

This is a wonderful, great big salad to serve as a centrepiece for a lunch with friends. Like any good salad, this one has a lovely balance of flavours and textures.

1 In a large bowl, mix together the chicken with the tarragon, 2 tablespoons of olive oil and the vinegar.

2 Cut the bacon rashers into 2cm (¾in) pieces. Quarter the cabbage lenthways, remove the core and finely slice the leaves.

3 Place a frying pan on a medium–high heat and pour in the remaining olive oil. Add the bacon and cook, stirring frequently, for 3–4 minutes or until the bacon is golden and crispy. Remove from the pan and drain on kitchen paper.

4 When the bacon is cooked, add it to the bowl with the chicken, followed by all the remaining ingredients. Season to taste with salt and pepper, then toss together and serve.

Thai noodle broth

....

SERVES 3-4

75g (3oz) egg or rice noodles
    (optional)
1 x 400ml tin of coconut milk
450ml (16fl oz) chicken stock
    (see page 51)
250g (9fl oz) peeled raw
    tiger prawns

For the paste
1 bunch of coriander
1 lemongrass stalk (outer layer
    removed), roughly chopped
3 cloves of garlic, peeled
2 tbsp light soy sauce
1 tbsp fish sauce (nam pla)
2 tbsp caster sugar
½ red chilli, deseeded

To serve
½ red chilli, deseeded
    and sliced
Juice of 1 lime
A few splashes of fish sauce
    (nam pla)

The Thai tradition of making a specially flavoured paste as a base for soups is a great way of dispersing flavours, but it's also such a convenient method for entertaining, as the paste can be made beforehand and will keep for a week or two. I've used tiger prawns here, but you could use any prawns or chicken.

1 Cook the egg or rice noodles (if using) following the instructions on the packet, then drain and rinse through with cold water. Drain again.

2 For the paste, remove the leaves from the coriander and chop 4 tablespoons of the leaves to serve. Set aside and put the stalks, together with the rest of the paste ingredients and 2 tablespoons of water, in a food processor. Whiz for 1–2 minutes or until smooth.

3 Pour into a large saucepan and cook for 1 minute on a medium heat, then add the coconut milk and stock and gently warm through for 5 minutes. Add the prawns and noodles (if using) and cook for a further 2 minutes.

4 To serve, stir in the chilli, chopped coriander leaves, lime juice and fish sauce, and pour into warmed bowls.

VARIATION
Thai chicken soup: Make the recipe as above, replacing the prawns with thin slices of raw chicken, adding the chicken 2 minutes before the noodles.

Pork rillettes

....

MAKES 1 LITRE
(1¾ PINTS)

500g (1lb 2oz) pork belly
500g (1lb 2oz) pork shoulder
200ml (7fl oz) dry white wine
6 cloves of garlic, peeled and
    roughly chopped
½ tsp freshly grated nutmeg
½ tsp ground black pepper,
    plus extra if needed
2 tsp sea salt, plus extra
    if needed
2 bay leaves
1 tbsp chopped thyme or
    rosemary leaves

Medium-sized casserole dish
    or ovenproof saucepan

*This has to be one of my very favourite things to eat! It's a sort of rough
pâté. Traditionally made just with pork, rillettes is now prepared with
other types of meat and even fish, but the original is the best in my
opinion. I usually pot it and serve it as a starter or for lunch with delicious
breads from the market and some cornichons on the side. It will keep for
a few months if left completely covered in the fat in a sealed jar.*

1 Preheat the oven to 150°C (300°F), Gas mark 2.

2 Remove the rind and fat from the top of the pork and cut the
flesh into 1–2cm (½–¾in) cubes. Also cut the pork shoulder into
1–2cm (½–¾in) cubes. Set the shoulder and flesh aside. Roughly
chop the pork belly rind and fat into a few pieces and place in a
roasting tin. Cook in the oven for ½–1 hour to render the fat, then
pour the liquid into a bowl and discard (or eat!) the cooked rind.
Set aside until later.

3 To make the rillettes, place all the remaining ingredients in
a casserole dish or ovenproof saucepan with the meat. Place on
a medium heat, stirring to mix everything together. Bring to
simmering point, then cover with a lid and transfer to the oven.
The rillettes need to cook for about 5 hours; all the fat on the meat
should be rendered into liquid and the meat should be flaky and
not at all chewy. You can break the meat up a little if you wish.

4 Taste for seasoning, then transfer to one or more sterilised
preserving jars (see tip below), packing the meat down tightly and
pouring over the rendered fat to just cover the meat. Allow to cool
to room temperature so the fat has solidified before serving.

RACHEL'S TIP

To sterilise jars and bottles, put them through a dishwasher cycle,
boil in a large saucepan filled with water for 5 minutes or place in
a preheated oven (150°C/300°F/Gas mark 2) for 10 minutes.

Game terrine with celeriac remoulade

....

SERVES AT LEAST 6

25g (1oz) butter, plus extra
    for greasing
1 large onion, peeled and
    very finely chopped
Salt and ground black pepper
300g (11oz) boneless mixed
    game bird meat, minced or
    pulsed in a food processor
200g (7oz) minced pork (at
    least 20% fat)
50g (2oz) streaky bacon,
    minced or pulsed in a food
    processor
Large pinch of freshly grated
    nutmeg
3 juniper berries, crushed
2 tsp chopped thyme leaves
8–10 rashers of streaky bacon,
    rind removed
25g (1oz) shelled pistachios
2 boneless game breasts
    (about 200g/7oz in total),
    such as pheasant, pigeon,
    partridge or woodcock,
    cut into strips
Bay leaves and juniper berries,
    to decorate

For the celeriac remoulade
½ celeriac
250ml (9fl oz) mayonnaise
    (see page 317)
Juice of ½ lemon
2 tsp wholegrain or
    Dijon mustard

13 x 23cm (5 x 9in) loaf tin
    or casserole dish

I adore this kind of food for casual entertaining: thick slabs of a wonderful rustic winter terrine sitting on slices of crusty white or sourdough bread and some tangy celeriac remoulade on the side. This is great to serve for lunch when having friends staying over for the weekend. If you have a mincer, the texture will be better, however, you can mince meat in a food processor by pulsing a few times to get very small pieces.

1 Melt the butter in a saucepan and add the chopped onion with some salt and pepper, then cover with a lid and cook on a low heat for about 8–10 minutes or until the onion is softened and slightly golden. Set aside to cool.

2 Meanwhile, in a large bowl, mix together the minced meats with the nutmeg, juniper berries and the chopped thyme and season with salt and pepper. Add the cooked onions, then fry a little bit of this mixture in a hot pan and taste for seasoning.

3 Preheat the oven to 180°C (350°F), Gas mark 4, and butter the loaf tin.

4 Place the bacon rashers between two sheets of cling film and roll out with a rolling pin to make the bacon slices thinner and longer. Peel away the cling film from the bacon and line a loaf tin or small casserole by placing the rashers slices side by side along its width, making sure that each piece hangs over each side as it will be folded back over the top of the terrine.

5 Spread one-third of the minced meat mixture over the bacon on the bottom of the tin, then scatter with half the pistachios and arrange half the pieces of game on top to cover the surface. Spread out a second third of the minced meat mixture, followed by another layer of the pistachios and game fillets. Fill with the remaining minced meat mixture, level out with the back of a

(continued overleaf)

spoon, then fold the overlapping bacon back over the top to cover.

6 Cover with foil, place in a bain-marie (a roasting tin filled to a depth of a few centimetres with boiling water) and bake in the oven for about 1½ hours or until cooked through or firm to the touch in the centre. (To check that it's cooked, insert a metal skewer into the centre of the terrine and leave for 10 seconds; the skewer, once removed, will then feel too hot to hold against the inside of your wrist.) Remove the foil after the first 45 minutes.

7 Let the terrine sit in the loaf tin for about 20 minutes before turning out onto a plate and allowing to cool to room temperature. Decorate with some bay leaves and juniper berries.

8 Meanwhile, make the remoulade. Peel and finely slice the celeriac into matchstick-sized pieces or grate using the roughest part of the grater or in a food processor. Then mix with the remaining ingredients in a bowl, seasoning to taste.

9 Cut the terrine into slices and serve with crusty white or sourdough bread and the celeriac remoulade.

RACHEL'S TIP

If you are using your own game meat, use it from the legs, thighs, kidneys, livers and hearts. If you or someone you know has shot a pheasant, pigeon or partridge, you could use up the whole bird in this dish: I tend to use two pheasants or one pheasant and one pigeon, but you could otherwise use a pack of mixed game from the butcher or a supermarket.

Penne with asparagus and Parma ham

....

SERVES 6

600g (1lb 5oz) dried penne
18 asparagus spears
Table salt, sea salt and ground
    black pepper
25g (1oz) butter
6 tbsp crème fraîche
8 large slices of Parma or
    Serrano ham, roughly cut
    into strips
A few shavings of Parmesan
    cheese per portion (shaved
    with a peeler)

Parma ham is one of the world's great foods, with an incredible complexity to its flavour. This is a simple lunch dish that is all about letting great ingredients speak for themselves.

1 Cook the penne following the instructions on the packet, then drain, reserving a few tablespoons of the cooking liquid, and return to the warm pan (off the heat).

2 While the pasta is cooking, snap off the tough woody part at the bottom of each asparagus spear and discard. Fill a large saucepan to a depth of 4–6cm (1½ –2½ in) with water, add some table salt and bring to the boil. Tip in the asparagus and cook in the boiling water for 4–8 minutes or until just cooked.

3 Drain the asparagus immediately, then cut each spear at an angle into 3–4 shorter lengths. Place in a bowl, add the butter and season with sea salt and pepper.

4 Add the crème fraîche to the drained pasta in the pan and toss to coat, then tip in the asparagus and Parma ham and season to taste with sea salt and pepper. Serve in warmed bowls with a few shavings of Parmesan on top of each portion.

Venison sausages
with celeriac purée

....

SERVES 4–6
MAKES 12 SAUSAGES

25g (1oz) butter
1 onion, peeled and diced
300g (11oz) venison, minced
   or pulsed in a food
   processor
200g (7oz) minced pork
   (at least 20% fat)
50g (2oz) fresh white
   breadcrumbs
1 egg, beaten
2 cloves of garlic, peeled and
   crushed or finely grated
1 tbsp chopped rosemary
   leaves
1 tbsp wholegrain mustard
Salt and ground black pepper
1–2 tbsp olive oil

For the celeriac purée
1 celeriac, peeled and chopped
   into 1–2cm (½–¾in) dice
2 floury potatoes, peeled and
   cut into 1–2cm (½–¾in)
   dice
400ml (14fl oz) milk
2 tbsp single or regular cream
15g (½oz) butter

These skinless sausages make a substantial, comforting meal – a great winter lunch. Celeriac is quite an ugly-looking vegetable – those gnarled roots look positively ancient. When peeling it, you'll find the skin goes quite deep in places. But beneath that knobbly armour is flesh that, when cooked, has a subtle flavour with just a hint of celery.

1 To make the sausages, melt the butter in a large frying pan on a medium–high heat, then add the onion and fry, stirring occasionally, for 8–10 minutes until slightly golden. Set aside.

2 Meanwhile, mix all the other ingredients except the seasoning and oil in a large bowl. Season with salt and pepper, then add the cooled onions to the mixture. If the mixture is very wet, add a few more breadcrumbs.

3 Preheat the oven to 200°C (400°F), Gas mark 6. Place a little bit of the mixture in the frying pan and cook for 1–2 minutes to check for seasoning. Shape the sausage mixture into about 12 sausages. Pour the olive oil into the frying pan and, on a medium heat, brown the sausages on every side. Then place on a baking tray and bake in the oven for 10 minutes or until cooked through.

4 For the purée, place the celeriac and potatoes in a large saucepan, then pour over the milk to just cover, simmer on a medium–low heat for about 15 minutes, then drain and mash very well. Season with salt and pepper, then add the cream and the butter. Unless serving immediately, place in a covered, ovenproof dish and keep warm in the oven after the heat has been switched off.

5 Serve the sausages with a spoonful of celeriac purée and a drizzle of cranberry sauce (see tip below).

RACHEL'S TIP

To make cranberry sauce, put 150g (5oz) cranberries in a saucepan with 50ml (2fl oz) water. Bring to the boil, then reduce the heat and simmer gently for 6–8 minutes until the cranberries have burst and are softened. Stir in 75g (3oz) caster sugar until dissolved.

Stocks

....

Many of the recipes in this book require stocks and nothing can compare to a homemade broth of boiled bones, vegetables and herbs. Stocks can be made in advance, stored in small containers and kept in the freezer for handy access. The recipes here are just a guideline but try not to add too much of any one vegetable or the flavour may dominate the stock. Livers are unwelcome as they will make the stock bitter, but necks, hearts and wing tips are perfect. Also avoid starchy vegetables, such as potatoes or parsnips, as they will turn the stock cloudy. Don't use salt when making a stock as if you eventually reduce it, the salt will remain and the liquid could be too salty. If you wish to concentrate the flavour, place the stock on a high heat and boil, uncovered, to reduce the liquid. To make your own frozen stock cubes, reduce the liquid to about a quarter of its original volume. Allow to cool and then pour into ice cube trays and freeze. Stocks can be refrigerated for three days or frozen for two months.

Vegetable stock

....

MAKES ABOUT 2 LITRES (3½ PINTS)
2 onions, peeled and roughly chopped
2 leeks, trimmed and roughly chopped
3 sticks of celery, trimmed and roughly chopped
3 carrots, peeled and roughly chopped
½ fennel bulb, roughly chopped
Bunch of parsley stalks
1 small sprig of rosemary
1 sprig of thyme

1 Place all the ingredients into a large saucepan or casserole dish. Add enough cold water to cover the ingredients by about 10cm (4in) and bring to a simmer.

2 Let the stock continue to simmer for an hour, then strain the liquid and discard the vegetables.

Beef stock

MAKES 3-4 LITRES (5-6 ¾ PINTS)
2kg (4lb 4oz) beef bones, preferably
    with a little meat still on
2 onions, peeled and cut in half
2 carrots, peeled and cut in half
2 sticks of celery, trimmed and
    roughly chopped
Bunch of parsley stalks
1 tbsp tomato paste
1 sprig of thyme
1 bay leaf

1 Preheat the oven to 230°C (450°F), Gas
mark 8. Place the bones on a roasting tray
and roast in the oven for about 30 minutes
until browned.

2 Transfer them to a large saucepan and
deglaze the roasting tray by placing it
on a medium heat on the hob. Pour a little
cold water into the tray (enough to cover
the bottom) and bring to the boil, scraping
the bottom with a whisk to dissolve the
caramelised juices that are stuck to the
tray. Then pour on top of the bones in the
saucepan with the rest of the ingredients.
Top up with enough cold water to cover
everything by a good 10cm (4in) and
bring to the boil. Reduce the heat and
bring the stock to a simmer.

3 Leave the saucepan to simmer gently for
5–6 hours, skimming the foam off the top
from time to time.

4 Strain the stock, discarding the bones and
vegetables. Allow to cool so the fat will rise
to the top where it is easy to skim off.

Chicken stock

MAKES 1-2 LITRES (1 ¾-3 ½ PINTS)
1 chicken carcass, cooked or raw
1–2 carrots, peeled and
    roughly chopped
1 onion or 4 spring onions,
    peeled and cut in half
1 leek or even just the green part,
    trimmed and roughly chopped
1 sticks of celery, trimmed and
    roughly chopped
Bunch of parsley stalks
1 sprig of thyme
1 small bay leaf

1 Place all the ingredients in a large saucepan
or casserole dish. Add enough cold water
to cover everything by about 8cm (3in) and
bring to the boil. Reduce the heat and bring
the stock to a gentle simmer and then leave
for about 2 hours. For the best flavour, skim
the foam off the surface from time to time,
though it's not completely necessary.

2 Strain the stock so you are left with
just liquid and discard the vegetables
and carcasses. Chill, then lift the fat off
the top and discard.

Polenta, orange and almond cake

....

This flourless cake is made with a mixture of ground almonds and polenta, which gives a texture that is dense yet soft. The hot syrup poured over at the end makes it incredibly moist.

SERVES 6-8
VEGETARIAN

375g (13oz) butter, softened, plus extra for greasing

200g (7oz) medium or coarse polenta, plus 1 tbsp extra for dusting

375g (13oz) caster sugar

5 eggs

Finely grated zest of 2 oranges

Juice of 1 orange

300g (11oz) ground almonds

1 tsp baking powder

4 tbsp chopped pistachio nuts, to serve

For the syrup

Juice and finely grated zest of 1 orange

50g (2oz) caster sugar

23cm (9in) diameter spring-form/loose-bottomed tin with 5cm (2in) sides

1 Preheat the oven to 170°C (325°F), Gas mark 3. Butter the cake tin, place a disc of greaseproof paper in the bottom and dust the tin with 1 tablespoon of polenta.

2 Cream the butter in a large bowl or in an electric food mixer until soft. Add the sugar and beat until the mixture is light and fluffy. Beat in the eggs, one at a time, then add the orange zest and juice. Fold in the remaining ingredients and spoon the mixture into the prepared tin. Place in the oven and cook for 80–90 minutes or until a skewer inserted into the centre of the cake comes out clean.

3 Remove the cake from the oven and allow it to cool in the tin for about 20 minutes before transferring to a serving plate. Using a skewer, make about eight holes, each around 2.5cm (1in) deep, across the surface of the cake.

4 To make the syrup, mix together the orange zest and juice with the caster sugar in a small saucepan. Bring to the boil and keep boiling for 2 minutes, then remove from the heat and immediately drizzle all over the polenta cake. Serve warm or at room temperature with a scattering of pistachio nuts and a dollop of crème fraîche.

RACHEL'S TIP
Depending on the oven, I sometimes quickly open it to place a piece of foil on top of the cake after 45 minutes, to prevent it from getting too brown.

Almond meringue
with apricot purée

....

SERVES 6-8
VEGETARIAN
3 egg whites
175g (6oz) caster sugar
100g (3½oz) nibbed or
  chopped almonds
200ml (7fl oz) double or
  regular cream
Icing sugar, for dusting

For the purée
2 tbsp lemon juice
100g (3½oz) caster sugar
225g (8oz) ready-to-eat
  dried apricots

The apricot purée is also divine served with natural yoghurt as a quick snack or for breakfast. It can be stored in the fridge in an airtight container and will keep for up to a week.

1 Preheat the oven to 150°C (300°F), Gas mark 2. Line two baking sheets with baking parchment.

2 Place the egg whites in a spotlessly clean dry bowl and whisk until the mixture is fairly stiff. Add a quarter of the sugar and continue to whisk until the mixture holds its shape. Gently fold in the remainder of the sugar, followed by the nibbed almonds.

3 Spoon half the meringue mixture onto each of the lined baking sheets and gently spread the meringue on each sheet to form a round 20–22cm (8–9in) in diameter. If you can fit both meringues on one tray, it's easier if you're not cooking in a fan oven.

4 Bake in the oven together for 25–30 minutes or until crisp on the outside and cream coloured. (If cooked, the meringue will lift easily off the paper.) Once the meringue is cooked, if possible leave it inside the oven for 1 hour to allow it to cool down slowly and lessen the risk of it cracking. Alternatively, remove it from the oven but don't put it anywhere too cold as soon as you take it out.

5 To make the purée, fill a large saucepan with 850ml (1½ pints) of water, add the lemon juice and sugar and bring to the boil. Add the apricots, return to the boil then reduce the heat and simmer, uncovered, for about 20 minutes or until the apricots are softened. Remove from the heat and allow to cool, then place in a blender or food processor and whiz to form a purée.

6 Place a meringue round onto a serving plate or cake stand. Whip the cream and spread onto the meringue round, pour over some apricot purée, then gently place the other round on top, saving the best-looking one for this. Dust with icing sugar and cut into slices to serve, with the remaining purée on the side.

Orange meringue roulade

SERVES 8–10
VEGETARIAN

Vegetable or sunflower oil,
    for oiling
4 egg whites
225g (8oz) caster sugar
Icing sugar, for dusting
200ml (7fl oz) orange curd
    (see page 56)
500ml (18fl oz) whipped
    cream

For the orange curd
2 eggs
1 egg yolk
100g (3½oz) butter
175g (6oz) caster sugar
Juice and finely grated
    zest of 3 oranges

20 x 30cm (8 x 12in) Swiss
    roll tin

Here is a light dessert with a lovely citrus zing. The orange curd is delicious and the quantity given here makes twice the amount you will need for the roulade filling. Either just make half the quantity given (using 1 whole egg and 1 yolk) or make the full amount and try it served on pancakes, toast or even ice cream. The curd can be stored in an airtight plastic container in the fridge for up to a week or in a sealed jam jar for two weeks.

1 First make the orange curd. Whisk together the egg and egg yolk. Then melt the butter in a saucepan on a low–medium heat. Add the sugar and orange juice and zest, and pour in the eggs.

2 Stir constantly with a wooden spoon, still over a low heat (if it is too high, the egg will scramble), for 10–15 minutes or until the mixture is fairly thick. If you find the egg does start to scramble, dip the bottom of the pan in very cold water and then sieve the mixture. The curd is ready when the mixture is thick enough to coat the back of the wooden spoon and leave a definite mark when you draw a line in it with your finger. It will thicken further once cool.

3 Remove the curd from the heat, pour into a bowl and allow to cool. If you wish to keep this for two weeks, store the orange curd in sterilised jars (see page 42).

4 To make the roulade, reheat the oven to 180°C (350°F), Gas mark 4. Line the Swiss roll tin with foil, then brush with a little vegetable or sunflower oil.

(continued overleaf)

5 Place the egg whites and sugar in the bowl of an electric mixer and whisk for about 10 minutes until the mixture forms stiff peaks.

6 Spoon the mixture into the tin and spread it out evenly. Place in the oven and cook for 15–20 minutes or until it looks marshmallowy and lightly springy to the touch in the centre.

7 Remove from the oven and turn the meringue out onto a sheet of baking parchment or foil that has been liberally dusted with icing sugar. Peel off the foil from the base and allow to cool.

8 To assemble the roulade, first spread the orange curd evenly to cover the meringue, then spread the whipped cream over the orange curd. Gently roll up the roulade starting at one of the long edges and rolling away from you, to form a log shape. Transfer to a long serving plate, making sure the 'join' is facing down, and dust with icing sugar. Cut into slices to serve.

Apple snow with shortbread biscuits

....

SERVES 6
VEGETARIAN
450g (1lb) cooking apples,
    such as Bramley, peeled,
    cored and cut into chunks
175g (6oz) caster sugar
2 egg whites
Shortbread biscuits
    (see below), to serve

This fantastically light meringue dessert is very quick to prepare, especially if you make the purée in advance and then just fold it into the whisked egg whites at the last minute. Eat on its own or with the shortbread biscuits. Once made, you can store these in a tin – if there are any left over! This recipe contains raw eggs, which should be avoided by pregnant women, the very young and the very old.

1 Place the apple chunks and sugar in a large saucepan with 100ml (3½ fl oz) water, cover with a lid and simmer on a low heat for 10 minutes or until the apples are quite soft. Remove the lid and continue to simmer for another 3–4 minutes or until the apples are quite mushy and all the liquid has evaporated.

2 Remove from the heat, allow to cool a little, then whiz in a blender or food processor for a few minutes to make into a purée. Taste the purée to make sure it is sweet enough, adding a little more sugar if needed. It should be slightly sweeter than you want it to be eventually as its flavour will be diluted by the egg whites. Transfer to a large bowl and allow to cool.

3 When you are ready to serve, whisk the egg whites in a spotlessly clean bowl until they form stiff peaks. Gently fold the egg whites into the apple purée. Serve in glass bowls or glasses with the shortbread biscuits on the side.

Shortbread biscuits

MAKES ABOUT
25 BISCUITS
VEGETARIAN
150g (5oz) plain flour, plus
    extra for dusting
50g (2oz) caster sugar
100g (3½oz) butter, softened
Icing sugar, for dusting
    (optional)

1 Preheat the oven to 180°C (350°F), Gas mark 4.

2 Place the flour and sugar in a large bowl, rub in the butter then bring the mixture together to form a stiff dough, or just whiz all the ingredients together briefly in a food processor until almost combined.

3 Pat out the dough into a round about 2cm (¾in) thick, then cover with greaseproof paper or cling film and chill in the fridge

for about 20 minutes. On a work surface lightly dusted with flour, roll out the dough to about 5mm (¼in) thick and cut into shapes – round, square, rectangular, heart-shaped, whatever takes your fancy. Place carefully on 2 baking sheets (no need to grease or line) and cook in the oven for 6–10 minutes or until pale golden.

4 Take out of the oven and allow to sit on the baking sheets for a few seconds to firm up slightly (don't leave them any longer or they will stick). Transfer to a wire rack to cool, then dust with icing sugar if eating with the Apple Snow.

Mango and raspberry Bellinis

SERVES 6
VEGETARIAN
1 x 750ml bottle of sparkling wine, such as Prosecco or Cava

For the fruit purée
1 mango, peeled, stone removed and flesh chopped
100g (3½oz) fresh or frozen and defrosted raspberries
3 tbsp lemon juice
4 tbsp caster sugar

6 champagne flutes

The classic Bellini cocktail – a divine combination of sparkling wine (normally Prosecco) and fresh peach juice – was invented in the 1940s by Giuseppe Cipriani, founder of the celebrated Harry's Bar in Venice. The cocktail's particular shade of pink supposedly reminded Cipriani of the colour of the toga worn by a saint in a painting by Renaissance artist Giovanni Bellini – hence the name.

1 Place all the ingredients for the fruit purée in a food processor and whiz for 1–2 minutes, then push through a sieve.

2 Mix in a jug or fill glasses with one-third purée and two-thirds sparkling wine, stirring gently to combine. Serve chilled.

VARIATIONS
Mango Bellinis: Purée the flesh of 1 large mango with 3 tablespoons of lime juice and 3 tablespoons of caster sugar, then mix with the sparkling wine, as above.

Raspberry Bellinis: Purée 250g (9oz) fresh or frozen and defrosted raspberries with 5 tablespoons of caster sugar and 5 tablespoons of lemon juice, then mix with the sparkling wine.

Apple and blackberry bread and butter pudding

....

SERVES 6-8
VEGETARIAN

Butter, for spreading
12 slices of white bread, crusts
   removed
200g (7oz) cooking apples,
   such as Bramley
150g (5oz) blackberries
450ml (16fl oz) single or
   regular cream
225ml (8fl oz) milk
4 eggs
150g (5oz) caster sugar
1 tbsp granulated sugar
Pinch of ground cinnamon
   (optional)

20 x 25cm (8 x 10in) square,
   round or oval ovenproof
   dish

This is a really comforting, autumnal dessert, delicious with a dollop of whipped cream. It's also a great excuse to get the family out picking blackberries. These can be substituted with raisins, however, if you prefer.

1 Preheat the oven to 180°C (350°F), Gas mark 4.

2 Butter the bread, cut into smaller pieces and arrange 6 in the ovenproof dish, butter side down. Peel and core the cooking apples and cut into 2cm (¾in) chunks. Place the pieces and blackberries in a layer on top of the bread. Then arrange the remaining bread, again butter side down and overlapping if necessary, to cover the fruit.

3 Pour the cream and milk into a saucepan, bring to just under the boil and remove from the heat.

4 While the milk and cream are heating up, whisk together the eggs and caster sugar in a large bowl. Add the hot cream and milk and whisk to combine, then pour this custard over the bread and leave to soak for 10 minutes. Sprinkle the granulated sugar over the top and the cinnamon (if using).

5 Put the dish in a bain-marie (a roasting tin filled with just enough boiled water to come halfway up the side of the dish). Place in the oven and bake for about 1 hour until the top is golden and the centre set.

RACHEL'S TIP

This can be prepared in advance and left in the fridge overnight, uncooked. If making it this way, don't heat up the milk and cream but add them cold to the whisked eggs and sugar.

MENU IDEAS FOR
BRUNCHES AND LUNCHES

Citrus honeyed fruit (page 16)
Skirt steak with spicy potatoes (page 25)
Lazy weekend Bloody Mary (page 19)

*

Spinach soup with rosemary oil (page 22)
Venison sausage with celeriac purée (page 48)
Apple snow with shortbread biscuits (pages 58–9)

*

Clams marinara (page 34)
Penne with asparagus and Parma ham (page 47)
Almond meringue with apricot purée (page 53)

*

Salade Niçoise (page 38)
Oven-baked courgette tortilla (page 26)
Polenta, orange and almond cake (page 52)

MAIN COURSES

Chilli sin carne

Sweet potato and chickpea tagine

Roasted vegetable coconut curry

Bean burritos with refried beans, guacamole and tomato salsa

Fish tacos with pepper and spring onion salsa

Fusilli with beans, smoked salmon and olives

Chicken and olive tagine

Chicken, pork and prawn paella

Beef and red wine stew

Chinese-style ribs with coleslaw

Mild lamb curry

Slow-roast ginger and citrus shoulder of pork

DESSERTS

Spiced poached pears

Ginger and treacle pudding

Apricot crumble

Cherry custard pudding

CASUAL MEALS

Sometimes you just want to get together with your friends
for no reason in particular. It might be a spontaneous thought,
and next thing you know you're on the phone to all your friends
asking if they can come over. Poker night? Movie night? Just because
it's Friday? There are so many reasons just to get a big pot of something
on the go. Here you'll find great ideas for simple but delicious meals
that you can serve at any time and to just about anyone – including
many which kids love. You won't find starters here because this
is 'tuck-in' food. Instead you'll find plenty of hearty and
comforting mains and desserts!

Chilli sin carne

....

SERVES 8-10
VEGETARIAN

4 tbsp olive oil

1 large onion, peeled and finely chopped

8 cloves of garlic, peeled and finely chopped

4 carrots, peeled and finely chopped

4 sticks of celery, trimmed and finely chopped

Salt and ground black pepper

2 large red chillies, deseeded and finely diced

2 tsp coriander seeds, ground (see page 25)

2 tsp cumin seeds, ground

200g (7oz) soya mince or TVP (textured vegetable protein), covered in cold water and soaked for 45 minutes

2 x 400g tins of red kidney or pinto beans, drained and rinsed, or 125g (4½oz) dried beans, soaked and cooked (see right)

2 x 400g tins of chopped tomatoes

200ml (7fl oz) vegetable stock (see page 50)

150ml (5fl oz) red wine

3 tbsp chopped coriander, to serve

Large casserole dish or saucepan

This vegetarian chilli is so bursting with flavours that even the most ardent meat lover will be impressed. Make sure to serve it with all the traditional chilli accompaniments, rice, guacamole and tomato salsa (see page 69), sour cream and tortilla chips.

1 Pour the olive oil into a large saucepan or casserole dish on a medium–low heat and add the onion, garlic, carrots and celery. Season with salt and pepper and cook, stirring occasionally, for about 20 minutes or until the vegetables are softened and golden. Stir in the chillies and spices and cook for a further 5 minutes.

2 Add all the remaining ingredients and taste for seasoning. Increase the heat to medium and cook, uncovered, for about 30 minutes or until thickened. Scatter with the chopped coriander and serve.

RACHEL'S TIP

To cook dried beans and pulses, soak them overnight in plenty of cold water, enough to cover the beans by a few centimetres, then drain and cook in fresh water until soft. It is best not to add salt to the cooking water as this toughens the beans.

Cooking time varies according to the type of bean and also how old they are:

Chickpeas = 45–75 minutes

Haricot or cannellini beans = 40–60 minutes

Pinto or kidney beans = 45–60 minutes

Note: 1 x 400g tin = 250g (9oz) drained, cooked beans or 125g (4½oz) dried beans.

Sweet potato and chickpea tagine

....

2 sweet potatoes (about 650g/1lb 7oz)
5 tbsp olive oil
Salt and ground black pepper
1 red pepper
1 yellow pepper
3 tbsp olive oil
1 large (300g/11oz) onion, peeled and thinly sliced
3 cloves of garlic, peeled and thinly sliced
3 tsp peeled (see page 27) and finely chopped root ginger
2 tsp cumin seeds, toasted and ground (see page 25)
2 tsp coriander seeds, toasted and ground
2 tsp paprika
1 x 400g tin of chickpeas, drained, or 125g (4½oz) dried chickpeas, soaked and cooked (see tip opposite)
100ml (3½fl oz) vegetable stock (see page 50)
1 tbsp honey
3 tbsp chopped coriander
75g (3oz) blanched almonds, toasted (see page 25) and roughly chopped

I absolutely adore this vegetarian tagine recipe; it has a spicy, sweet complexity that might be bullied out of the way were any meat added. Chickpeas are better friends with the canning process than any other pulse, though they are also delicious cooked from dry (see tip opposite).

1 Preheat the oven to 230°C (450°F), Gas mark 8.

2 Peel and cut the sweet potatoes into 2cm (¾in) cubes. Put them in a bowl, mix with 2 tablespoons of olive oil and season with salt and pepper. Spread the potato pieces out in a large roasting tin, place the whole peppers at one end, on the same tin, and roast in the oven for about 20 minutes or until the sweet potato is tender. When cooked, transfer the sweet potatoes to a bowl and set aside.

3 The peppers will need an additional 10–20 minutes to roast, depending on their size. They are ready when the skin has slightly blackened and the flesh feels soft underneath. When cooked, remove and place in a bowl covered with cling film – this makes the skins easier to remove. When the peppers are cool enough, peel off the skin. Cut the peppers in half and remove all the seeds, then chop the flesh into roughly 2cm (¾in) pieces.

4 While the sweet potatoes and peppers are cooking, pour the remaining olive oil into a casserole dish or large saucepan and place on a medium heat. Add the onion, garlic, ginger, ground cumin and coriander and the paprika, and season with salt and pepper. Cook for 10–12 minutes or until the onions are soft and beginning to brown.

5 Add the drained chickpeas with the vegetable stock, bring to the boil, then reduce the heat and simmer for 5 minutes. Next add the cooked sweet potatoes, roasted peppers, honey and half the chopped coriander, stir gently to combine and taste for seasoning.

6 Transfer to a warmed serving bowl, scatter over the remaining coriander and toasted almonds and serve with couscous.

65

Roasted vegetable coconut curry

SERVES 8-10
VEGETARIAN

2 x 400ml tins of coconut milk
600ml (1 pint) vegetable stock
    (see page 50)
4 large carrots
6 parsnips
700g (1½lb) sweet potatoes
4 onions
150g (5oz) spinach (any
    large stalks removed
    before weighing)
400ml (14fl oz) natural
    yoghurt

For the paste
1 tbsp coriander seeds
2 tsp cumin seeds
2 tsp chana masala
50g (2oz) root ginger, peeled
    (see page 27) and chopped
12 cloves of garlic, peeled
4 red chillies, deseeded
200g (7oz) onions, peeled
    and quartered
50ml (2fl oz) vegetable oil
1 tbsp ground turmeric
2 tsp caster sugar
2 tsp salt

To serve
Bunch of coriander, chopped
100g (3½oz) cashew nuts,
    toasted (see page 25) and
    chopped
200ml (7fl oz) natural yoghurt
    or crème fraîche

Large casserole dish
    or saucepan

The creamy coconut milk and myriad spices grant these vegetables both elegance and luxury. Roasting the vegetables in the paste really brings out their sweetness. Making your own curry paste only takes a few minutes and the complex depth of flavour means it's always worth doing.

1 Preheat the oven to 170°C (325°F), Gas mark 3.

2 First make the paste. Place a small frying pan on a medium heat and add the coriander, cumin and chana masala. Cook, tossing frequently, for about 1 minute or until they start to pop, then crush (see page 25).

3 Place the ginger, garlic, chillies, onions and vegetable oil in a food processor and whiz for 2–3 minutes or until smooth. Pour into a large saucepan or casserole dish and stir in the ground spices, along with the turmeric, sugar and salt. Place on a medium–low heat and cook, stirring occasionally, for about 5 minutes or until the mixture has reduced slightly.

4 Remove the mixture from the heat and pour half into a large bowl. Pour the coconut milk and stock into the remaining half in the saucepan or casserole dish, stirring to combine. Leave to simmer for 15 minutes to reduce.

5 Meanwhile, prepare the vegetables. Peel the carrots, parsnips and sweet potatoes and cut into 2cm (¾in) cubes. Peel the onions and cut into eighths and chop the spinach.

6 Stir the yoghurt into the spice paste in the bowl, then add the vegetables and onions and stir to coat. Tip into 1–2 roasting tins and cook in the oven for about 1 hour or until lightly browned.

7 Remove the vegetables from the oven and add to the saucepan or casserole dish. Place on a medium heat for a few minutes to warm through, then stir in the spinach and spoon into bowls with a sprinkling of fresh coriander, a scattering of the toasted nuts and a spoonful of yoghurt or crème fraîche.

Bean burritos with refried beans, guacamole and tomato salsa

....

These burritos are great for a casual crowd. Children will especially love creating their own at the table, choosing from a variety of fillings for the tortillas. I love to see everyone passing around various bowls and plates. This is what communal food is all about.

SERVES 8
VEGETARIAN
1 quantity of guacamole
(see opposite)
1 quantity of tomato salsa
(see opposite)
1 x 200g jar of jalapeño
peppers (optional)
250g (9oz) Cheddar or
Gruyère cheese, grated
250g (9oz) crème fraîche
16 tortillas
1 quantity of refried beans
(see opposite)

1 Preheat the oven to 150°C (300°F), Gas mark 2.

2 Place the guacamole, salsa, peppers (if using), grated cheese and crème fraîche in separate serving bowls on the table.

3 Put the tortillas in a roasting tin, cover with foil or an upturned bowl and place in the oven for 5–10 minutes or until warmed through, then divide between plates. Reheat the beans, pour into a serving dish and place on the table with the other bowls. People can help themselves and assemble their own burritos by spooning each of the fillings in a line on their tortilla, then rolling up and eating!

Refried beans

SERVES 8 AS A SIDE DISH
VEGETARIAN
25g (1oz) butter
1 onion, peeled and finely chopped
4 cloves of garlic, peeled and finely chopped
½–1 red chilli, deseeded and finely chopped
2 x 400g tins of pinto or kidney beans, drained
    and rinsed, or 250g (9oz) of dried beans,
    soaked and cooked (see page 64)
100ml (3½fl oz) beef or chicken stock
    (see page 51)
1 tsp ground cumin
1 tsp ground coriander
Salt and ground black pepper

1 Melt the butter in a large frying pan on
a medium heat, add the onion, garlic and
chilli and cook for about 8–10 minutes or
until softened and a little golden around
the edges.

2 Add the beans, stock, cumin and coriander
and season with salt and pepper. Cook,
stirring occasionally and mashing the beans
every so often using a potato masher, for a
further 7–8 minutes or until the sauce has
reduced slightly, then remove from the
heat and allow to cool.

Guacamole

SERVES 8 AS A SIDE DISH
VEGETARIAN
2 ripe avocados, peeled and stones removed
2 cloves of garlic, peeled and crushed
    or finely grated
2 tbsp extra-virgin olive oil
2 tbsp chopped coriander
Salt and ground black pepper
Juice of ½ lime or lemon

1 Place the avocado flesh in a large bowl,
add the garlic, olive oil and coriander and
mash together, seasoning to taste with salt,
pepper and lime juice.

2 Cover the bowl with cling film to stop
the mixture going brown and set aside
until it is needed.

Tomato salsa

SERVES 8 AS A SIDE DISH
VEGETARIAN
4 ripe tomatoes, cut into 1cm (½in) cubes
1 tbsp chopped red onion
1 clove of garlic, peeled and crushed
    or finely grated
½–1 red chilli, deseeded and finely chopped
2 tbsp chopped coriander
Juice of ½ lime
Salt and ground black pepper
Pinch of sugar

1 Mix all the ingredients together, seasoning
with salt, pepper and a pinch of sugar.

Fish tacos with pepper and spring onion salsa

....

SERVES 8

750g (1lb 10oz) filleted round
    white fish, such as haddock,
    whiting, hake or cod, in
    small fillets or one big piece
2 tbsp olive oil
Salt and ground black pepper

To serve
16 taco shells
1 quantity of guacamole
    (see page 69)
1 quantity of pepper and
    spring onion salsa
    (see below)
250g (9oz) crème fraîche

The first bite into a fish taco immediately transports me to the white sands of Puerto Escondido in Mexico. The flavours here are all so evocative: crunchy taco shells enveloping a crisp, refreshing salsa, a smooth and creamy guacamole (see page 69) and delicate flakes of fish. I can practically smell the sea!

1 Preheat the oven to 180°C (350°F), Gas mark 4.

2 Put the fish in a roasting tin, drizzle with the olive oil and season with salt and pepper. Place in the oven and cook for 10–20 minutes, depending on the size of the fish piece or pieces, until the flesh is opaque all the way through.

3 A few minutes before the fish are cooked, place the tacos in the oven to warm through, then bring to the table with bowls of the guacamole, salsa and crème fraîche. Cut or break up the fish into bite-sized chunks and place in a warmed serving bowl on the table. People can help themselves: just spoon a little from each bowl to fill the tacos, and eat!

Pepper and spring onion salsa

SERVES 8 AS A SIDE DISH
VEGETARIAN

2 yellow peppers (or 1 red and
    1 yellow), very finely sliced
8 spring onions, trimmed
    and sliced
8 radishes or ⅓ cucumber,
    left unpeeled and cut into
    thin strips
½–1 red chilli, deseeded
    and finely diced
Juice of 2 limes
2 tbsp extra-virgin olive oil
2 ripe tomatoes, finely diced
2 tbsp chopped coriander
Salt and ground black pepper

1 Mix all the ingredients together in another bowl and season to taste with salt and pepper.

Fusilli with beans, smoked salmon and olives

....

This dish is perfect for any form of casual entertaining. If made in advance, it can be chilled and brought back up to room temperature.

SERVES 8-10

300g (11oz) smoked salmon
500g (1lb 2oz) dried fusilli
4 tbsp olive oil
Salt and ground black pepper
1 red pepper, deseeded and
   finely sliced
1 x 400g tin of kidney beans,
   drained and rinsed
½ red onion, peeled and
   sliced
Handful of chopped mint
Handful of chopped coriander
Juice of 2 limes or 1 lemon
16 olives, pitted (see page 38)
   and roughly chopped
125ml (4½fl oz) crème fraîche

1 Preheat the oven to 200°C (400°F), Gas mark 6. Place the smoked salmon on a baking sheet in the oven and roast for about 10 minutes or until it turns pale coral. Break the salmon into roughly 2cm (¾in) pieces, then set aside to cool.

2 Cook the fusilli following the instructions on the packet, but remove it from the pan when it is al dente. Drain the pasta, reserving about 25ml (1fl oz) of the cooking water. Pour this back into the fusilli along with the olive oil, and season. Transfer to a large bowl and allow to cool to room temperature.

3 Add the remaining ingredients, apart from the salmon, and mix together. Scatter the salmon pieces over the top and serve.

Chicken and olive tagine

....

This take on a classic Moroccan dish has a real elegance to it despite the fact that it's incredibly easy to make.

SERVES 6-8

3 tbsp olive oil
200g (7oz) peeled and sliced
   onions
4 large cloves of garlic,
   peeled and chopped
2.5cm (1in) piece of root
   ginger, peeled and chopped
Salt and ground black pepper
600g (1lb 5oz) chicken meat
400ml (14fl oz) chicken stock
   (see page 51)
Good pinch of saffron
2 tbsp chopped parsley
2 tbsp chopped coriander
16 olives, pitted

1 Pour the olive oil into a large frying pan on a medium heat, then add the onions, garlic and ginger. Season with salt and pepper and fry for about 5 minutes, stirring occasionally, until the onions have almost softened and are a little golden around the edges.

2 Cut the chicken into bite-sized chunks, add to the pan and cook for 2 minutes before adding the stock and saffron. Stir to combine then bring to the boil, reduce the heat and simmer for about 15 minutes or until the chicken is cooked all the way through.

3 Stir in the remaining ingredients and taste for seasoning and serve immediately. This goes very well with couscous.

Chicken, pork and prawn paella

....

SERVES 10-12
2 tbsp olive oil
250g (9oz) chorizo sausage, chopped into 1cm (½in) chunks
1 large Spanish or red onion, peeled and finely chopped
4 cloves of garlic, peeled and chopped
300g (11oz) chicken meat from the leg or breast, cut into bite-sized pieces
300g (11oz) pork meat from the leg, cut into bite-sized pieces
Salt and ground black pepper
500g (1lb 2oz) paella rice
150ml (5fl oz) dry white wine
1.2 litres (2 pints) chicken stock (see page 51)
4 large very ripe tomatoes, peeled (see tip below) and cut into chunks
1 tsp caster sugar
450g (1lb) peeled raw whole prawns, large ones halved lengthways
150g (5oz) baby spinach, removing any stalks from larger leaves
Juice of ½–1 lemon
1 tbsp chopped parsley
1 tbsp chopped chives

40cm (16in) diameter paella pan or wide, heavy-based frying pan

This rice dish originated in Valencia but can now be found all over Spain and the Balearics. Paella is a wonderful dish for entertaining as it is just as easy to make for 12 people as it is for four, provided you have a pan large enough. Should you ever be in Spain, I would recommend purchasing an authentic paellera, which come in many sizes.

1 Pour the olive oil into the paella pan or frying pan on a medium heat. Tip in the chorizo chunks along with the onion and garlic and cook for 6–7 minutes, stirring regularly, until the oils have come out of the chorizo and the onion is softened and golden.

2 Remove the chorizo, onion and garlic from the pan, leaving any oils behind. Turn the heat up to high, then when the pan is hot, add the chicken and pork and, tossing regularly, cook for 3–4 minutes or until the meat is golden. Season to taste with salt and pepper.

3 Reduce the heat to low, add the rice and stir for 1–2 minutes before adding the cooked chorizo, onion and garlic with the wine, stock, tomatoes and sugar. Continue to cook, uncovered, for 20 minutes, stirring every now and then, until the rice is just cooked. If the paella begins to look a little dry, add some more hot stock.

4 Next add the whole or halved prawns and the spinach and cook for another 2–3 minutes or until the prawns are cooked (opaque and firm to the touch) and the spinach leaves are wilted. Add some lemon juice to taste and half the chopped herbs and taste for seasoning. Scatter the remaining herbs over the top and serve.

RACHEL'S TIP

To peel tomatoes, cut an 'X' in the skin of each one, place in a bowl and cover with boiling water. Leave for 10–15 seconds, then drain, leave to cool and peel off the skin. If you can't get hold of good-quality tomatoes, replace them with a 400g tin of cherry tomatoes.

Beef and red wine stew

....

There's nothing better than a big hearty casserole filled with tender meat and delicious veggies, all in a robust red wine sauce. This makes for great winter entertaining, and reheats perfectly. Serve with a big bowl of mashed potato (see page 191) or the Roast Garlic Colcannon on page 244.

(see page 191) ... on page 244.

25g (1oz) butter

300g (11oz) streaky bacon in the piece or 6 rashers, cut into 2cm (¾in) dice

1kg (2lb 3oz) stewing beef, cut into 2cm (¾in) cubes

Salt and ground black pepper

800g (1¾lb) carrots, peeled and sliced

10 small onions, peeled and halved

3 tbsp chopped herbs, such as thyme, rosemary or tarragon

600ml (1 pint) chicken stock (see page 51)

425ml (15fl oz) red wine

500g (1lb 2oz) white mushrooms, sliced

25g (1oz) roux (made with 10–15g (⅓–½oz) each of butter and plain flour; see tip below)

Large flameproof casserole dish

1 Preheat the oven to 140°C (275°F), Gas mark 1.

2 Melt half the butter in a casserole dish on a medium heat. Add the bacon and cook for 2–3 minutes until almost golden. Turn up the heat to high and add half the cubed beef and seasoning and cook for 5–6 minutes, tossing regularly, until browned all over. Tip the bacon and beef onto a plate and cook the remaining beef, adding a little more butter if the dish or pan is too dry.

3 Remove the meat from the casserole dish onto the plate, then toss the carrots and onions in the juices on a high heat for 4–5 minutes before adding the herbs and putting the meat back in. Pour in the stock and the wine, cover and bring to simmering point. Place in the oven and cook for 1½–2 hours or until the meat is tender. If you have the time, let it simmer at an even lower temperature – 130°C (250°F), Gas mark ½ – for about 2½–3 hours.

4 Just before the stew has finished cooking, melt the remaining butter in a frying pan on a high heat, add the mushrooms and seasoning and sauté for 3–4 minutes until golden.

5 Take the casserole dish from the oven, remove 2–3 ladlefuls of the sauce and bring to the boil in a small saucepan. Whisk in the roux and allow to boil for 2–3 minutes or until the sauce has thickened. Pour back in the dish and stir in the mushrooms. Taste for seasoning, then serve straight from the casserole dish.

RACHEL'S TIP

A roux is a simple sauce thickener that is made with equal quantities of flour and butter. For the recipe above, melt 15g (½oz) butter in a small saucepan on a medium heat, add 15g (½oz) plain flour and allow to cook for 2 minutes, stirring regularly. Use immediately.

Chinese-style ribs
with coleslaw

....

SERVES 6-8

2kg (4lb 4oz) baby back ribs
    of pork
6 spring onions, trimmed
    and finely sliced, to serve

For the spice mixture
3 tbsp cornflour
2 tbsp light brown sugar
1 tbsp peeled (see page 27)
    and finely grated root ginger
2 tsp Chinese five-spice powder
4 tbsp hoisin sauce
3 tbsp rice wine or dry sherry
Pinch of salt

For the coleslaw
400g (14oz) white cabbage,
    quartered lengthways,
    core removed and leaves
    finely sliced
1 large carrot, peeled and grated
1 onion, peeled and finely sliced
1 stick of celery, trimmed and
    finely sliced
200ml (7fl oz) mayonnaise
    (see page 317)
2 tbsp chopped coriander
    or parsley
Salt and freshly ground pepper

*Ribs are one of those foods that demand to be eaten with your hands.
It is just not possible to effectively eat a rib with a knife and fork. Perhaps
for this reason, as well as the fabulous sweet-sour Chinese flavours,
adults and children will happily devour entire piles of these ribs. For the
hungrier among your guests, bake some potatoes to serve alongside.*

1 Preheat the oven to 220°C (425°F), Gas mark 7.

2 In a bowl, stir together all the ingredients for the spice mixture.
Arrange the ribs in a roasting tin in a single layer and rub the spice
mixture all over. Place in the oven and bake for 30–35 minutes or
until slightly crispy and a deep golden brown.

3 While the ribs are cooking, make the coleslaw. Mix all the
ingredients together in a large bowl, seasoning to taste with
salt and pepper.

4 Remove the ribs from the oven, scatter with the spring onions
and serve with the coleslaw.

Mild lamb curry

....

SERVES 8-12

4–6 tbsp vegetable oil

1.5kg (3lb 5oz) stewing lamb,
   cut into 2cm (¾in) cubes

900g (2lb) peeled and sliced
   onions

8 cloves of garlic, peeled and
   crushed

2 tsp cumin seeds, ground
   (see page 25)

2 tsp coriander seeds, ground

2 tsp fennel seeds, ground

1 tsp ground turmeric

1 tsp ground nutmeg

Salt and ground black pepper

800ml (1 pint 9fl oz) coconut
   milk (or 2 x 400ml tins)

400ml (14fl oz) chicken stock
   (see page 51)

1 x 400g tin of chopped
   tomatoes

Juice of 2 limes

4 tbsp chopped mint

Lime wedges, to serve

Large saucepan or casserole
   dish

This curry isn't spicy and the coconut milk makes it so creamy that our children love it too.

1 Pour about 4 tablespoons of the vegetable oil into a large saucepan or casserole dish on a medium heat. Add the lamb and fry on all sides for 3–4 minutes, stirring frequently.

2 Add the remaining oil, if necessary, then tip in the onions, garlic and spices and add seasoning. Cook for 15 minutes, stirring occasionally, until the onions are soft and beginning to brown.

3 Add the coconut milk, stock and tomatoes, stir well and reduce the heat to low. Gently simmer, uncovered and stirring regularly, for 1¼–2 hours or until the meat is meltingly tender.

4 When the lamb is cooked, stir in the lime juice and chopped mint, taste for seasoning and then serve immediately with some lime wedges.

Slow-roast ginger and citrus shoulder of pork

....

SERVES 6-8
2–3kg (4lb 4oz–6½lb)
  shoulder of pork on the
  bone, with the rind still on
Sea salt

For the marinade
8 cloves of garlic, peeled and
  crushed or finely grated
1 tsp ground star anise
2 tbsp peeled (see page 27) and
  finely chopped root ginger
Finely grated zest of 2 oranges
  and juice of 1 orange
150g (5oz) light soft brown
  sugar
75ml (3fl oz) sherry vinegar
4 tbsp chopped coriander
Juice of 1 large lemon
1 tsp salt
1 tsp ground black pepper

Although this is not a quick supper, it is still perfect for an informal meal. It really isn't difficult to prepare and, once cooked, it is an unfussy dish. The shoulder is a cut of meat that requires slow cooking. The marinade imparts its sweet, citrus notes to the pork, while the slow cooking breaks down all the fat and fibres to leave incredibly flavourful and succulent meat. This recipe is delicious served with broccoli and Celeriac Purée (see page 48).

1 Using a craft knife or a very sharp knife, score the rind of the pork, making incisions (about 5mm/¾in deep) all across the surface of the meat in a criss-cross pattern.

2 Next make the marinade by simply mixing all the ingredients in a bowl. Place the pork shoulder in a sealable plastic bag and pour in the marinade, rubbing it into the pork and into any seams or cuts. Chill in the fridge overnight or for at least 12 hours.

3 Preheat the oven to 220°C (425°F), Gas mark 7.

4 Place the pork shoulder on a roasting tray and pour over any of the marinade that hasn't soaked in. Place in the oven and cook for 10 minutes, then reduce the heat to 110°C (225°F), Gas mark ¼, and cook, basting with the juices from time to time, for 12 hours or until the meat feels completely soft and yielding. Take the pork out of the oven and turn the heat up to 220°C (425°F), Gas mark 7. Sprinkle the rind generously with sea salt then pop it back into the oven and cook for a further 10 minutes to crisp up the skin.

5 Remove from the oven, place on a baking tray or carving board and allow to rest for at least 30 minutes. Put in the oven with the heat turned off. While the meat is resting, degrease the cooking juices (see page 226), then pour them back into the roasting tin in which the pork was cooked. Set on a medium heat and cook for about 5 minutes to reduce the liquid and concentrate the flavours. Carve the meat into thick slices or chunks and serve with the sauce.

Spiced poached pears

....

SERVES 6
VEGETARIAN
300ml (½ pint) red wine
110g (4oz) caster sugar
1.5cm (2in) cinnamon stick
1 clove
Juice and finely grated zest
   of 1 orange
6 firm (but not rock-hard)
   pears

A spicy version of classic poached pears, these are lovely with vanilla or cinnamon ice cream, or try with a tangy blue cheese.

1 Pour the wine and 300ml (½ pint) water into a large saucepan and add the sugar, cinnamon stick, clove, orange juice and zest. Place on a medium heat and stir until the sugar dissolves.

2 While the sugar is dissolving, peel the pears, leaving the stalks on, and place upright in the saucepan. They should fit snugly, but if they fall over because the pan is too big, place a folded strip of greaseproof paper or baking parchment around them.

3 Cover the saucepan with a lid and bring to the boil, then reduce the heat and allow to simmer on a low heat for 30–40 minutes. Spoon the red wine syrup over the pears once or twice during this time.

4 To test whether the pears are ready, gently press one with your finger: there should be a little bit of give without being too soft to the touch. Remove from the heat and discard the cinnamon and clove. Spoon the syrup over the pears once more and put into the fridge to chill overnight.

5 When you are ready to serve, take the pears out of the syrup and cut a slice off the bottom of each pear – this will ensure they stand upright on the serving plates. Serve each pear with some spicy syrup drizzled over.

Ginger and treacle pudding

SERVES 8–10
VEGETARIAN

250g (9oz) butter, softened,
    plus extra for greasing
150g (5oz) caster sugar
4 tbsp treacle/molasses
2 eggs
Grated zest and sieved
    juice of 1 orange
200ml (7fl oz) milk
250g (9oz) plain flour
2 tsp baking powder
1 tsp ground cinnamon
75g (3oz) crystallised ginger,
    finely chopped
Icing sugar, for dusting

This moist, delicious pudding can be made a few days in advance and heated gently before serving. It is yummy served with Orange Ice Cream (see page 258) or whipped cream mixed with some grated orange zest.

1 Preheat the oven to 180°C (350°F), Gas mark 4, and line a 30 x 20 x 6cm (12 x 8 x 2½in) ovenproof dish or deep baking tin with non-stick baking paper.

2 Cream the butter in a large bowl or in an electric food mixer until soft. Add the sugar and treacle and beat until the mixture is light and fluffy. Beat in the eggs, one at a time, then whisk in the orange zest and juice and milk. Sift over the flour, baking powder and ground cinnamon, then fold in with the chopped ginger.

3 Spoon the mixture into the baking tin and bake for 40 minutes or until a skewer inserted into the centre comes out clean. Allow to cool for a few minutes before cutting the pudding into squares. Place each square onto a serving plate and dust with icing sugar.

Apricot crumble

SERVES 6
VEGETARIAN

110g (4oz) wholemeal flour
25g (1oz) plain flour
75g (3oz) porridge oats
110g (4oz) butter, cubed
250g (9oz) demerara or light
    soft brown sugar
600g (1lb 5oz) fresh apricots,
    halved and stones removed
100g (3½oz) flaked almonds,
    toasted (see page 25), to
    decorate

23 x 25cm (9 x 10in)
    ovenproof dish

This delicious crumble is wonderful served with homemade custard or vanilla ice cream.

1 Preheat the oven to 180°C (350°F), Gas mark 4.

2 To make the topping, place the flours in a large bowl, add the oats and mix together. Using your fingertips, rub the butter into the flour and oatmeal mixture until it resembles coarse breadcrumbs. Add 110g (4½oz) of the sugar and mix well.

3 Place the apricots, cut side up, in the ovenproof dish. Sprinkle over the remaining sugar and then the crumble mixture to cover the fruit. Cook for 30–40 minutes or until golden and bubbling Serve the crumble warm from the oven, scattering a few toasted almonds on top.

Cherry custard pudding

....

SERVES 6-8
VEGETARIAN

250ml (9fl oz) double or
    regular cream
1 generous tbsp caster
    sugar or vanilla sugar
2 tbsp Kirsch (optional)
450g (1lb) black cherries,
    pitted

For the custard
200ml (7fl oz) milk
1 vanilla pod, split in
    half lengthways
25g (1oz) cornflour
50g (2oz) caster sugar
3 egg yolks

Large glass bowl or 6-8
    individual glasses

Our lovely German au pair Rebecca Zemeitat made this for us at home. The custard is quite thick so the cherries can be added in layers. It can be made in one large glass bowl or in individual glasses. It can also be assembled earlier in the day and kept covered in the fridge until needed.

1 First make the custard. Pour the milk into a saucepan on a low heat, add the vanilla pod, cornflour and half the sugar, and gently heat, stirring constantly, until the sugar has dissolved.

2 In a bowl, beat the egg yolks with the remaining sugar until pale in colour and creamy in consistency. Slowly pour in the hot milk mixture, whisking as you add it in, then pour back into the saucepan (having washed it first to help prevent the custard sticking and scrambling).

3 Whisk well and cook on a low–medium heat for 2–3 minutes, stirring constantly with a wooden spoon (to get to the mixture in the corners of the pan), until the custard has thickened. Now remove the vanilla pod, scrape out some of the seeds and stir these back into the custard. Remove from the heat and allow to cool.

4 In a separate bowl, whip the cream with the vanilla or caster sugar until slightly thickened, then fold in the Kirsch (if using) and the custard.

5 Pour half of the custard cream into a serving bowl, or divide the mixture between individual glasses. Add a layer of cherries, then pour the remaining mixture on top and add the rest of the cherries. Chill in the fridge for 30 minutes before serving.

MENU IDEAS FOR
CASUAL MEALS

Slow-roast ginger and citrus shoulder of pork with green salad (pages 80 and 239)
Apricot crumble (page 83)

*

Roasted vegetable coconut curry (page 66)
Mild lamb curry with boiled rice and naan bread (page 78)
Ginger and treacle pudding (page 83)

*

Chinese-style ribs with coleslaw and baked potatoes (page 77)
Cherry custard pudding (page 84)

STARTERS
Middle Eastern chilled cucumber soup
Harissa roasted vegetables
Tomato and lentil couscous salad
Pan-fried mackerel with panzanella salad

MAIN COURSES
Southeast Asian grilled fish
Salmon teriyaki
Marinades
Spiced barbecued lamb with potato salad and mint raita
Honey, mustard and ginger pork skewers
Lamb and lentil salad with olives and roast red peppers

SALADS AND SIDE DISHES
Broad bean and pancetta salad
Fennel, orange and hazelnut salad
Sue's aubergine, yoghurt and harissa salad
Beetroot slaw
Garlic and herb mushrooms
Grilled asparagus
Barbecued corn on the cob

DESSERTS
Blueberry and custard tart
Strawberries in rosé wine
Strawberries and blueberries with Grand Marnier
Peaches with mascarpone, walnuts and honey

EATING OUTDOORS

When the weather is nice, it's great to throw open the doors and gather one's friends and family around to enjoy time together outside. Picnics, barbecues, dinners in the garden, even beach parties if you're lucky – there are so many options. These are some of my favourite, sunny recipes for when you just don't want to eat indoors! But don't let a little rain stop you from trying them at any time of year – you might just need to keep under cover…

Middle Eastern chilled cucumber soup

....

SERVES 4-6
VEGETARIAN

1 large cucumber, peeled,
   if you wish, and grated
200ml (7fl oz) single or
   regular cream
200ml (7fl oz) natural yoghurt
2 tbsp white wine vinegar
Small handful of coriander,
   plus small sprigs to serve
1 clove of garlic, peeled and
   crushed or finely grated
1 tbsp finely grated gherkins
Salt and ground black pepper

This is an elegant soup. Each ingredient highlights the cucumber's fresh flavour, perfect for a summer's day.

1 Mix all the ingredients, keeping back 4–6 teaspoons cucumber, together in a large bowl and season to taste with salt and pepper, then chill in the fridge for at least 1 hour before serving.

2 Serve in small chilled bowls with a few coriander sprigs and the remaining cucumber sprinkled on top.

Harissa roasted vegetables

....

SERVES 6-8
VEGETARIAN

Good pinch of salt
450g (1lb) new potatoes,
    unpeeled and halved
    or quartered
5 carrots, peeled and cut
    into 1cm (½in) slices
1 head of broccoli, cut into
    large bite-sized chunks
2 red or yellow peppers,
    deseeded and cut into
    bite-sized chunks
2 large courgettes, cut into
    bite-sized chunks
2 tbsp chopped coriander
    or parsley, to serve

For the harissa dressing
1 red pepper
250ml (9fl oz) extra-virgin
    olive oil, plus extra for
    drizzling
2 tbsp coriander seeds,
    ground (see page 25)
1½ tbsp cumin seeds, ground
1 red onion, peeled and
    quartered
3 cloves of garlic, peeled
2 red chillies, deseeded
1 dried red chilli
1 tbsp tomato purée
2 tsp smoked paprika
Juice of 1 lemon
½ tsp salt
1 tsp sugar

*Harissa is a North African chilli sauce with paprika and tomatoes.
If you don't like your food too spicy, just use fewer chillies. It will keep
for a couple of months in the fridge and you can use it to flavour both
meat and fish either as a marinade or as a sauce.*

1 Preheat the oven to 220°C (425°F), Gas mark 7.

2 First make the harissa dressing. Place the red pepper in a
roasting tin, drizzle with a little oil and cook for 40–45 minutes
or until completely softened and the skin blackened. Remove
from the oven and place in a bowl covered with cling film –
this makes the skin easier to remove. When the pepper is cool
enough to handle, use your fingers to peel off the skin, then
cut the pepper in half, deseed and roughly chop.

3 Place all the ingredients except the olive oil in a food processor
and whiz until smooth. With the machine still running,
gradually pour in the olive oil to make a paste, adding more
oil if the dressing is too thick.

4 Fill a large saucepan with water, add the salt and bring to
the boil. Tip in the potatoes, blanch for 4 minutes then add the
carrots and boil for another 3 minutes before removing from
the water and leaving to drain. Add the broccoli to the boiling
water and blanch for 2 minutes, then drain and set aside.

5 Place the blanched potatoes and carrots in a roasting tin
and add the peppers and courgettes. Pour over half the harissa
dressing and mix to thoroughly coat the vegetables. Place in
the oven for 15–20 minutes or until the potatoes are tender,
add the blanched broccoli, mix together and return to the
oven for a further 5 minutes.

6 Remove from the oven, stir in the remaining harissa dressing
and serve, either hot or at room temperature, with the chopped
herbs scattered over the top.

Tomato and lentil couscous salad

....

SERVES 4
VEGETARIAN

5 tbsp olive oil, plus extra
   for drizzling
1 large onion (400g/14oz),
   peeled and sliced
100g (3½oz) Puy lentils
1 tbsp lemon juice
Sea salt and ground black
   pepper
300g (11oz) cherry tomatoes,
   halved widthways
150ml (5fl oz) couscous
150ml (5fl oz) hot vegetable
   stock (see page 50)
2 tbsp each of chopped
   coriander and mint,
   to serve

To serve
3 tbsp thick natural Greek
   yoghurt
1 clove of garlic, peeled and
   crushed or finely grated

The different elements of this salad combine together beautifully, the nutty grains dispersed among the sweet onions and tomatoes and intensely savoury garlic yoghurt. This dish also has the advantage of being able to be made a good few hours in advance.

1 Pour 2 tablespoons of the olive oil into a frying pan on a low heat, add the onion and cook, stirring occasionally, for about 45 minutes until completely soft and caramelised.

2 While the onions are caramelising, cook the lentils. Rinse and place in a saucepan with enough water to cover by 1cm (½in) and simmer for 20–30 minutes until soft. Drain, then add the lemon juice and remaining olive oil and season with salt and pepper.

3 Meanwhile, preheat the oven to 220°C (425°F), Gas mark 7.

4 Place the tomatoes in a roasting tin cut side up, drizzle with a little olive oil and season with salt and pepper, then place in the oven for about 15 minutes or until softened and a little scorched at the edges.

5 In a large bowl, mix the couscous with the hot stock and leave to sit for 5 minutes or until absorbed and soft, then allow to cool. When cooled, mix together with the lentils, tomatoes and onions and stir in the chopped herbs.

6 In a separate small bowl, mix together the yoghurt and garlic and season with sea salt. Disperse teaspoonfuls of the garlic yoghurt throughout the couscous salad without mixing them in and serve.

Pan-fried mackerel with panzanella salad

2 generous tbsp plain flour
8 mackerel fillets, with the
  skin still on
1 tbsp olive oil

For the panzanella salad
3 slices of ciabatta or white
  bread, preferably a couple
  of days old
4 tbsp extra-virgin olive oil
4–6 ripe tomatoes
12 black olives, such as
  kalamata, pitted
  (see page 38)
8 tinned anchovies,
  drained, rinsed and
  roughly chopped
1 heaped tbsp capers,
  drained and rinsed
2 tbsp torn or roughly
  chopped basil
2 tbsp red wine vinegar
  or balsamic vinegar
Sea salt and ground
  black pepper
Pinch of sugar (optional)
Basil leaves, to decorate

This is inspired by a dish we ate at Over the Moon in Skibbereen, a West Cork restaurant gem. The mackerel is perfectly complemented by the bread salad, its oiliness counterbalanced by the punchy anchovies, olives and capers.

1 First make the panzanella salad. Break the bread into chunks and place in a shallow-sided serving dish then drizzle with the extra-virgin olive oil.

2 Cut the tomatoes in half and squeeze out the seeds – not every single one, but just enough to ensure the bread doesn't get too soggy. Chop the tomato flesh and add to the bread along with the remaining ingredients. Season to taste with salt and pepper; it may also need a pinch of sugar.

3 Next prepare the mackerel. Sprinkle the flour onto a plate and season generously with salt and pepper, then place a griddle pan or frying pan on a high heat. While it is heating, dip the mackerel fillets into the flour to coat both sides, shaking off any excess flour.

4 To cook the fish, add the olive oil to the hot pan. Lay the fish in the pan (or as many that will fit in a single layer – the fillets may need to be cooked in a couple of batches), flesh side down. Cook for just a minute or two on each side, then transfer to individual warmed plates and serve with the panzanella salad decorated with some basil leaves on the side.

Southeast Asian grilled fish

....

SERVES 6-8

2cm (¾in) piece of root
 ginger, peeled (see page 27)
 and sliced thinly
1 stick of lemongrass (outer
 layer removed), bruised
 and sliced
2 spring onions, trimmed
 and sliced
1 red chilli, deseeded
 and sliced
2 tbsp light soy sauce
1 tbsp fish sauce (nam pla)
1 tsp caster sugar
2 mackerel or 1 whole small–
 medium fish (½–1kg/1lb
 2oz–2lb 3oz in total), such
 as sea bream, scaled and
 gutted (ask your
 fishmonger to do this)
1–2 tbsp sunflower oil,
 for frying (optional)

To serve
1 tbsp sesame oil
A few drops of fish sauce
 (nam pla)
Squeeze of lemon or
 lime juice
1 tbsp chopped coriander

*Ever since spending a few months travelling around southeast Asia,
I've been enamoured with the flavour combinations in their food.
These ingredients work fantastically well as they bring an array
of salt, sweet, sour and spicy flavours to the fish.*

1 Place half of each of the ginger, lemongrass, spring onions
and chilli into a food processor, along with all of the soy, fish
sauce and sugar, and whiz for 1–2 minutes to form a paste.

2 Score the fish by making cuts about 5mm (¾in) deep at
an angle in the skin and rub in the paste. Fill the cavity with
the remaining ginger, lemongrass, spring onions and chilli,
cover and leave to marinate for 1–2 hours in the fridge.

3 Cook on a moderately hot barbecue – or in a large griddle
pan or frying pan brushed with sunflower oil and placed on
a medium–high heat – for 3–5 minutes on each side or until
the skin is crispy and the fish is opaque all the way through.

4 To serve, drizzle with the sesame oil and fish sauce, squeeze
over some lemon or lime juice and scatter over the coriander.

RACHEL'S TIP

If you are cooking this dish for quite a few people, you can lay the
fish on an oiled oven tray, drizzle a little oil over the top of each
fish, and cook under a hot grill for 3–5 minutes on each side or
until the skin is crispy and the fish opaque all the way through.

Salmon teriyaki

....

SERVES 6-8

8 salmon steaks (200g/
    7oz each)
150ml (5fl oz) dark soy sauce
100g (3½oz) caster sugar
50ml (2fl oz) mirin
1 tsp salt
1 tbsp sunflower oil,
    for frying (optional)

Teriyaki is a famous Japanese cooking technique. It refers to food that is marinated in sweet soy sauce and grilled in the marinade. This traditional sauce is delightfully simple and utterly delicious.

1 Put the salmon in a shallow dish. Place the remaining ingredients, except the sunflower oil, in a small saucepan and heat gently until the sugar has dissolved, then remove from the heat and allow to cool. Pour over the salmon, cover and leave to marinate in the fridge for 2 hours.

2 Remove the salmon from the marinade and place on a moderately hot barbecue (or in a griddle pan or frying pan brushed with sunflower oil and set on a medium–high heat), reserving the marinade. Cook, brushing continuously with the marinade, for 2–3 minutes on each side or until the fish is opaque all the way through. Remove to serving plates and pour over any remaining marinade.

Marinades

························

When barbecuing or oven-roasting a piece of meat, it is often necessary to marinate it first. This means soaking it in a flavoured liquid – the 'marinade' – before cooking. As well as herbs and spices, this usually contains an acidic ingredient – such as citrus juice, vinegar, yoghurt, wine or soy sauce – to help tenderise the meat. Usually no salt is included in the marinade as this can draw out much needed moisture during the soaking time, so unless a recipe calls for salt, don't add it until just before cooking. In order for the marinade to really soak into the meat – especially a large joint – it's generally a good idea to score the surface a few times before adding the marinade.

HOW LONG TO MARINATE MEAT

All the marinades that follow are enough for about 1kg (2lb 3oz) meat, which will serve about 6 people. Once combined with the marinade – in a sealable plastic bag or a covered shallow dish – the meat should be left to marinate in the fridge for at least 2 hours or overnight.

Provençal marinade

....

TO GO WITH BEEF OR LAMB
2 sprigs of thyme
2 sprigs of rosemary
2 bay leaves
4 cloves of garlic, peeled and
    crushed or finely grated
10 whole black peppercorns
150ml (5fl oz) olive oil
50ml (2fl oz) red wine vinegar

1 Put all the ingredients except the vinegar
in a saucepan and place on a medium heat.
Cook until the olive oil just comes to a
simmer then remove from the heat – the
simmering process will allow the flavour
of the herbs to infuse.

2 Add the vinegar and allow to cool, then
combine with the meat.

Char sui marinade

....

FOR PORK, CHICKEN OR BEEF
4 cloves of garlic, peeled and crushed
    or finely grated
2 tbsp light soft brown sugar
2 tbsp peeled and finely chopped root ginger
    (for peeling ginger, see page 27)
2 tbsp runny honey
50ml (2fl oz) light soy sauce
50ml (2fl oz) rice wine or dry sherry
2 tbsp hoisin sauce
2 tsp vegetable oil

1 Mix everything together in a bowl, then
combine with the meat. Don't discard this
marinade after marinating the meat – you
can use it as a sauce.

2 Simply pour into a saucepan, bring to the
boil and cook for 3–4 minutes, then drizzle
over the cooked meat.

Port and orange marinade

....

TO GO WITH BEEF, PORK OR DUCK
2 tbsp peeled and finely chopped root ginger
    (for peeling ginger, see page 27)
4 cloves of garlic, peeled and sliced
Juice of 1/2 lemon
Juice of 1 orange
100ml (3 1/2 fl oz) olive oil
100ml (3 1/2 fl oz) port

1 Mix everything together in a bowl,
then combine with the meat.

Smoked paprika and rosemary marinade

....

TO GO WITH LAMB OR CHICKEN LEGS
2 cloves of garlic, peeled and crushed
    or finely grated
2 tsp smoked paprika
3 tbsp finely chopped rosemary leaves
1/2 tsp ground black pepper
100ml (3 1/2 fl oz) sherry vinegar
2 tbsp olive oil

1 Mix everything together in a bowl,
then rub all over the meat.

Saffron yoghurt marinade
....

TO GO WITH LAMB OR CHICKEN LEGS
2 cloves of garlic, peeled and crushed
1 tsp saffron threads
½ small onion, peeled and finely grated
75ml (3fl oz) natural Greek yoghurt
25ml (1fl oz) olive oil
Juice of 1 lemon
Ground black pepper

1 Mix everything together in a bowl,
then combine with the meat.

Greek marinade
....

TO GO WITH LAMB, CHICKEN OR PORK
2 cloves of garlic, peeled and crushed
2 tbsp finely chopped marjoram
Juice of ½ lemon
100ml (3½fl oz) olive oil
Ground black pepper

1 Mix everything together in a bowl,
then combine with the meat.

Cider marinade
....

TO GO WITH PORK
2 tbsp raisins
2 tbsp light soft brown sugar
Pinch of ground cloves
1 tsp ground cinnamon
½ tsp cardamom seeds
250ml (9fl oz) cider

1 Put all the ingredients in a saucepan
and cook just below simmering point
for 5 minutes or until the raisins have
expanded slightly.

2 Remove from the heat and allow to
cool, then combine with the meat.

Mint yoghurt marinade
....

TO GO WITH CHICKEN OR LAMB
2 tbsp chopped mint
Finely grated zest of 1 lemon
2 tsp each of coriander and cumin seeds,
    ground (see page 25)
Pinch of cayenne pepper
200ml (7fl oz) natural yoghurt

1 Mix everything together in a bowl,
then combine with the meat.

Lemongrass marinade
....

TO GO WITH CHICKEN OR BEEF
4 lemongrass stalks (outer layer removed),
    finely chopped
Zest of ½ lemon
2 cloves of garlic, peeled and crushed
    or finely grated
2 shallots, peeled and finely chopped
1 red chilli, deseeded and finely chopped
2 tsp light soft brown sugar
3 tbsp fish sauce (nam pla)
3 tbsp lime juice

1 Mix everything together in a bowl,
then combine with the meat.

Spiced barbecued lamb with potato salad and mint raita

SERVES 8–12
1 leg of lamb (2.2–2.5kg/
    5–5½lb), butterflied
    (ask you butcher to do this)
3 tbsp chopped coriander,
    to serve

For the marinade
2 tsp each of coriander
    and cumin seeds
1 tsp green cardamom seeds
2 tsp ground turmeric
1 red chilli, deseeded and
    finely chopped
2 tsp salt
4 tbsp olive oil
1 tbsp white wine vinegar
5 garlic cloves, peeled and
    grated or crushed
1 tbsp peeled (see page 27) and
    finely grated root ginger

To serve
450ml (16fl oz) cucumber,
    tomato and mint raita
    (see opposite)
1 quantity of Indian potato
    salad (see opposite)

A leg of lamb steeped in this wonderfully aromatic marinade is ideal for feeding lots of people, whether cooked on the barbecue or in the oven indoors. The meat can be marinated the day (or even two days) before cooking, making it a really entertaining-friendly dish. Serve with the Indian potato salad and the cucumber, tomato and mint raita (see opposite).

1 First make the marinade. Toast and crush the coriander, cumin and cardamom seeds following the tip on page 25. Mix together with all the other marinade ingredients, then massage into the lamb and place in a sealed plastic bag or a covered dish and leave to marinate in the fridge overnight or for at least 8 hours.

2 Take the lamb out of the bag or dish, reserving the marinade, and place on a hot barbecue, quite far from the coals. It should take about 50–65 minutes to cook, depending on how pink you like it, basted from time to time with the reserved marinade. Alternatively, you can cook the lamb in the oven, preheated to 200°C (400°F), Gas mark 6, where it will take about 1–1½ hours, again basted regularly.

3 Remove the lamb from the oven and allow the meat to rest for at least 15 minutes. Serve with the chopped coriander sprinkled on top, Indian potato salad and a bowl of raita on the side.

Indian potato salad with turmeric, chilli and ginger

....

SERVES 8-10
VEGETARIAN
2kg (4lb 4oz) new potatoes
Salt and ground black pepper
75ml (3fl oz) extra-virgin olive oil
2 tsp ground turmeric
3 cloves of garlic, peeled and
   crushed or finely grated
3 tsp peeled (see page 27) and
   finely grated root ginger
¼–½ red chilli, deseeded and chopped
Juice of ½ lemon
1 tbsp chopped coriander, to serve

1 Place the potatoes in a large saucepan of boiling, salted water and cook for 20 minutes or until tender. While the potatoes are boiling, pour the olive oil into a bowl and add the remaining ingredients. Stir to mix.

2 When the potatoes are cooked, drain, peel and chop into 2cm (¾in) pieces. While they are still hot, pour over the oil mixture and gently mix. Season to taste with salt and pepper, sprinkle with chopped coriander and serve at room temperature.

Cucumber, tomato and mint raita

....

MAKES 450ML (16FL OZ)
VEGETARIAN
250g (9oz) natural Greek yoghurt
1 small–medium or ½ large cucumber,
   peeled (optional), deseeded and finely diced
4 large ripe tomatoes, cut into 1cm (½in) dice,
   or 16 cherry tomatoes, halved or quartered
2 tbsp chopped coriander or mint
1 tsp cumin seeds, ground (see page 25)
Salt and ground black pepper

1 Mix all the ingredients together in a bowl, seasoning to taste with salt and pepper.

Honey, mustard and ginger pork skewers

....

MAKES 12 SKEWERS
SERVES 6-8

900g (2lb) lean pork, such as pork fillet, trimmed and cut into 2cm (¾in) cubes

6cm (2½in) piece of root ginger, peeled and cut into fine matchstick pieces (see page 27)

For the marinade

6cm (2½in) piece of root ginger, peeled and finely grated

3 cloves of garlic, peeled and crushed or finely grated

2 tbsp sunflower or vegetable oil

2 tbsp dark soy sauce

1 tbsp runny honey

1 tbsp Dijon mustard

1 tbsp cider vinegar

1 tsp salt

½ tsp ground black pepper

12 metal skewers, or 12 wooden satay sticks (soaked in cold water for 30 minutes to prevent burning)

In this dish I've spiced up the timeless combination of honey, mustard and pork with a little ginger. The crispy ginger topping isn't essential, but it does add a lovely crunch. The ginger is first boiled to take away some of its heat.

1 First make the marinade by mixing all the ingredients together in a large bowl. Add the pork, mixing it with the marinade so that it is well coated, and place in the fridge for at least 1 hour or even overnight.

2 When you are ready to cook the pork, preheat the oven to 200°C (400°F), Gas mark 6, and make the crispy ginger topping.

3 Place a small saucepan of water on the hob and bring to the boil. Add the ginger pieces and boil for 1 minute, then drain, dry with kitchen paper and place in a single layer on a baking tray or roasting tin. Bake in the oven for 5–8 minutes (depending on how thick they are) until golden. Remove from the oven and allow to cool, then set aside.

4 Remove the pork from the fridge and thread onto the skewers or satay sticks.

5 Heat a griddle pan or frying pan on a medium–high heat until very hot, or allow the barbecue to heat up. Place the skewers on the pan or barbecue grill and cook for 3–4 minutes on each side or until cooked all the way through. Sprinkle each skewer with the crisp ginger topping and serve.

Lamb and lentil salad with olives and roast red peppers

....

SERVES 8-10

2 red peppers

6 tbsp olive oil, plus 2 tsp for brushing the red peppers

800g (1¾lb) Puy lentils

200g (7oz) olives, pitted (see page 38) and roughly chopped

150g (5oz) cold roast lamb (see page 337), sliced

25g (1oz) anchovies from a tin, drained, rinsed and chopped

1 tsp Dijon mustard

2 tbsp finely chopped tarragon

Salt and ground black pepper

Squeeze of lemon juice

This is a fantastic way of using any leftover lamb. Anchovies and lamb might seem like a strange combination, but it's actually a classic. The anchovies don't make it fishy, they just add a fullness and depth to the flavour.

1 Preheat the oven to 220°C (425°F), Gas mark 7.

2 First roast the red peppers. Place in a small roasting tin and brush lightly with 1 teaspoon of olive oil, then cook in the oven for 40–45 minutes or until the skins are blackened and charred and the flesh is soft. Remove from the oven and place in a bowl covered with cling film to cool (this makes the skin easier to peel).

3 While the red peppers are roasting, rinse the lentils thoroughly and place in a saucepan. Add enough water to cover by a few centimetres, cover loosely and bring to the boil, then reduce the heat and simmer for 15–20 minutes or until soft. Drain and set aside to cool for 5–10 minutes.

4 Peel the red peppers, removing all the seeds, and cut the flesh into 2cm (¾in) pieces. Place the pepper pieces in a large bowl and add the lentils, 3 tablespoons of olive oil, pitted olives, lamb, anchovies, mustard and tarragon. Mix together well, seasoning to taste with salt, pepper and lemon juice. Serve slightly warm or at room temperature.

Broad bean and pancetta salad

SERVES 6–8 AS A SIDE DISH

1 tbsp olive oil

200g (7oz) pancetta or 5
  rashers of streaky bacon,
  cut into 1cm (½in) dice

400g (14oz) shelled fresh
  or frozen broad beans

1 tbsp chopped mint

125g (4½oz) soft goat's cheese

For the dressing

2 tbsp extra-virgin olive oil

1 tsp finely grated lemon zest

1 tbsp lemon juice

Salt and ground black pepper

A gorgeously summery salad, this is perfect for al fresco entertaining. If your broad beans are small – no bigger than your thumbnail – then it may not be necessary to peel off their skins after cooking. You can use a harder cheese, such as feta or pecorino instead of the soft goat's cheese if you prefer.

1 First make the dressing by mixing together all the ingredients and seasoning with salt and pepper.

2 Place a frying pan on a high heat, then once the pan is good and hot, pour in the olive oil, add the pancetta or bacon and fry until crispy and golden. Drain on kitchen paper and set aside.

3 Meanwhile, bring a large saucepan of water to the boil. Add the beans and boil for ½–1 minute or until they are just cooked, then drain. If the beans are quite big, peel them at this stage (they'll pop out of their skins easily); this isn't essential but I think it's well worth it as the skins can be tough.

4 Dress the beans while they are still warm, then leave to macerate for 15–20 minutes. Finally, add the cooked pancetta and the mint to the beans, crumble the cheese over the top and serve.

Fennel, orange and hazelnut salad

....

SERVES 6-8
VEGETARIAN

4 oranges
Juice of 1 lemon
2 fennel bulbs
110g (4oz) hazelnuts,
  toasted, peeled (see
  page 29) and chopped
2 tbsp chopped mint

I love this salad – it's fantastically fresh and crunchy, and great as a starter before serving something rich like duck or goose. It's also good served with barbecued meats.

1 Peel the oranges (see tip below) and cut across the width of each fruit to make slices about 5mm (¼in) thick. Squeeze out the juice from any flesh still left on the peel and pour it into a large bowl with the lemon juice, then discard the peel.

2 To prepare the fennel, slice off the tops and the fronds (save the feathery fennel bits for scattering over the salad when serving), then thinly slice lengthways using a sharp knife or a mandolin.

3 Finally, add the orange and fennel slices to the bowl with the lemon and orange juices, and mix together. Scatter with the hazelnuts and the chopped mint and serve on individual plates or a single serving dish. (This can be prepared in advance up to the point of scattering the hazelnuts and chopped mint over the top. Chop the mint closer to the time, however, otherwise it will turn black.)

RACHEL'S TIP

A good way of peeling an orange, especially the thinner-skinned varieties, is to first slice the top and the bottom off the fruit just below the pith and into the flesh (but trying not to cut into the flesh too much). Next stand the orange on a chopping board and, using a small sharp knife, slice off the peel in strips following the curvature of the orange.

Sue's aubergine, yoghurt and harissa salad

....

SERVES 6-8 PEOPLE
VEGETARIAN

3 aubergines
75ml (3fl oz) olive oil
4 tsp cumin seeds, ground
    (see page 25)
Salt
25ml (1fl oz) natural yoghurt
3–4 tsp harissa dressing
    (see page 90)
3 tbsp chopped coriander,
    plus 1 tbsp whole coriander
    leaves, to serve

One of the teachers at the Ballymaloe Cookery School, Sue Cullinane, makes this delicious Middle Eastern-inspired salad. It's warm and spicy, and the roasted aubergines give it a wonderful sweetness.

1 Preheat the oven to 230°C (450°F), Gas mark 8.

2 Cut the aubergines into 2cm (¾in) chunks, then place in a roasting tin. Add the olive oil and cumin and toss to coat. Place in the oven and roast for 10–12 minutes or until soft and golden, then season with salt and allow to cool.

3 Meanwhile, mix the yoghurt, harissa and chopped coriander. Drizzle the mixture over the cooked aubergines and scatter with the whole coriander leaves to serve.

Beetroot slaw

....

SERVES 6-8
VEGETARIAN

100g (3½oz) raw beetroot
100g (3½oz) carrot
100g (3½oz) green leafy
    cabbage, such as Savoy
50g (2oz) raisins
100g (3½oz) pecans, toasted
    (see page 25) and roughly
    chopped
2 tbsp walnut, hazelnut or olive
    oil (in order of preference)
1–2 tbsp lemon juice
Salt and ground black pepper

This is a colourful, crunchy salad that looks great in a big bowl. Watch out when grating the beetroot as it can stain quite easily, so wear rubber gloves (if you want to avoid having cerise-pink hands) and an apron.

1 Peel and grate the beetroot and carrot and quarter the cabbage lengthways. Remove the core and finely slice the leaves.

2 Mix all the ingredients together, seasoning to taste with the lemon juice and salt and pepper.

Garlic and herb mushrooms

....

SERVES 6-8
VEGETARIAN
6-8 large flat or portabello
   mushrooms (1 per person)
60-75g (2½-3oz) garlic and
   herb butter (see below)

Very simple to make and so delicious, these mushrooms are lovely cooked on the barbecue instead of in the oven, and are particularly good with lamb chops or steaks. You can easily make larger quantities of the garlic and herb butter and freeze it for up to two months. It's so handy to have in the freezer, to use for anything from a cooked juicy steak or lamb chops to a simple baked potato. You can then slice off pieces as you need them. Leave out the garlic, if you wish, or feel free to add other ingredients, such as chilli, mustard, olives or sun-dried tomatoes.

1 Preheat the oven to 230°C (450°F), Gas mark 8.

2 Wipe the mushrooms clean, then remove the stem from each mushroom, leaving a small well in the centre of the mushroom. Fill this with 1–2 teaspoons of the garlic and herb butter, then place on a baking tray and cook in the oven for 10–20 minutes or until the mushrooms are cooked through and browned. Alternatively, wrap the mushrooms in foil and cook on a hot barbecue for 20–35 minutes. Serve immediately.

Garlic and herb butter

SERVES 8-10
VEGETARIAN
100g (3½oz) butter, softened
2 tbsp finely chopped parsley
1 tbsp lemon juice (or to taste)
3 cloves of garlic, peeled and
   crushed
2 tbsp chopped herbs, such
   as tarragon, marjoram,
   chives, parsley, watercress,
   rocket or thyme, or a
   mixture of these

1 Beat the butter in a bowl until very soft then add the rest of the ingredients and mix thoroughly.

2 Serve like this or place on a piece of cling film or baking parchment and roll into a sausage shape about 3cm (1¼in) in diameter and store in the fridge or freezer.

Grilled asparagus

....

SERVES 6–8
VEGETARIAN
16 asparagus spears
Salt and ground black pepper
4–6 tbsp olive oil, plus extra
   for frying (optional)

A light grilling gives gentle scorch marks to the asparagus and adds just a little smokiness to the flavour.

1 Rub the asparagus all over with olive oil and season with sea salt and pepper.

2 Place on a moderately hot barbecue – or griddle pan or frying pan brushed with oil and set on a medium–high heat – and cook for just about 7–10 minutes, turning regularly.

Barbecued corn on the cob

....

SERVES 6–8
VEGETARIAN
8 corn on the cob
Olive oil, for drizzling
Salt and ground black pepper

Using different flavoured butters is a great way of enlivening corn on the cob. Here are two ideas, but it's fun to experiment.

1 Drizzle the corn with a little olive oil, season with salt and pepper and place on a hot barbecue.

2 Cook for 10–15 minutes, turning every so often, until the kernels are slightly soft and charred in places.

3 Remove from the barbecue and serve by brushing with one of the flavoured butters (see below).

FLAVOURED BUTTERS

Cumin and fresh coriander butter: Mix together 200g (7oz) butter (softened) with 2 teaspoons of ground cumin seeds (for grinding, see tip on page 25) and 2 tablespoons of chopped coriander, seasoning to taste with salt and ground black pepper.

Lemon and marjoram butter: Mix together 200g (7oz) butter with 2 teaspoons each of lemon zest and juice and 2 tablespoons of chopped marjoram, seasoning to taste with salt and pepper.

Blueberry and custard tart

....

SERVES 6-8
VEGETARIAN

375g (13oz) fresh blueberries
2 tsp redcurrant jelly
   (see page 337)
2 tsp water, just boiled

For the sweet shortcrust pastry
175g (6oz) plain flour
100g (3½oz) chilled butter,
   cubed, plus extra for
   greasing
25g (1oz) caster sugar
1 egg, separated and the
   white lightly whisked

For the custard
200ml (7fl oz) milk
1 vanilla pod, split in half
   lengthways
25g (1oz) cornflour
50g (2oz) caster sugar
3 egg yolks
200ml (7fl oz) whipped cream

23cm (9in) diameter loose-
   bottomed shallow tart tin

This is a great dessert for summer entertaining. The pastry can be made a day in advance of filling and serving, and if you'd rather use raspberries, there's nothing to stop you.

1 Begin by making the pastry. Place the flour, butter and sugar in a food processor and whiz briefly until the butter is in small lumps. Add the egg yolk and continue to whiz for another few seconds or until the mixture looks as though it may just come together. (Bear in mind that prolonged processing will only toughen the pastry, so don't whiz it up to the point where it forms a ball of dough.) If the pastry is still too dry, you can add a small amount of the egg white, but not too much as the mixture should be just moist enough to come together. If making by hand, sift the flour and salt into a large bowl. Rub the butter into the flour until the mixture resembles coarse breadcrumbs. Add the sugar and gently mix in using a fork. Drizzle in the egg yolk and lightly stir it in with a knife until the mixture comes together, adding more egg yolk if necessary.

2 With your hands, flatten out the ball of dough until it is about 2cm (¾in) thick, then cover with cling film or greaseproof paper and chill for at least 30 minutes in the fridge.

3 When you are ready to roll out the pastry, butter the tart tin and remove the pastry from the fridge, placing it between two sheets of cling film (each wider than your tart tin). Using a rolling pin, roll out the pastry until it's about 3mm (⅛in) thick and wide enough to line the base and sides of the prepared tin. Make sure to keep it in a round shape as well as large enough to line both the base and sides of the tin.

4 Remove the top layer of cling film, slide your hand, palm upwards, under the bottom layer of cling film, then flip the pastry over (so that the cling film is now on top) and carefully lower it into the tart tin. Press into the edges (with the cling film still

attached) and, using your thumb, 'cut' the pastry on the edge of the tin to give a neat finish. Remove the cling film, prick over the base with a fork and chill the pastry in the fridge for a further 30 minutes or in the freezer for 10 minutes (it can keep for weeks like this in the freezer).

5 Meanwhile, preheat the oven to 180°C (350°F), Gas mark 4.

6 Remove the pastry from the fridge or freezer and line with foil, greaseproof paper or baking parchment, leaving plenty to come over the sides of the tin. Fill with baking beans or dried pulses (you can use these over and over again) and bake 'blind' for 15–20 minutes or until the pastry feels dry to the touch in the base. Remove the foil/paper and beans, brush with a little egg white and return to the oven for a further 5–8 minutes or until the pastry is lightly golden. Remove from the oven and allow to cool.

7 To make the custard, pour the milk into a saucepan on a low heat, add the vanilla pod, cornflour and half the sugar and gently heat for 1–2 minutes, stirring to combine.

8 In a bowl, beat the egg yolks with the remaining sugar until they turn creamy in consistency and pale in colour. Slowly pour in the hot milk mixture, whisking as you add it, then pour back into a clean saucepan. (It's best to use a fresh or cleaned pan to lessen the chance of the sauce sticking and scrambling.)

9 Whisk well and place over a low–medium heat, then cook for 2–4 minutes, stirring constantly with a wooden spoon, until the custard has thickened. Now remove the vanilla pod, scrape out some of the seeds and stir these back into the custard. Remove from the heat and allow to cool. Fold in the whipped cream.

10 To assemble the tart, spoon the cooled custard cream into the pastry case and top with the blueberries. Dissolve the redcurrant jelly in the just-boiled water. Using a pastry brush, gently coat the blueberries with this glaze, taking care not to move the blueberries or disturb the custard. This will give the tart a lovely finishing gloss.

11 To serve, remove the tart from the tin (with the base of the tin still attached, if that's easier) and carefully transfer it to a serving plate or cake stand.

Strawberries in rosé wine

....

SERVES 4
VEGETARIAN
275g (10oz) strawberries,
    hulled and quartered
    lengthways (or halved
    if they are small)
50g (2oz) caster sugar
4 tbsp rosé or white wine

4 wine glasses or bowls

This is a very simple recipe – a classic French way to dress up strawberries. Of course, this is at its best in summer when strawberries are locally grown and perfectly ripe. Serve the marinated strawberries in champagne flutes or delicate bowls, either on their own or with meringues and cream or shortbread biscuits (see page 58).

1 Place the strawberries in a bowl with the sugar, add the wine and stir gently to combine the ingredients.

2 Cover and place in the fridge for at least 2 hours, preferably overnight. If possible, give the bowl a little swirl once or twice during that time.

3 Serve chilled, divided between the wine glasses or bowls.

Strawberries and blueberries with Grand Marnier

....

SERVES 4
VEGETARIAN
225g (8oz) strawberries,
    hulled and sliced
75g (3oz) fresh or frozen
    and defrosted blueberries
Juice of 1 orange
4 tsp Grand Marnier or
    Cointreau
Crème fraîche, to serve

4 glasses or decorative bowls

This gorgeous summery dessert is so easy to put together.

1 In a large bowl, gently mix together all the ingredients.

2 Serve in the glasses or bowls with a dollop of crème fraîche.

Peaches with mascarpone, walnuts and honey

....

SERVES 10
VEGETARIAN

Butter, for greasing
10 peaches
6 tbsp mascarpone
6 tbsp runny honey, plus
    extra to serve
75g (3oz) shelled walnuts or
    pecans, toasted (see page 25)
    and chopped

Medium-sized gratin or
    ovenproof dish

Mascarpone is a mild, slightly sweet flavoured soft cheese from Italy. Essential to many Italian desserts, especially tiramisu, here it enriches sweet ripe peaches. This elegant dish is delicious served simply on its own, or with vanilla ice cream.

1 Preheat the oven to 200°C (400°F), Gas mark 6, and butter the gratin or ovenproof dish.

2 Cut a cross at the bottom of each peach and place them into a heatproof bowl. Pour over freshly boiled water to cover and leave for a minute or two. Carefully remove the peaches from the bowl and, using a sharp knife, peel off the skins. Halve and stone each peach, remove the stone and place, cut side up, in the gratin dish.

3 In a separate bowl, mix together the mascarpone and honey, then spoon this into the cavity of each peach, dividing the mixture equally between the peach halves. Cover the dish with foil and bake in the oven for 20–25 minutes or until the peaches are soft.

4 Serve the peaches with a good drizzle of honey and some toasted walnuts or pecans scattered on top.

MENU IDEAS FOR
EATING OUTDOORS

Tomato and lentil couscous salad (page 91)
Southeast Asian grilled fish with fennel, orange and hazelnut salad (pages 94 and 108)
Blueberry and custard tart (pages 114–15)

*

Harissa roasted vegetables (page 90)
Spiced barbecued lamb with potato salad and mint raita and
barbecued corn on the cob (pages 100 and 113)
Strawberries in rosé wine (page 117)

*

Middle Eastern chilled cucumber soup (page 88)
Honey, mustard and ginger pork skewers with
broad bean and pancetta salad (pages 102 and 107)
Peaches with mascarpone, walnuts and honey (page 118)

*

Pan-fried mackerel with panzanella salad with
beetroot slaw, grilled asparagus and
barbecued corn on the cob (pages 92, 110 and 113)
Strawberries and blueberries with Grand Marnier (page 117)

SAVOURY CANAPÉS

Moroccan tomato and yoghurt shots

Spicy pastry straws

Black pudding, blue cheese and beetroot toasts

Caramelised onion, blue cheese and walnut tarts

Gently spiced prawn and bacon skewers

Smoked salmon tartlets

Buckwheat blinis with smoked salmon, crème fraîche and caviar

Crab, chorizo and anchovy toasts

Potato soup with chorizo and parsley pesto

Thai chicken cakes with sweet chilli jam

Duck and Chinese five-spice spring rolls

Mini Yorkshire puddings with peppered steak and onion jam

COCKTAILS

Watermelon margaritas

Elderflower champagne

Negroski

Summer punch

Tropical fruit fizz

Apple, rum and ginger

SWEET CANAPÉS

Mendiants

Chocolate, pecan and meringue squares

Pistachio and cranberry chocolates

Crystallised ginger fudge

Mini coffee cupcakes

CANAPÉS AND SMALL BITES

Canapés and cocktails are a fun way to start a dinner party, especially for a special occasion. You can also have a canapés-only party, including dessert, rather than a sit-down meal. You and your guests can mingle and chat, which isn't always possible sitting at a table, and everyone loves the surprise of what comes out of the kitchen next! Ask a family member or friend to help serve, and remember to have enough large platters or trays so that as one goes around, you're getting the next one ready.

Moroccan tomato and yoghurt shots

....

MAKES 10–12 SHOTS
VEGETARIAN

250g (9oz) very ripe tomatoes
Juice of ½ lemon
2 tsp finely chopped mint
2 cloves of garlic, peeled
and crushed
Salt and freshly ground pepper
Good pinch of sugar
450ml (16fl oz) natural
yoghurt

10–12 chilled shot glasses

This is best made in summer with really good red ripe tomatoes. Serve before a meal as a little amuse-bouche – which literally means 'mouth amuser', to get your taste buds tingling. They are pictured here with Spicy Pastry Straws (see page 124).

1 Roughly chop the tomatoes and place in a blender with the lemon juice, mint and garlic. Season with salt, pepper and sugar and blend for 2–3 minutes.

2 Push through a sieve, discarding the pulp, and whisk in the yoghurt. Serve in chilled shot glasses. Alternatively, layer the yoghurt and sieved tomatoes and mint in the shot glasses and serve with a swizzle stick.

Spicy pastry straws

....

MAKES ABOUT
40 PASTRY STRAWS
VEGETARIAN

Plain flour, for dusting
150g (3oz) ready-made
    puff pastry

Flavouring choices
1 tsp each of ground cumin
    and coriander and sea salt
50g (2oz) Parmesan or
    Parmesan-style cheese,
    finely grated and mixed
    with a pinch of cayenne
    pepper
1 x 25g tin of anchovies,
    drained, rinsed and finely
    chopped and mixed with
    2 tbsp sesame seeds
3 tbsp tapenade (see page 163),
    mixed with 25g (1oz) finely
    grated Parmesan or
    Parmesan-style cheese

These are an ideal finger food to serve with drinks (see the picture on page 123). You can use pre-rolled puff pastry to make them. If you have any leftover pastry scraps after making the Raspberry Millefeuille (see page 304), use them for this!

1 Preheat the oven to 220°C (425°F), Gas mark 7.

2 On a work surface lightly dusted with flour, roll the pastry into a rectangle about 20 x 40cm (8 x 16in) and about 3mm (1/8 in) thick.

3 Sprinkle one half of the pastry sheet evenly with your chosen flavouring, then fold over the other half of the pastry to completely cover the scattered ingredients. Roll out the pastry again to the same dimensions as before (20 x 40cm/8 x 16in), so that the scattered ingredients become embedded in it. If it is quite warm and sticky by this stage, you may need to place it on a baking sheet (the metal will help to chill it quickly) and place in the fridge for about 15 minutes.

4 Using a pastry wheel or a knife, cut the pastry into strips about 1cm (1/2 in) wide and 15cm (6in) long and give them a little twist if you like. Place on a baking sheet or two and cook in the oven for about 8 minutes or until golden brown and crisp. Take out of the oven and cool on a wire rack.

RACHEL'S TIP
These can be prepared in advance and frozen while raw. A good way to do this is to tray-freeze them first (i.e. freeze them on a baking sheets/trays). Once they have frozen solid, take them off the sheet or tray (if you need the space in the freezer), carefully transfer them to a plastic bag or box and put back in the freezer (they will keep like this for up to three months). When baked from frozen, they will take only an extra minute or two in the oven to cook.

Black pudding, blue cheese and beetroot toasts

....

MAKES 10 TOASTS

Olive oil, for drizzling
    and frying
10 slices of black pudding,
    7mm–1cm (3/8–1/2in) thick
10 slices of baguette, 1cm
    (1/2in) thick
10 slices of blue cheese, 5mm
    (1/4in) thick
10 slices of pickled beetroot,
    5mm (1/4in) thick

On a trip to San Sebastian in Spain, we ate a great many excellent pintxos (pronounced 'pinchos'), the local version of tapas, and this recipe was inspired by one of them. The flavours of the blue cheese and black pudding are balanced perfectly by the tangy pickled beetroot. Serve warm, or at room temperature, as little bites to enjoy with drinks, or as a starter.

1 Preheat the grill to hot and place a large frying pan on a medium heat and pour in a small drizzle of olive oil. Add the black pudding slices and cook on both sides for 4 minutes then drain on kitchen paper.

2 Toast the bread on both sides under the grill until golden, then drizzle each side with a little olive oil.

3 On each baguette toast, arrange first a piece of black pudding, then a piece of cheese and finally a slice of pickled beetroot. Serve immediately.

RACHEL'S TIP

If you're entertaining lots of people and need to get ahead, the toasts can be made earlier in the day and just slightly warmed through before serving.

Caramelised onion, blue cheese and walnut tarts

....

MAKES ABOUT
50 MINI TARTS
VEGETARIAN

4 large onions (about
400g/14oz each)
6 tbsp olive oil
Salt and ground black pepper
Plain flour, for dusting
300g (11oz) all-butter
puff pastry
4 tbsp roughly chopped
walnuts, toasted
(see page 25)
150g (5oz) blue cheese, cut
into 1cm (½in) cubes

These are great to serve as canapés with drinks. You can also make them in advance and store them in the freezer. (For convenience tray-freeze them first – see page 124 – before transferring into a freezer bag.) If cooking from frozen, they'll take an extra minute or two in the oven.

1 Preheat the oven to 220°C (425°F), Gas mark 7.

2 Peel the onions, then cut in half lengthways through the root and thinly slice along the width, parallel to the root.

3 To caramelise them, pour the olive oil into a large frying pan on a low heat, add the sliced onions, season with salt and pepper and stir to combine. Cook, uncovered, for 40–50 minutes, stirring occasionally (you may need to scrape the bottom of the pan to remove the lovely sweet golden bits and mix them in with the rest), until the onions are golden, completely soft and sweet. Remove from the heat and set aside. (The onions can be kept in the fridge for up to a week.)

4 On a work surface lightly dusted with flour, roll out the pastry into a rectangle about 20 x 40cm (8 x 16in) in size and 3mm (⅛in) thick. Next cut the rectangle into fifty 4cm (1½in) squares.

5 Arrange the squares on the baking sheets, turn each one over (this helps them to really puff up), then add 1 teaspoon of the caramelised onions in the centre of each square, 2–3 pieces of chopped walnut and a cube of cheese. (The tarts can be frozen – and cooked from frozen – or refrigerated for up to 48 hours, at this point.)

6 Cook in the oven for 7–10 minutes or until golden, crispy and puffed up.

Gently spiced prawn and bacon skewers

....

MAKES 30
30 medium-sized prawns
   or langoustines
6 tbsp olive oil
1 tbsp chopped thyme leaves
1 tbsp chopped rosemary
   leaves
1 tsp paprika
1 tsp ground coriander
1 tsp coriander seeds, ground
   (see page 25)
4 large cloves of garlic, peeled
   and finely chopped
15 rashers of streaky bacon,
   cut in half
Lime slices, to serve

10 metal skewers, or 10
   wooden satay sticks, soaked
   in water for 30 minutes

Prawns and bacon make a delicious combination. Serve two or three on each skewer or satay stick and accompany with some slices of fresh lime.

1 Place the prawns in a freezer bag with the olive oil, herbs, spices and garlic and leave to marinate for about 2 hours.

2 Before cooking, wrap each prawn in half a piece of streaky bacon. Place three prawns on a skewer and cook under a hot grill or on the barbecue, or in a griddle pan on a medium–high heat, for 4–5 minutes on each side or until the bacon is crispy and the prawns are firm all the way through.

3 Serve immediately decorated with a slice of lime.

Smoked salmon tartlets

....

For the shortcrust pastry (if using)
125g (4½oz) plain flour, sifted
75g (3oz) chilled butter, cubed, plus extra for greasing
Pinch of salt
1 egg, beaten

For the filo pastry (if using)
3 sheets
50g (2oz) butter, melted, plus extra for greasing

For the filling
1 egg
125ml (4½fl oz) single or regular cream
2 tsp chopped herbs, such as chives, parsley, dill or fennel
100g (3½oz) smoked salmon, chopped into 5mm (¼in) pieces
Squeeze of lemon juice
Salt and ground black pepper

6cm (2½in) pastry cutter and a 24-hole mini-muffin tin

You can use either shortcrust or filo pastry for these tartlets. Shortcrust is a little more substantial, while filo is more delicate. These can be made about 24 hours in advance. If you like, you can replace the smoked salmon with smoked mackerel or pre-cooked chicken and/or bacon.

1 If making shortcrust pastry, place the flour, butter and salt in a food processor and whiz briefly until the butter is in small lumps. Add half the beaten egg and continue to whiz for just another few seconds or until the mixture looks as though it may come together when pressed. (Prolonged processing will only toughen the pastry, so don't whiz it up until it is a ball of dough.) You might need to add a little more egg, but not too much as the mixture should be just moist enough to come together. If making by hand, rub the butter into the flour and salt until it resembles coarse breadcrumbs, then add just enough egg to bring the mixture together.

2 With your hands, flatten out the ball of dough into a round about 2cm (¾in) thick, then wrap in cling film or place in a plastic bag and leave in the fridge for at least 30 minutes.

3 While the pastry is chilling, make the filling. Whisk together the egg, cream and herbs, stir in the smoked salmon and lemon juice and taste for seasoning.

4 Preheat the oven to 180°C (350°F), Gas mark 4, and butter the muffin tin.

5 Remove the pastry from the fridge and place between two large sheets of cling film. Using a rolling pin, roll the pastry out until it is very thin (about 3mm/⅛in thick), then remove the top layer of cling film and, using the pastry cutter, cut into 24 rounds. If using

filo pastry, cut the sheets into 72 x 6cm (2½ in) squares (three squares per tartlet).

6 If using shortcrust pastry, lightly push down the pastry rounds into the muffin moulds to form cups. If using filo pastry, take one square, brush with melted butter, then place in a muffin mould.

7 Repeat with another square and place in the same mould, perpendicular to the previous square. Repeat once more so there are there three layers of pastry in each mould. Then repeat for all 24 moulds.

8 Next add the filling. Pour 1–2 tablespoons into each mould, then place the tin in the oven for 15–20 minutes or until the filling has set and the pastry is golden and crisp.

VARIATION

These can also be lovely made without any pastry at all. Just grease the muffin tin with a little melted butter, add a tablespoon or two of the filling straight into each mould and bake for 15–20 minutes or until set. Remove and allow to slightly cool before serving.

Buckwheat blinis with smoked salmon, crème fraîche and caviar

....

MAKES ABOUT 40 BLINIS
VEGETARIAN

50g (2oz) buckwheat flour
100g (3 oz) strong white flour
tsp salt
1 x 7g sachet fast-acting yeast
2 eggs, separated
150ml (5fl oz) milk, at room temperature
150ml (5fl oz) crème fraîche, at room temperature
25g (1oz) butter

For the topping
110g (4oz) smoked salmon, cut into small slices
200ml (7fl oz) crème fraîche
25g (1oz) caviar
Dill sprigs, to decorate

A traditional Russian treat, these lightly leavened pancakes use buckwheat flour, which has an earthy taste. Topped with caviar and/ or smoked salmon, they marry the luxurious with the rustic. These mini-blinis can be popped in the mouth with your fingers.

1 Sift the two flours and the salt together into a bowl and stir in the yeast.

2 In another bowl, whisk the egg yolks with the milk and crème fraîche, and pour over the flour mixture. Whisk everything together, then cover with cling film or a clean tea towel and leave in a warm place for about 1 hour or until the mixture is bubbling.

3 In a separate, spotlessly clean bowl, whisk the egg whites until they form stiff peaks, then gently fold into the batter. Cover again and leave for a further hour.

4 To fry the blinis, melt some of the butter in a large, non-stick frying pan on a medium heat, using a little kitchen paper to spread the butter around the pan – you need just enough to cover the base. When the pan is hot and the butter beginning to turn brown, add 1 teaspoon of batter per blini and cook for 30–40 seconds or until bubbles appear on top and the underside is golden, then turn oven and fry on the other side until golden.

5 As each blini is cooked, transfer to a wire rack to cool while you cook the remaining batter, adding more butter to the pan as you need it.

6 To serve, top each blini with a slice of salmon, 1 teaspoon of crème fraîche followed by 1 teaspoon of caviar and a piece of dill.

Crab, chorizo and anchovy toasts

....

MAKES 10 TOASTS
10 slices of baguette,
   1cm (½in) thick
Olive oil, for drizzling
150g (5oz) crab meat,
   shredded (for how to
   cook a crab, see page 36)
2 tsp mayonnaise (see
   page 317)
2 tsp peeled and finely
   grated onion
1 tsp Dijon mustard
Salt and ground black pepper
Small squeeze of lemon juice
   (optional)
20 slices of chorizo sausage,
   about 5mm (¼in) thick
A few lettuce leaves
10 tinned anchovies, drained
   and rinsed

All the components for these tasty little morsels can be prepared and cooked in advance, but you'll need to assemble them closer to the time you want to eat them – an hour or two beforehand. (Pictured with the Potato Soup with Chorizo and Parsley Pesto, see overleaf.)

1 Preheat the grill to hot and toast the baguette slices on both sides until golden. Drizzle each side with olive oil, and set aside.

2 In a bowl, mix together the crab meat, mayonnaise, grated onion and mustard. Taste for seasoning; it may need a small squeeze of lemon juice. Once made, this can sit in the fridge for up to 24 hours.

3 Place a large frying pan on a medium heat, then add a tiny drizzle of olive oil. Tip in the chorizo slices and fry on both sides for 2–3 minutes or until cooked, then drain on kitchen paper and allow to cool.

4 When you are ready to serve, assemble the toasts by first placing the baguette croutons on a large plate. Arrange a small piece of lettuce on each crouton, followed by two chorizo slices, a small dollop of the crab meat mixture and an anchovy carefully laid across the top to finish.

Potato soup with chorizo and parsley pesto

....

SERVES ABOUT 50
25g (1oz) butter
425g (15oz) potatoes,
    peeled and chopped
150g (5oz) onions, peeled
    and chopped
Salt and ground black pepper
750ml (1⅓ pints) chicken
    or vegetable stock
    (see pages 50–1)
250ml (9fl oz) milk, or
    half milk and half single
    or regular cream

To serve
250g (9oz) chorizo, cut into
    5mm (¼in) cubes
1 tbsp olive oil
100ml (3½fl oz) parsley pesto
    (see below)

This delicious soup an be made in advance and looks wonderful served with the parsley pesto and chorizo (see picture on page 134). Pour into espresso cups to serve as a canapé. Stored in a jar in the fridge, parsley pesto will keep as long as it's always re-covered with oil for a few months.

1 Melt the butter in a large saucepan on a medium heat. Add the potatoes and onions and seasoning, stir well and cover with a butter wrapper or greaseproof paper. Put the lid on the pan, turn down the heat and sweat for 10 minutes, stirring regularly.

2 Add the stock, cover again, bring to the boil then reduce the heat and simmer for 5–10 minutes until the vegetables are soft. Pour in the milk, bring back to the boil and liquidise in a blender (or use a hand-held blender). You may need to add more stock to thin it to a velvety and smooth consistency. Season to taste.

3 Fry the chorizo in the olive oil in a frying pan on a medium heat for 2–3 minutes. Remove from the pan when it is crisp and drain on kitchen paper, reserving the rich-coloured oil left in the pan.

4 To serve, pour the hot soup into espresso cups, drizzle with a little parsley pesto, then top with a few cubes of cooked chorizo and a drizzle of the chorizo oil from the pan.

Parsley pesto

MAKES 150ML (5FL OZ)
VEGETARIAN
25g (1oz) parsley, chopped
25g (1oz) Parmesan or
    Parmesan-style cheese,
    grated
25g (1oz) pine nuts
2 cloves of garlic, peeled
    and crushed
75ml (3fl oz) extra-virgin
    olive oil, plus extra
Good pinch of salt

1 Place all the ingredients except the olive oil in a food processor and whiz together. Add the oil and a good pinch of salt and taste for seasoning.

2 Pour into a screw-top jar (for sterilising jars, see page 42), cover with 1cm (½in) of oil and store in the fridge.

RACHEL'S TIP
I pour this soup into a jug and top up guests as they like.

Thai chicken cakes with sweet chilli jam

....

MAKES 20

Sunflower oil, for greasing
1 lemongrass stalk
500g (1lb 2oz) minced chicken
2 tsp peeled (see page 27) and finely chopped or grated root ginger
4 spring onions, trimmed and finely sliced
1 clove of garlic, peeled and crushed
1 tbsp roughly chopped coriander
½ red chilli, deseeded and finely chopped
75g (3oz) fresh white breadcrumbs
1 egg
2 tbsp fish sauce (nam pla)
Salt and ground black pepper
100ml (3½ fl oz) sweet chilli jam (see below), to serve

Nowadays, foods that would once have been considered exotic, tasted only on far away trips to Asia, are easily available and routinely cooked at home. The sweet chilli jam is a perfect accompaniment to the Thai flavours in the chicken cakes. You can make it in advance and it will keep for a few months.

1 Preheat the oven to 200°C (400°F), Gas mark 6, and oil a baking tray with sunflower oil.

2 Prepare the lemongrass by peeling off the outer later and finely chopping the inside of the stalk. Place all the ingredients in a bowl, season with salt and pepper and mix to combine.

3 Wet your hands then shape the mixture into 20 balls each about 2cm (¾in) in diameter. Transfer these to the prepared baking tray and lightly flatten to form small patties.

4 Place in the oven and cook for 10–12 minutes or until lightly browned and cooked through. Remove from the oven and serve with the sweet chilli jam.

MAKES 1 X 400G (14OZ) JAR
VEGETARIAN

25g (1oz) root ginger, peeled (see page 27) and roughly chopped
3 cloves of garlic, peeled
2 red chillies, deseeded
2 tbsp fish sauce (nam pla)
375g (13oz) tomatoes or cherry tomatoes, peeled (see page 74) and chopped
200g (7oz) caster sugar
75ml (3fl oz) sherry vinegar or white wine vinegar

Sweet chilli jam

1 Put the ginger, garlic, chillies and fish sauce into a blender (or use a hand-held blender) and whiz to a purée. Place the purée in a saucepan with the tomatoes, sugar and vinegar and bring to the boil. Reduce the heat and simmer, stirring regularly, for 8–10 minutes or until thick and jam-like in consistency.

2 Place in a sterilised jar (for sterilising jars, see page 42), cover with a lid and allow to cool, or pour straight into a bowl to cool, if serving with the Thai Chicken Cakes (see above).

Duck and Chinese five-spice spring rolls

....

MAKES 32 SPRING ROLLS

Vegetable oil, for stir-frying
   and deep-frying
1 tbsp peeled (see page 27) and
   finely grated root ginger
3 garlic cloves, peeled and
   finely chopped
100g (3½oz) mushrooms,
   chopped
150g (5oz) cooked duck,
   finely shredded
½–1 tsp Chinese five-spice
   powder
1 tbsp sesame oil
100g (3½oz) green cabbage,
   such as Savoy, quartered
   lengthways, core removed
   and leaves finely chopped
100g (3½oz) carrots, cut
   into matchsticks
2 tbsp light soy sauce
2 tbsp hoisin sauce
4 spring onions, trimmed
   and finely sliced
100g (3½oz) cornflour
8 square spring roll wrappers

Spring rolls are the perfect food for entertaining. With each one carefully hand-folded it's like giving guests their own little parcels of delight. Chinese five-spice is widely used in Chinese cuisine, it is most commonly a mixture of star anise, cloves, cinnamon, Sichuan pepper and fennel.

1 Place a large frying pan or wok on a high heat. When it is hot, pour in 2 tablespoons of vegetable oil, then add the ginger and garlic and cook on a high heat for 1 minute. Add the mushrooms, duck, five-spice powder and sesame oil and cook, tossing regularly, for 5 minutes.

2 Add the cabbage and carrots and the soy and hoisin sauces and continue to cook for 1–2 minutes or until the cabbage has just wilted. Next remove the wok or pan from the heat and mix in the spring onions. Taste for seasoning, adding more soy sauce, if necessary, then set aside.

3 To fill the spring rolls, first make the cornflour paste by mixing together the cornflour and 10mlg (3½fl oz) of water. Cut a spring roll wrapper into quarters, making sure to cover the remaining wrappers in a clean damp tea towel while you work so that they don't dry out.

4 Using a pastry brush, paint the wrapper all over with the cornflour paste, then place 1–2 teaspoons of the mixture in a sausage shape near the foot of the wrapper, 2.5cm (1in) in from the edges and base of the sheet. Carefully roll the wrapper with your hands, then fold in the edges, roll again and seal to form a sausage shape. Repeat with the remaining spring roll wrappers.

5 Heat the vegetable oil in a deep-fat fryer to 180°C (350°F).

Alternatively, pour the oil into a large saucepan to a depth of 2cm (¾in) and bring to the same temperature on the hob (checking with a sugar thermometer, or see tip below).

6 Deep-fry only 2–3 spring rolls at a time as you don't want to overcrowd the fryer and adding too many spring rolls at once will reduce the temperature of the oil. Cook for 3–5 minutes or until golden and crispy. Drain on kitchen paper and serve while hot.

RACHEL'S TIP
An easy way of checking if cooking oil is hot enough for deep-frying is to drop in a cube of bread. If it comes back up to the top relatively quickly, the oil is the perfect temperature. If it immediately burns, the oil is too hot.

Mini Yorkshire puddings with peppered steak and onion jam

....

MAKES 24 YORKSHIRE
PUDDINGS
1 sirloin steak (200g/7oz)
Olive oil, for drizzling
1 tsp black peppercorns,
   coarsely crushed using
   a pestle and mortar
   or rolling pin
Sea salt
4–5 tbsp onion jam
   (see opposite)
24 small rocket leaves,
   to decorate

For the Yorkshire puddings
75g (3oz) strong white
   flour, sifted
1 egg
1 egg yolk
150ml (5fl oz) milk
½ tsp salt
Vegetable oil, for oiling

24-hole mini-muffin tin

I love the idea of shrinking a main course into a canapé; here, as bite-sized Sunday roasts! I use strong white flour for Yorkshire puddings because the high gluten content means they really rise in the oven and keep their structure. These Yorkshires should form nice cups for the onion jam and beef to sit in, but if they're fully risen and fluffed on top, you can just poke a little hole in the top.

1 Place all the ingredients for the Yorkshire puddings into a bowl, along with 150ml (5fl oz) water, and whisk together just until it firms a smooth batter. Pour into a jug and set aside.

2 Preheat the oven to 200°C (400°F), Gas mark 6. Add 1 teaspoon of the vegetable oil into each hole of the muffin tin.

3 Meanwhile, place a griddle pan or cast-iron frying pan on a high heat. Put the steak on a plate, drizzle with olive oil then sprinkle the black pepper and some sea salt generously over both sides. Place the steak in the dry pan once it's smoking hot and cook for 2–4 minutes on each side, depending on how well done you like it. Once the steak is cooked, remove from the pan, cover it with foil and allow to rest, somewhere warm, for at least 15 minutes.

4 Place the oiled muffin tin in the oven for about 5 minutes until the oil is just smoking. Remove from the oven and quickly fill each hole about two-thirds full with the Yorkshire pudding batter, then immediately return to the oven and cook for about 20 minutes or until they are risen and golden.

5 While the Yorkshire puddings are cooking, cut the steak into 24 slices, 5mm (¼in) thick, making sure to remove any excess fat.

6 As soon as the puddings are cooked, take them out of the oven and transfer them onto a large serving plate.

7 To serve, add a generous half teaspoon of onion jam and a slice of steak to each and decorate with a small rocket leaf.

50g (2oz) butter

700g (1½lb) red onions, peeled and finely sliced

150g (5oz) caster sugar

1 tsp salt

2 tsp ground black pepper

100ml (3½fl oz) sherry vinegar or balsamic vinegar

250ml (9fl oz) full-bodied red wine

2 tbsp crème de cassis (blackcurrant liqueur)

Onion jam

1 Melt the butter in a saucepan on a medium high heat, holding your nerve until it becomes a deep nut-brown colour – this will give the onions a delicious rich flavour but be careful not to let it burn. Add the onions, sugar, salt and pepper and stir well. Cover with a lid, reduce the heat to low and cook for 30 minutes, keeping an eye on the onions and stirring from time to time, until the onions are completely soft and caramelised.

2 Next add the vinegar, red wine and the cassis and cook, uncovered, for another 30 minutes, still on a low heat and stirring every now and then. Pour into a serving bowl to use immediately or place in storage jars (for sterilising jars, see page 42).

Cocktails

If you're having a canapé party, you probably want to serve at least one cocktail. Here are some of my favourites.

Watermelon margaritas

SERVES 4-6
VEGETARIAN
450g (1lb) peeled and deseeded watermelon
Juice of 4–5 limes
100ml (3½fl oz) tequila
50ml (2fl oz) Cointreau or Triple Sec
2–3 tbsp caster sugar
Handful of ice cubes
Salt, to serve

4–6 cocktail glasses

1 Place all the ingredients, including the ice, in a blender or food processor and whiz for about 1 minute.

2 To serve, scatter a little salt onto a plate, dip the rim of each chilled glass into the margarita mixture (to a depth of about 5mm/¼in), then dip in the salt to form a salted rim. Divide the drink between the glasses.

Elderflower champagne

MAKES 5 LITRES (8¾ PINTS) OR
ALMOST 7 X 750ML WINE BOTTLES
VEGETARIAN
1 large lemon
4 large elderflower heads
500g (1lb 2oz) caster sugar
25ml (1fl oz) white wine vinegar

1 Wash the lemon and remove the peel using a peeler, then cut in half and squeeze out the juice, discarding the peeled halves.

2 Rinse the elderflower heads and check for insects, then place in a very large bowl or saucepan (in either case just over 5 litres/8¾ pints in capacity) with the lemon peel and juice, sugar, vinegar and 5 litres (8¾ pints) of cold water. Stir to combine, then cover with cling film or a lid and leave in a cool place for 24 hours, stirring every now and again.

3 Pour the cordial through a sieve and into sterilised screw-top wine bottles (for sterilising bottles, see page 42). Secure the tops and store somewhere quite cool, but not the fridge. The 'champagne' is ready after two weeks but will keep for up to two years. Serve chilled.

Negroski

SERVES 4
VEGETARIAN
110ml (4fl oz) vodka
110ml (4fl oz) sweet red Martini
50ml (2fl oz) Campari
8 ice cubes
Peel of 1 orange, cut using a peeler, to serve

4 cocktail glasses

1 Mix the vodka, Martini and Campari together, pour into a cocktail shaker, add the ice cubes and shake, then strain into the glasses.

2 Decorate each with a twist of orange peel.

Summer punch

SERVE 4–6
VEGETARIAN
300ml (½ pint) lemonade
300ml (½ pint) apple juice
110ml (4fl oz) rum
110ml (4fl oz) Triple Sec or Cointreau
500ml (18fl oz) brandy
A few mint leaves, to serve

4–6 highball glasses

1 Pour all the ingredients into a jug and stir to mix. Serve chilled over ice with a few mint leaves.

Tropical fruit fizz

SERVES 4–6
VEGETARIAN
400ml (14fl oz) lemonade

For the fruit purée
1 mango, peeled and stone removed
600g (1lb 5oz) peeled and deseeded watermelon
200ml (7fl oz) pineapple juice
200g (7oz) fresh or frozen and defrosted strawberries
2 tbsp lemon juice
2 tbsp caster sugar

4–6 highball glasses

1 Place all the ingredients for the fruit purée in a blender or food processor and whiz together for 1–2 minutes. Mix with the lemonade and serve chilled over ice.

Apple, rum and ginger

SERVES 4
VEGETARIAN
600ml (1 pint) apple juice
110ml (4fl oz) rum
1 tbsp peeled (see page 27) and finely grated root ginger

4 highball glasses

1 Simply mix everything together, pour into the glasses and serve chilled over ice.

Mendiants

....

MAKES ABOUT 20
CHOCOLATE DISCS
VEGETARIAN
100g (3½oz) dark, milk
or white chocolate,
broken into pieces

Mendiants are a traditional French treat and make a perfect dessert canapé or to serve with coffee at the end of a meal. They are unbelievably fast and easy to make, yet they look so elegant. The French use different nuts and dried fruits to represent the four mendicant or monastic orders of the Dominicans (raisins), Augustinians (hazelnuts), Franciscans (dried figs) and Carmelites (almonds). You can use these or any of the toppings I've suggested below. The salt flakes in particular create a fascinating taste sensation. These can be made a few days in advance; make sure to store them somewhere cool, but preferably not the fridge as they will 'sweat'.

1 Place the chocolate in a heatproof bowl set over a saucepan of water. Heat the water until it just begins to boil, then remove from the heat and allow the chocolate to melt slowly in the bowl, stirring from time to time.

2 Line a baking tray with baking parchment. Carefully drop a teaspoonful of liquid chocolate on one corner of the paper – it will spread out slightly to form a small disc. Repeat with the rest of the chocolate, then carefully, while the chocolate is still liquid, add any of a variety of toppings (see below). Place somewhere cool to set, then carefully lift them off the paper and serve.

TOPPINGS
Dried fruit such as cranberries, raisins, sultanas or candied peel
Chopped crystallised ginger
Nuts such as shelled whole (or chopped) almonds, hazelnuts, pistachios, walnuts or pecans
Pinch of dried chilli flakes
Pinch of ground cinnamon or ginger
Sea salt flakes
A little edible gold leaf!

Chocolate, pecan and meringue squares

....

MAKES 30-36 SQUARES

VEGETARIAN

25g (1oz) raisins

½ tbsp brandy or rum

175g (6oz) dark chocolate,
broken into pieces

50g (2oz) butter, cubed

½ tbsp golden syrup

25g (1oz) shelled pecans,
toasted (see page 25)
and roughly chopped

2 leftover meringue halves,
broken into small pieces
(about 150ml/5fl oz in
volume)

13 x 23cm (5 x 9in) loaf tin

These are delicious served as a sweet canapé. They also make a beautiful gift – just pop into a decorative bag and tie up with some pretty ribbon.

1 Line the loaf tin with baking parchment, allowing the paper to come over the sides of the tin.

2 Place the raisins in a small bowl and pour over the brandy or rum. Stir to coat the raisins and then put to one side.

3 Place a heatproof bowl over a saucepan of barely simmering water on a low–medium heat, then add the chocolate, butter and golden syrup. Gently heat, stirring occasionally, for 4–5 minutes or until they have melted.

4 Remove from the heat and add the raisins, with the brandy or rum, together with the pecans and broken meringue pieces. Mix well, then pour the mixture into the lined tin and gently press down. Chill in the fridge for 2–3 hours or overnight until hardened.

5 Carefully lift the hardened chocolate mixture and paper out of the tin and cut, using a sharp knife, into small squares. Store in an airtight plastic container in the fridge until needed. They will keep for a week or two if you can resist them!

Pistachio and cranberry chocolates

....

MAKES ABOUT
40 CHOCOLATES
VEGETARIAN

200g (7oz) white chocolate,
    broken into pieces
75g (3oz) shelled pistachios
50g (2oz) dried cranberries
50g (2oz) milk or dark
    chocolate, chopped or
    roughly broken into
    small pieces

13 x 23cm (5 x 9in) loaf tin

These little chocolates are a real cinch to make and so lovely to serve as a canapé or with coffee as petits fours at the end of a meal, or to give as gifts.

1 Place the white chocolate pieces into a heatproof bowl set over a saucepan of water. Heat the water until it just begins to boil, then remove from the heat and allow the chocolate to melt slowly, stirring it from time to time.

2 While the chocolate is melting, line the loaf tin with one piece of baking parchment, allowing the paper to come over the sides of the tin.

3 When the chocolate has melted, stir in the pistachios and cranberries. Pour into the lined loaf tin and allow to cool.

4 As the white chocolate cools, melt the milk or dark chocolate in the same way in a separate bowl. When the white chocolate has almost set (but not completely, or the top layer of chocolate will not adhere to the white chocolate layer), but is still slightly shiny in places, pour the milk or dark chocolate over the top to make a second layer.

5 Allow to cool completely, then cut into about 40 squares and store in the fridge.

Crystallised ginger fudge

....

MAKES 64 SQUARES
VEGETARIAN

1 tbsp vegetable oil, for oiling
1 x 375ml tin of sweetened
  condensed milk
100g (3½oz) butter
450g (1lb) soft light brown
  or caster sugar
4 tbsp finely chopped
  crystallised ginger

18 x 18cm (7 x 7in) square cake
  tin with 2.5cm (1in) sides

I love these sweet, gingery little mouthfuls. They can be made a couple of weeks in advance and stored in an airtight box. They also make a lovely gift. Your guests will be impressed, as fudge is much easier to make than they (or you) might imagine!

1 Oil the cake tin with a little of the oil, line with baking parchment and oil again.

2 Place the condensed milk, butter and sugar in a saucepan on a medium heat, stir together as the butter melts, and bring to the boil, stirring frequently to prevent the sugar from sticking and burning on the bottom of the pan.

3 Reduce the heat to low and simmer for about 15 minutes, stirring all the time, until a sugar thermometer dipped into the mixture reads 113°C (235°F). Alternatively, drop a ½ teaspoon of the fudge into a bowl of cold water and test it with your fingers. It should be malleable to the touch: too soft and the fudge will not set; too hard and the fudge is overcooked. The fudge should also have darkened in colour to a rich golden brown.

4 Remove from the heat and stir in the crystallised ginger, then sit the bottom of the saucepan in a large bowl of cold water that comes 2–3cm (¾–1¼in) up the outside of the pan. Stir vigorously until the fudge cools down – it will go from smooth, shiny and toffeeish in appearance, to thick, grainy and matt-looking.

5 Scrape the contents of the saucepan into the oiled cake tin – the fudge should be about 1–1.5cm (¾– ⅝in) thick. Allow to cool, then cut into squares.

Mini coffee cupcakes

....

75g (3oz) butter, softened
75g (3oz) caster sugar
2 eggs
2 tsp coffee essence or espresso
   or very strong coffee
125g (4½oz) plain flour
1 tsp baking powder
Chocolate covered espresso
   beans, to serve (optional)

For the icing
200g (7oz) icing sugar, sifted
2 tbsp coffee essence or very
   strong coffee

24-hole mini-muffin tin

I adore this twist on after-dinner coffee. The coffee essence (called Camp in England and Irel in Ireland) is very useful because it provides coffee flavour without adding too much liquid to your cake mixture. If you can't get hold of it, you can always substitute very strong coffee for the essence.

1 Preheat the oven to 180°C (350°F), Gas mark 4 and line the muffin tin with paper cases.

2 Cream the butter in a large bowl or in an electric food mixer until soft. Add the sugar and beat until the mixture is light and fluffy. Whisk in the eggs, one at a time, followed by the coffee essence, then sift over the flour and baking powder and fold in.

3 Divide between the paper cases in the muffin tin and bake in the oven for 8–10 minutes or until risen and springy to the touch.

4 While the cupcakes are baking, make the icing. Place the icing sugar and the coffee essence in a bowl, mix together and add a little water (about ½–1 tbsp) and mix until smooth, adding more water if necessary, it should be spreadable.

5 Remove the cupcakes from the oven and allow to cool on a wire rack, then top each with a generous teaspoonful of icing or pipe a swirl of icing. Serve with a chocolate covered espresso bean placed on top, if you wish.

MENU IDEAS FOR CANAPÉS AND SMALL BITES

Moroccan tomato and yoghurt shots (page 122)
Gently spiced prawn and bacon skewers (page 129)
Crab, chorizo and anchovy toasts (page 135)
Duck and Chinese five-spice spring rolls (pages 138–9)
Chocolate, pecan and meringue squares (page 148)

*

Potato soup with chorizo and parsley pesto (page 136)
Caramelised onion, blue cheese and walnut tarts (page 129)
Mini Yorkshire puddings with peppered steak and onion jam (pages 140–1)
Pistachio and cranberry chocolates (page 149)

*

Spicy pastry straws (page 124)
Buckwheat blinis with smoked salmon, crème fraîche and caviar (page 132)
Thai chicken cakes with sweet chilli jam (page 137)
Mendiants (page 146)
Mini coffee cupcakes (page 152)

STARTERS

Scallops with Brussels sprouts, bacon and orange
Asparagus on toast with hollandaise sauce
Warm winter green salad with Caesar dressing, smoked bacon and a poached egg
Tomato, mozzarella and tapenade crostini
Gratins of butternut squash and leek
Halloumi with Greek salad and roasted pitta wedges

MAIN COURSES

Summer pea and mint ravioli
Pan-fried tuna with olive, sun-dried tomato and caper salsa
Poached monkfish with tomato, sherry vinegar and toasted hazelnut salsa
Pan-grilled chicken breasts with basil cream sauce and roast cherry tomatoes
Rack of lamb
Chicken confit
Garlic and herb pork chops
Steak au poivre
Pheasant casserole with chorizo, cream and thyme
Roast duck breasts

SIDE DISHES

Watercress mousse
White bean purée
Pea guacamole
Potato and anchovy gratin
Cucumber with mint
Buttered courgettes
Fluffy mashed potato
Creamy lentils with rosemary and tomatoes
Creamy polenta
Sauteed rosemary potatoes

DESSERTS

Chocolate crèmes brulées
Iles flottantes
Coffee zabaglione with tuiles biscuits
Orange sorbet with Campari

SMALL CELEBRATIONS
(2 – 4 PEOPLE)

There are occasions when you want to put a little extra effort into a special meal, whether for a romantic dinner for two or a quiet celebration with your closest friends. This is your chance to show off a little. The recipes here aren't difficult, but a few just take a little more time or have special ingredients, so be sure to give yourself enough time when planning. You don't have to serve three courses, but for an important occasion you may want to have a little more fun and go for it.

Scallops with Brussels sprouts, bacon and orange

....

SERVES 2
3 rashers of streaky bacon
    (100g/3½oz), cut into 2cm
    (¾in) dice
100g (3½oz) Brussels sprouts,
    outer leaves discarded,
    sliced about 5mm (¼in)
    thick
Sea salt and ground black
    pepper
4 prepared scallops, including
    the corals
15g (½oz) butter
1 large orange, peeled,
    segmented and juice
    reserved (see tip on
    page 108)
2 tsp sherry vinegar or lemon
    juice

These sprouts are decidedly different. Fried rather than boiled, they retain a crisp crunch and marry beautifully with the salty bacon and rich scallops, while the orange provides sweet citrus notes. If you can, try to use scallops that haven't been frozen, otherwise they may leak too much water and end up poached rather than fried.

1 Place a frying pan on a medium–high heat, add the bacon and cook for about 5 minutes, tossing regularly, until golden and very crispy. Drain on kitchen paper then transfer to a plate and keep warm in a low oven, reserving the fat in the pan.

2 Place the pan back on a medium–high heat and allow to get hot, then add the sprouts, season with salt and pepper and cook, tossing frequently, for about 3 minutes or until the sprouts have coloured and slightly softened. You may need to add 1 tablespoon of water if the sprouts dry out too much. Transfer to a bowl and keep warm in the oven with the bacon.

3 Season the scallops, including the corals, with a little salt and pepper. Place a non-stick frying pan on a medium–high heat (add a small knob of butter if using a pan) and put the scallops directly into it in a single layer. Cook on one side for 1–2 minutes or until light golden, before turning over to cook the other side for the same length of time.

4 In a large bowl, mix together the warm sprouts with the bacon, orange segments and sherry vinegar or lemon juice. Taste for seasoning and divide between plates. Add the scallops and serve.

RACHEL'S TIP
To open the scallops (this can be done earlier in the day and the scallops stored, covered, in the fridge), place each scallop on a board with the flat shell pointing up. Insert the point of a knife between the shells and slice across the underside of the top shell to cut through the internal muscle, then pull the shells apart. Pull off the outer membrane with your fingers, remove the coral, keeping it intact. Dry the scallops and corals on kitchen paper.

Asparagus on toast with hollandaise sauce

....

With the welcome arrival of spring comes the first of the new season's asparagus, and my very favourite way to enjoy it is on buttered toast with lashings of hollandaise sauce.

SERVES 4
VEGETARIAN
16–20 asparagus spears
Good pinch of salt and
  ground pepper
4 slices of bread
Butter for spreading
Hollandaise sauce (see below)

1 Snap off the tough woody part at the bottom of each asparagus stalk and discard. Fill a large saucepan to a depth of 4–6cm (1½ – 2½in) with water, add the salt and bring to the boil. Tip in the asparagus and cook in the boiling water for 4–8 minutes or until tender when pierced with a sharp knife. Drain immediately.

2 While the asparagus is cooking, toast the bread, then spread with the butter and remove the crusts, if you wish. For each person, place a piece of toast on a warmed plate, put 4–5 asparagus spears on top and spoon over a little hollandaise sauce.

Hollandaise sauce

MAKES 75ML (3FL OZ)
VEGETARIAN
1 egg yolk
50g (2oz) butter, diced
Squeeze of lemon juice
Salt and ground black pepper

1 Place a heatproof bowl over a saucepan of simmering water on a medium heat. (The water must not boil. If it does it may heat the sauce so much that it will scramble or curdle – so take the pan off the heat every so often.) Add the egg yolk and 1 tablespoon of cold water and whisk together. Gradually add the butter, a few bits at a time, until each addition has melted and emulsified as it is whisked in, before adding the next.

2 Once all the butter has been incorporated, cook for a couple of minutes more, stirring constantly, until the sauce has thickened enough to coat the back of a spoon. Season to taste with lemon juice and salt and pepper. Remove from the heat, and keep warm if necessary, by covering with cling film and leaving to sit over the warm water, until you're ready to serve.

Warm winter green salad with Caesar dressing, smoked bacon and a poached egg

....

SERVES 4

4 high-quality eggs

1 tbsp sunflower oil, for frying

8 rashers of smoked streaky bacon, cut into 1cm (½in) dice

4 handfuls of mixed lettuce leaves, including rocket and winter greens such as kale, spinach, mustard greens or small beetroot leaves

For the dressing

175ml (6fl oz) sunflower or vegetable oil

50ml (2fl oz) extra-virgin olive oil

1 x 50g tin of anchovies, drained and rinsed

2 egg yolks

1 clove of garlic, peeled and crushed

2 tbsp lemon juice

1 tsp Dijon mustard

Pinch of salt

1 tbsp Worcestershire sauce

1 tsp Tabasco sauce

To serve

50g (2oz) Parmesan cheese, grated

1 tbsp chopped chives

This recipe is a gorgeous twist on a classic Caesar salad. The dressing makes more than you will need but it keeps in the fridge for a week, if covered.

1 First make the dressing, which you can do either in a food processor or by hand. Pour both oils into a jug. If making the dressing by hand, mash the anchovies with a fork then place in a bowl with the remaining ingredients and whisk together. As you are whisking, add the mixed oils very slowly and gradually. It will become creamy as the emulsion forms. When all the oil has been incorporated, whisk in 50ml (2fl oz) water to make it the consistency of double cream, then add extra seasoning to taste.

2 Alternatively, place all the ingredients, except the mixed oils, in a food processor and whiz together, then gradually add the oil and the water as above, pouring them in through the feed tube of the machine.

3 To poach the eggs, first place a saucepan of water on a high heat to come to the boil. Meanwhile, pour the oil into a frying pan on a high heat, add the bacon and fry for 3–5 minutes or until golden brown and crispy. Drain on kitchen paper and set aside.

4 While the bacon is frying, tear the mixture of lettuce and winter greens into large bite-sized pieces and place a handful on each plate. Drizzle with 1–2 tablespoons of the dressing and sprinkle with the crispy bacon pieces.

5 Once the egg-poaching water has come to the boil, turn the heat down to low. Crack each egg into the lightly simmering water and poach for 3–4 minutes or until the white is set and the yolk still a little soft. Turn the heat off under the saucepan and carefully lift each egg out one by one, allowing all water to drain from the egg.

6 Arrange one egg in the centre of each salad, sprinkle with grated Parmesan and the chopped chives and serve immediately.

Tomato, mozzarella and tapenade crostini

....

SERVES 2-4
12 slices of baguette
100ml (3½ fl oz) tapenade
  (see below)
4 large ripe tomatoes, cut
  widthways into 6 slices
4 tbsp extra-virgin olive oil
Juice of ½ lemon
Salt and ground black pepper
Pinch of sugar
Handful of chopped basil,
  plus leaves to decorate
2 x 125g balls of mozzarella
  cheese, each cut into 6 slices

The Italian flavours here are a timeless combination and the presentation is sure to impress. Get hold of buffalo mozzarella if you can as it is made only from buffalo milk, which is richer than cow's milk. The flavour is more delicate and the texture much softer. This is best made in the summer with perfectly ripe and sweet tomatoes.

1 Toast the baguette slices, spread 1 teaspoon of tapenade on each slice and arrange three pieces on each individual plate.

2 On a large flat plate spread the sliced tomato out in a single layer, drizzle with 3 tablespoons of the olive oil and the lemon juice, then season with salt, pepper and sugar. Add the basil and toss together gently.

3 Mix together the remaining olive oil with 1 tablespoon of the tapenade, then build three 'towers' on each plate. Add a slice of tomato to each piece of toast, followed by a slice of mozzarella and another slice of tomato. Finish with a small drizzle of the tapenade oil, either on top of the crostini or around the plate, and decorate with the basil leaves.

MAKES 150ML (5FL OZ)
100g (3½ oz) pitted black
  olives (for pitting olives,
  see tip on page 38)
1 x 25g tin of anchovies,
  drained and rinsed
1 tbsp capers, drained
  and rinsed
1 tsp Dijon mustard
1 tsp lemon juice
4 tbsp extra-virgin olive oil
Ground black pepper
  (optional)
Salt (optional)

Tapenade

1 Place all ingredients apart from the olive oil into a food processor. Whiz for a minute or two to form a rough paste, then, with the machine still running, pour in the olive oil.

2 Taste for seasoning: you may need pepper but probably won't need salt.

Gratins of butternut squash and leek

SERVES 4
VEGETARIAN

75g (3oz) hazelnuts, toasted
and peeled (see page 29)

75g (3oz) fresh white
breadcrumbs

75g (3oz) Parmesan or
Parmesan-style cheese,
finely grated

25g (1oz) butter, melted

Salt and ground black pepper

600g (1lb 5oz) butternut
squash, peeled and cut
into 1cm ($\frac{1}{2}$in) cubes

4 tbsp olive oil

400g (14oz) leeks, trimmed
and finely sliced

25g (1oz) butter

4 cloves of garlic, peeled and
finely chopped

25g (1oz) kale or spinach
(any large stalks removed
before weighing), broken
into bite-sized pieces or
roughly chopped

100ml (3$\frac{1}{2}$fl oz) dry
white wine

$\frac{1}{2}$ tsp Dijon mustard

2 sprigs of thyme

75ml (3fl oz) double or
regular cream

For the sauce
50ml (2fl oz) vegetable stock
(see page 50)

(ingredients continued overleaf)

This dish is a variation of a dish I've eaten at Denis Cotter's restaurant Café Paradiso in Cork. It is a perfect example of Denis' cooking; vegetarian food that is so flavourful and luxurious that even the most ardent carnivore will want to indulge. Stainless steel rings are certainly worth using for presenting this dish. The end result is an elegantly layered and colourful presentation. However, you can just use individual ovenproof bowls – it will taste just the same.

1 Preheat the oven to 220°C (425°F), Gas mark 7.

2 Roughly crush the toasted hazelnuts with a rolling pin, then combine in a bowl with the breadcrumbs, Parmesan cheese and butter, and season to taste with salt and pepper.

3 Next roast the squash. In a bowl, mix together the squash and olive oil, and season with salt and pepper. Place in a roasting tin in a single layer and cook in the oven for 20–25 minutes or until the squash is soft and slightly golden.

4 While the squash is roasting, cook the leeks. Melt the butter in a frying pan on a medium–high heat, add the leeks and garlic, season with salt and pepper, and cook, stirring frequently, for 2–3 minutes or until the leeks have softened.

5 Stir in the kale or spinach, followed by the wine, mustard and thyme, and cook for a further 2 minutes. Add the cream and let it bubble for another 2 minutes or until the kale is wilted, then transfer to a bowl.

6 Turn the oven down to 180°C (350°F), Gas mark 4.

7 To assemble the gratins, place the metal rings on a baking tray lined with baking parchment, or use four ovenproof bowls also

(continued overleaf)

50ml (2fl oz) dry white wine
150ml (5fl oz) double or
  regular cream
75g (3oz) Parmesan or
  Parmesan-style cheese,
  finely grated

4 stainless-steel rings (such as
  10cm/4in cookie cutters) or
  individual ovenproof bowls

placed on a baking tray. Divide the leek and kale mixture between the rings or bowls and then top with the squash, leaving a gap of about 5mm (¼in) from the top. Add a layer of the hazelnut mixture to fill the rings or bowls. Place in the oven and cook for about 20 minutes or until the top is brown and crispy and the mixture is hot inside.

9 While the gratins are baking, make the sauce. Pour the stock and wine into a small–medium saucepan and set on a high heat. Boil for 2–3 minutes or until the liquid has reduced significantly. Add the cream and boil for a further 2–3 minutes or until it has thickened again, then remove from the heat and stir in the Parmesan, seasoning to taste with salt and pepper.

10 To serve, use a fish slice or spatula to carefully place on plates, then remove the rings (if using). Pour the sauce around each gratin and serve immediately. Otherwise serve in the bowls (if using), with the sauce in a jug.

VARIATION
You can always mix together the leek and kale with the butternut squash before putting them into the metal rings.

Halloumi with Greek salad and roasted pitta wedges

....

SERVES 4
VEGETARIAN

1 x 250g (9oz) halloumi
  cheese, cut into 4 pieces
2 pitta breads, cut into wedges
Olive oil, for drizzling
Sea salt

For the marinade
1 red or green chilli, deseeded
  and finely chopped
25ml (1fl oz) extra-virgin
  olive oil
1 clove of garlic, peeled and
  finely chopped
1 tsp finely chopped oregano
  or marjoram
Salt and ground black pepper

For the Greek salad
100g (3½oz) baby spinach
  leaves
50g (2oz) cherry tomatoes,
  halved
½ cucumber, peeled,
  deseeded and sliced
50g (2oz) black olives, such
  as kalamata, pitted
  (see page 38)
1 tbsp extra-virgin olive oil
Salt and ground black pepper

Halloumi is a Cypriot cheese with a high melting point, which means you can cook it and get a nice golden crust long before it melts. This marinade adds flavour and interest to the salty cheese. Some people call halloumi 'squeaky cheese' – try eating it and you'll see why!

1 In a bowl, mix together all the ingredients for the marinade. Add the halloumi, mix with the marinade and leave to marinate for 1 hour.

2 Meanwhile, preheat the oven to 220°C (425°F), Gas mark 7.

3 Place the pitta bread wedges in a separate bowl, toss together with enough olive oil to coat and season with sea salt. Spread out flat on a baking tray and cook in the oven for about 5 minutes or until pale golden (keep an eye on them as they cook as they burn quickly).

4 While the pittas are roasting, mix together all the ingredients for the Greek salad, seasoning to taste with salt and pepper.

5 Place a griddle pan or frying pan (cast iron if possible) on a high heat and allow to get very hot. Add the halloumi and fry on each side for just 30 seconds until golden. Divide between individual plates, adding some of the Greek salad and a few roasted pitta wedges to each plate.

Summer pea and mint ravioli

....

MAKES ABOUT 50 RAVIOLI
SERVES 3-4
VEGETARIAN

For the ravioli
250g (9oz) Italian Tipo '00'
    flour or strong white flour,
    plus extra for dusting
Salt and ground black pepper
2–3 eggs
250g (9oz) frozen peas
    (preferably petits pois)
2 tbsp olive oil
3 tbsp chopped mint
Squeeze of lemon juice

For the Alfredo sauce
25g (1oz) butter
200ml (7fl oz) double
    or regular cream
50g (2oz) Parmesan or
    Parmesan-style cheese,
    grated
Salt and ground black pepper

To serve
15g (½oz) butter
50g (2oz) frozen peas
    (petits pois)
Small handful of mint leaves
    or pea shoots, if available

I think this dish should only be made on a beautiful day with the sun cascading into the kitchen. Unless they are very fresh, frozen peas will have more flavour so they are perfectly fine to use here. Peas are the essence of the season and each ravioli is a tiny pillow of summer. The joy of making fresh pasta is that you can fill ravioli or tortellini with a freshly made filling of your choice. Pasta machines are inexpensive and make the process much, much easier, though you can use just a rolling pin.

1 To make the pasta for the ravioli, first sift the flour and salt together into a bowl. Whisk the eggs together in a separate bowl, then make a well in the centre of the flour and add half the beaten eggs. Mix into a dough using your hands, adding the remainder of the egg only if you need it. The pasta should just come together, but shouldn't stick to your hands; if it does, add a little more flour.

2 Knead in the bowl for a few minutes until smooth, then cover with cling film and set aside to rest for 30 minutes–1 hour to relax. (It will keep for about two days in the fridge.) The dough can also be made in an electric food mixer or food processor, again being careful not to add too much egg.

3 Next make the pea purée for filling the ravioli. Bring a saucepan of water to the boil and add 1 teaspoon of salt. Tip in the peas and boil for about 2 minutes or until just cooked (don't overcook them!), then drain. Place in a food processor with the remaining ingredients (or use a hand-held blender) and whiz for a couple of minutes or until smooth, then season to taste. Set aside to cool.

4 To make up the ravioli, divide the dough into quarters and, using a pasta machine, roll out each piece at a time, starting with the widest setting and ending with the narrowest by which time

(continued on page 170)

you should be able to read the headline print on a newspaper through the pasta. You may need a light dusting of flour if your pasta is slightly wet. You can also use a rolling pin, though it is more labour intensive. As you finish rolling each piece, make sure you cover it with a tea towel as the pasta will quickly dry out.

5 Lay two sheets of pasta on a floured work surface and, with a sharp knife, lightly mark each into a grid (5 squares across and 5 squares down) of 5cm (2in) squares, but don't cut through the dough yet. Place ½ teaspoon of the pea purée in the middle of each square, then use a pastry brush to wet the spaces in between the heaps of purée with a littler water. Lay the second sheet of pasta over the top and use your fingers to press the pasta together around the purée and seal. Be careful to press only in between the mounds of purée and try to ensure each ravioli doesn't contain too much air.

6 Using either a pastry wheel (I like to use a fluted one), a pizza cutter or a sharp knife, cut the ravioli into 25 x 5cm (2in) squares so that each ravioli contains a mound of pea purée. Dust 2 baking trays with flour and place the ravioli on the tray in a single layer. (They can be refrigerated for a few hours or frozen at this point.) Repeat steps 4 and 5 with the remaining two pasta sheets.

7 To make the Alfredo sauce, place the butter and cream in a saucepan on a medium–low heat, and bring to a simmer. Cook for about 5 minutes until the sauce has slightly thickened, then remove from the heat and mix in the grated Parmesan cheese. Season to taste and set aside.

8 In a frying pan on a medium heat, melt the 15g (½oz) butter, then add the 50g (2oz) peas and cook for about 2 minutes, tossing occasionally. Set aside somewhere warm until ready to serve.

9 To cook the pasta, bring a large saucepan of water to the boil and add 2 teaspoons of salt. Add the ravioli and cook for about 2 minutes or until the pasta is just al dente. Drain then place on kitchen paper briefly to get rid of any excess water and divide between warmed bowls. Pour over the Alfredo sauce, then scatter over a few peas and some mint leaves, and serve immediately.

Pan-fried tuna with olive, sun-dried tomato and caper salsa

....

SERVES 4

4 x 150–175g (5–6oz) tuna
    fillets
2 tbsp olive oil
Salt and ground black pepper

For the salsa
100g (3½oz) pitted black
    olives (see page 38)
150g (5oz) pitted green olives
4 tbsp chopped sun-dried
    tomatoes
1 tbsp capers
2 cloves of garlic, peeled and
    crushed or finely grated
8 basil leaves, torn
100ml (3½fl oz) extra-virgin
    olive oil

The colour contrast of this tuna looks beautiful on the plate. The outside is cooked and full of flavour while the inside remains pink, moist and succulent. Served at room temperature, pan-fried tuna goes to perfection with the Salade Niçoise (see page 38). The salsa also complements everything from steak to mackerel.

1 First make the salsa. Place all the ingredients apart from the oil in a food processor and whiz for a few seconds, leaving it still slightly chunky.

2 Pour in the olive oil and whiz for a few seconds until combined. This will keep, covered, in the fridge for a couple of weeks. Let it come back up to room temperature before serving.

3 To cook the tuna, place a large frying pan or griddle pan on a high heat and allow it to get very hot. Brush each side of the tuna fillets with the olive oil and season with salt and pepper.

4 Place on the pan and cook for 2–3 minutes on each side – the centre should still be pink.

5 Remove from the heat and allow the tuna to sit for a few minutes before serving with the salsa.

Poached monkfish with tomato, sherry vinegar and toasted hazelnut salsa

....

SERVES 2-4
450g (1lb) monkfish tails,
    filleted and trimmed
    of skin and membrane
1 tsp salt

For the toasted hazelnut salsa
3 large ripe tomatoes, or 20
    cherry tomatoes, cut into
    1cm (1/2 in) pieces
2 tbsp peeled and finely
    chopped red onion
3 tbsp extra-virgin olive oil
2 tbsp chopped coriander
    or parsley
1 tbsp sherry vinegar or
    balsamic vinegar
50g (2oz) hazelnuts, peeled,
    toasted (see page 29) and
    chopped
Sea salt and ground
    black pepper

Poached monkfish is quite easy to cook when entertaining as it just needs a few minutes in boiling, salted water, and can be prepared in advance. The salsa is lovely with the monkfish; it's fresh, light and very gently warms through from the hot fish. If you are making the salsa in advance, don't put it in the fridge but keep it at room temperature.

1 Cut the monkfish into 1cm (1/2 in) slices and refrigerate in a covered bowl until needed.

2 To make the salsa, mix the tomatoes, onion, olive oil, coriander or parsley, vinegar and half the hazelnuts in a bowl, then season to taste with salt and pepper. (The salsa can be made up to about 1 hour in advance.)

2 Bring 1.2 litres (2 pints) of water to the boil in a large saucepan and add the salt. Add the monkfish and simmer very gently for 4–5 minutes or until completely white and no longer translucent.

3 Drain well and place on kitchen paper to dry. Arrange on warmed plates and drizzle over some of the salsa, then scatter with the remaining hazelnuts and serve immediately.

RACHEL'S TIP
If you want to keep the monkfish warm for a short while before serving (up to 10 minutes), remove the fish but don't drain the boiling water from the saucepan. Turn the lid upside down over the pan (off the heat), place a double layer of kitchen paper on the flat, upturned lid and sit the cooked monkfish on top.

Pan-grilled chicken breasts with basil cream sauce and roast cherry tomatoes

....

SERVES 2
2 skinless chicken breasts
1 tbsp olive oil

For the roast cherry tomatoes
About 10 small or cherry
    tomatoes (5 per person)
Olive oil, for drizzling
Sea salt and ground
    black pepper

For the basil cream sauce
175ml (6fl oz) double
    or regular cream
150g (5oz) butter, cut into
    1cm (½in) cubes
Squeeze of lemon juice
2 tbsp sliced or torn basil

The deliciously creamy sauce in this recipe transforms a simple supper of grilled chicken breasts into a luxurious treat. I like to serve this with some supremely fluffy mashed potato (see page 191) to soak up all of the sauce. For the roast tomatoes, try to get hold of cherry tomatoes or small tomatoes that are still attached to the stalk. These look good and the stalk can be cut with scissors into portions before cooking. If the tomatoes are off the stalk, you can cook them whole or cut in half.

1 Preheat the oven to 200°C (400°F), Gas mark 6. Place the tomatoes on a baking tray (if they are cut in half, place them cut side up), drizzle with olive oil and season with salt and pepper. Cook in the oven for about 10 minutes or until the skin is a little blistered and the flesh soft on the inside. Take out of the oven and keep warm until serving – they will sit happily for up to half an hour in the oven with the heat turned off to keep warm before serving.

2 Place a cast-iron griddle pan or a frying pan on a high heat and allow it to get quite hot – it should be just smoking. Rub the chicken breasts with the olive oil, and season with salt and pepper. Place the chicken in the pan serving side down (the side that is cooked first always looks the nicest) and cook for 3–4 minutes or until the one side is a deep golden or has good scorch marks (if using the griddle pan).

3 Turn the chicken over and reduce the heat, continuing to cook for 5–10 minutes or until the chicken is cooked through (it should be opaque in the middle). The chicken can also be browned on one side, then turned over and finished in the oven, preheated to 200°C (400°F), Gas mark 6, for about the same amount of time. This is especially useful if you are making more than 2–3 servings.

4 Meanwhile, make the sauce. Pour the cream into a small saucepan, bring just to boiling point, then reduce the heat and

(continued overleaf)

simmer until it has reduced to about 4 tablespoons and is very thick. Remove from the heat and allow to cool for 30 seconds–1 minute (if the cream is too hot when you add the butter, the mixture will curdle), then whisk in the butter bit by bit. When all the butter has been incorporated, season to taste with salt (if necessary), pepper and lemon juice, and stir in the basil.

5 To serve, place the chicken breasts, whole or sliced, on warmed plates, spoon some sauce over the top or around the edge and place a portion of cherry tomatoes on the side.

RACHEL'S TIP

If the sauce is kept warm, it will keep for a couple of hours. Place in a heatproof ceramic bowl or jug (a metal bowl might get too hot) immersed in a saucepan of hot water. Heat up the water every so often to prevent the sauce from becoming to cold, but make sure the water isn't boiling as if it's too hot the sauce will curdle.

Rack of lamb

....

SERVES 2-4
1 rack of lamb
Salt and ground black pepper

A rack of lamb is so easy and is perfect for serving two to four people, depending on the size of the chops and how many there are of them on the rack. It goes very well with the Watercress Mousse and Potato and Anchovy Gratin (see pages 185 and 188) as lamb tastes gorgeous with anchovies.

1 Preheat the oven to 220°C (425°F), Gas mark 7.

2 Remove the papery skin if it is still attached, then score the fat in a criss-cross pattern with lines 1–2cm (½–¾in) apart, trying not to cut into the meat. Sprinkle with salt and pepper, then place in a roasting tin and cook in the oven for 25–35 minutes, depending on the weight of the lamb and how pink you like it to be.

3 Leave in the oven, covered in foil, with the heat turned off, then cut between the chops and give each person 2–3 each.

Chicken confit

....

SERVES 2
2 chicken legs (including
 the thighs)
1 tbsp thyme leaves
2 bay leaves, broken in half
1 tbsp salt
½ tsp ground black pepper
6 cloves of garlic
8 black peppercorns
500ml (18fl oz) duck or goose
 fat (or olive oil), to cover

*It is usually duck legs that are cooked in this way, but all fowl taste
pretty good cooked in half a litre of duck fat! It adds wonderful moisture
and a rich texture to pheasant, guinea fowl or even pigeon. I usually
double or even treble the quantities (but keeping roughly the same
amount of fat, which just needs to cover the meat in the saucepan)
as it makes no difference to the amount of work involved and it keeps
in the fridge, covered in the fat, for up to a year.*

1 Place the chicken legs in a bowl and sprinkle over the thyme,
1 of the bay leaves, salt and pepper, rubbing the herbs and
seasoning into the meat. Cover and place in the fridge overnight.

2 When you are ready to cook the chicken, preheat the oven
to 110°C (225°F), Gas mark ¼.

3 Remove the chicken legs from the fridge. Discard any liquid from
the bowl and rinse the meat to wash off the salt and pepper. Pat
very dry with kitchen paper, then place in a saucepan large enough
to fit both chicken legs snugly. Add the garlic, peppercorns and
remaining bay leaf to the pan, then pour over enough duck fat to
cover the chicken. (If there is not enough duck fat to cover them,
add a little olive oil to make sure they're covered.)

4 Place in the oven and cook for about 7 hours or until the chicken
is completely tender and easily comes away from the bone.
Remove from the oven and allow to cool.

5 To serve, first remove the chicken from the fat. Place a frying
pan on a medium–high heat, then drop in about 1 tablespoon of
the fat and cook the chicken on each side for 4–5 minutes or until
the skin is crisp and golden in colour and the meat heated right
through. Serve hot with the Creamy Lentils with Rosemary and
Tomatoes and the Crunchy Coriander Roast Potatoes (see pages
192 and 297), or at room temperature, broken into large bite-sized
pieces on a salad, such as the Winter Leaf Salad (see page 273).

RACHEL'S TIP
Once you've used the chicken, reserve the fat as it can be reused,
either for this recipe again or for roasting potatoes.

Garlic and herb pork chops

SERVES 4
4 large pork loin chops or
  12 small cutlets

For the marinade
50ml (2fl oz) olive oil
Juice of 1 lemon
1 tbsp chopped sage
1 tbsp chopped rosemary
  leaves
25ml (1fl oz) balsamic vinegar
4 cloves of garlic, peeled and
  crushed or finely grated

Sage has such a distinctive flavour that pairs very well with pork. If you can, marinate the chops for at least a couple of hours, as it gives the flavours and oils enough time to penetrate deep into the meat. Try serving with the Creamy Lentils with Rosemary and Tomatoes on page 192.

1 Combine all the marinade ingredients in a large bowl and add the pork chops, turning them in the marinade so that they are coated in the mixture. Cover the bowl with cling film or place in a sealed plastic bag, then refrigerate overnight or for at least 2 hours.

2 Preheat the oven to 220°C (425°F), Gas mark 7.

3 When you're ready to cook, remove the chops from the marinade. Place a cast-iron griddle pan or ovenproof frying pan on a high heat and when it begins to smoke, add the chops. Cook for 2–3 minutes on each side to brown the meat, then roast in the oven for 7–9 minutes or until the pork is cooked through. Remove from the oven and allow to rest for a few minutes before serving.

Steak au poivre

....

SERVES 4

2 tbsp whole black
 peppercorns
1 tsp sea salt
4 sirloin, rump or fillet steaks
 (150–200g/5–7oz each)
2 tbsp olive oil
50ml (2fl oz) brandy
150ml (5fl oz) beef stock
125ml (4½fl oz) double
 or regular cream
½ tsp Dijon mustard

One of my favourite ways to serve steak is this traditional French bistro method. Pepper, a seasoning that often hides in the background barely noticed, is thrust onto centre stage. Where normally we grind peppercorns into a fine powder, here they are left in larger chunks so you notice the flavour and texture as well as the heat.

1 Use a pestle and mortar to coarsely crush the peppercorns, leaving quite large chunks of pepper. Alternatively, place the peppercorns in a plastic bag and use a rolling pin to coarsely crush them. Tip into a sieve with a bowl underneath and shake out the powdered pepper. You can use the finer pepper grounds for seasoning something else but they would make the steaks too hot if combined with the larger pieces of pepper.

2 Place a frying pan (cast-iron if possible) on a high heat, allowing it to get very hot. While the pan is heating, mix the larger pieces of pepper with the salt, spread this out on a plate and dip each steak into it so that the meat is completely coated in salt and pepper.

3 The pan should be very hot by now, so pour in the olive oil. Add the steaks (cook them in batches if necessary) and cook for 2–4 minutes on each side, depending how rare or well done you like them. Then remove to warmed plates and allow to rest.

4 While the steaks are resting, make the sauce. With the pan still on a high heat, pour in the brandy (taking care as you pour it in as it may flame), boil for 30 seconds, then add the stock, cream and mustard. Whisk to combine and boil for 2–3 minutes or until it thickens slightly. Taste the sauce for seasoning then spoon over the steaks and serve immediately with mashed potato to soak up the sauce.

Pheasant casserole with chorizo, cream and thyme

....

SERVES 3-4

1 tbsp olive oil

350g (12oz) chorizo, cut into slices 8mm (3/8 in) thick

275g (10oz) onions, peeled and cut into wedges, or baby onions, peeled and cut in half

1 pheasant, cut into portions, still on the bone

Salt and ground black pepper

4 sprigs of thyme, plus 1 tsp chopped thyme leaves

150ml (5fl oz) chicken stock

125ml (4½ fl oz) double or regular cream

4 tsp roux (made with 2 tsp butter and 2 tsp flour – see page 76) (optional)

Medium-sized casserole dish or ovenproof saucepan with a lid

Luxurious comfort food for a cold day, this casserole is intensely flavoured, with a lovely warm kick from the chorizo sausage. Serve over Creamy Polenta (see page 193).

1 Preheat the oven to 150°C (300°F), Gas mark 2.

2 Place a casserole dish or ovenproof saucepan on a medium heat, pour in the olive oil, then add the chorizo and onions and cook for 3–5 minutes or until the oils from the chorizo have drained into the dish and the onions are slightly golden Remove the chorizo and onions and set aside, leaving the oils in the pot.

3 Add the pheasant pieces to the casserole dish or saucepan and fry for about 5 minutes or until golden on both sides, being careful not to burn the pot, then season with salt and pepper. Drain any excess oils from the dish or pan, then add the cooked chorizo and onions, along with the thyme sprigs and the stock.

4 Bring to simmering point on top of the stove, then place in the oven and cook for about 45 minutes or until the meat is tender. The cooking time will depend on how long the pheasant pieces were sautéed.

5 When the casserole is cooked, scoop out the pheasant, onions and chorizo and thyme sprigs. Strain off the cooking liquid and return the meat, onions and thyme sprigs to the pot. Degrease the cooking liquid (see tip on page 226) and pour into a separate saucepan, then add the cream, bring to the boil and boil, uncovered, for about 4 minutes or until the sauce has slightly thickened (if you would like a thicker sauce, you can whisk in a little roux). Add the chopped thyme and taste for seasoning, then pour back over the meat, onions and thyme sprigs in the casserole. Serve bubbling hot.

Roast duck breasts

....

SERVES 2
2 duck breasts
Salt and ground black pepper

Duck breasts make a glorious meal, their pink juicy flesh topped by a layer of undeniably appealing crispy skin. Take care to ensure the skin is crisp and inviting rather than thick and flabby. The low heat at the start of cooking brings out the excess fat, then the higher temperature of the oven gives that crispiness. These are delicious served with redcurrant jelly, White Bean Purée (see pages 337 and 186) and crispy roast potatoes made using the fat rendered from the duck breasts during cooking.

1 Preheat the oven to 220°C (425°F), Gas mark 7.

2 Score the duck breasts by making cuts, about 1cm (½in) apart, in the fat along the width of the breast, trying not to cut into the meat. Season with salt and pepper, briefly massaging the seasoning into the fat.

3 Place an ovenproof frying pan or griddle pan on a low heat, and immediately add the duck breasts, fat side down. When cooked like this all the excess fat will drain out of the scored skin, leaving you with deliciously crisp skin and only the bare minimum of fat underneath. Cook for 10–20 minutes or until the fat is golden underneath, then turn over, transfer to the oven and cook for 6–8 minutes. It should still be pink inside.

4 Remove from the oven and allow to rest for at least 10 minutes before serving. Serve whole or cut into slices.

Watercress mousse

SERVES 3
VEGETARIAN

25g (1oz) butter, plus extra
    for greasing
125g (4½oz) watercress
    (large stalks removed),
    chopped
1 egg
1 egg yolk
50ml (2fl oz) double or
    regular cream
Small pinch of grated nutmeg
Salt and ground black pepper

Six 5cm (2in) diameter,
    100ml (3½fl oz) ramekins
    or a six-hole muffin tin

These individual mousses are particularly good as a side dish served with lamb, but also work well with chicken or turkey. Remove any large tough stalks from the watercress before cooking.

1 Preheat the oven to 200°C (400°F), Gas mark 6, and butter the ramekins or muffin tin.

2 Melt the butter in a large saucepan on a medium heat, then add the watercress and cook for 2–4 minutes or until the leaves are wilted. Meanwhile, whisk together the eggs and egg yolk in a bowl and set aside.

3 Add the cream to the watercress, then purée in a food processor (or use a hand-held blender), for 2–3 minutes until smooth. When the purée has cooled right down, whisk in the beaten eggs, add the nutmeg and season to taste with salt and pepper.

4 Divide the mixture between the ramekins or muffin tin and place in a bain-marie – a roasting tin filled with enough water to come about halfway up the ramekins or muffin tin. Place in the oven and bake for about 20 minutes or until just set. When you gently press the centre of each mousse, it should be lightly springy to the touch. Serve 2 per person.

VARIATION
Spinach/kale mousse: Replace the watercress with the same quantity of spinach or kale.

White bean purée

This rich garlicky purée, scented with rosemary, is wonderful served with Roast Duck Breasts (see page 184).

(see page 184)

SERVES 2–4
VEGETARIAN
1 x 400g tin of haricot or
  cannellini beans, drained
  and rinsed, or 125g (4½oz)
  dried beans, soaked and
  cooked (see page 64)
2 tbsp olive oil
1 clove of garlic, peeled and
  crushed or finely grated
2 tsp chopped rosemary leaves
50–75ml (2–3fl oz) vegetable
  stock (see page 50)
Salt and ground black pepper

1 Pour the beans into a saucepan, add the remaining ingredients and season to taste with salt and pepper. Place on a low–medium heat and simmer for 8–10 minutes.

2 Take the pan off the heat and either roughly mash the beans with a potato masher, or place in a food processor and whiz to form a smooth purée. Serve while still warm.

Pea guacamole

Not strictly a guacamole, this is a pea purée packed with flavour. It is delicious with the Pan-fried Tuna with Olive, Sun-dried Tomato and Caper Salsa on page 171.

SERVES 4 AS A SIDE DISH
VEGETARIAN
450g (1lb) shelled fresh
  or frozen peas
Salt
2 tbsp extra-virgin olive oil
2 tbsp lime juice
2 tbsp finely chopped
  coriander
½–1 red chilli, deseeded
  and finely chopped
½ tsp cumin seeds, ground
  (see page 25)
½ tsp coriander seeds,
  ground

1 Cook the peas in boiling, salted water for 3–4 minutes for fresh peas, 2–3 minutes for frozen. Refresh under cold water and drain.

2 Place in a food processor with the remaining ingredients and a good pinch of salt (or use a hand-held blender) and whiz for 1–2 minutes or until almost smooth. Taste, adjusting the seasoning if necessary, then put into a bowl, cover and refrigerate until needed. Bring back up to room temperature before serving, if not using immediately.

Potato and anchovy gratin

....

SERVES 4
Butter, for greasing
1kg (2lb 3oz) potatoes,
    peeled and cut into
    5mm (¼ in) slices
3 x 50g tins of anchovies,
    drained and rinsed
Salt and ground black pepper
5 cloves of garlic, peeled and
    finely chopped
400ml (14fl oz) single or
    regular cream
100g (3½ oz) Parmesan
    cheese, grated
100g (3½ oz) Gruyère
    cheese, grated

18 x 26cm (7 x 10½ in)
    gratin or similar-sized
    ovenproof dish

This side-dish is based on the famous Swedish dish 'Jansson's Temptation', though Jansson (a nineteenth-century opera singer) would call for sprats rather than anchovies. It goes very well with meat such as lamb.

1 Preheat the oven to 200°C (400°F), Gas mark 6, and butter the gratin or ovenproof dish.

2 Divide the potatoes into four lots, and the anchovies into two. Arrange a quarter of the potatoes in the bottom of the dish, then place half of the anchovies on top of these, in three lines evenly spaced across the width of the dish. Season with salt (not too much as the anchovies will be quite salty) and pepper.

3 Add another layer of potatoes, then three more lines of anchovies perpendicular to the ones in the previous layer. Season again, then add another layer of potatoes. Next add the chopped garlic, sprinkled evenly across the potatoes, season again, then add the last layer of potatoes. Pour the cream into the dish, then sprinkle the grated cheeses over the top.

4 Cover the dish in foil and place in the oven. After 30 minutes remove the foil and cook for a further 30 minutes or until the potatoes are tender when pierced with a skewer and the surface of the dish is golden brown and bubbling.

Cucumber with mint

....

SERVES 2-3
VEGETARIAN
10g (⅓oz) butter
1 cucumber, peeled, deseeded
    and cut into 1cm (½in) dice
1 tsp white wine vinegar
1 tbsp finely chopped mint
Salt and ground black pepper

It's surprising how delicious cucumber is when cooked. This side dish is fresh and light and is a great accompaniment to fish or chicken.

1 Melt the butter in a frying pan on a low heat, add the cucumber and vinegar and cook, stirring occasionally, for 2–3 minutes or until the cucumber has softened slightly.

2 Stir in the chopped mint, season to taste with salt and pepper and serve while warm.

Buttered courgettes

....

SERVES 2-4
VEGETARIAN
2 courgettes
25g (1oz) butter or 3 tbsp
    olive oil
Salt and ground black pepper

Primarily to go with fish, this dish is extremely quick and simple to prepare. It is delicious as it is, but feel free to add a sprinkling of chopped herbs when serving, such as marjoram, tarragon, basil or mint.

1 Peel the courgettes, then slice in half lengthways and remove and discard the soft inner seeds. Next carefully cut the flesh into 1cm (½in) cubes or slices.

2 To cook, place a frying pan on a high heat. Once hot, add the butter or olive oil and when the butter has melted tip in the courgette pieces. Sauté for 2–3 minutes until just softened, tossing regularly, and season to taste with salt and pepper. Serve immediately.

VARIATION
Buttered cucumber: Replace the courgettes with 1 medium cucumber and then prepare and cook as above.

Fluffy mashed potato

....

SERVES 4
VEGETARIAN

1 kg (2lb 3oz) floury potatoes,
    unpeeled
Salt and ground black pepper
About 150ml (5fl oz) milk,
    or 110ml (4 fl oz) milk and
    50ml (2fl oz) single or
    regular cream
25g (1oz) butter
2 egg whites, lightly beaten

The egg whites in this recipe give the potatoes volume, structure and –
most importantly – fluffiness. You can also stir in chopped herbs once
mashed; parsley, tarragon, marjoram or chives all work well. I find
partially steaming floury potatoes is the best way to cook them. If you
want to make this dish in advance, add a little extra milk or, as it will
dry out as it sits. It will keep really well, covered, in a warm oven for
an hour or so.

1 Place the potatoes in a large saucepan of cold water with a good
pinch of salt. Bring to the boil and cook for 10 minutes, then pour
all but about 4cm (1½in) of the water out of the pan and continue
to cook the potatoes on a very low heat. (Don't be tempted to
stick a knife into them as the skins will break and they will just
disintegrate and get soggy if you do.)

2 About 20 minutes later, when you think the potatoes might
be cooked, test them with a skewer: if they are soft, take them
off the heat. Peel the potatoes while they are still hot and mash
them immediately, either by hand or using the paddle
attachment in an electric food mixer.

3 Bring the milk (or milk and cream) to the boil in a small
saucepan. Add the butter and some salt and pepper to the
potatoes, but don't add any milk until they are free of lumps.
When the potatoes are fully mashed, add the boiling milk (or
milk and cream) and stir to a smooth consistency. You might
not need all the milk/cream or you might need a little more
– it depends on how dry the potatoes are.

4 Next add the egg whites and beat well either with a wooden
spoon or in the food mixer with the paddle attachment. Keep
going for a couple of minutes or until the mixture is light and
fluffy. Add some more salt and pepper if necessary and serve
immediately.

Creamy lentils with rosemary and tomatoes

....

SERVES 4
VEGETARIAN
2 tbsp olive oil
½ onion (150g/5oz),
    peeled and finely chopped
1 clove of garlic, peeled and
    finely chopped
3 tsp chopped rosemary leaves
200g (7oz) Puy lentils, rinsed
1 x 400g tin of chopped
    tomatoes
150ml (5fl oz) single or
    regular cream
Salt and ground black pepper
Pinch of sugar

Lentils are often thought of as a cheap source of protein without much excitement for the cook. Yet this couldn't be further from the truth for they have a gloriously earthy flavour that here is enriched with cream and tomatoes, enough to convert even the most ardent lentil hater. These work brilliantly with Chicken Confit or Garlic and Herb Pork Chops (see pages 177 and 179).

1 Pour the olive oil into a large saucepan on a medium heat, add the onion and garlic and cook, stirring occasionally, for about 5 minutes. Stir in 1 teaspoon of the chopped rosemary and continue cooking for a further 5 minutes or until the onion is very soft and lightly golden.

2 Add the lentils, tomatoes and 250ml (9fl oz) of water, cover with a lid, bring to the boil, then reduce the heat and simmer for about 50 minutes or until the lentils are quite soft. Add the cream and remaining rosemary, allowing the cream to bubble for about 3 minutes, then season to taste with salt, pepper and sugar. Serve while warm.

Creamy polenta

SERVES 2-4
VEGETARIAN
Salt and ground black pepper
100g (3½oz) medium or
coarse polenta
25g (1oz) butter
50g (2oz) Parmesan or
Parmesan-style cheese,
finely grated

Traditional Italian polenta makes a lovely soothing side dish. Like a good mash, the texture and flavour of polenta accommodates any sauce it meets. This recipe works to perfection with the Pheasant Casserole with Chorizo, Cream and Thyme with which it is photographed on page 183.

1 Place 800ml (1 pint 9fl oz) of water and 1 teaspoon of salt in a large saucepan and bring to the boil. Add the polenta, whisking constantly, then bring back up to the boil and as soon as it begins to bubble, turn the heat down as low as possible. Cook for 30–40 minutes, stirring very frequently (this time with a wooden spoon). The polenta is cooked when it is very thick and porridge-like; the fine grains should be fully softened, not al dente.

2 Stir in the butter, grated Parmesan and season generously with pepper, adding a little more salt if necessary.

Sautéed rosemary potatoes

SERVES 2-4
VEGETARIAN
Salt and ground black pepper
500g (1lb 2oz) potatoes, cut
into 1-2cm (½–¾in) dice
50ml (2fl oz) olive oil
2 cloves of garlic, peeled and
crushed or finely grated
1 tbsp chopped rosemary

This is a lovely quick way of getting soft and crispy potatoes and would go very well with Chicken Confit and Creamy Lentils with Rosemary and Tomatoes (see page 177 and opposite). If the potatoes are new and small, keep their skins on, otherwise peel them.

1 Place a saucepan of lightly salted water over a high heat and bring to the boil. Add the potatoes and cook for 2–5 minutes (floury potatoes will cook faster) until they have slightly softened, then drain before tipping onto kitchen paper to dry completely.

2 Place a large frying pan over a high heat, add the olive oil and when hot, add the potatoes and cook, tossing frequently, for 3–4 minutes until they begin to turn a light golden. Add the garlic and rosemary and cook for a further 3–5 minutes until the potatoes are golden and crispy. Season with salt and pepper and serve immediately, or keep warm, uncovered, to prevent softening.

Chocolate crèmes brûlées

SERVES 4
VEGETARIAN

4 egg yolks
40g (1½oz) caster sugar
½ tsp vanilla extract
350ml (12fl oz) double
  or regular cream
4 tsp cocoa powder
4 tsp demerara sugar

Four small ramekins or
  similar-sized
  ovenproof dishes

My brother-in-law makes this divine chocolate variation of the classic crème brûlée. It is such a pleasing thing to eat, using your spoon to break the crisp sugar barrier to invade the creamy chocolate custard it protects.

1 Place the egg yolks in a large bowl with the caster sugar and vanilla extract, and whisk until combined.

2 Pour the cream into a saucepan and bring to the boil. As it is heating, whisk in the cocoa powder until the cream is just about to boil. Remove from the heat and slowly pour into the bowl with the egg mixture, whisking constantly.

3 Pour the egg and cream mixture into the saucepan (having washed it first to help prevent the custard sticking and scrambling) and place on a low heat (any hotter and it will scramble easily). Cook the custard, stirring constantly, for a couple of minutes or until it thickens. (Stir first with the whisk, then, as it heats up, change to a wooden spoon so you can get into the corners of the saucepan and avoid uneven cooking.) As the custard starts to 'shiver' on top and comes almost to the boil, remove immediately from the heat. At this point, speed is crucial as the custard could turn into sweet scrambled eggs!

4 Pour the mixture into the ramekins, allow to cool and then cover and place in the fridge to chill for at least an hour (or they will be fine left overnight). Make sure when you are covering them with cling film that you do not touch the surface of the crèmes: you need a skin to form as this is what will hold the sugar on top – so no dipping fingers in to taste!

5 When you're ready to serve, sprinkle 1 teaspoon of demerara sugar over each crème, spreading it out evenly so that it's one grain thick across the whole surface. With a cook's blow-torch on full heat, caramelise the sugar, keeping the flame just over the sugar and moving in slow circular movements, taking take care not to burn the sugar. Alternatively, cook for 20–60 seconds under a very hot grill until the sugar has caramelised and is bubbling. Set aside for a few minutes to allow the caramel to cool and set and then serve.

Îles flottantes

....

SERVES 4
VEGETARIAN

For the crème anglaise
3 egg yolks
75g (3oz) caster sugar
1 vanilla pod, with a line
    scored down the side,
    or ½ tsp vanilla extract
250ml (9fl oz) milk

For the islands
1 egg white
50g (2oz) caster sugar

For the caramel
50g (2oz) caster sugar

4 glass bowls, wide cocktail
    glasses or champagne cups

*Floating in a sea of rich vanilla custard, these meringue islands are
the most delicate sweet dumplings imaginable.*

1 First make the crème anglaise. In a large bowl, whisk the egg
yolks with the sugar until light and thick. Place the vanilla pod
(if using) in a saucepan with the milk and slowly bring just up
to the boil. Remove the vanilla pod and pour the milk onto the
egg yolks and sugar, whisking all the time.

2 Return the mixture to the saucepan with the vanilla extract
(if using) and stir over a low heat until it has thickened sufficiently
to lightly coat the back of a spoon. (Don't allow it to boil.) Remove
the pan from the heat and pour into a bowl, then cover with cling
film (to prevent a skin forming) and allow to cool.

3 While the crème anglaise is cooling, you can make the 'islands'.
In a spotlessly clean, dry bowl, whisk the egg white until it is
nearly at the stiff stage, then add half of the sugar and whisk until
the mixture forms stiff peaks. Fold in the remaining sugar.

4 Place a wide, shallow saucepan or roasting tin on the stove and
pour in enough cold water to a depth of 3–4cm (1¼–1½in). Bring
to simmering point, then turn the heat down to low and use a
dessertspoon to scoop up four equal blobs of meringue mixture
to place in the water to poach.

5 Allow the meringues to poach for 3 minutes before carefully
turning them over to poach for a further 3 minutes. When cooked
they will feel spongy if prodded gently with your finger. Remove
the islands from the water, then drain on kitchen paper.

6 Make the caramel at the last moment. Put the sugar into a
heavy-based saucepan and place on a medium heat. Stir until the
sugar dissolves, then continue to stir for 2–3 minutes (don't worry
if it begins to look almost lumpy – this will go) or until it turns a
golden caramel. Remove from the heat while you quickly divide
the crème anglaise between the four bowls or glasses and carefully
place an island on top of each portion of custard. Drizzle some hot
caramel over each island and serve straight away.

Coffee zabaglione
with tuiles biscuits

....

SERVES 4
VEGETARIAN
4 egg yolks
50g (2oz) caster sugar
2 tbsp strong black coffee,
    such as espresso
1 tsp double or regular cream
3 tbsp Marsala or medium
    sherry
Tuiles biscuits (see below),
    to serve

4 small glasses

If you love coffee, you will adore this intense dessert. I like to serve it in glasses with tuiles biscuits on the side. Any leftover tuiles can be stored in an airtight container, where they will keep for a couple of days.

1 Place the egg yolks and the sugar in a heatproof bowl sitting over a saucepan of simmering water on a low–medium heat. Whisk together over the heat until the sugar dissolves. The mixture will be runny at this point: continue to whisk for another 5 minutes or until the mixture thickens and becomes quite pale in colour.

2 Now add the remaining ingredients and whisk again for a further 10 minutes or until the mixture is thick and fluffy. Remove from the heat and allow to rest for 10 minutes before pouring into the sherry glasses and serving with the tuiles biscuits on the side.

MAKES 17-20 BISCUITS
VEGETARIAN
2 egg whites
110g (4oz) caster sugar
50g (2oz) plain flour, sifted
½ tsp vanilla extract
50g (2oz) butter, melted
    and cooled

Tuiles biscuits

1 Preheat the oven to 180°C (350°F), Gas mark 4. Line two baking sheets with baking parchment.

2 Place the egg whites in a spotlessly clean, dry bowl and whisk for 1–2 minutes or until they are foamy and just turning white. Gently fold in the remaining ingredients.

3 For each biscuit, spoon 1 teaspoon of the mixture onto a baking sheet and gently spread into a circle, about 5cm (2in) in diameter. The biscuits will spread a little while baking, so do leave space between them. Place in the oven and bake for 3–6 minutes or until they turn light golden brown around the edge and still pale in the middle.

4 Remove from the oven and very gently lift off each biscuit from the baking parchment. Lay while still warm over a rolling pin or

(continued overleaf)

the side of a wine bottle to give a curved shape (tuile means 'tile' in French, as in a curved roof tile) and place on a wire rack to cool. If you would prefer flat biscuits, just place the tuiles straight on the wire rack without curving them first. The tuiles need to be warm to be pliable so keep the rest warm on the baking sheets – in the oven with the heat off and the door open – as you mould each biscuit.

RACHEL'S TIP
Take care not to leave the tuiles in a steamy atmosphere as they will soften very quickly; make sure they are stored somewhere dry.

Orange sorbet with Campari

....

VEGETARIAN
300ml (½ pint) freshly
    squeezed orange juice
    (from about 5 oranges)
Finely grated zest of 1 orange
100g (3½oz) caster sugar
3–4 tbsp Campari, to serve

3–4 chilled cocktail glasses

A delightful little twist on my favourite drink, this can be served as a starter, a palate cleanser during the meal before the main course or for dessert.

1 Place a saucepan on a low heat, add the orange juice, zest and sugar and gently warm through, stirring frequently, until the sugar has dissolved. Remove from the heat and allow to cool. Place in an ice-cream machine and churn for 20–30 minutes or until it has thickened.

2 If you don't have an ice-cream machine, place the sorbet in the freezer for 2–3 hours or until it begins to set around the edges, then, using a fork, stir to break up the frozen crystals. Put the lid back on and continue to freeze for a further hour. Remove from the freezer and stir again, then freeze for another hour, remove and stir one final time.

3 Meanwhile, place a bowl in the freezer that will hold all the sorbet. Once the sorbet has thickened, transfer to the frozen bowl, cover and pop straight into the freezer and leave overnight.

4 When ready to serve, place the frozen sorbet in the fridge for about 10 minutes to soften ever so slightly, before scooping into the chilled glasses and topping with about 1 tablespoon (or more if preferred) of Campari. Serve immediately.

MENU IDEAS FOR
SMALL CELEBRATIONS

Serve all menus with a green salad (see page 239)

Warm winter green salad with Caesar dressing, smoked bacon
and a poached egg (page 160)
Rack of lamb with watercress mousse and potato and
anchovy gratin (pages 176, 185 and 188)
Chocolate crèmes brûlées (page 195)

*

Scallops with Brussels sprouts, bacon and orange (page 157)
Chicken confit, creamy lentils with rosemary and tomatoes
and sautéed rosemary potatoes (pages 177, 192 and 193)
Coffee zabaglione with tuiles biscuits (page 199)

*

Tomato, mozzarella and tapenade crostini (page 163)
Summer pea and mint ravioli (page 168)
Orange sorbet with Campari (page 200)

*

Asparagus on toast with hollandaise sauce (page 159)
Roast duck breasts with white bean purée (pages 184 and 186)
Îles flottantes (page 196)

STARTERS

Ballycotton prawn soup with rouille and toasts
Chicken liver pâté with sweet apple relish
Fish mousse with shrimp beurre blanc
Smoked mackerel and goat's cheese soufflé
Decadent mushroom tart
Beef carpaccio
Sesame and mint chickpea pancakes

MAIN COURSES

Summer vegetable stew
Jerusalem artichokes, toasted hazelnuts and goat's cheese with pasta ribbons
Bulgar wheat pilaf
Miso salmon steaks
Fragrant coconut prawns
Fish stew
Pot-roast pheasant with bacon and brandy
Beef Wellington
Roast pork belly with a fennel and garlic rub
Roast loin of lamb with a spicy rub
Coq au vin
Roast duck legs

SIDE DISHES

Lentils with red wine
Braised chicory
Green salad dressings
Spinach and mint orzo
Creamy potato and Gruyère gratin
Ribboned carrots with honey and parsley
Butternut squash and chickpeas with cumin and coriander
Roast garlic colcannon
French beans with lemon and pine nuts
Soy and sesame pak choi

DESSERTS

Maple pecan toffee tart
Blackberry mousse
Raspberry and amaretto tart
Peach jelly pannacotta pots
Tiramisu
Spiced raisin tart
Almond and orange cake
Orange ice cream
Cinnamon ice cream
Gin and tonic lemon sorbet
Choosing a cheese board
Paper-thin crispbreads

DINNER
PARTIES

(4–8 PEOPLE)

Ah, the classic dinner party. Don't let them scare you! They can
be as relaxed or dressed-up as you want, and you can ask friends
to help or to bring a dish, especially if they love cooking! As with
Small Celebrations, you may wish to serve either two or three
courses, depending on your time available. You may also wish
to have fun decorating your table with more than just candles,
or to give people name tags at their place settings
(see page 8 for ideas).

Ballycotton prawn soup
with rouille and toasts

SERVES 4-6

100g (3½oz) tomatoes,
    chopped
1 carrot (about 100g/3½oz),
    peeled and chopped
1 onion (about 100g/3½oz),
    peeled and chopped
1 tbsp olive oil
Salt and ground black pepper
Pinch of sugar
25g (1oz) butter
300g (11oz) peeled prawns
    (raw or cooked), roughly
    chopped 100ml (3½fl oz)
    dry white wine
300ml (½ pint) Crab or
    Prawn/Shrimp Stock
    (see page 37) or fish stock
125ml (4½fl oz) single
    or regular cream
Chervil, to decorate (optional)

For the rouille and toast
1 baguette
25ml (1fl oz) Crab or Prawn/
    Shrimp Stock (see page 37)
    or fish stock
4 cloves of garlic, peeled and
    crushed or finely grated
1 large egg yolk
¼ tsp whole saffron strands
75ml (3fl oz) olive oil

This is a heavenly and quite rich soup that is great to serve as a starter for a dinner party. The sweetness of the prawns in the soup gets a good garlicky kick from the rouille.

1 Place the tomatoes, carrot and onion in a large saucepan with the olive oil. Season with salt, pepper and sugar, and gently sweat, covered, on a low heat for 40–45 minutes, stirring regularly, until the carrot is completely soft.

2 While the vegetables are cooking, make the rouille. Cut a large slice, about 2cm (¾in) thick, from the baguette, reserving the remainder for later. Break up the slice into chunks and place in a small bowl with the crab or prawns (shrimps) stock.

3 Allow the bread to soak up the stock so that it becomes completely mushy. Add the garlic, egg yolk and saffron and mix together. Then, whisking all the time, add the olive oil very slowly, as though you were making mayonnaise. Indeed, the rouille should look like a thick, deep yellow mayonnaise. Place in a bowl and set aside. (You could make the rouille in advance as it will keep, covered, in the fridge for a couple of days.)

4 Preheat the grill to hot. Cut the remaining baguette into slices about 1cm (½in) thick and toast on both sides under the grill until light golden.

5 To finish making the soup, melt the butter in another saucepan on a medium heat. When it starts to foam, add the prawns and cook for about 2 minutes until cooked through. Next add the wine, stock and the cooked tomato mixture, then simmer, still on a medium heat, for about 10 minutes.

6 In a blender (or use a hand-held blender), liquidise the soup until it's smooth, then stir in the cream and season to taste.

7 Serve the soup hot. Spread a generous amount of the rouille on each piece of toast and either place in the bowl of soup as croutons decorated with chervil leaves, or eat as an accompaniment.

Chicken liver pâté with sweet apple relish

....

The combination of port, brandy and thyme gives this rich, smooth pâté bags of flavour –fabulous as a dinner party starter on toast, crusty bread or thin crackers and with a dollop of the sweet apple relish.If you are cooking for larger numbers, this recipe doubles up very easily. It keeps for three days in the fridge.

SERVES 4-6

250g (9oz) chicken livers
110g (4oz) butter
50g (2oz) peeled and finely chopped shallots
2 cloves of garlic, peeled and finely chopped
2 tsp chopped thyme leaves
75ml (3fl oz) port
25ml (1fl oz) brandy
Salt and ground black pepper
250ml (9fl oz) sweet apple relish (see opposite), to serve

1 Trim off any greenish or white sinewy bits from the livers.

2 Melt 15g (½oz) butter in a large frying pan on a low–medium heat and, when it starts to foam, add the chicken livers. Cook for 2–4 minutes on each side; cooking time will depend on the thickness of the livers, but they should still be slightly pink inside. Remove the livers to the bowl of a food processor and set aside.

3 Melt a further 15g (½oz) butter in the same frying pan over a medium heat, add the shallots and garlic and cook for 6–8 minutes until slightly golden. Tip in the thyme, port and brandy and continue to cook until the liquid has reduced to approximately 2 tablespoons. (Be very careful when adding the alcohol, as it may flame, so stand well back and make sure you pre-measure it – don't hold the bottle of brandy or port directly over the hob.)

4 Place the shallot mixture in the food processor with the chicken livers, making sure to scrape the pan to get all the juices in. Whiz everything together for a good few minutes until smooth then allow to cool completely. Cut the remaining butter into cubes and add to the chicken livers, whiz together again and season to taste with salt and pepper.

5 Spoon into a bowl, smooth the top and store, covered in cling film, in the fridge. Allow to come up to room temperature before serving with the sweet apple relish.

MAKES 250ML (9FL OZ)
VEGETARIAN

25g (1oz) butter
2 eating apples, peeled,
    cored and chopped into
    5mm (¼in) dice
50g (2oz) caster sugar
25ml (1fl oz) sherry vinegar
75ml (3fl oz) red wine
Pinch of salt

Sweet apple relish

In addition to serving this relish with the chicken liver pâté, opposite, it would also be lovely with the Game Terrine with Celeriac Remoulade or the Venison Sausages with Celeriac Purée (see pages 45 and 48), or serve it with cheese on the cheeseboard. Stored in a sterilised jar, this relish will keep for several weeks.

1 Melt the butter in a saucepan on a medium heat. When it has melted and begins to foam, add the apples and cook for 2–3 minutes or until the apples turn slightly golden around the edges.

2 Add the remaining ingredients, stir thoroughly and cook over a low–medium heat for 5–8 minutes or until reduced and jam-like, the apples cooked through but not mushy.

3 Allow to cool before serving, or store in a sterilised jar (for sterilising jars, see page 42).

Fish mousse with shrimp beurre blanc

....

SERVES 6

For the shrimp beurre blanc
3 tbsp dry white wine
3 tbsp white wine vinegar
1 tbsp peeled and finely
   chopped shallots
1 tbsp double or regular
   cream
175g (6oz) chilled butter,
   cubed
Freshly ground white pepper
Freshly squeezed lemon juice
A small knob of butter
75g (3oz) cooked shrimps
   or prawns, peeled

For the mousse
175g (6oz) fillets of whiting,
   pollack, cod or haddock,
   skinned and free of bone
   or membrane
½ tsp salt
Pinch of freshly ground
   white pepper
1 egg
Melted butter, for greasing
300ml (½ pint) double or
   regular cream, chilled

Six 100ml (3½fl oz) ramekins

The purpose of a mousse is to take the essence of a flavour and create something that is both light and luxurious at the same time. This is my husband's favourite starter ever; it's been made at Ballymaloe since he was a boy. It's best to have everything as cold as possible to begin with, even the bowl of the food processor, as this helps keep the texture of the mousse as light as possible.

1 To make the beurre blanc, place the wine, vinegar and shallots into a heavy-based saucepan and boil, uncovered, for about 5 minutes to let the mixture reduce to about half a tablespoon.

2 Pour in the cream and boil again until it thickens. Whisk in the chilled butter in little pieces, keeping the sauce just warm enough to absorb the butter.

3 Strain out the shallots, season with white pepper and lemon juice and keep warm in a bowl over hot, not simmering, water. The sauce should not be too thick, only slightly thicker than double cream; if you need to thin it, just add some warm water.

4 Place a frying pan on a medium heat and allow to get hot. Add the knob of butter and toss the shrimps or prawns in the butter for 1 minute until warmed through. Then set aside for a few seconds to slightly cool before stirring through the sauce.

5 Before making the mousse it is best to have everything well chilled to start with, including the bowl of the food processor. Cut the fish fillets into small dice and purée the pieces in the food processor. Add the salt and pepper, then the egg, and continue to purée until the ingredients are well mixed, though not for any

(continued overleaf)

longer or the mixture will curdle and become rubbery in texture. Chill in the fridge for 30 minutes.

6 Preheat the oven to 200°C (400°F), Gas mark 6, and brush the ramekins with melted butter.

7 When the fish has rested for 30 minutes, remove from the fridge, pour in the cream and whiz again in the food processor just until it is well incorporated. Check the seasoning. (The mousse can be prepared to this point several hours ahead. Cover and place in the fridge until needed.)

8 Divide the mousse mixture between the ramekins and place them in a deep roasting tin. Pour enough boiling water in the tin to come halfway up the outside of the ramekins. Cover with a sheet of perforated foil or greaseproof paper (using a skewer or sharp knife to make about 10 holes all over) and transfer to the oven to bake for about 20 minutes. When cooked the mousses should feel just firm in the centre. They will keep perfectly for 20–30 minutes in a low oven.

9 Turn out onto warmed plates then spoon over some shrimp beurre blanc to serve.

Smoked mackerel and goat's cheese soufflé

....

SERVES 6-8
50g (2oz) butter, plus
    extra for greasing
50g (2oz) plain flour
250ml (9fl oz) milk
4 eggs, separated
100g (3½oz) smoked
    mackerel, skin removed
    and flesh chopped
100g (3½oz) soft goat's
    cheese, broken into 1cm
    (½in) pieces
2 tbsp chopped chives
1 tsp chopped dill
2 tbsp lemon juice
Salt and ground black pepper
25g (1oz) grated Parmesan
    cheese

Six 100ml (3½fl oz) or eight
    75ml (3fl oz) ramekins

Cheese soufflé is a classic and not nearly as scary a dinner party prospect as you might imagine. This version, with goat's cheese and smoked mackerel, is a fantastic variation on the theme.

1 Preheat the oven to 220°C (425°F), Gas mark 7. Butter the ramekins and place a baking sheet in the centre of the oven to heat up.

2 Melt the butter in a large saucepan on a medium heat, then add the flour and stir for 1 minute, being careful not to let it burn. Turn the heat down and whisk in the milk gradually, stirring until you have a thick white sauce, then remove the pan from the heat.

3 Beat in the egg yolks, then fold in the smoked mackerel, goat's cheese and herbs. Season to taste with lemon juice and salt and pepper. It should taste highly seasoned as adding the egg white will dilute the flavour.

4 Whisk the egg whites in a spotlessly clean, dry bowl until they form stiff peaks, then take 2 tablespoons of the egg white and mix it into the sauce. Very carefully fold in the remaining egg white, making sure not to over-mix it.

5 Divide the mixture between the ramekins, filling each to the top, then scatter with the grated Parmesan. Place the cheese soufflés on the hot baking sheet in the oven and cook for 12–15 minutes or until well risen and golden. Serve immediately.

VARIATION
Twice-baked soufflé: If you have any cheese soufflés left over, tip each out of its ramekin and place in a buttered shallow baking dish. Pour over 50ml (2fl oz) cream per soufflé and bake in the oven, preheated to 200°C (400°F), Gas mark 6, for 6–8 minutes.

Decadent mushroom tart

....

SERVES 8
VEGETARIAN

For the shortcrust pastry
200g (7oz) plain flour, sifted
100g (3½oz) chilled butter,
    cubed, plus extra for
    greasing
½–1 egg, beaten

For the filling
15g (½oz) butter
100g (3½oz) shallots, peeled
    and finely chopped
200g (7oz) button or large
    flat mushrooms, finely
    chopped
Salt and ground black pepper
25g (1oz) dried mushrooms,
    such as porcini
250ml (9fl oz) boiling water
2 eggs
1 egg yolk
250ml (9fl oz) double
    or regular cream

For the tarragon hollandaise
3 egg yolks
175g (6oz) butter, diced
Squeeze of lemon juice
¼ tsp Dijon mustard
3 tbsp chopped tarragon

23cm (9in) diameter loose-
    bottomed tart tin

Porcini are one of the most prized mushrooms. They are dried for preservation and when rehydrated in water they bestow their powerful, almost meaty flavour to the liquid. This tart uses that liquid and other mushrooms, as well as the porcini themselves, so it is crammed with mushroom flavour. Drizzled with tarragon hollandaise, it becomes the height of luxurious sophistication.

1 Place the flour and butter in a food processor and whiz briefly until the butter is in small lumps. Add half the beaten egg and continue to whiz for another few seconds or until the mixture looks as though it may just come together when pressed. (Prolonged processing will only toughen the pastry, so don't whiz it up until it is a ball of dough.) You might need to add a little more egg, but not too much as the mixture should be just moist enough to come together. If making by hand, rub the butter into the flour until it resembles coarse breadcrumbs then, using your hands, add just enough egg to bring it together. Reserve any leftover egg to use later.

2 With your hands, flatten out the ball of dough until it is about 2cm (¾in) thick, then wrap in cling film or a plastic bag and leave in the fridge for at least 30 minutes.

3 When you are ready to roll out the pastry, butter the tart tin and remove the pastry from the fridge, placing it between two sheets of cling film (each larger in size than your tart tin). Using a rolling pin, roll the pastry out to no thicker than 5mm (¼in). Make sure to keep it in a round shape as well as large enough to line both the base and the sides of the tin.

4 Remove the top layer of cling film, slide your hand, palm upwards, under the bottom layer of cling film, then flip the pastry over (so that the cling film is now on top) and carefully lower it into the tart tin. Press the pastry into the edges of the tin (with the cling film still attached) and, using your thumb, 'cut' the pastry along the edge of the tin for a neat finish. Remove the cling film,

prick over the base with a fork and chill the pastry in the fridge for another 30 minutes or in the freezer for 10 minutes (it can keep for weeks like this in the freezer).

5 Preheat the oven to 180°C (350°F), Gas mark 4.

6 Remove the pastry from the fridge and line with foil, greaseproof paper or baking parchment, leaving plenty over the sides. Fill with baking beans or dried pulses (all of which can be reused repeatedly), then place in the oven and bake 'blind' for 15–20 minutes or until the pastry feels dry in the base. Take out of the oven, remove the baking beans and foil/paper, brush the base of the pastry with any leftover beaten egg, then bake for another 3 minutes or until lightly golden. Remove from the oven and set aside.

7 Next make the filling. Melt the butter in a large frying pan on a medium heat, add the shallots, cover with a lid and cook for 7–8 minutes or until soft but not browned. Stir in the mushrooms, season with salt and pepper and cook, uncovered, for 8–10 minutes or until soft and dark and any juices that have come out during cooking have evaporated.

8 While these are cooking, soak the dried mushrooms in the boiling water for 10 minutes. Drain, reserving the soaking liquid, then finely chop the soaked mushrooms and add to the shallot and mushroom mixture along with the soaking liquid. Continue to cook, stirring occasionally, for about 10 minutes or until the liquid has completely evaporated. Remove from the heat and allow to cool for a few minutes.

9 Meanwhile, whisk together the eggs, egg yolk and cream, then add to the mushrooms. Mix together and then pour into the pre-baked tart case. Place in the oven and cook for about 30 minutes or until the filling has completely set.

10 While the tart is baking make the hollandaise sauce following the instructions on page 159, stirring the mustard and tarragon into the cooked sauce just before seasoning.

11 Remove the tart from the oven, cut into slices while warm and serve with a generous drizzle of the tarragon hollandaise.

Beef carpaccio

....

SERVES 8
350g (12oz) fillet of beef
Extra-virgin olive oil, for
    oiling and drizzling
Rocket leaves (about
    5 per person)
Shavings of Parmesan cheese
    (cut using a peeler)
18 black olives, pitted
    (see page 38) and
    finely chopped
Sea salt and ground black
    pepper

This classic starter uses raw beef (it's perfectly safe if you use good, very fresh quality beef). The fillet is so tender it doesn't need cooking to tenderise, but do try and cut the slices as thinly as possible. When raw beef tastes this good it's almost enough to make me wonder why we ever cook it at all!

1 Chill the meat by placing it on a baking tray in the fridge for an hour or so, then remove and slice widthways as thinly as possible with a very sharp knife.

2 Place each slice on a piece of oiled cling film, then cover with another piece of oiled cling film (you can reuse these for each slice of beef). Roll gently with a rolling pin until the meat is paper thin. Peel the cling film off the top, then flip the meat over onto a plate so that the lower layer of cling film is facing upwards. Gently peel away this piece of cling film. (If you want to prepare this an hour or two in advance, keep the beef slices covered with cling film in the fridge – with cling film between each layer of beef to prevent the slices sticking together – then remove about 20 minutes before serving to bring back up to room temperature.)

3 Scatter the rocket leaves, Parmesan shavings and chopped olives over the beef, then season with salt and pepper. Drizzle with olive oil and serve immediately with crusty bread.

Sesame and mint chickpea pancakes

....

MAKES 6
VEGETARIAN

2 tomatoes, deseeded
  and cubed
½ cucumber, peeled,
  deseeded and sliced
½ red onion, peeled and
  finely sliced
2 tbsp olive oil
1 tbsp sesame seeds, toasted
  (see page 25), to serve

For the dressing
50ml (2fl oz) natural yoghurt
1 tbsp extra-virgin olive oil
1 tsp chopped mint
1 tsp lemon juice
Salt and ground black pepper

For the pancakes
1 x 400g tin of chickpeas,
  drained and rinsed, or 125g
  (4½oz) dried chickpeas,
  soaked and cooked
  (see page 64)
2 tsp chopped mint
2 tsp chopped parsley
2 tsp sesame oil
1 egg
100g (3½oz) fresh white
  breadcrumbs
Juice of ½ lemon

*I absolutely adore the Middle Eastern flavours in this starter.
The pancakes contrast perfectly with the moist and crunchy salad,
while the mint brings a real freshness.*

1 Whisk all the dressing ingredients together, seasoning to taste
with salt and pepper, then stir in the vegetables and set aside.

2 Next make the pancakes. Place the chickpeas in a food processor,
along with the mint, parsley, sesame oil and egg. Whiz for
1–2 minutes to form a rough paste, then add the breadcrumbs,
season with salt and pepper, add the lemon juice and pulse
a few times until everything comes together.

3 Shape into six even-sized pancakes about 6cm (2½in) wide
and 1.5cm (⅝in) thick. Pour the olive oil into a large frying pan
on a medium heat. When the oil is hot, add half the pancakes and
fry on each side for about 3 minutes or until golden brown and
crispy. Repeat with the remaining pancakes, adding a little more
oil first.

4 Place on individual plates with some salad on the side, then
scatter with the toasted sesame seeds.

Summer vegetable stew

....

SERVES 4-6
VEGETARIAN

350g (12oz) small new
   potatoes, left unpeeled and
   cut into 2cm (¾in) cubes
7 tbsp olive oil
Sea salt and ground black
   pepper
1 red pepper
1 yellow pepper
1 small aubergine, cut into
   2cm (¾in) cubes
200g (7oz) cherry tomatoes,
   halved across the middle
1 onion (300g/11oz in weight),
   peeled and thinly sliced
2 cloves of garlic, peeled and
   finely sliced
1 tbsp sherry vinegar or red
   wine vinegar
3 generous tbsp roughly
   chopped or torn basil

*This dish has echoes of a ratatouille, but because in this recipe all the
components are roasted, it has a lovely sweet and intense flavour. As
with most stews, this is very good reheated when all the flavours have
had time to marry and infuse.*

1 Preheat the oven to 230°C (450°F), Gas mark 8.

2 In a bowl, mix the potatoes with 2 tablespoons of the olive oil
and season with salt and pepper. Place on a large roasting tin
with the whole peppers and roast in the oven for 15 minutes.

3 Meanwhile, in the same bowl, mix together the aubergine
and tomatoes with 3 tablespoons of olive oil. Season with salt
and pepper and set aside.

4 After 15 minutes, add the aubergine and tomatoes to the
potatoes and return to the oven. Cook for a further 20–25 minutes
or until the aubergine is completely soft and beginning to brown
at the edges. Remove the tin from the oven and set aside.

5 The peppers should be completely soft and the skin slightly
blackened. Transfer to a bowl and cover with cling film – this
makes the skin easier to remove. When the peppers are cool
enough to handle, peel them, remove all the seeds and cut
the flesh into pieces roughly 2cm (¾in) square.

6 Meanwhile, place a large saucepan on a medium heat and pour
in the remaining olive oil. Add the onion and garlic and cook for
10 minutes or until soft and beginning to brown. Add the roasted
vegetables, together with the vinegar and basil, and stir gently to
combine. Taste for seasoning and serve while warm.

Blackberry mousse

....

SERVES 6

450g (1lb) blackberries, plus
   extra to decorate (optional)
110g (4oz) caster sugar
1 rounded tsp powdered
   gelatine
300ml (½ pint) double
   or regular cream

This is a gorgeous autumnal dessert with a wonderful pink colour. It's also a great excuse to go out foraging for blackberries! The shortbread biscuits on pages 58–9 are the perfect accompaniment.

1 Place the blackberries in a large saucepan and add the sugar and 2 tablespoons of water. Cook over a low heat for 10–12 minutes or until the blackberries are soft.

2 Pour the blackberries into a large sieve set over a bowl and push through all the liquefied fruit that you can, leaving the seeds in the sieve. Remember to scrape the underside of the sieve too and add this into the purée in the bowl.

3 Pour 1 tablespoon of water into a small bowl, sprinkle over the powdered gelatine and set aside for 5 minutes.

4 Pour the blackberry purée into a saucepan and add the soaked gelatine. Stir the syrup over a low heat for 2–3 minutes or until the gelatine has dissolved.

5 In a separate bowl, whip the cream until it forms stiff peaks, then gently fold in the purée. Pour into a serving bowl, pretty glasses or, if you have them, old-fashioned tea cups. Cover with cling film and chill overnight or for 2–3 hours until set. You could sprinkle a few blackberries on top just before serving.

Raspberry and amaretto tart

SERVES 6-8
VEGETARIAN

225g (8oz) deep-golden
   amaretti biscuits
125g (4½oz) butter
½ tsp ground cinnamon
250g (9oz) natural Greek
   yoghurt, pushed through
   a sieve
350g (12oz) fresh raspberries
Icing sugar, for dusting
   (optional)

23cm (9in) diameter loose-
   bottomed tart tin

At the height of the raspberry season I can think of few more delightful or indeed any easier ways to present them than this tart. The crunchy texture and almond flavour of the amaretti complement the velvety sharpness of the fruit.

1 To make the tart base, first place the amaretti in a clean plastic bag and crush into fine crumbs using a rolling pin. Alternatively, you can whiz the biscuits in a food processor for a second or two.

2 Melt the butter in a large saucepan over a medium heat, then remove from the hob and stir in the biscuit crumbs. Pour the biscuit mixture into the tin, then use the back of a spoon to flatten it into the base and up the sides of the tin by 3cm (1¼in). (I find using my fingertips for this gives the edges a good finish.) Put the biscuit base in the fridge to chill for 1½–2 hours.

3 When you are ready to serve, mix the cinnamon with the yoghurt, then spoon the mixture into the chilled tart base and simply top with the fresh raspberries, lightly dusted with icing sugar, if wished.

Peach jelly pannacotta pots

....

SERVES 6
Sunflower oil, for oiling

For the peach syrup jelly
110g (4oz) caster sugar
3 peaches, left unpeeled but
    halved and stones removed
1 tbsp powdered gelatine

For the pannacotta
300ml (½ pint) double or
    regular cream
25g (1oz) caster sugar
1 vanilla pod, split lengthways
1 rounded tsp powdered
    gelatine

Six 100ml (3½fl oz) ramekin
    dishes or glasses

This divine dessert is a twist on the classic combination of peaches and cream. The bright translucent fruit jelly looks gorgeous perched on the rich smooth pannacotta.

1 Lightly oil the inside of each ramekin, then carefully line with cling film, allowing extra to hang over the sides for covering the top of the dish when it has been filled, then lightly oil the inside of the cling film.

2 Begin by making the peach syrup jelly. Fill a large saucepan with 300ml (½ pint) water and add the sugar. Set on a medium heat and stir until the sugar is dissolved. Then bring to boiling point, add the halved peaches, then reduce the heat and allow to simmer for 5–8 minutes or until the peaches are soft.

3 Take the pan from the heat, carefully remove the peaches from the syrup and gently peel away their skins, which should slip off easily. Place each peach half, cut side up, in one of the lined ramekins.

4 Pour 2 tablespoons of water into a small bowl, sprinkle over the gelatine and set aside for 5 minutes. Next add the soaked gelatine to the peach syrup in the saucepan and stir over a low heat for 2–3 minutes or until dissolved.

5 Divide the syrup equally between the six ramekins, making sure you keep the peaches as central and upright as possible in each dish, then chill in the fridge for 2 hours to set the jelly.

6 To make the pannacotta, place the cream, sugar and vanilla pod in a saucepan and slowly bring to boiling point, then turn off the heat and allow the vanilla to infuse.

7 Pour 2 teaspoons of water into a clean bowl, add the gelatine and set aside for 5 minutes. Add the soaked gelatine to the hot cream mixture, stirring gently until the gelatine dissolves. (If the cream

has cooled down too much, you may need to reheat it slightly once the gelatine has been added.)

8 Allow to cool to room temperature, remove the vanilla pod then pour the pannacotta over the set peach jelly in the ramekins. Gently cover each dish with the excess cling film hanging over the sides, then place in the fridge to chill for 2–3 hours or overnight until set.

9 To serve, turn each ramekin upside down onto a plate, carefully remove the ramekin and then very gently peel off the cling film.

RACHEL'S TIP
Sometimes creased cling film can leave marks on the pannacotta. So if you would like yours to be completely smooth, very gently smooth the edges with a metal spatula dipped in hot water.

Tiramisu

....

SERVES 6
VEGETARIAN
1 egg yolk
1 tbsp caster sugar
1 tsp vanilla extract
1 x 250g tub of mascarpone
200ml (7fl oz) double or
    regular cream
200ml (7fl oz) strong black
    coffee, such as espresso
2 tbsp brandy
10–12 boudoir biscuits
    (sponge fingers), each
    broken into 3 pieces
1–2 tbsp cocoa powder,
    for dusting

Six medium glasses

This classic Italian dessert is very straightforward to prepare yet looks impressive layered up in individual glasses.

1 Place the egg, sugar and vanilla extract in a large bowl and whisk to a creamy consistency. Add the mascarpone and cream and continue to whisk until smooth and creamy.

2 In a separate bowl, mix together the coffee and brandy. Dip 2–3 pieces of the boudoir biscuits into the coffee and brandy (just long enough to absorb the liquid, but not so long that they fall apart) and put into the bottom of one of the six glasses. Repeat for the remaining glasses.

3 Add 1 tablespoon of the mascarpone and cream mixture to cover the biscuits in each glass. Follow this with another layer of 2–3 biscuit pieces, dipped again in the coffee and brandy, finishing with another layer of mascarpone and cream.

4 Dust each glass with cocoa powder and place in the fridge to chill for at least 1 hour (or up to 24 hours). Take out of the fridge 10 minutes or so before serving (so they aren't too chilled) and dust with a little more cocoa powder to serve.

Spiced raisin tart

VEGETARIAN

110g (4oz) butter, plus extra
  for greasing
225g (8oz) digestive biscuits
225g (8oz) raisins
1 tsp cornflour
½ tsp ground cinnamon
110g (4oz) demerara or light
  soft brown sugar

23cm (9in) diameter loose-
  bottomed tart tin

*A favourite recipe of my mum's from the 70s, this is fabulously retro.
My sister and I used to love eating the leftovers (if there were any!)
from my parents' dinner parties. It's great served with the Cinnamon
Ice Cream on page 258. Because of the dried fruit and spice filling, it
works particularly well as a Christmas dessert. If there's any left over,
it's also delicious with a cup of coffee.*

1 Start by making the biscuit base. Butter the tart tin, then
place the digestive biscuits in a clean plastic bag and, using a
rolling pin, crush into fine crumbs. Alternatively, you could
whiz the biscuits in a food processor for a minute or two.

2 Melt the butter in a saucepan over a medium heat, remove
from the heat and stir in the biscuit crumbs. Pour the mixture
into the prepared tin and, using the back of a spoon, flatten the
crumbs into the base and up the sides of the tin. (I find using
your fingertips gives the sides a good finish.) Place in the fridge
to chill for 1½–2 hours.

3 Meanwhile, fill a separate saucepan with 300ml (½ pint) of
water and add the raisins. Bring to a simmer and cook for about
10 minutes or until the raisins have plumped up.

4 Place the cornflour in a small bowl, add 2 teaspoons of water and
mix to a smooth consistency. Pour this into the cooked raisins and
continue to stir gently over a low heat for about 2 minutes or until
the liquid thickens slightly.

5 Next add the cinnamon and sugar and continue to stir over
a low heat for about 2 minutes or until the sugar has dissolved.
Remove from the heat and allow the raisin mixture to cool.

6 Once it has cooled, pour the mixture into the biscuit base and
pop the tart back into the fridge for 1–2 hours before serving.

Almond and orange cake

....

SERVES 6-8
VEGETARIAN

100g (3½oz) butter,
  softened, plus extra
  for greasing
175g (6 oz) caster sugar
3 eggs
Juice and finely grated
  zest of 1 orange
50g (2oz) plain flour
1 tsp baking powder
100g (3½oz) ground almonds

For the syrup
75g (3oz) icing sugar
Juice of 1 orange
1 tbsp Cointreau or
  Grand Marnier

20cm (8in) diameter spring-
  form/loose-bottomed tin

This is a really moist cake that will keep for up to a week – if you can resist eating it! It is divine served with Orange Ice Cream (see page 258) or some whipped cream mixed with a little icing sugar and Cointreau or orange zest.

1 Preheat the oven to 180°C (350°F), Gas mark 4. Butter the tin and line the base with baking parchment.

2 Cream the butter in a large bowl or in an electric food mixer until soft. Add the sugar and beat until the mixture is light and fluffy. Beat in the eggs, one at a time, then whisk in the orange juice and zest. Sift in the flour and baking powder and fold into the cake batter, then fold in the ground almonds.

3 Spoon the mixture into the prepared tin and bake in the oven for 30–40 minutes or until the cake is golden and a skewer inserted into the middle comes out clean.

4 While the cake is baking, make the syrup. Place the icing sugar and orange juice in a small saucepan and stir over a low heat for 1–2 minutes or until the sugar has dissolved. Remove from the heat and add the Cointreau or Grand Marnier.

5 When you remove the cake from the oven, leave it in the tin and use a skewer to make holes, about 2cm (¾in) deep and 3cm (1¼in) apart, across the surface of the cake. Gently drizzle the warm syrup over the top of the cake, allowing it to soak in. Allow to cool slightly before removing it from the tin, and serve warm. This cake is also delicious cold.

Orange ice cream

SERVES 6-8
VEGETARIAN
300ml (½ pint) double or
    regular cream
4 eggs, separated
100g (3½oz) caster sugar
Juice and finely grated zest
    of 2 oranges

The beauty of this ice cream is that you don't need an ice-cream machine to make it. It is yummy with the Almond and Orange Cake or used in the recipe for Amaretti with Brandy and Ice Cream (see pages 257 and 300).

1 Pour the cream into a bowl and whisk until thickened. In a separate bowl, whisk together the egg yolks and the sugar until thickened and creamy in colour. Add the orange juice and grated zest and whisk to combine.

2 In a spotlessly clean, dry bowl, whisk the egg whites until they form stiff peaks. Fold the cream into the egg and sugar mixture, then gently fold in the egg whites. Pour into an airtight plastic container with a lid or into a serving bowl and cover with cling film. Freeze overnight.

VARIATION

Lemon ice cream: Make the recipe in the same way, simply replacing the orange juice and zest with the juice and zest of 2 lemons.

Cinnamon ice cream

SERVES 6-8
VEGETARIAN
300ml (½ pint) double
    or regular cream
4 eggs, separated
100g (3½oz) caster sugar
1 tsp ground cinnamon

A very easy ice cream to make, and you don't need an ice-cream machine. Delicious on its own and particularly good served with the Spiced Raisin Tart or the Spiced Poached Pears (see pages 256 and 82).

1 In a bowl, whip the cream until thickened. In another bowl, whisk together the egg yolks with the sugar until thickened and creamy in colour. Add the cinnamon and whisk again to combine.

2 In a separate, spotlessly clean, dry bowl, whisk the egg whites until they form stiff peaks. Fold the cream into the egg and sugar mixture, and then gently fold in the egg whites.

3 Pour the mixture into an airtight plastic container with a lid or into a serving bowl. Cover with cling film and freeze overnight.

Gin and tonic lemon sorbet

250ml (9fl oz) freshly
   squeezed lemon juice
   (from about 4 lemons)
400g (14oz) caster sugar
750ml (1⅓ pints) tonic water

To serve
8 slices of lemon
About 8 tbsp gin

8 chilled cocktail glasses

I love this playful twist on the timeless drink. Like the Orange Sorbet with Campari (see page 200), this can be served as a starter, a palate cleanser during the meal before the main course or even for dessert.

1 Place a saucepan on a low heat, add the lemon juice and sugar and gently warm through, stirring frequently, until the sugar has dissolved. Remove from the heat, stir in the tonic water and allow to cool. Place into an ice-cream machine and churn for 20–30 minutes or until the mixture has thickened.

2 If you don't have an ice-cream machine, place the sorbet in the freezer for 2–3 hours or until it begins to set around the edges, then, using a fork, stir to break up the frozen crystals. Put the lid back on and continue to freeze for a further hour. Remove from the freezer and stir again, then freeze for another hour, remove and stir one final time.

3 Meanwhile, place a bowl in the freezer that will hold all the sorbet. Once the sorbet has thickened, transfer to the frozen bowl, cover and pop straight into the freezer and leave overnight.

4 When ready to serve, place the frozen sorbet in the fridge for about 10 minutes to soften ever so slightly, before scooping into the glasses and topping with a slice of lemon and about 1 tablespoon (or more if preferred) of gin. Serve immediately.

Choosing a cheese board

....

I love to serve a cheese course as part of a dinner party, sometimes before dessert, as is the custom in France; sometimes instead of a dessert course; but more often than not I prefer to serve cheese at the very end of the meal to enjoy with the last of the red wine. People may feel apprehensive about serving a cheese board, uncertain as to what goes with what. They needn't be, as there are no solid rules, but here are a few guidelines.

* I think while a selection can be nice, your money would be better spent on fewer, better cheeses. I would be happier with just a couple of great cheeses from a good cheese shop than a number of mediocre, unripe cheeses.

* A little honey is a nice contrast to the intense savoury flavour of a goat's cheese or blue cheese.

* Some fruit, especially figs or grapes, work well with cheese – hard varieties in particular.

* A fruit paste (such as quince membrillo) is very nice with semi-hard to hard cheeses.

* Fresh bread is delicious with cheese, as are oatcakes, crispbreads (see page 262) or crackers. Serve one or a selection.

* Cheese is much better served at room temperature, so take it out the fridge at least 1 hour before serving.

* It's a good idea to ask your cheesemonger the best way to store each variety as some are best stored, covered, outside the fridge.

Paper-thin crispbreads

....

MAKES ABOUT
15 LARGE CRISPBREADS
VEGETARIAN

375g (13oz) plain flour OR
   225g (8oz) plain flour and
   150g (5oz) wholemeal flour
1 tsp salt
1 tbsp sesame seeds or
   poppy seeds
2 tsp crushed cumin,
   fennel, black pepper or
   coriander seeds or sea salt,
   or herbs (all optional)
1 egg
1 tbsp olive oil
125ml (4fl oz) water

This super-thin crispbread is amazingly versatile and goes really well with any cheese board.

1 Place the dry ingredients in a large bowl and mix together.

2 Whisk the egg in another bowl, add the olive oil and water and mix well. Pour the wet ingredients into the dry ingredients and, using your hands or in the bowl of a food processor, mix to a dough. Knead for 2 minutes until the dough is smooth, then wrap in cling film and set aside to rest for 20 minutes.

3 Preheat the oven to 200°C (400°F), Gas mark 6 (if using a fan oven, see below) and lightly oil several baking trays.

4 Divide the dough into two and roll out each piece until it is about 20cm (8in) wide. Fold the dough in half, then in half again and continue to roll until the dough is paper thin, like pasta, about 1–2mm ($^1/_{16}$in) thick. The pieces should be about 45cm (18in) square. You may need to use some flour while rolling out.

5 Cut the dough into rectangles approximately 8 x 14cm (5½in) in size and place in a single layer on the prepared baking trays. If you want to sprinkle sea salt or seeds on top of the crispbreads, then brush the top of the raw crispbreads with olive oil before sprinkling over so that they stick to the surface.

6 Bake in the oven for 10–14 minutes or until pale golden brown and slightly curled up at the edges. They will feel dry when cooked, but will only really crisp up when they have cooled. Check after 8–10 minutes of cooking and if they are golden brown underneath, but still quite pale on top, then turn them over. Allow to cool on wire racks.

RACHEL'S TIP

If you have a fan oven, you can bake the crispbreads on more than one baking tray at a time. Preheat it to 180°C (350°F), Gas mark 4.

MENU IDEAS FOR DINNER PARTIES

Serve all menus with a green salad (see page 239)

Smoked mackerel and goat's cheese soufflé (page 211)
Roast loin of lamb with a spicy rub and spinach and mint orzo (pages 232 and 240)
Almond and orange cake (page 257)

*

Beef carpaccio (page 214)
Miso salmon steaks (page 222)
French beans with lemon and pine nuts (page 245)
Peach jelly pannacotta pots (pages 252-3)

*

Chicken liver pâté with sweet apple relish (pages 206-7)
Roast pork belly with a fennel and garlic rub, butternut squash
and chickpeas with cumin and coriander and ribboned carrots
with honey and parsley (pages 231, 242 and 241)
Spiced raisin tart (page 256)

*

Ballycotton prawn soup with rouille and toasts (page 204)
Roast duck legs with lentils with red wine and braised chicory (pages 236 and 238)
Tiramisu (page 254)

STARTERS

Chilled avocado soup with red and yellow pepper and coriander salsa
Roast wedges of butternut squash with goat's cheese and spinach pesto
Zingy Asian prawns
Lamb cutlets with spinach pesto
Winter leaf salad with pomegranate, apple and walnuts
Smoked fish platter with Ballymaloe cucumber relish

MAIN COURSES

Greek red peppers
Baked beetroot risotto with Parmesan crisps
Zesty pine nut-crusted fish with salsa verde
Soy-poached fish with avocado salsa
Spiced chicken with red pepper and almonds
Conchiglie pasta with chicken livers, bacon and port
Winter herb and sausage pasta
Cassoulet
Beef and wild mushroom lasagne
Roast haunch of venison

SIDE DISHES

Wilted greens with garlic and anchovy breadcrumbs
Roast Jerusalem artichokes
Rosemary and garlic bread
Parsnip, mustard and parsley mash
Crunchy roast coriander potatoes
Potato and mushroom gratin
Cucumbers with tomatoes, cream and mint

DESSERTS

Amaretti with brandy and ice cream
Iced strawberry parfait with strawberry sauce
White chocolate and ginger parfait with dark chocolate sauce
Raspberry millefeuille
Salted caramel chocolate tart
Rhubarb and ginger crumble cake
Passion fruit and orange granita
Chocolate roulade

LARGER GATHERINGS

(8–12 PEOPLE)

I won't lie, cooking for a larger group for a party or get-together
takes a little extra planning and effort, so here I've given you recipes
that are easier to cook for a bigger group. As ever, remember that
cooking for a crowd is great fun, and the satisfaction from
having fed so many friends and family goes a long way
to making you feel great.

Chilled avocado soup with red and yellow pepper and coriander salsa

....

The vivid colours of this soup make it a perfect dish for a dazzling dinner party.

4 very ripe avocados
15g (½oz) peeled and
 sliced onion
100ml (3½fl oz) French
 dressing (see page 318)
2–4 tsp lemon juice
600ml (1 pint) cold chicken
 or vegetable stock
 (see pages 50–1)

For the red pepper salsa
1 red pepper, deseeded
 and chopped into 3mm
 (⅛in) dice
1 yellow pepper, deseeded
 and chopped into 3mm
 (⅛in) dice
1 red onion, peeled and
 chopped, or 2 spring
 onions, trimmed and
 finely chopped
2 generous tbsp chopped
 coriander (or mint or basil),
 plus some leaves
8 tbsp extra-virgin olive oil
Salt and ground black pepper
Juice of ½–1 lemon

1 Peel and roughly chop the avocados and place in a food processor. Add the onion, French dressing and lemon juice, whiz to a purée, then pour in enough of the stock to bring it to the consistency of thick double cream. Depending on the size of your avocados you may need more or less of the stock to achieve the desired consistency, keeping in mind that it needs to be thick enough so that the salsa will not sink when serving.

2 Taste for seasoning, adding more lemon juice if needed. Push through a sieve then pour into a container for the fridge, cover and chill for ½–1 hour or up to about 4 hours before serving.

3 Meanwhile, make the salsa. Place the red and yellow peppers, onion, chopped coriander and olive oil in a bowl, mixing together and seasoning to taste with salt, pepper and lemon juice.

4 When ready to serve, pour the soup into individual bowls with a spoonful of salsa added to the centre of each and scatter over the coriander leaves.

Roast wedges of butternut squash with goat's cheese and spinach pesto

....

VEGETARIAN
½ tsp black peppercorns
2 butternut squash
4 tbsp olive oil
1 tbsp sherry vinegar
   or balsamic vinegar
Sea salt

To serve
150ml (5fl oz) spinach pesto
   (see page 270)
2 large handfuls of rocket
   leaves
250g (9oz) soft goat's cheese,
   broken into 2cm (¾in)
   chunks
3 tbsp pumpkin seeds, toasted
   (see tip on page 25)

The substantial nature of this dish makes it a hearty vegetarian starter. I'm often surprised at just how sweet butternut can be; the roasting draws out and caramelizes the sugars. The sweetness is countered by the savouriness of the goat's cheese and spinach pesto (see overleaf). It is a beautiful combination on the plate as well as in the mouth. It also makes a delicious accompaniment for roast meat. I like to serve it slightly warm, but it can be served at room temperature too.

1 Make the spinach pesto (see overleaf) and place to one side.

2 Preheat the oven to 220°C (425°F), Gas mark 7.

3 Coarsely crush the peppercorns using a pestle and mortar, or place in a small plastic bag and crush with a rolling pin. Peel the butternut squash using a sharp knife, cut in half lengthways and discard the seeds (or see tip below).

4 Cut the butternut squash into wedges just less than 1cm (½in) at the thickest part. Place in a wide bowl and drizzle with the oil and vinegar, seasoning with a good pinch of sea salt and the pepper. Toss with your hands then tip into a roasting tin or baking tray, making sure to pour in all the oil and seasoning. Spread out into a single layer and roast in the oven for 10–15 minutes or until the squash is tender and a little crisp at the edges. Remove from the oven and allow to cool slightly.

5 To serve, divide the butternut squash between individual plates and scatter the rocket leaves on top. Scatter over the goat's cheese, drizzle with the spinach pesto (1–2 teaspoons per plate) and sprinkle over the pumpkin seeds.

RACHEL'S TIP
If you are feeling ambitious, you can wash the squash seeds, roast them in the oven for about 8 minutes or until golden, then peel them and use in place of the pumpkin seeds.

MAKES ABOUT 300ML
(½ PINT)
VEGETARIAN

100g (3½oz) spinach
(any large stalks removed
before weighing)
50g (2oz) pine nuts
50g (2oz) Parmesan or
Parmesan-style cheese,
finely grated
1 clove of garlic, peeled and
crushed or finely grated
150ml (5fl oz) extra-virgin
olive oil, plus extra for
adding to the jar
Salt and ground black pepper

Spinach pesto

Baby spinach is best for this; if you are using a larger-leafed variety, make sure the leaves aren't too large or tough, and remove any stalks. In addition to the Roast Wedges of Butternut Squash with Goat's Cheese (see page 268), the pesto is also delicious with roasted root vegetables, or roast lamb or chicken. It will keep for a few months stored in a jar in the fridge.

1 Place all the ingredients, except the seasoning, in a food processor, adding only a little of the olive oil at this stage. Whiz together for a minute or two to form a rough paste.

2 Mix in the remaining oil, pouring it in through the tube of the food processor, and add salt and pepper to taste. If the pesto is too thick to drizzle, add a little more olive oil, taking care the pesto does not split.

3 Pour into a sterilised jar (for sterilising jars, see tip on page 42) and cover with a layer of olive oil.

Zingy Asian prawns

SERVES 8-12
600g (1lb 5oz) peeled cooked
  prawns
8 cloves of garlic, peeled and
  crushed
2 tsp peeled and finely grated
  root ginger (see page 27)
2 tbsp chopped mint
2 tbsp chopped coriander
2 tsp finely chopped
  lemongrass
4 tbsp fish sauce (nam pla)
2 tbsp soft light brown sugar
½–1 red chilli, deseeded and
  chopped
Juice of 1 lemon

To serve
1 Cos lettuce
Whole coriander leaves

The combination of mint and coriander in this great southeast Asian starter make it wonderfully light and fresh tasting. Serve it on a sunny summer's day, followed by the Spiced Chicken with Red Pepper and Almonds (see page 284).

1 Place all the ingredients in a large bowl and mix together. Taste for seasoning, adding more fish sauce if it's not salty enough, then leave to marinate for at least 20 minutes before serving.

2 To serve, shred the lettuce and divide between individual plates or bowls, then spoon the prawns on top, scattering over a few coriander leaves.

Lamb cutlets with spinach pesto

SERVES 8
24 lamb cutlets
3 tbsp olive oil
Salt and ground black pepper
150ml (5fl oz) spinach pesto
  (see opposite)

If you can, use a cast-iron griddle pan for cooking the cutlets. The pans are heavy but extremely useful in the kitchen. They can get very hot and the criss-cross marks they leave don't just look great, they really enhance the flavour of the meat.

1 Drizzle the cutlets with olive oil and season with salt and pepper. Place a griddle pan or frying pan on a high heat and allow to get quite hot, then add the cutlets and cook for 2–4 minutes on each side depending on how well done you like them.

2 Allow to rest for a few minutes before serving with a drizzle of the spinach pesto.

Winter leaf salad with pomegranate, apple and walnuts

SERVES 8
VEGETARIAN

2 large handfuls of salad
 leaves, such as mustard
 greens, rocket, small baby
 chard, kale, beetroot or
 spinach, larger leaves sliced,
 small leaves kept whole
2 large handfuls of radicchio,
 sliced
4 tbsp chopped walnuts,
 toasted (see page 25)
Seeds from 1 pomegranate
2 small crisp eating apples,
 unpeeled, cored and
 chopped

For the dressing
8 tbsp extra-virgin olive oil
3 tbsp lemon juice
Sea salt and ground black
 pepper

This is an incredible, multi-flavoured, multi-textured salad, the slightly bitter flavour of the radicchio is offset by the tangy apple and pomegranate and the earthy crunchiness of the walnuts.

1 To make the dressing, pour the olive oil and lemon juice into a bowl or screw-top jar, season with sea salt and pepper and mix or shake together. (This will sit happily for a few days in the fridge.)

2 Place all the salad ingredients in a large bowl, pour over the dressing and toss everything together, then serve immediately.

RACHEL'S TIP
To remove the seeds from a pomegranate, simply cut into quarters and bend the skins to push out the seeds. Make sure you discard all of the white inner membrane as it is quite bitter.

Smoked fish platter with Ballymaloe cucumber relish

....

SERVES 8

2 fillets of smoked mackerel,
    skinned and cut into slices
    about 1cm (½in) thick
8 slices of smoked salmon,
    cold or hot smoked
1 smoked eel fillet, sliced
    into 8 x 4cm (1½in) batons
1 smoked trout fillet, divided
    into 8 pieces
16 smoked mussels
8 thin slices of smoked tuna
    or hake

To serve
8 lemon wedges
8 tbsp cucumber relish (see
    below)
8 tbsp horseradish sauce (see
    page 341)
8 tbsp sweet dill mayonnaise
    (see page 317)

This is less of a cooking recipe and more of a guide to assembling delicious smoked fish to serve as a starter for a larger dinner party. I've given a few suggestions as to which smoked fish to use; you can serve all six or just one or two, depending on what's available. Smoked fish goes beautifully with sweet-sour flavours – hence the cucumber relish below. Serve with slices of bread – brown (yeast or soda) or rye is best, or a good crusty white loaf.

1 Simply divide the portions of fish between individual plates or servings plates for guests to help themselves, adding a wedge of lemon, 1 tablespoon each of the cucumber relish and horseradish sauce and a drizzle of the mayonnaise.

RACHEL'S TIP

When storing smoked fish in the fridge, make sure it is covered, and make sure to take it out of the fridge at least 10 minutes before serving.

MAKES ABOUT 1 LITRE
(1¾ PINTS)
VEGETARIAN

900g (2lb) cucumber, unpeeled
1 medium onion, peeled,
    halved and very thinly sliced
350g (12oz) caster sugar
1 tbsp salt
225ml (8fl oz) cider vinegar
    or white wine vinegar

Ballymaloe cucumber relish

1 Using a food processor or mandolin, slice the cucumber and place in a large bowl with the onion.

2 Add the remaining ingredients and mix well to combine.

275

Greek red peppers

....

SERVES 8
VEGETARIAN
600g (1lb 5oz) feta cheese,
   crumbled into 5mm–1cm
   (¼–½in) pieces
2 red onions, peeled and diced
300g (11oz) cherry tomatoes,
   quartered
50g (2oz) capers, drained,
   rinsed and chopped
6 tbsp chopped mint
Salt and ground black pepper
Pinch of sugar
8 peppers (red or yellow),
   halved lengthways,
   retaining the stalks,
   and deseeded
150g (5oz) fresh white
   breadcrumbs
75ml (3fl oz) olive oil

*A substantial, yet refined, main course, peppers can be stuffed with
a huge variety of fillings. Here the breadcrumbs provide crunch and
the salty feta balances the sweetness of roasted peppers.*

1 Preheat the oven to 180°C (350°F), Gas mark 4.

2 In a large bowl, mix together the feta, onions, tomatoes, capers
and mint and season with salt and pepper and a pinch of sugar.
Divide this mixture between the pepper halves.

3 Top with the breadcrumbs and drizzle with olive oil, then place
in the oven and bake for 45–55 minutes or until the peppers are
soft and the crumbs on top are deep golden and crunchy.

Baked beetroot risotto with Parmesan crisps

....

SERVES 8-12
VEGETARIAN

For cooking the beetroot
1kg (2lb 3oz) beetroot,
  unpeeled
2 tbsp olive oil, plus
  extra for roasting
Salt and ground black pepper
2 tsp balsamic vinegar

For the Parmesan crisps
100g (3½oz) Parmesan or
  Parmesan-style cheese,
  finely grated

For cooking the risotto
2 tbsp olive oil
2 onions (300g/11oz in total),
  peeled and finely chopped
Salt and ground black pepper
700g (1½lb) risotto rice, such
  as Arborio or Carnaroli
300ml (½ pint) dry
  white wine
2 litres (3½ pints) chicken
  or vegetable stock
  (see pages 50-1)
150g (5oz) Parmesan or
  Parmesan-style cheese,
  finely grated
100g (3½oz) butter, diced

With its amazing deep pink colour, this is a fun-looking dish with a seriously delicious taste. A risotto cooked in the traditional way can be a pain to prepare for a party. You have to be on hand to stir the stock constantly into the rice when you'd much rather be dazzling your guests with witty repartee. This baked recipe offers an easy alternative to all that stirring. For added convenience, the beetroot can be cooked up to two days in advance and the Parmesan crisps kept for up to eight hours if stored in an airtight box.

1 Place the beetroot in a large saucepan of water, bring to the boil then reduce the heat and simmer covered loosely for about 30 minutes or until the beetroot is very tender when pierced with a sharp knife and the skins feel loose to the touch.

2 Drain the beetroot and peel off the skins with your fingers (you may want to wear some rubber gloves for this), then place half the beetroot in a food processor, add the 2 tablespoons of olive oil and whiz to form a smooth purée. Season to taste with salt and pepper and set aside.

3 Cut the other half of the cooked beetroot into bite-sized chunks, or wedges if you prefer, and set aside.

4 Preheat the oven to 180°C (350°F), Gas mark 4.

5 To make the Parmesan crisps, arrange the grated cheese in about 20 small disc-shaped mounds (3–4cm/1¼–1–1½in in diameter and 2–3mm/⅛in thick) on a baking sheet lined with baking parchment. (You can do this very easily by using a round cookie cutter as a stencil.) Cook for 6–8 minutes or until the cheese has melted and is golden in colour. Take out of the oven and carefully

(continued overleaf)

The 'Kings,' 'Castles,' Gresley Pacifics and Southern 'Lord Nelsons' were all recognizable as developments of what had gone before on their respective railways, particularly the 'Castles' and 'Kings' with their traditional Great Western copper-capped chimney, polished brass safety-valve casing, and polished brass beading over the splashers. The 'Kings' added another touch of color with the brass of their outside axleboxes for the leading bogie axle. This arrangement was necessary in order to provide independent springing for all wheels of the bogie. The springs for the leading wheels had to be outside the bogie frame in order to clear the inside cylinders, while those for the other pair of wheels were inside to be clear of the outside cylinders.

In contrast to the rest, the fifth of the big express passenger engines of the late 1920s was startlingly different from anything seen before on the main line from London Euston station to the north and Scotland. This was the 'Royal Scot' 4–6–0 of the London Midland & Scottish Railway, a design produced in some haste to fill a gap in that company's motive power resources.

The LMS authorities were interested in the performance of the GWR 'Castles' and in 1926 borrowed No 5000, *Launceston Castle*, for trials between Euston station, Crewe and Carlisle in the north. The results convinced them of the need for a new 4–6–0 conceived in the modern manner, but they had left things late considering the developments on the other lines. The design office was put urgently to work, and

Above: The first British Pacific locomotive, Great Western No 111, *The Great Bear*, built to the design of G J Churchward in 1908, heads a Cheltenham tea-car express on the Paddington-Swindon portion of its journey.
Above left: After the first batch of Gresley Pacifics, a second series was built with higher boiler pressure. One of this later batch, No 2547, *Donovan*, heads the up 'Flying Scotsman' shortly after being fitted with a corridor tender for making the nonstop run between London and Edinburgh.
Left: LNER Pacific No 4472, *Flying Scotsman*, leaves King's Cross with the 'Flying Scotsman' express on its first nonstop run to Edinburgh on 1 May 1928. No 4472 was the second of Gresley's Pacifics, the first being No 4470, *Great Northern*. It is now preserved and in private ownership.

Left: There was a short period during the end of the 1950s/early 1960s when British Rail paid considerable attention to liveries and smartness. Here, at Newcastle, BR 0–6–0T No 68723 shunts resplendent in North Eastern Railway green.
Right: Ex-Great Western Railway No 6960, *Raveningham Hall,* as preserved on the Severn Valley Railway at Bridgnorth.
Below: An unknown GWR 'Castle' heads a down express out of Box Tunnel on the main line to Bristol during the early days of British Rail.
Bottom: LNER A4 class Pacific No 4498, *Sir Nigel Gresley,* at Carnforth Depot.

the Southern Railway collaborated by loaning drawings of its 'Lord Nelson' class. Certain constructional features were copied from this source, but the major influences on the design of the new LMS 4–6–0 were those aspects of the Great Western 'Castle' which made it so effective in the generation and use of steam, as demonstrated by *Launceston Castle* in the trials. The contract for production was put out to the North British Locomotive Company Limited and by the autumn of 1927 the first 'Scots' were reaching the LMS. Tractive effort for this three-cylinder locomotive was 33,150 lb (15,036.6 kg) and the boiler pressure 250 lb per square inch (17.6 kg/sq cm). It was an impressive locomotive but distinctive rather than handsome, its appearance spoiled by a very small chimney perched on a very large-diameter smokebox. The boiler was similarly rotund, and the top of the firebox sloped down toward the cab to help in accommodating the whistle within the loading gauge; even then it had to be mounted horizontally.

In this busy period of new locomotive types, many important services were still being worked by locomotives of various wheel arrangements, built by the pre-'Grouping' companies. The Great Northern Atlantics, for example, still had a distinguished future before them, and a wide variety of 4–6–0s and 4–4–0s still carried around with them the atmosphere of an earlier railway era.

At the end of its independent life, the London & South Western Railway introduced 20 4–6–0 locomotives which inspired the development of one of the most admired classes of the Southern Railway during the steam era. Designed by R W Urie, the last Motive Power Superintendent of the LSWR, the 20 4–6–0 outside-cylinder engines, with his charac-

Above: A Great Western 'Castle' class 4–6–0 speeds the 'Cheltenham Flyer' toward London.

Below: An up LNER express in 1935 waits to leave Doncaster with Gresley Pacific No 4479, *Robert the Devil*.

Below right: The eaves of a characteristic Great Western station platform awning frame 'Castle' class 4–6–0 No 7019, *Fowey Castle*.

Right: After C B Collett's 'Castles' came his larger 4–6–0s, the 'Kings.' No. 6027, *King Richard 1*, hurries down the Cornish Riviera Express past Reading West station in 1938.

teristic high running plate emphasizing their 6-foot 7-inch (2007-mm) driving wheels, all went into service between 1918 and 1923. When R E L Maunsell became Chief Mechanical Engineer of the Southern Railway in 1923 he took Urie's design as the basis of a new express passenger 4–6–0, the 'King Arthur' class, and introduced some improvements of his own. The new class was launched with ten brand-new engines built at Eastleigh. The 20 Urie engines were brought into line with them and 30 more were ordered from the North British Locomotive Company Limited. With further construction at Eastleigh, the class eventually numbered 74 engines, the last appearing in 1927. Maunsell altered the smokebox arrangements to improve the draft compared with the original Urie engines, reduced the cylinder diameter from 22 inches to 20.5 inches (559 mm to 521 mm) and raised the boiler pressure from 180 lb per square inch (12.7 kg/sq cm) to 200 lb per square inch (14.1 kg/sq cm). The valve gear was also altered to give a longer travel.

It was an astute move on the part of the Southern Railway to name express engines after the semilegendary personage of King Arthur and his wholly legendary entourage of knights and ladies whose domain spread west from Winchester. And so the holiday trains from London's Waterloo station set out behind engines with resonant names like *Sir Mador de la Porte* or *Sir Cador of Cornwall*. Their widely scattered 'through' portions, shed at intervals as they made their way westward, sometimes came to rest at places so remote that it was hard to imagine a continuous line of rails stretching back to the banks of the Thames in London.

Far left: Britain's final prenationalization design of Pacific was Bulleid's 'West Country' class – an engine with a comparatively light axle-loading enabling it to work over the branches in the West Country and on the 'Southern's' main lines. It was, in the main, rebuilt as No 34044 *Woolacombe*.
Left: The last steam locomotive to be built for British Rail No 92220 at Shildon, 1975.
Below: British Railways' only steam-operated line, the 2-foot gauge Vale of Rheidol section out-of-Aberystwyth train.

Above: The first of Riddles' standard designs for British Railways was the 'Britannia' class medium Pacific. Produced to run over most of Britain's main lines with all but the heaviest expresses, these engines found their way from Devon to Scotland. The majority of the class carried names but the later engines were distinguishable only by their numbers, such as No 70045 standing at Skipton with a northbound fast freight.

Right: Perhaps Sir Nigel Gresley's masterpiece was this A4 class streamlined Pacific introduced in 1935 for the famous 'Silver Jubilee' express from London (King's Cross) to Edinburgh. British Rail painted the class in their standard dark green as shown here adorning No 60029, *Woodcock*.

The prize of three guineas went to a guard at Waterloo whose entry was the first received, the others being rewarded with paperweight models of a 'King Arthur' class locomotive. The name lasted until 1964, when 'through' services between Waterloo and the West Country were terminated at Exeter. For most of its life the train carried coaches for Plymouth and the south Devon resorts of Seaton, Sidmouth and Exmouth as well as those for the Atlantic Coast, giving it the largest number of through portions of any train in the country. In the 1930s it was often powered by 'Lord Nelson' class locomotives between London and Salisbury, where 'King Arthurs' took over. They in turn were replaced by 4—4—0 or 2—6—0 engines of lighter axle-load for the final stages of the journey with the portions that continued past Exeter for destinations further west.

The 'King Arthurs' could not work over the main line from Tonbridge to Hastings because of restricted clearances. This was a route with heavy gradients, and the problems it presented were the primary reason for the development of a new 4—4—0 locomotive that was required to be, as far as possible, the equivalent of a contemporary 4—6—0 in all respects except adhesion. Maunsell achieved this in his 'Schools' class 4—4—0 by combining a shortened version of the 'King Arthur' boiler with the cylinders, valves and front-end design of a 'Lord Nelson' but using three cylinders instead of four. The 'Schools,' introduced in 1930, were the most powerful 4—4—0s in Europe. They equalled the 'King Arthurs' in nominal tractive effort but weighed 75 US tons/67 UK tons/68 tonnes as against the 91 US tons/81 UK tons/82 tonnes of the 4—6—0.

As well as relieving older 4—4—0s on the Hastings line, the 'Schools' enabled the Southern to increase the loading of its 80-minute Charing Cross—Folkestone trains and allowed the nonstop Waterloo—Portsmouth time to be cut to one and one-half hours for the 79.3 miles (127.6 km) in the summer timetables of 1935.

When the 'Schools' appeared in 1930 the most interesting developments in Southern steam practice were still in the future, but on one section of the railway steam was already seeing an Indian Summer. The Central Section of the Southern comprised the former London, Brighton & South Coast Railway, whose main line to Brighton was being electrified. Completion of the work at the end of 1932 made the last of the LBSCR's express locomotive designs redundant. These were the Baltic (4—6—4) tank engines designed by L Billinton, and were the ultimate expression of the old Brighton company's policy of building tank engines for its relatively short-distance express traffic as well as those for suburban services. It should be noted that it is only 51 miles (82.1 km) from London's Victoria station to Brighton but the route required smart locomotive performance to keep to the 60-minute commuter schedule as signal checks and stops in the inner-London suburban traffic area were inevitable and lost time had to be recouped in the 40 miles (64.4 km) south of East Croydon station where there were fewer junctions and speed restrictions. Billinton's Baltics were converted to 4—6—0 tender engines in 1934 and transferred to the former LSWR lines.

As electrification was extended progressively to the coastal towns of Eastbourne, Hastings and Portsmouth, other ex-Brighton passenger engines were turned over to secondary routes but the Atlantic

Above: Southern Railway 4—6—0 No 850, *Lord Nelson,* **heads for London with the 'Golden Arrow' boat train in the shadow of the famous Dover cliffs. Above left: In this 1951 view of the 'Cornish Riviera Express' near Starcross, No 6023,** *King Edward II,* **is painted in a blue livery. Left: In the early 1900s the Great Western Railway experimented briefly with compounding on the de Glehn system. No 104,** *Alliance,* **seen at Snow Hill station, was one of three 4—4—2 compounds built in France for the GWR to the order of G J Churchward for comparative trials.**

The Southern was equally fortunate in finding a romantic-sounding name for its premier service from Waterloo station to the West. In LSWR days there had been fierce competition with Great Western for Plymouth traffic, but the South Western route suffered the combined disadvantages of length and difficulty. On the other hand the company could offer a competitive service to Ilfracombe in Devon – SW had its own line to that seaside resort over which it worked through portions of Great Western trains from Paddington station in London. Further west, Bude and Padstow looked out over the Atlantic Ocean (Ilfracombe could claim to do the same if one looked in the right direction). Named trains had not proliferated in the early years after 'Grouping' though Great Western's 'Cornish Riviera Limited' was well established. A competition to find a suitable name for the mid-morning express from Waterloo to the West was launched in the *Southern Railway Magazine* and no fewer than four entrants proposed 'Atlantic Coast

**Above: The LMS entered
the 'big engine' league
with the 'Royal Scot' class
4–6–0 in which certain
features of Southern 'Lord
Nelsons' and Great
Western 'Castles' were
combined. No 6102,** *Black
Watch,* **is at Euston in the
late 1920s, when horse
cabs were still to be seen
on the arrival side of the
old station.**
**Top: Southern Railway
'King Arthur' class 4–6–0,**
Sir Bors de Ganis, **in
British Railways days,
renumbered as Southern
Region No 30763.**

locomotives designed by D E Marsh, who had been
closely associated with development of the large-
boilered engines of the same wheel arrangement on
the Great Northern Railway, were still to be seen
on the main line on the Newhaven boat train. In
Southern Railway days the class was rebuilt with
superheaters. They were then named after coastal
headlands, including the one which had previously
been *La France* in honor of the visit of the President of
France in 1913. In a second series of Atlantics Marsh
provided superheaters from the outset. None were
named by the LBSCR but further 'headland' names
were given them by the Southern.

The Southern Railway's electrification schemes
only involved passenger services – freight continued
to be steam hauled – and so the 2–6–0 goods engines
brought out by Billinton for the LBSCR in 1913 continued in the role for which they were intended until
the end of their days under British Railways.

For some reason which is hard to define, the
London, Brighton & South Coast Railway enjoyed a
charisma all its own. This was most deeply felt by

those who lived in or near its territories, but others
could sense it. Partly perhaps it was the glamor
of the all-Pullman London–Brighton express, the
'Southern Belle,' advertised as 'the most luxurious
train in the world' and surviving into the electric
era as the 'Brighton Belle.' However, some think the
powerful Brighton appeal began with the very high
standard of cleanliness insisted on for engines.
Drivers were assigned their own engines and each
man's name was shown on a plate fixed in the cab.

World War I was a watershed in many ways. On
the railways the Chief Mechanical Engineers who
took over at 'Grouping' inevitably found gaps in the
capabilities of the motive power they inherited when
it came to working a railway in the postwar world,
and serving a public that tended to expect more
and to be more critical. The move toward more
powerful locomotives has been noted already. On
the Great Northern section of the LNER the requirement for power gave birth to the Gresley Pacifics, but
on the Great Eastern section of the same railway a
4–6–0 design was needed which would have reserve

power over existing locomotives but have the same clearance restrictions. Gresley's answer was the 'Sandringham' class, a three-cylinder locomotive using his own derived drive for the center cylinder valve gear as on his Pacifics. The first series of 'Sandringhams' were named after what are now called 'stately homes.' To meet GE section requirements they were equipped with short tenders to keep within the overall length of their predecessors. This rather spoiled their appearance, but the improvement of 19 percent over existing Great Eastern 4—6—0s was ample compensation from the point of view of the operators. Later, additional locomotives of the same class were built for the Great Central section of the LNER and fitted with much larger tenders of modern design, so that both looks and performance were of high standard.

Although Great Central was a commercial problem in that many of its services duplicated those of other main lines with shorter routes, it brought with it to the LNER some noteworthy locomotive classes. They were the legacy of J G Robinson, Chief Mechanical

Engineer of the GCR, who had given that railway a fleet of good-looking locomotives which must have done much to endow it with an up-to-the-minute image in contemporary eyes. Gresley was sufficiently impressed by the Robinson 'Director' class 4—4—0s for express traffic and his 4—6—2 tanks for fast commuter services to have more locomotives of both classes built, the 4—4—0s to supplement motive power inherited by the LNER from the North British Railway in Scotland and the tank engines to work on short distance passenger duties in the North Eastern area. In building his own 'Hunt' class 4—4—0s at a later date, Gresley chose three cylinders and his own derived valve motion for the inside cylinder but the engines embodied certain 'Director' features, particularly in the boiler proportions. A later series of 'Hunts,' beginning in 1932, was fitted with poppet valve gear.

One of Robinson's designs for Great Central was later to be seen widely on the LNER. This was his 2—8—0 freight locomotive, first put to work in 1911 on the GCR and later built in large numbers by private

Above: C J Bowen Cooke's 'Claughton' class 4—6—0 of 1913 was the ancestor of the much more successful LMS 'Patriots' of the 1930s. 'Claughton' No 5964, *Patriot,* was named as a memorial to the LNWR employees who fell in World War I.

firms for the requirements of the Railway Operating Division during World War I. Many of them were acquired by the LNER in the postwar years. In 1930, however, six-coupled classes still predominated for freight traffic, with the inside-cylinder 0–6–0 as the classic British type. The LMS had built an inside-cylinder 0–8–0 in 1929 but this was, in many respects, a development of an earlier design for the London & North Western Railway.

By 1930 the first fruits of a new motive power policy were becoming visible – namely the development of the general purpose or mixed traffic locomotive. In some quarters the 2–6–0 wheel arrangement was favored for motive power in this category. British manufacturers had long experience in building the 2–6–0 for overseas markets, where it was popular from an early period. Its beginnings in Great Britain were tentative and two of the earliest had been built for an overseas company which found itself unable to take delivery. They were bought from the builder, no doubt on favorable terms, by the impecunious Midland & South Western Junction Railway in England and when they were put into service in 1895 and 1896 they were the only representatives of this wheel arrangement in the country. Later the 2–6–0 was to be widely used, and the Great Western was building outside-cylinder 2–6–0s as early as 1911. At 'Grouping,' incidentally, it inherited the two pioneers from the MSWJR, one of which lasted until 1930.

In the early 'Grouping' years the LMS produced the versatile class of 2–6–0s popularly known as 'Crabs.' A high running plate exposed the inclined outside cylinders, valve gear and 5-foot 6-inch (1676-mm) coupled wheels. When all the rods and cranks of the Walschaerts gear were in motion the effect presumably recalled the movements of a crab's pincers to some imaginative observer.

An alternative approach to mixed traffic design was the small-wheeled version of a 4–6–0 passenger locomotive. Great Western in 1924 rebuilt a 'Saint'

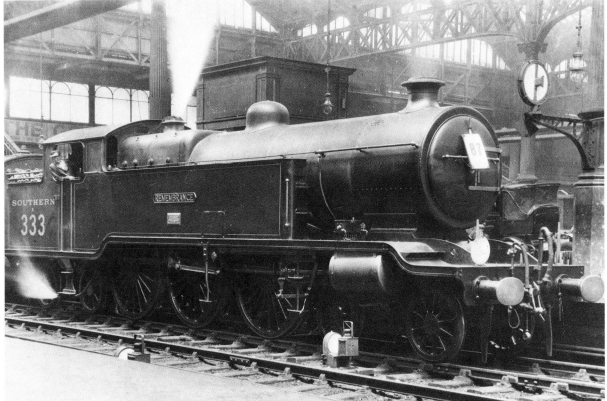

Above: SR 'Schools' class
4–4–0 No 930, *Radley*,
waits for the starting signal
at Waterloo in the 1930s.
Above right: Ex-LBSC K
class 2–6–0 No 32349
heads an Eastleigh-to-
Fratton goods train on the
single line from Knowle
Junction to Fareham.
Left: After the Brighton
main-line electrification,
LBSC main-line classes
found employment on
secondary routes. Marsh
Atlantic No 32421 leaves
Selsdon with a slow train
from Brighton in 1950.
Right: Soon to be displaced
by electrification and
rebuilt as a 4–6–0 tender
engine, the former London,
Brighton & South Coast
Railway's war memorial
engine, 4–6–4T No 333,
Remembrance, waits with
lifting safety valves to
leave Victoria Station.

Left: A 'Director' class
4–4–0 of the Great Central
Railway's first series. The
second series and those
built subsequently by the
LNER had side-window
cabs. No 5436, *Sir
Berkeley Sheffield*, belonged
to LNER class D10.
Far left: An ex-Great
Central 4–6–2T, No 5447
of LNER class A5, passes
Chorleywood on the
Metropolitan & Great
Central Joint line with a
local train in June 1934.
Below: The 'Lord
Faringdon' 4–6–0s of the
Great Central Railway
were renowned for their
looks, but their performance
was marred by an
inadequate grate area.
Under Grouping, when
they became LNER class
B3, they worked on other
sections of the LNER. No
6164, *Earl Beatty*, on the
East Coast Main Line, has
a heavier load than it
would normally encounter
on its home metals.

class 4–6–0 with coupled wheels of 6 feet (1829 mm)
diameter instead of 6 feet 8 inches (2032 mm). It was
a successful experiment, and two years later the railway began production of the numerous 'Hall' class.
The 'Halls' carried the same boiler as the Churchward
passenger 4–6–0s and could give a good account of
themselves on fast passenger work. Many mixed
traffic 4–6–0s followed them in the course of the
1930s. The general-purpose locomotive was an
operator's ideal which was just coming within his
reach at the beginning of the decade.

It was some time before the Pacific wheel arrangement was widely adopted in Great Britain. The Great
Western never returned to it after *The Great Bear*. A
class of five 'Pacifics' was designed for the North
Eastern Railway by Sir Vincent Raven and introduced
on the eve of 'Grouping.' They came into LNER
ownership in 1923 but all were withdrawn in 1936–
37. Apart from these, Gresley's Pacifics were the only
representatives of this wheel arrangement in a tender
locomotive for a decade. The LMS soldiered on for a
time with its 'Royal Scot' 4–6–0s as its first line
express locomotives, but when Sir Henry Fowler was
succeeded by W A (later Sir William) Stanier it
received its first Pacific design.

Observers at the first appearance of the Stanier
Pacific saw not only a pair of wheels under the firebox
but also a tapered boiler, the hallmark of a Great
Western locomotive. The first two Stanier Pacifics
were not outstandingly successful. They had a
moderate degree of superheat, the idea being to
improve thermal efficiency by minimizing waste heat
in the exhaust. In Great Western conditions, the firm
from which Stanier had come, this practice had
worked well, but on the much less homogeneous
LMS, where the quality of coal often differed from
area to area and there was a diversity of driving
practice, Stanier's designs tended at first to be un-
satisfactory steamers. Later engines of the class were
given higher superheat and in due course the two
originals were modified accordingly. This improved
version was the basis of the ultimate in express locomotive development by Sir William Stanier.

In the 1920s the emphasis had been on locomotive power but at the turn of the decade railway
publicity changed to concentrate on the more market-
able commodity of speed. There had been numerous
speed highlights already, but the overall pattern was
patchy and in 1931 the mileage scheduled to be
covered daily at speeds between 60 and 70 mph
(97 and 113 kph) was only 861 miles (1385.6 km).
A year later it rose to 2134 miles (3434.3 km).

For some years after World War I the fastest
scheduled run in the British Isles was made by a
train on the North Eastern Railway which was
required to cover the 44.1 miles (70.9 km) from
Darlington to York in 43 minutes (61.7 mph/99.3
kph). In 1923 when the North Eastern had become
part of the LNER Group, the Great Western took the
record from it by booking the 14.30 from Cheltenham
to run the 77.1 miles (124.1 km) from Swindon to
Paddington in 75 minutes (61.8 mph/99.4 kph). This
was before the advent of the 'Castles' but Great
Western 4–6–0s of earlier classes often improved
on the scheduled time.

When new engines were available, Great Western
in 1929 was able to schedule the train to run from
Swindon to Paddington in 70 minutes, pushing the
average speed up to 66.3 mph (106.7 kph), and
enabling Great Western to claim ownership of 'the

Above: A local train on
the Somerset & Dorset
Joint line in British
Railways days is headed by
an example of the classic
British inside-cylinder
0–6–0 for freight work.
No 44102 in this picture
was an LMS development
of a Midland Railway
design.
Above right: 'Hunt' class
4–4–0 No 235, *The
Bedale,* was one of a series
of engines designed by
Gresley in which he used
three cylinders and his own
valve gear but incorporated
certain features of the GC
'Director' class.
Right: A Great Western
'43' 2–6–0 No 4367 looks
as much at home under
express headcode as on any
of the duties this versatile
early mixed-traffic class
was called upon to
undertake.

fastest train in the world.' The title suddenly slipped
away, however, for in Canada at this time the fierce
competition for traffic between Montreal and Toronto
led the Canadian Pacific Railway to accelerate two
trains to run the 124 miles (200 km) between Smith's
Falls and Toronto at average speeds of 68.9 and 67.6
mph (110.9 and 108.8 kph). In response the Great
Western reacted by cutting three minutes off the
Swindon–Paddington schedule, achieving an average
speed of 69.2 mph (111.4 kph). Once more it had 'the
fastest train in the world' and in case the fact was
overlooked by the public, a headboard suitably in-
scribed was carried by the locomotive. The train had
become generally known as the 'Cheltenham Flyer'
although the name did not appear in the timetable.
The final acceleration came in 1932 when the time
for the 77.1 miles (124.1 km) was cut to 65 minutes
and the average speed rose to 77.1 mph (124.1 kph).
All these scheduled times and speeds were improved
upon on various occasions, culminating in the so-
called 'record of records' of 5 June 1932 when
Number 5006, *Tregenna Castle,* took the train from
Swindon to Paddington in 56 minutes 47 seconds,
giving an average of 81.7 mph (131.4 kph).

The 'Cheltenham Flyer' was not balanced by a
corresponding service in the opposite direction, and
in any case it only 'flew' from Swindon to London on
generally falling gradients. Its schedule from Chelten-

ham to Swindon was quite mundane.

Although the Anglo-Scottish services were the
most prestigious of the British express trains, their
speed was restrained for many years by an agreement between the West Coast and East Coast companies following an accident at Preston in 1895 when
a West Coast express had been derailed by taking the
curve through the station at excessive speed.

For 37 years the companies concerned limited
their London–Glasgow and London–Edinburgh trains
to a minimum time of 8.25 hours. The advent of larger
locomotives in the 1920s inevitably brought a new
stirring of the competitive spirit, but at first it had to
be expressed in a different way. In 1927 an advance
portion of the 'Flying Scotsman' King's Cross (London)-
Edinburgh express of the LNER began running nonstop between London and Newcastle (268.5 miles/
432.1 km) behind Gresley's Pacifics. The rival LMS
responded by deleting from the public timetable all
intermediate stops by its 10.00 express in each
direction between Euston and Glasgow. These trains
were also shown in the timetable for the first time as
the 'Royal Scot,' which eventually ran nonstop from
Euston to Kingmoor (Carlisle), a distance of 301 miles
(484.4 km).

Early in 1928 the LNER announced that beginning
with the summer timetable the 'Flying Scotsman'
would run nonstop in both directions between King's

Cross and Edinburgh. This was to be a genuine non-stop run of 393 miles (632.5 km). For its daily performance provision had to be made for changing engine crews *en route*, and for this purpose certain Pacifics were equipped with tenders having a corridor along one side and the usual form of intercoach vestibule connection at the rear, so that a relief crew riding in the leading compartment of the train could walk through to the footplate and take over at the halfway point of the journey.

Nonstop runs to Scotland by its rival put the LMS in a difficult position because the 'Royal Scot' had to stop *en route* to Glasgow to detach the Edinburgh portion. But the company was determined not to be outdone: a few days before the nonstop 'Flying Scotsman' was introduced, the 'Royal Scot' was run from Euston in two portions, one for Edinburgh and one for Glasgow, and both were worked to their destinations without a stop. Each locomotive carried a crew of three, one man as a reserve. The eight-coach Glasgow portion was worked by 'Royal Scot' class 4–6–0 No 6113, *Cameronian*, but the lighter six-coach portion for Edinburgh was headed by compound 4–4–0 No 1054. The 393.7 miles (633.6 km) nonstop from Euston to Edinburgh's Princes Street on this occasion exceeded any previous nonstop run by a British four-coupled locomotive by 100 miles (161 km).

Left: A long-lived Great Western 'Saint' class 4—6—0 No 2915 heads an express near Knowle & Dorridge on 14 May 1949. A rebuild of a 'Saint' in 1924 paved the way to the 'Hall' and other GW 4—6—0 general-purpose classes.

Such a lengthy stint for the enginemen could not become a permanent feature and the LMS reverted to engine-changing outside Carlisle until the coming of the first Stanier Pacifics on the LMS in 1933.

When the anomalous 8.25-hour agreement between companies was dropped from the summer of 1932, the 'Royal Scot' ran to Glasgow in 7 hours 40 minutes and the 'Flying Scotsman' to Edinburgh in 7 hours 30 minutes. Both timings had been improved by 1939 when the outbreak of war put an end to competitive acceleration, but by that time the fastest Anglo-Scottish journeys were being made by new streamlined trains.

By 1938 the mileage run at over 60 mph (97 kph) in Great Britain had risen to 11,665 miles (18,773 km); and at over 70 mph (113 kph) to 730 miles (1174.8 km), all with steam traction.

Gresley of the LNER had been attracted by the idea of a high-speed business service and had an open mind over the choice of steam or diesel-electric as motive power. In 1934 he made a report to the LNER Board which led to a party of the company's officers, including himself, visiting Germany to explore the possibility of high-speed diesel-electric services on the East Coast main line, initially between London, Leeds and Newcastle, modelled on those of the Deutsche Reichsbahn. However, Gresley then decided against a gamble with untried engines and decided to see what could be done with steam traction and a locomotive-and-coaches train.

The first experiment was made on 30 November 1934 with the Pacific locomotive No 4472, *Flying Scotsman* and a four-coach train on a journey from London to Leeds and back. Going north the train covered the 185.7 miles (298.8 km) in 152 minutes and ran for over 70 miles (112.6 km) at an average speed in excess of 80 mph (129 kph). The maximum attained was 95 mph (153 kph). The homeward

trip was distinguished by a brief 100 mph (161 kph) burst of speed recorded in the dynamometer car while descending a 1-in-200 gradient. Probably the maximum was not held for more than 600 yards (550 m) but it caused great excitement because of the rarity of authenticated three-figure speeds in British railway history. (A maximum of 102.3 mph [164.6 kph] attained early in the century on the Great Western Railway, and long accepted, was closely scrutinized in later years and some doubt was cast on its accuracy.)

On 5 March 1935 a further high-speed trial was conducted, this time between London and Newcastle, 268.3 miles (431.8 km) each way. The locomotive, heading a six-coach train, was Pacific No 2750, *Papyrus*, one of the later Gresley Pacifics with a 220 lb per square inch (15.5 kg/sq cm) boiler. The schedule in both directions was 240 minutes, which was cut to 237 minutes going north and 232 minutes returning, but the climax of the day occurred as the train hurried south through Lincolnshire, once more aided by the descent at 1-in-200 from Stoke tunnel. A commentator wrote, 'At last the magic "hundred" has been passed, and this time in a way that admits of no dispute. Not only was the enormously high figure of 108 mph (174 kph) maintained for ten seconds continuously, but for 12.3 miles (19.8 km), from Corby down to Tallington, the speed *averaged* 100.6 mph (161.9 kph).'

At the LNER annual general meeting in 1935 the company's chairman cautiously announced that 'serious consideration' would be given to the 'possible' introduction of four-hour services between London's King's Cross and Newcastle in the next timetable. Matters were, in fact, advancing rapidly. The suggestion of a high-speed steam train for the London—Newcastle service was made by Sir Ralph Wedgwood, Chief General Manager of the LNER, after the trial

Below: A southbound train via Oxford and Reading waits at Birmingham Snow Hill behind GW 'Hall' class 4–6–0 No 5959, *Mawley Hall*, in 1955.

runs of 5 March. Gresley submitted an outline diagram of a suggested train on 11 March, which was shown to the Board and approved on 28 March. The necessary orders for the design and construction of locomotives and coaches were given to the works at Doncaster forthwith. No doubt the haste was due in part to the fact that 1935 was the Silver Jubilee of the reign of King George V and therefore a fitting occasion for demonstrating British engineering skill and inventiveness.

The new train of seven coaches and streamlined Pacific locomotive was ready for a demonstration run on 27 September 1935. It entered public service with the name 'Silver Jubilee' three days later. The demonstration run showed that 100 mph (161 kph) speeds could soon become commonplace on special streamlined trains of restricted weight. The 100 mph (161 kph) mark was passed going north only 30 miles (48.3 km) out of London and speed did not fall below that level for the next 25 miles (40.2 km). A maximum of 112.5 mph (181 kph) was reached at two separate points.

The four new Pacific locomotives built initially for the streamlined trains had similar valve gear, driving wheel diameter and wheelbase spacing to the standard engines but some boiler proportions were

Far left below: The smokebox nameplate of streamlined Pacific No 4496, *Golden Shuttle*, is clearly visible in this view of the down 'Coronation' King's Cross–Edinburgh express about to be engulfed in a tunnel. *Golden Shuttle* was allocated to the West Riding Limited streamliner (King's Cross–Leeds–Bradford) in September 1937.

Below: LNER streamlined Pacific No 2510, *Quicksilver*, heads the 'Silver Jubilee' King's Cross–Newcastle express. Far left above: This early view of No 2510 at rest recalls the period when the names of the first streamliners were painted at the center of the boiler casing instead of appearing on a smokebox nameplate.

changed. In the design of steam and exhaust passages Gresley followed principles which had been successfully applied by André Chapelon in rebuilding Pacific locomotives in France. It was not, in fact, Gresley's first venture in this direction, for he had acted similarly in building his large 2–8–2 express locomotives for Scotland's Edinburgh–Aberdeen route. There was much argument as to whether this 'internal streamlining' was not more important than the external streamlining. Comparative wind-tunnel tests on wooden models of streamlined and nonstreamlined locomotives were carried out at the National Physical Laboratory and the results suggested that streamlining could be worth a saving of 100 hp in the average output required between London's King's Cross station and Newcastle but it proved difficult to substantiate this figure in practice.

In 1937 streamlining spread to the Anglo-Scottish services, already lively compared with their long slumber under the 8.25-hour agreement. Now the LMS entered the field, building five new Pacific locomotives basically similar to those introduced by Stanier in 1933 but with certain modifications and a beautiful streamlined exterior. Their immediate purpose was to work the 'Coronation Scot' streamlined express between London and Glasgow, but more were built later, both with and without streamlining, for general heavy express passenger duties. King George V had died in 1936. The following year saw the coronation of King George VI, hence the name of the new LMS Anglo-Scottish streamliner

and one of the LNER's 'Coronation' streamlined London–Edinburgh expresses which entered service at the same time, again hauled by Gresley's streamlined Pacifics. More of these engines were being built at the time and those allocated to the 'Coronation' service were painted Garter blue. The 'Coronation Scot' ran between London's Euston Station and Glasgow in six and one-half hours and the 'Coronation' between King's Cross Station and Edinburgh in only six hours.

Stanier's Pacifics for the 'Coronation Scot' were more than a streamlined version of his earlier 'Princess Royal' class 4–6–2s. Instead of four sets of Walschaerts valve gears, the gears for the outside cylinders operated the valves of the inside cylinders through rocking levers, and the piston valves were of 9-inch (229 mm) diameter instead of 8 inches (203 mm). Coupled wheel diameter was increased from 6 feet 6 inches to 6 feet 9 inches (1981 mm to 2057 mm). As Gresley had done in his streamliners, Stanier paid special attention to the free flow of steam. The locomotives for the 'Coronation Scot' service had a streamlined external casing and were known as the 'Princess Coronation' class, a name which linked them with their 'Princess Royal' predecessors. Further locomotives of the same design were built without streamlining. These were the 'Duchess' class. In the 'Princess Coronations' and the 'Duchesses' the heating surface was increased from the previous 2967 square feet (275.6 sq m) in the 'Princess Royals' to 3637 square feet (337.9 sq m). By using

Above: One of the early Stanier Pacifics, No 6204, *Princess Louise,* takes a northbound LMS express past Linslade, Buckinghamshire, in 1936. A rather dirty 'semaphore'-type Scottish route indicator is just visible on the smokebox.

Above: One of the
streamlined versions of the
Stanier Pacifics No 6223,
Princess Alice, heads the
LMS 'Coronation Scot'
London–Glasgow service
in 1938.

nickel steel the thickness of the boiler and firebox plates was significantly reduced, and in spite of the larger heating surface a nonstreamlined 'Duchess' weighed slightly under a ton more than a 'Princess Royal' weighed.

The 'Coronation Scot' made a demonstration run from Euston (London) to Crewe and back on 29 June 1937. The occasion is remembered for the dramatic acceleration over the last eight miles (12.8 km) into Crewe. As far as Whitmore the train had not exceeded 87.5 mph (140.8 kph) at any point but the authorities were evidently determined to make the most of the favorable conditions between Whitmore and Crewe in order to surpass the 112.5 mph (181 kph) achieved by LNER's 'Silver Jubilee' on its demonstration run two years earlier. The goal was reached, but only at the last moment, a peak of 114 mph (184 kph) being attained with the train already uncomfortably close to Crewe. With only a half-mile (0.8 km) left before reaching the crossovers at the approach to the station the train braked very sharply and lurched over the crossovers in dramatic style.

But Gresley was not content to leave speed honors with the LMS. The role of the brakes in high-speed running is often overlooked, but stopping distances are of the utmost importance and it is equally important to minimize the delay in application of brakes between front and rear vehicles, inherent in the vacuum system. In 1938 the LNER was conducting trials with a new type of brake valve. The locomotive

in use for this purpose on 3 July was streamlined Pacific No 4468 *Mallard* with a train of six 'Coronation' coaches. While descending the 1-in-200 of Stoke bank the engine was opened up to the limit and for a moment the speed recorder in the dynamometer car showed 126 mph (203 kph). However, during the run a big end on *Mallard* overheated and the engine was taken off the train at Peterborough.

The plaque commemorating the 'famous victory' was not affixed to *Mallard* until 1948. It can still be seen on the locomotive, now preserved in the National Railway Museum at York, and reads, 'On the 3rd July 1938 this locomotive attained a world speed record for steam traction of 126 miles per hour.'

The golden age of the streamlined train ended with the outbreak of World War II but the locomotives built to work them gave good service for many years, with their streamlining either modified to allow easier access to working parts or removed entirely.

Although the LMS waited until the Coronation year, 1937, to introduce a streamliner, it had marked the Silver Jubilee year, 1935, by naming one of its new 4—6—0 express passenger locomotives, *Silver Jubilee*. This was No 5552 of the class introduced by Stainier in 1934 and soon known universally as the 'Jubilees.' It appeared in a black and silver livery instead of the normal LMS red with yellow lining. The Jubilees were part of the huge program of updating LMS motive power which Stainier shouldered on his appointment to the railway.

After Fowler's 'Royal Scots,' further 4—6—0s had

31

been provided by rebuilding certain engines of the former LNWR 'Claughton' class and by new construction programs. They became known as the 'Baby Scots,' a name deplored by the LMS but which proved hard to stamp out in favor of the officially preferred 'Patriot' class. The 'Patriots' were successful engines, but they had their roots in the past, and Stanier's job was to produce a new range of modern, standard types. His 'Jubilees' were intended as an improvement on the 'Patriots' and in the long term they proved an admirable express engine for duties below the Pacific level, although they had steaming problems in their early days and underwent a number of boiler modifications.

In the 1930s the economic problems of running a railway were beginning to bite. The ideal of a general-purpose locomotive able to turn its hand to most types of work and so be productive *throughout* its hours in steam, was becoming increasingly attractive in railway board rooms. The Great Western had moved in this direction as early as 1911 with its 4300 class 2–6–0, an efficient performer on slow or express freights or on passenger trains at speeds up to 70 mph (113 kph). In the 1930s numbers of mixed-traffic 4–6–0s were built for the GWR, equally adaptable and better equipped for the higher-speed end of their duties by reason of the leading bogie. In

this climate a mixed-traffic design was an obvious necessity for the new locomotive program on the LMS, and in 1934 Stanier produced the first of his mixed-traffic 4–6–0s of a class which ranged widely over the whole LMS system, and indeed was to become ubiquitous on British Railways until the end of steam. It was known to its admirers as the 'Black Fives.' The official classification of these engines was 5P5F, that is power class 5 for passenger and freight duties. Coupled wheel diameter was 6 feet (1829 mm) as against the 6 feet 9 inches (2057 mm) of the 'Jubilees' but they were timed on many occasions at speeds of 90 mph (145 kph) and over.

The free flow of steam obtained by 'internal streamlining' of the steam passages made high piston speeds possible. Designers could therefore use wheels of smaller diameter in locomotives which would spend some of their time on express work, and at the same time the smaller wheels gave increased tractive effort. These factors helped to create the much-desired 'general purpose' locomotive. In later years the description 'general purpose' was preferred to 'mixed-traffic' because the latter had come, by association, to imply suitability for two classes of freight work – the slow goods not fitted with continuous brakes and the fitted express freight train – rather than the whole range of duties.

Above: With streamlining removed after the war, Stanier Pacific No 46220, *Coronation,* passes Bulkington with the up 'Royal Scot' in 1949.
Above right: Stanier 'Jubilee' class 4–6–0 No 5649 stands at Derby shortly after delivery and still without its 'Hawkins' nameplates.
Right: The name of LMS No 5902, *Sir Frank Ree,* is the only recognizable sign of its being reconstructed from the similarly-named LNWR 'Claughton.' The early rebuilds and later new locomotives formed the LMS 'Patriot' class. Views such as this, before smoke deflectors were fitted, are rare.

Gresley's general-purpose locomotive for the LNER evoked considerable interest when it appeared in 1936 because it had the unusual wheel arrangement, for a tender engine, of 2–6–2, which had previously been used in Great Britain only for tank engines. The first of the class was named *Green Arrow*, identifying the design closely with the 'Green Arrow' express freight service. However, the locomotives also took their share of fast passenger trains. Gresley had already introduced his 'Cock o' the North' class of 2–8–2 passenger engines for the heavy trains on the steeply graded Edinburgh–Aberdeen route, using 6 feet 2 inches (1880 mm) coupled wheels, and he used the same wheel diameter on the 'Green Arrows' (otherwise known as the Y2 class). The 'Green Arrow' boiler was a shortened version of the one used in his second series of Pacifics and the same wide firebox made a trailing axle necessary. At the front end he placed a two-wheel truck of the same design as in an earlier and numerous class of 2–6–0s. The cab front was wedged shaped, as in the streamlined Pacifics, where the shape had been adopted for aerodynamic reasons.

A few years after their introduction the 'Green

Arrows' were called upon to perform prodigious feats of haulage in wartime traffic. One noteworthy occasion was reported in a contemporary magazine in 1940:

> 'Whilst it has recently been necessary to place a limit on the size of trains, there have been occasions during the past few months when LNER locomotives have accomplished stupendous feats of strength.
>
> Greatest of all was when Green Arrow type mixed traffic locomotive No 4800 recently *hauled a passenger train of 26 vehicles weighing 762 tons from Peterborough to London*. With passengers and luggage the load hauled *exceeded a total of 800 tons and easily eclipsed all previous records*.'

The Southern Railway at this period had some small-wheeled versions of express passenger engines in service for fast freight traffic but they did not show the versatility of the specialized general-purpose design. However, a locomotive of this category was in the offing when war was declared in 1939 for Maunsell's successor, O V S Bulleid, was building a Pacific to improve on the haulage power and speed of the 'Lord Nelsons.' He chose 6-foot 2-inch (1880-mm) coupled wheels, which had by then shown themselves adequate for speeds in the 90 mph (145 kph) range, and it was fortunate that he did so for it enabled the engines to be classed as 'general purpose' so that construction was allowed to continue in the war years, when the building of locomotives purely for express passenger traffic was halted.

The first Bulleid Pacific came out in 1942. Its exterior was 'streamlined' in the eyes of the multitude, but the Southern preferred to call it 'air-smoothed.' There was a certain angularity about it, and in later years the various versions of the design came to be known as 'Spam cans,' recalling a canned meat consumed, *faute de mieux*, in large quantities during World War II. More formally, the first engines were the 'Merchant Navies,' being named after the famous shipping lines.

There were several unusual features in this class which at once earned its designer a reputation for originality. The most debatable was the special design of valve gear adopted to allow the sets for the three cylinders all to be accommodated between the frames. The gear was operated from a crankshaft which was chain driven from the main crank axle and the whole mechanism was enclosed in an oil bath. Problems ensued and the arrangement was not popular with maintenance staff. Two series of lighter 'air-smoothed' Pacifics – the 'West Country' and 'Battle of Britain' classes – followed at the end of the war, but their maintenance record was poor and in the end all the originals and many of their smaller successors were rebuilt with conventional valve gear, and the air-smoothing construction removed.

Other departures from standard British practice in the years between the two World Wars may be noted. Gresley decided to experiment with a water tube boiler and built a 4–6–4 locomotive to take it, the boiler itself being built by an outside engineering firm. Pressure was 450 lb per square inch (31.6 kg/sq cm). In 1930 the locomotive worked passenger turns from Gateshead (Newcastle) and on one occasion made a return trip from Edinburgh to London with the non-stop 'Flying Scotsman.' Practical problems soon arose in maintaining a marine-type boiler in railway service and the experiment was short-lived, but the locomotive was rebuilt with a conventional Pacific boiler and streamlining and continued in service until 1938. A still higher working pressure – 900 lb per square inch (63.3 kg/sq cm) – was chosen for an experiment with a 'Royal Scot' type locomotive of the LMS. The locomotive was a compound; the center cylinder took high-pressure steam and exhausted it into a mixing chamber where it met with steam generated at 250 lb per square inch (17.6 kg/sq cm) in the part of the boiler built on conventional lines. During trials a pipe in the high-pressure section failed, causing an explosion in which a member of the test staff was killed. The experiment was then halted and never resumed.

A more successful venture was Stanier's turbine-driven Pacific locomotive for the LMS, built in 1935. The 'Turbomotive' as it was called showed itself able to perform as well as the best of the standard Pacifics but unfortunately much of its working life occurred under war conditions when its availability did not match that of the conventional machines and, since the turbines were made by an outside firm which was heavily engaged in war work, there were problems in obtaining spare parts. Many engineers would have liked to see the locomotive working under normal conditions after initial difficulties had been solved, but in 1946 it was rebuilt as a standard LMS Pacific. Six years later it was wrecked in a three-train collision at Harrow and had to be scrapped.

Above left: Bulleid's 'Merchant Navy' Pacifics for the Southern Railway were deemed general-purpose locomotives when they came out in the war years, but from 1946 were soon at the head of the company's crack passenger trains. In British Rail days No 35009, *Shaw Savill*, starts the up 'Atlantic Coast Express' after the Salisbury stop.
Above: Stanier turbine-driven Pacific No 6202 (the 'turbomotive') is at Rugby with a down Liverpool express in 1945.
Right: LNER general-purpose 2–6–2 No 4771, *Green Arrow*, first of a class which performed notably both on express freight and fast passenger work.

2. Last Steam in Britain

On 1 January 1948 the principal railways in Great Britain were nationalized. There was some joyful tooting of engine whistles at midnight on New Year's Eve, for such an event had long been desired in some quarters and there were many on the railways who had come to look upon it as a solution to all problems. Some problems, however, could not be solved overnight such as the fact that British railway motive power had been overworked for six years and had suffered from restricted maintenance.

Steam clearly had a continuing role but opinions differed as to how long. The steam locomotive was approaching the limits of what could be extracted from a mobile steam-generating plant subject to limitations on its size. It had been shown that the steam locomotive was capable of improvement beyond what had once been thought possible, but its performance in these higher regions was dependent on expert handling. In postwar conditions a locomotive would inevitably be driven by a number of crews of varying capability; simplicity rather than refinement would have to be the keynote of future design.

British Railways, as the nationalized undertaking was called, took over some 20,000 locomotives of 448 different types from the previous four railway companies. Many of these dated back to the 120 individual companies which had been amalgamated to form four 'Groups' in 1923. Such variety was unacceptable for the new unified system, where uniform maintenance procedures were to be followed and reductions in the variety of spare parts were imperative.

The first move was to decide which of the more recent locomotive classes had the best claim to become the basis for future building. This was to be settled by interchange trials in which locomotives would operate on routes outside their normal territories, and all aspects of performance would be carefully monitored. The comparisons were not made using data gleaned from special test runs, but from performance statistics taken from trains on the normal timetable. The trials took place in 1948, but revealed that no one class was outstandingly superior over all the others. Accordingly it was decided to develop a range of new standard designs to work alongside the more recent existing classes and to compensate for the withdrawals of obsolescent types.

There was some criticism of the decision to build new steam locomotives in such numbers at so late a date, but the railways had to be kept going and there was little experience of diesel or electric traction to

Left: Thompson B1 class general-purpose 4—6—0 No 1159 stands at Leicester Central station in 1947.

Above: British Railways Class A1 Pacific No 60126, *Sir Vincent Raven*, **heads the up 'Queen of Scots' (Glasgow–Edinburgh–King's Cross) Pullman. The A1s were new locomotives built by A H Peppercorn as a development of E Thompson's conversion of the original Gresley Pacific** *Great Northern.*

build on. Diesel development had concentrated on shunting units. Main-line electrification had been confined to passenger services on short-distance routes between London and the south coast, using multiple-unit trains exclusively until early in the war – after the war the grand total of three electric locomotives appeared. Moreover, Great Britain was rich in coal and, although some of the best quality grades for raising steam were running out or were reserved for export, what remained was still the envy of many Continental and overseas railwaymen.

By the time the first of the new standard locomotives was ready, modifications to certain classes

of prewar locomotives had already taken place giving them a new lease of life. Sir Nigel Gresley, Chief Mechanical Engineer of the London & North Eastern Railway, had died in 1941. He was succeeded by Edward Thompson, who had to tackle a problem which had developed in Gresley's type of valve gear for three-cylinder locomotives. With the inevitable lowering of standards and infrequency of maintenance during the war years, play had developed in the joints of the lever system which worked the valves of the inside cylinder so that the distribution of steam to all three cylinders was unbalanced. In Gresley's layout the connecting rods of the outside and inside cylinders were of unequal length – the inclined inside cylinder was shorter than the outside ones. Thompson adopted the principle that all coupling rods should be of equal length and rebuilt one of Gresley's 2–8–2s as a Pacific with an altered cylinder layout to give this effect, with separate valve gear for the inside cylinder. The difficulty experienced with Gresley's gear was removed and the other 2–8–2s were rebuilt, followed by some new Pacifics built along similar lines in 1946.

A year later A H Peppercorn succeeded Thompson as Chief Mechanical Engineer. He introduced a new Pacific in which he returned to a more orthodox cylinder layout but retained the separate gear for the inside cylinder valves.

Admirers of Sir Nigel Gresley outside the railway industry were aghast at Thompson's treatment of his locomotives and indignation reached a crescendo when he laid his hands on the historic *Great Northern*, first of the Gresley Pacifics, to modify it according to his own ideas. It seems that eyebrows were discreetly raised within the industry as well, for Sir Ronald Matthews, Chairman of the London and North Eastern Railway, was once heard to say that 'the LNER could not build a locomotive policy on the basis that everything that Gresley did was wrong.' It must be said in Thompson's defense that he acted as he did in pursuance of a policy of standardization to make the best use of available funds, which on the LNER were less than those available to Stanier on the LMS. Thompson therefore proposed to introduce certain new classes for future building, to select others which would be retained in service by reboilering, and to designate others which would only be kept in traffic until the stocks of boilers on hand were used up.

His own original contribution was the class B1 general-purpose 4–6–0 of 1942, which filled a gap in the motive power left by Gresley in that it was more closely equivalent than any of Gresley's designs to the LMS 'Black Five.' The B1 was a straightforward two-cylinder locomotive which implemented Thompson's standardization ideas by embodying many parts corresponding to existing classes so that little new machinery was needed to produce it. Over 200 B1s were built and they did excellent and varied work both during and after the war.

With the return of more normal conditions in 1945, both in maintenance and train loading, the Gresley valve gear was no longer a problem and the earlier Pacifics returned to the lighter and faster passenger services. The Thompson and Peppercorn classes had met the needs of their day but in the more tranquil postwar environment they proved less economical in fuel consumption than the older engines because of the large grate areas with which they had been endowed to meet the demands of heavy wartime traffic. Nonstop running between London's King's Cross and Edinburgh, resumed in 1948, was always entrusted to the Gresley streamlined A4 Pacifics and these engines worked the 'Elizabethan' 6.5-hour London–Edinburgh express which was the postwar equivalent of the 'Coronation' although no longer formed of special streamlined stock.

On the LMS a 'Royal Scot' locomotive had been rebuilt with an improved steam circuit and tapered boiler in 1935. The experiment was successful, and in 1943 the rebuilding of the class on similar lines but with further improvements based on the Stanier Pacifics was undertaken. In their rebuilt form the 'Royal Scots' put up some of the best performances

Left: Rebuilt 'Royal Scot' class 4–6–0 No 6108, *Seaforth Highlander,* leaves Carlisle. The locomotive is in the glossy black livery once used by the London & North Western Railway and revived for a time by the LMSR.

Above: In early BR days several Stanier 'Black Fives' were experimentally modified in various ways to improve their efficiency. No 44755 has been equipped with Caprotti valve gear, Timken roller bearings and double chimney.

of their career. Similar success attended the rebuilding of the 'Patriot' class from 1946 with tapered boilers, larger cylinders and a double blastpipe.

The postwar rebuilding of Southern's 'Merchant Navy' and subsequent Pacifics designed by O V S Bulleid was mentioned in Chapter One. During the war Bulleid again showed his originality and disregard for convention when he designed an 0–6–0 goods engine which had the widest possible route availability on the Southern Railway. Instead of building more of Maunsell's Q class engines, he decided that a larger boiler and firebox would be desirable. In so doing he used up a higher proportion of the overall weight than usual and so had to cut down in other directions. He eliminated the running plates and developed a cab fabricated from thin sheet. The result was very much a 'basic' locomotive, the Q1 class, with its wheels fully exposed. To go with the multiple-jet blastpipe there was a stubby chimney and the dome was similarly austere. Both of these boiler fittings were the antithesis of the shapely appurtenances on which many locomotive designers prided themselves and which were characteristic of the British locomotive for many years. Bulleid did

not do these things to shock. He had the practical end of weight saving in view. It seems likely that criticisms of the appearance of the Q1 locomotive did not cause him much concern; his son, H A V Bulleid, recorded years later that his father was not greatly interested in the aesthetics of industrial design. Probably his most successful essay in this direction was his choice of bright malachite green as the Southern main-line locomotive livery. To some eyes even the Q1 was not out of the ordinary. The Bulleid family were having breakfast in their home adjacent to the line from Redhill to Reading outside London when the first Q1 passed the bottom of the garden. Everyone rushed out to see it, but the comment from the female side was that it was 'just an ordinary engine' – presumably no excuse for precipitate departure from the breakfast table.

Bulleid made another more radical break with steam locomotive convention in his 'Leader' class design of 1949. This was a steam equivalent of the power bogie electric locomotive except that the axles were not individually driven as in modern electric traction practice. The locomotive was carried on two three-axle bogies. In each of these bogies there was a

Left: 'Black Five' No
44766, seen here in British
Rail livery, was modified
with Timken roller bearings
and a double chimney in
1947, the last year of the
LMS.
Far right: Bulleid light
('West Country') Pacific
No 21C140, *Crewkerne*,
takes the 'Golden Arrow'
boat-train out of Victoria
shortly after the postwar
restoration of the express
by the Southern Railway.
Below: The streamlining of
the light Pacifics was later
removed, as seen in this
view of No 34100,
Appledore, again on the
'Golden Arrow' but in
British Rail days.

three-cylinder steam engine with sleeve-valve distribution driving the center axle; outer axles were coupled to the center axle by chain drives. There was a driver's cab at each end and a separate position for the fireman approximately at the middle of the locomotive as the boiler was off-center on the main frames and fired from the side. The discomfort of working in this position would have been serious, but could have been overcome for oil-firing. A more serious problem proved to be stretching of the chains and a consequent uneven distribution of the load between them (particularly when starting) which led to excessive wear. Work was put in hand on four locomotives of this type, but only one was completed and tested. The trials revealed too many problems to be overcome and the project was abandoned in 1951. The completed locomotive and those still under construction were scrapped.

Bulleid set out his philosophy of locomotive design in a paper written for the Institution of Mechanical Engineers entitled 'Stages in the Development of the Steam Locomotive to Restore It to Its Supremacy as the Ideal Railway Traction Unit.' The paper was never presented, at the request of British Railways, which was highly sensitive to criticism of spending money on experiments of doubtful value and by no means convinced that Bulleid's assessment of the status of the steam locomotive in railway traction was correct.

On the Great Western Railway, consideration of postwar requirements had revived the idea of a Great Western Pacific, and C B Collett's successor, F W Hawksworth, prepared a Pacific design using a 280 lb per square inch (19.7 kg/sq cm) boiler. No work on engines purely for express passenger traffic could be undertaken in the war years, but when, toward the end, the building of more mixed traffic locomotives was permitted Hawksworth introduced his 'County' class, a mixed-traffic 4–6–0 with the boiler pressure and wheel diameter (6 feet 3 inches/ 1905 mm) that had been proposed for the Pacific. The first of the series went into service in 1945. In the previous year Hawksworth had begun construction of a new batch of 'Hall' class 4–6–0s – the

Great Western's pioneer general purpose design – in which a higher degree of superheat was used. These 'modified Halls' continued the success of their predecessors in the new postwar environment.

After the war all the 'King' class locomotives on the Western Region were fitted with double blastpipes and chimneys. Similar fitments were applied to new series of 'Castles' built in postwar years, and some of the earlier locomotives were similarly modified.

The first of the BR standard locomotive classes appeared in 1951. The 'Britannia Pacific' set the trend – it was a two-cylinder design with the emphasis on easy maintenance. The frames were massive, bearing surfaces of ample proportions and all running gear outside. Equipment included a self-cleaning smokebox, a rocking grate and hopper ashpan to lighten the tasks of the shed staff attending to the locomotive after its spell of duty. Self-cleaning devices had been fitted in some locomotive smokeboxes much earlier than this, but they were operated by the driver. During World War II certain locomotives were fitted with equipment which performed the function automatically and continuously. Wire mesh screens were fitted in the path of the gases from the fire where they emerged from the boiler tubes. These screens served to break down the larger cinders to a size which could be ejected through the chimney, instead of accumulating in the bottom of the smokebox to be cleared by the shed staff. Shed-staff duty was one of the less attractive aspects of attending to the steam locomotive and the railway companies were under no illusions about the difficulty of attracting labor to the railways. Railroad companies had to compete with newer industries which often offered less arduous working conditions. First experiments with the screens showed a detrimental effect on power obtained from the steam and it became evident that the insertion of these fittings in the smokebox made adjustments to the design and dimensions of blastpipe and chimney necessary. The lessons were learned and were applied to the design of the Standard classes.

The 'Britannia' Pacific, with 6-foot 2-inch (1880-mm) diameter wheels, was a general-purpose loco-

Far right: GW 'King' No 6010, *King Charles I*, pilots 'Britannia' No 70019, *Lightning*, on a down express near Aller Junction, where the Torquay branch diverges from the main line to Penzance.

Bottom: The 'basic steam locomotive,' exemplified by Bulleid Q1 class 0–6–0 No 33007 heading a ballast train. The class was introduced in 1942 and 40 were built.

Right: The last Great Western main-line locomotive design was F W Hawksworth's 'County' class 4–6–0, partly derived from a contemplated Pacific which was never built. No 1011, *County of Chester*, passes Bath with a Taunton–London (via Bristol) train on 11 August 1961.

Below: The 'Britannia' Pacifics were the first of the British Rail Standard classes, beginning with No 70000, *Britannia*, in 1951. No 70054, *Dornoch Firth*, was the last of the line.

motive. After some initial problems had been overcome it gave excellent service, even holding its own on express duties with other classes designed specifically for that type of work. The class first made its name on the completely recast and accelerated timetable between London, Norwich and other points in East Anglia, which was introduced soon after the new locomotives became available. A lighter version of the class with smaller cylinders was also built. During its short life the 'Britannia' was widely used in many parts of the BR system; migratory habits were forced upon it as more and more main-line diesels came into service.

Other classes in the first production of Standards were two 4—6—0s based on the celebrated LMS 'Black Five' of Stanier's day: a 2—6—4T also of LMS conception and a 2—6—2T based on a Great Western design. These were followed by three 2—6—0 mixed-traffic classes and a further 2—6—2T, but this time with LMS antecedents. The largest of the mixed-traffic 2—6—0s, with 5-foot 3-inch (1600-mm) coupled wheels and 225 lb per square inch (15.8 kg/sq cm) boiler pressure showed itself highly competent on light express duties on cross-country routes, with a good turn of speed.

High speeds with relatively small coupled wheels reflected the progress that had been made in improving the locomotive steam circuit and hence the ability to admit and exhaust steam adequately at high piston speeds. Perhaps the most remarkable demonstration of this capability was given by the last of the Standard classes to be produced in quantity, a 2—10—0 with 5-foot (1524-mm) coupled wheels intended for freight work plus general duties in the lower speed range. In practice these engines showed themselves capable of 90 mph (145 kph) on at least two well-attested occasions when put on to express passenger turns in an emergency.

The first of the 2—10—0s came out in 1954. A year later British Railways announced its Modernization Plan, one ingredient of which was the complete replacement of steam by diesel or electric traction. Despite the threat of extinction, however, efforts to improve the efficiency of steam traction continued, one of which was the building of ten of the 2—10—0s with Crosti boilers in 1955. The object of this type of boiler, used with some success in Italy and Germany, was to improve thermal efficiency by preheating the water fed into the boiler. The preheater was in effect a smaller boiler with flue tubes underneath the main boiler, into which the hot gases from the fire were directed on reaching the front smokebox. They then flowed back through the tubes in the preheater to a final smokebox at the firebox-end of the boiler, where they escaped to the atmosphere through a chimney. Exhaust steam from the cylinders was also piped back to the rear smokebox and expelled through the same chimney to create a draft, and a proportion passed through a jacket around the preheater to assist in raising the temperature of the feedwater by heat exchange. In British Rail locomotives the chimney was on the running plate on the right-hand side, adjacent to the firebox, but there was also a small chimney in the usual position on the front smokebox. This, however, was used only when lighting up the locomotive for initial steam-raising and was not in the exhaust steam circuit. All ten locomotives with Crosti boilers were eventually rebuilt with conventional exhaust arrangements.

Until World War II there had been only two

Above: A standard class 2 2–6–2T No 84005 leaves Manton Tunnel with the Stamford branch push-pull train on 3 April 1965. Left: A BR Standard class 4 4–6–0 No 75005 brings an unusual touch of modernity to the Cambrian section of the Western Region.

previous ten-coupled locomotives in Great Britain. The first had been a 0–10–0 tank engine built in 1903 by the Great Eastern Railway to demonstrate that a steam locomotive could accelerate a train as well as electric traction. The company was being pressed to electrify its London suburban services out of Liverpool Street and the slogan '30 mph in 30 seconds from rest' was the battle-cry of the campaign. The Great Eastern's 'Decapod' did even better with a load of about 280 US tons/250 UK tons/254 tonnes. Apparently the demonstration silenced the pressure group and the railway was saved from having to face the huge capital cost of electrification. Presumably this saving was compensation for the expense of building a locomotive which was of little practical use after having proved its point, for its weight, distributed over a wheelbase of only 19 feet 8 inches (5.9 m) was too great for the permanent way and it never went into regular service.

The Great Eastern continued to work its intensive suburban services with steam locomotives of more modest size, earning much admiration for its smart operating, notably the speed with which incoming trains were provided with new engines to take them out again, while engines which had just arrived were deftly dispatched to their next duties. Rush-hour signalling at Liverpool Street must have been an exhausting occupation, particularly in the days of hand-worked points and signals.

47

Above: Standard
locomotives of power class
2 included a light 2—6—0
tender engine. No 78000,
the first of the class, is at
Shrewsbury in 1961.

Although the immediate demand for electrification had been silenced, however, it was revived from time to time and when government finance for new railway works was made available in the middle 1930s one of the approved schemes was the electrification of the line from Liverpool Street through the eastern suburbs of London to Shenfield in Essex, 20.25 miles (32.6 km). War postponed the work in 1939 and it was not completed until ten years later.

The second British ten-coupled locomotive was an 0—10—0 banking engine built by the Midland Railway for assisting trains on the Lickey Incline on its main line from Birmingham to Gloucester. It had a long and useful life and was still working in 1914 when a series of 2—10—0 locomotives was built by the North British Locomotive Company for the British War Department. It was the good performance of this class which led to the choice of the same wheel arrangement for the standard BR heavy freight locomotive – originally a 2—8—2 had been in mind. The last steam locomotive built for British Railways was one of the Standard 2—10—0s. It was named *Evening Star* and has been preserved in running order.

Although the 'Britannias' met most fast passenger train requirements on British Railways, the range of standard types was extended to include a design specifically made for express traffic. It was again a Pacific, but differed from all the others in that it had a three-cylinder engine. Wheel diameter was the same as in the 'Britannia' class, as this had been found satisfactory for free running at speeds up to 90 mph

(145 kph). The valve gear, however, was different from all the other standard engines, consisting of cam-operated poppet valves, and the locomotive was fitted with a double blastpipe. Only one engine was built to this design. Trials and service experience showed the need for some modifications on the steam-generating side, for the locomotive was less effective in this respect than the 'Britannias,' and relatively heavy on fuel. Already, however, the decision to abolish steam traction on British Railways had been taken and there was little incentive for further experiment and development of the design.

If its maximum steaming capacity was unimpressive, this Pacific, named *Duke of Gloucester*, was highly efficient in using what it did produce, improving by about 1 lb/ihp-hr on most contemporary simple-expansion designs and being bettered by the most advanced French compounds only to the same degree. Unfortunately it needed a different driving technique from the other Pacifics with which it was housed at Crewe North Motive Power Depot and, in the absence of a regular crew who could have learned its idiosyncracies, its performance did not do justice to its sophisticated design. It was withdrawn at the end of 1962 and its cylinders removed to be sectioned and displayed in the Science Museum in London. Over a decade later the other remains were rescued from a scrapyard in South Wales by a preservation society which began the formidable task of reconditioning it for a working life on a private railway.

In 1956, after the decree that steam was to be

48

phased out but before quantity production of mainline diesels had begun, there was a proposal to build more locomotives of the same class, and these would no doubt have improved on the original. However the plan did not materialize and the solitary *Duke* made its contribution to the last years of steam by providing information obtained from scientific testing of its performance on a stationary plant and on the road. As a result a similar poppet-valve gear was fitted to 30 BR standard class 5 locomotives built at Derby in 1956–57 and there were numerous applications of its double-exhaust system. Had steam survived, the influence of *Duke of Gloucester* would have been more durable.

Much was learned about the steam locomotive during its last years in Britain. World War II saw widespread development of measurement and recording systems, and of transducers for converting physical quantities into electrical signals. Locomotive testing went back many years, but these new scientific resources enabled it to be carried out on a greater scale and with more significant results. British Railways tested a number of the more recent locomotive classes and published bulletins giving findings that could have had a considerable effect on future design had steam locomotive building continued.

In earlier years one of the problems of locomotive testing on the road had been to find stretches of line where a locomotive could run in constant conditions long enough for useful measurements to be taken and without hindrance to other traffic. Early in the century Dr G V Lomonossoff had been a pioneer of locomotive testing in Russia, where long stretches of

level track with only light traffic could be found. The tests were considered to be of national importance and test trains were given the same priority as the Czar's own train. Similar advantages were not enjoyed elsewhere, and it was many years before a procedure was developed to obtain similar results without interfering with other traffic in Great Britain. This was the Controlled Road Testing System used on the Great Western Railway and the Western Region of British Railways. The essential feature of the system was measurement of the rate of steaming by detecting the fall of pressure across the blastpipe. A corresponding indication was given in the cab, and the driver held the instrument reading steady by adjustment of the cut-off, using the brakes to check speed when necessary, while the fireman maintained a constant rate of firing. In this way a test train could run at varying speeds without upsetting the measurements and could more easily be fitted into the timetable by the operating department. On the Great Western Railway these road tests supplemented tests on a stationary plant at Swindon. In 1939 a more advanced stationary installation for use by all the railways was being built at Rugby, but the work was held up by the war. After the war rehabilitation of the railways was given priority and the Rugby plant did not come into operation until 1950.

Although the end of steam had been decreed in the British Railways Modernization Plan in 1955, steam locomotives remained at work until August 1968. The effects of the new policy were barely noticeable until the early 1960s, when the pace of withdrawals accelerated. Early in 1961 there were still 241 loco-

Below: The 'Austerity' 2–10–0s built by the Ministry of Supply during the war were bought by British Railways. No 73788 is at the Rugby testing station in 1949, awaiting tests on the roller test plant. These locomotives led to the design of the 9F Standard 2–10–10s.

motives of the traditional British 4–4–0 wheel arrangement on the BR books, but all except one earmarked for preservation had been condemned by the end of 1962. Withdrawals then came so fast that they have been described as a 'massacre.' While lamented by enthusiasts, these events were little noticed by the travelling public at large who were more concerned at the shrinkage of the railway system itself under the proposals of a report, *The Re-shaping of British Railways*, prepared under the aegis of Dr (later Lord) Beeching, who became Chairman of the newly-formed British Railways Board on 1 January 1963. Rationalization weeded out or downgraded routes which had been built for competitive reasons but now simply duplicated facilities.

Surprisingly, the last London terminus to see main-line steam was Waterloo, Southern Region, which for many years had been the focus of an extensive electrified network. In the 1960s the Southern was busy completing electrification between Waterloo and the coastal resort of Bournemouth, and until this work was finished BR Standards and rebuilt Bulleid Pacifics continued to work the Bournemouth and Weymouth line trains. The end came on 8 July 1967 when 'West Country' Pacific No 34037, *Clovelly*, took the last steam-hauled passenger train out of the terminus on its way to Southampton Docks.

A dwindling band of steam locomotives carried on in northwest England until 11 August 1968. British Railways marked the end with a 'Last Day of Steam'

Below: Before the 'Austerities' and the 9Fs, the longest-lived British ten-coupled locomotive was the banking engine built by the Midland Railway for assisting trains on the Lickey Incline at Bromsgrove on the Derby–Bristol main line. In this view the banker, No 22290, is at Derby in LMS days after a major overhaul. Right: The only BR standard engine designed specifically for express traffic rather than general duties was No 71000, *Duke of Gloucester*. It was overtaken by the diesel program and withdrawn in 1962, but while at work contributed useful data under test which could have influenced future steam-locomotive design in Great Britain.

special from Liverpool to Carlisle and back. On the previous weekend enthusiasts' societies had chartered steam-hauled trains for commemorative trips from Birmingham to Huddersfield and from Manchester to Blackpool. Then, there was only the throb of the diesel or the hum of the traction motor through the length and breadth of British Railways.

Some would say that the world of steam is not quite lost, pointing to the achievements of the many preservation societies in reclaiming locomotives from the scrapyards and restoring them to running order to operate on lines long-since abandoned by British Railways. This is indeed a splendid and an international enterprise, and many barely of an age to remember the steam locomotive in its prime are ensnared by its fascination. What is more they pass on the same spirit to their children. Only the old and churlish occasionally prick the bubble by paraphrasing Marshal Bosquet's comment as he watched the Charge of the Light Brigade at Balaclava —

'C'est magnifique, mais ce n'est pas le chemin de fer.'

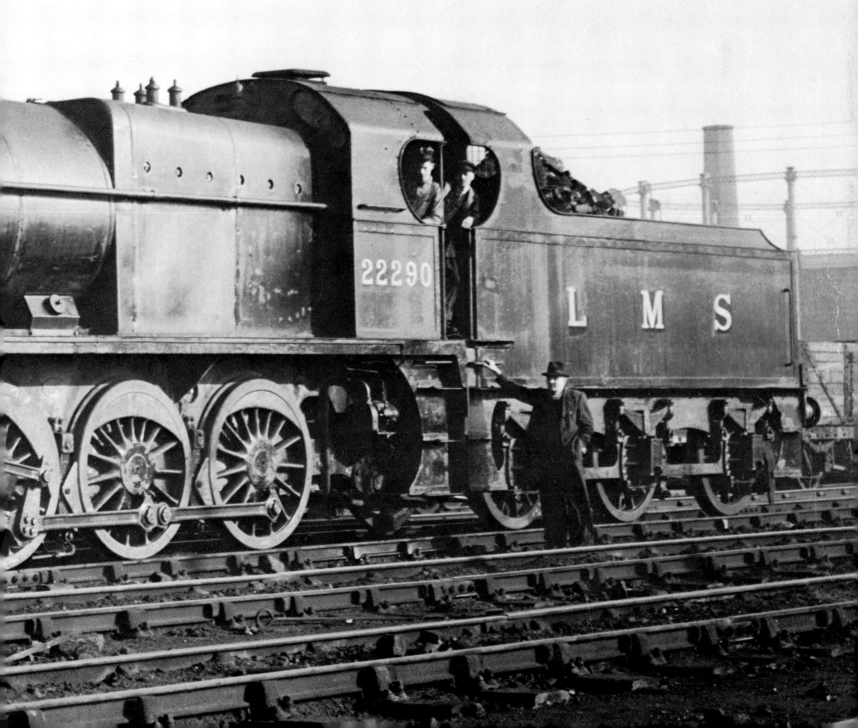

3. North American Steam

Though it was a British-made locomotive which was the first to run on an American railroad line, the development of railways in North America followed a very different pattern to that in Britain, just as the evolution of the locomotive turned the American versions into a distinctive creature well suited to the characteristics of the country.

Apart from the sheer size of the continent which required the building of lines over vast distances and adverse geological conditions, the railways of America were constructed under entirely different social conditions. In the 'old countries' railway companies found that their lines usually had to be built to fit into – or around – established communities and they became involved in complicated negotiations over land rights. In North America there were considerably fewer long-established communities and there were vast tracts of land on which there were no rights of ownership. In the old world the railroads were used to connect existing towns and cities; in America the railroads were not only a means of communication between communities but also served to open up the country and actually attracted the development of new settlements.

The historic first run by a locomotive in the USA was made by Horatio Allen of the Delaware and Hudson Canal Company on board the *Stourbridge Lion* which had been built for Allen by Foster, Rastrick

& Company of Stourbridge, England to operate on a 16-mile (25.7-km) line between Carbondale coal mines and the canal at Honesdale, Pennsylvania. Allen, who had never driven a locomotive before, confessed later to having been fearful of making that first run and in fact insisted that he make it alone on the basis that 'If there is any danger on this ride it is not necessary that the life and limb of more than one be subjected to danger.' The journey of three miles (4.8 km) was completed successfully but neither the *Lion* nor the *America*, which had been ordered from Robert Stephenson & Company together, proved suitable for the track and were taken out of service.

The real development of railways in the early days of steam locomotion in the United States was undertaken by the Baltimore & Ohio Railroad and the South Carolina Railroad. The latter was the first passenger line in America, and second in the world to the British Liverpool and Manchester line, to rely entirely on steam locomotion. However, it was on the former that steam locomotion in North America really began, although when the line was inaugurated in 1829 it was built to use horse traction. When Peter Cooper of New York demonstrated his *Tom Thumb* vertical-boilered engine to the directors, they were sufficiently impressed to organize a locomotive competition, similar to the famous 'Rainhill trials' held in England in 1829.

Right: The Santa Fe Express halts at Virginia City in 1885, headed by Virginia & Truckee 4–4–0 No 11, *Rene*.
Below left: 'American' 4–4–0s at a busy junction in New York State are depicted in an engraving of 1874. The vehicle on the extreme right is a 'Pullman Palace Drawing Room and Sleeping Car.'
Below: An impression of a train on the Hudson River Railroad (later absorbed into the New York Central & Hudson River) shows the ornamentation of locomotives that was practiced in the nineteenth century and the prevalence of bogie vehicles at a period when British travellers generally rode on six wheels.
Below right: Shunting at a yard on the Central Pacific Railroad about 1869. The site is probably near Salt Lake City, Utah.

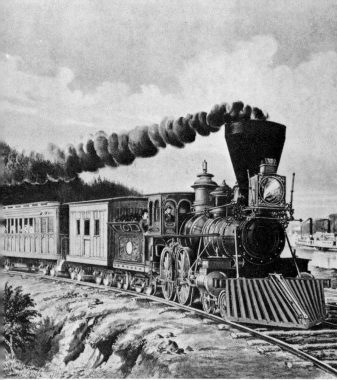

Above: A New York Central Hudson (4–6–4) cautiously approaches a maze of crossings.
Top left: Two 2–10–2 locomotives of the standard gauge Colorado & Southern leave Denver, Colorado, with a freight for Cheyenne, Wyoming.
Left: Streamlined 4–8–4 No 607 of the Norfolk & Western Railroad is typical of the cleaner lines achieved in US locomotive design toward the end of steam.

The Baltimore trials in 1831 had a more practical basis than those at Rainhill. Rather than a straightforward speed test the American contestants were required to submit their locomotives to a month's service hauling traffic. From the five entrants the vertical boiler *York*, designed by Phineas Davies, a watchmaker, was judged the winner of the $4000 first prize and the locomotive became the prototype for a fleet of 18 engines, the last of which did not retire until 1893 and was the oldest working locomotive in the world at that time.

The success of the Baltimore & Ohio and the South Carolina Railroads led to a burst of activity; a host of new companies sprung up to thrust out lines into the virgin lands of North America. While British railway builders may have been staggered by the enormity of the task of building railroads in North America they might also have been horrified by the standard of construction. In Britain and Europe lines were robustly built to careful specifications but in North America the keynote was speed and cheapness. The rush was on to open up the country as quickly as possible and only when lines had proved themselves economically viable were improvements made to the original, often dangerously flimsy, constructions. The hasty and haphazard approach by so many independent companies led to a complete lack of standardization in gauges. Many early lines in the northern states were built to a 3-foot (914-mm) gauge, while the southern states adopted South Carolina's 5-foot (1524-mm) gauge and the Erie

Railroad of 1841 was started with a gauge of 6 feet (1829 mm). Eventually, when the first transcontinental railroad came to be built, Congress approved a standard gauge of 4 feet 8.5 inches (1435 mm). Such was the rate of construction that even by 1835 railroads in the Eastern States accounted for more than half the world's total track length of 1600 miles (2575 km).

The idea of a transcontinental railroad had been the dream of pioneers and a few impractical theorists since early in the century but it became a political and economic necessity with the rapid population growth in the West coupled with the discovery of gold in the 1840s. Even then the political and commercial maneuverings rumbled on for years while rival factions suggested various routes and schemes, frequently without the backing of accurate surveys. Finally the Senate passed the Pacific Railroad Act in June 1862, granting two charters: one to the Union Pacific to build west from a suitable terminus in the center of the continent and the other to the Central Pacific Railroad to build east from Sacramento. The following year Union Pacific began building from Omaha, Nebraska and Central Pacific from Sacramento. The two lines eventually met at Promontory in May 1869. Over the years other companies completed their transcontinental lines – the Atchison Topeka & Santa Fé, the Southern Pacific, the Northern Pacific and the Chicago, Milwaukee, St Paul & Pacific – but their histories are well documented elsewhere.

The golden age of steam for the United States was

in the early years of this century. By this time the worst features of 'jerrybuilding' had been corrected, routes improved and locomotives of juggernaut proportions had evolved into what was to be their final form. Valves had changed from the 'flat-iron' slide version to less friction-bound piston types; fireboxes had deepened to give more heat and hence more power.

It was this big grate which was to give the world a new railroad language. The deep fireboxes left no room for driving wheels underneath and so small carrying wheels on a pony truck at the rear were added to the guiding wheels on a front truck to provide the common wheel arrangements which became a worldwide method of identification associated forever with the names of the types which first carried them. Hence we had the 4–4–2 Atlantics, the 4–6–2 Pacifics, the 2–6–2 Prairies and the less widely known 2–8–2 Mikados, which, with the Pacifics, became the standard freight locomotives in the United States for over 20 years. Those names were a reference to the first orders for the locomotives:

Right: The 'Hiawatha' with a Hudson at the head runs through the outskirts of Chicago at the start of its 410-mile journey to St Paul.

Left: Ready for the return trip to Chicago, the 'Hiawatha's' Hudson waits with its train for the rightaway from St Paul.
Below: A Chicago & North Western streamlined Hudson locomotive pauses at Cedar Rapids, Iowa, with the eastbound Pacific Limited (Los Angeles–Chicago). These engines performed briefly on the 400 (Chicago–St Paul) express but were superseded after a year by diesels.
Below right: One of the streamlined Atlantics built for the 'Hiawatha' express sets out on the high-speed run with its train of matching coaches.

the first 4–6–2 crossed the Pacific to New Zealand, the first 2–8–2 went to Japan and the first 4–4–2 was ordered by the Atlantic Coast line.

Enlargement of the grate obviously meant that larger stocks of coal had to be carried, to the extent that it was sometimes impossible for the fireman to keep up with the demands of the firebox. The answer was automatic stoking. A screw-feed mechanism powered by a small steam donkey engine became the most usual method, the coal being distributed evenly within the grate by jets of steam.

By the end of World War I North America had 72,000 working locomotives. Thereafter the number began, slowly, to decline but improvements in details of design continued to meet demands of speed and higher performance standards. One of the major alterations involved adding extra driving wheels while another involved articulation, which called for even more wheels! This 'stretching' of locomotives led to the giant locomotives with eight-coupled driving wheels for passenger work and ten or 12

for freight work. The ultimate was the 4–8–8–4 'Big Boy,' first produced for Union Pacific in 1941 for freight service. We shall return to this later.

Although the locomotives of North America had, like all others, evolved directly from Stephenson's *Rocket*, their appearance by the end of World War I was a clear indication of the different line of evolution which North American designers had taken to that of their British and European cousins. However, British design *did* have some influence on the external appearance of many locomotives after 1927. It was in that year that the famous British 4–6–0 of the Great Western Railway, *King George V*, visited North America and left a lasting impression for its clean lines. Thereafter there was a determined effort on the part of many railroads to conceal the extraneous pipework of their locomotives under boilerjackets and generally to smooth down and improve their external appearance. The end result tended to be a cleaner-looking breed of locomotive which, nonetheless, retained its distinctive workman-like appearance.

Left: One of the New York Central's streamlined Hudsons approaches Chicago with a passenger train.

The coming of the 1930s saw the introduction of the great steam-hauled express trains of North America. Chicago & North Western announced that it was going to launch an express that would cover the 408.6 miles (657.6 km) between Chicago and St Paul in seven hours, cutting the previous best time by 170 minutes. The new train, called the '400,' first ran on 6 January 1935. Over the 209.5 miles (337.2 km) from Chicago to Adams the train had to average 63.8 mph (102.7 kph) to the first stop at Milwaukee, 85 miles (136.8 km) from Chicago, and then cover the remaining distance to Adams at the same average speed. In its early days the train was formed of five air-conditioned steel coaches headed by an oil-burning Pacific locomotive which had been modified for the service by the substitution of 6-foot 7-inch diameter (2007-mm) driving wheels for those of 6-foot 3-inch (1905-mm) diameter originally fitted. The '400' triggered a railway 'race' between Chicago and the Twin Cities of St Paul and Minneapolis.

This was a less well-known but more significant phase in railway history than the railway races in Great Britain from London to Edinburgh and to Aberdeen in the previous century. It is true that the earlier British events had a commercial motive in that the company making the fastest run would gain prestige, but to the ordinary traveller the frequent changes in schedules must have been irritating, while the 'racing' trains often landed him at his destination at an inconveniently early hour. Moreover, the companies involved were unlikely to make their best performance the standard for everyday running in future. On the other hand the schedules of the American expresses were a regular offer and planned for the convenience of the railway customer.

The other line using steam traction between Chicago and the Twin Cities was the Chicago, Milwaukee, St Paul and Pacific, which, not unreasonably, preferred to call itself in its publicity simply 'The Milwaukee Road.' Response from this quarter to the '400' was swift. A new service called the 'Hiawatha' was scheduled to run from Chicago to St Paul in 6.5 hours for the journey by this route of 410.5 miles (660.6 km), with four intermediate stops. The 'Hiawatha' service was introduced on 29 May 1935 and immediately attracted attention by a very fast start-to-stop timing – 62 minutes for the 78.3 miles (126 km) from Sparta to Portage, representing an average of 75.8 mph (121.9 kph) and the fastest steam run in the world at that time.

The Chicago & North Western's '400' was not a streamliner. Locomotives and coaches were of conventional outline and the locomotives were normal members of their class except for the larger driving wheels already mentioned. For the 'Hiawatha,' however, new streamlined locomotives and coaches were built. The American Locomotive Company at Schenectady built two Atlantics for the service in 1934, and added two more shortly afterward. The engines had the high working pressure of 300 lb per square inch (21.1 kg/sq cm) and driving wheels of 7 feet (2134 mm) diameter. Oil-firing was chosen because it was feared that on a long high-speed run of over 400 miles (643 km) the ash accumulation would be excessive. Two outside cylinders drove the leading pair of coupled wheels, which was unusual in American Atlantics, but in other respects the engines were in line with well-established design practice.

The first streamlined 'Hiawatha' trains were six-car formations weighing 351 US tons/313 UK tons/318 tonnes and seating 376 passengers. In 1938 new stock was introduced and normally formed into nine-car trains weighing 482 US tons/430 UK tons/437 tonnes with seating for 499. Each train comprised a combined baggage and buffet car, four luxury cars for 'coach' class passengers (equivalent to second class), a café-dining car, two parlor cars and a parlor observation car. The last-named had a 'beaver tail' end and a somewhat unusual array of fins which served both to shield the rear windows from the sun and to strengthen the car at the back against the effects of possible impact. Special attention was paid to the suspension system so that shocks were absorbed and vibration suppressed.

From 1935 to 1939 there was one 'Hiawatha' train in each direction, both leaving the respective terminals at 1 pm. From 21 January 1939 an additional morning service was introduced and by that

Right: Closeup of a Pennsylvania T–1 4–4–4–4 showing the characteristic Raymond Loewy style of streamlining and the 16-wheel tender.
Below: A Pennsylvania Railroad K4 Pacific assists one of the T–1 class 4–4–4–4s with a heavy train on the Horseshoe Curve.

time the popularity of the train had grown to the extent that sometimes 15 cars had to be run. To meet these developments the railway commissioned six more powerful locomotives of the 4–6–4 wheel arrangement and put them into traffic in 1938. These were the new F7 class Hudsons, which became among the United States' finest locomotives. Normally they worked the morning 'Hiawathas' – the midday trains continued to run with the original Atlantics. From 28 January 1940, when the services were accelerated, one of the 4–6–4s had the task of making the Sparta–Portage run with the eastbound morning 'Hiawatha' in only 59 minutes, giving an average speed of 79.6 mph (128.1 kph) which put it far ahead of any contemporary steam competitor.

The 4–6–4s were coal-fired with automatic stokers. Boiler pressure and wheel diameter were the same as in the Atlantics. Diesels began to appear on the 'Hiawatha' in 1941, by which time the speed over the fastest stretch had been raised to 81 mph (130 kph). Perhaps spurred by diesel competition, the 4–6–4s now gave some of their best performances. They could, and did, sustain a speed of 100 mph (161 kph) over long distances with loads of 784 US tons/700 UK tons/711 tonnes. On one occasion an engine of this class hauling 874 US tons/780 UK tons/792.9 tonnes averaged 100.5 mph (161.7 kph) for 62 miles (99.8 km) continuously. In spite of these performances, the engine crews preferred the Atlantics, which gave them a smoother ride, and these locomotives continued to work on the service when loads did not exceed nine cars. During the war years, the use of diesels increased, although steam continued to share the work until 1945. Thereafter the Atlantics and Hudsons appeared in emergencies only and all engines of both classes had gone by 1951.

Nine streamlined 4–6–4s were built for the Chicago & North Western in 1938 to take over the '400' from the original Pacifics but a year later this train became regularly diesel-hauled. Like both classes of high-speed engines on the Milwaukee, the C&NW had 7-foot (2134-mm) diameter driving wheels.

The revival of the Atlantics for high-speed service in the USA and in Belgium aroused considerable

Right: T–1 4–4–4–4 No 5537 leaves Fort Wayne with the Pennsylvania's 'Fast Mail.'
Below: A Southern Pacific streamlined 4–8–4 of class GS3, in distinctive livery to match the coaches of the 'Daylight' express behind its tender, on its journey from Los Angeles to San Francisco.

Bottom: The Pennsylvania adopted the 'duplex' arrangement of the T–1s for freight service as well, building first a 4–6–4–4 design (class Q–1) and then a 4–4–6–4 here. These 26 engines formed class Q–2.

Left: Double-heading was
necessary on nearly all
trains from Cheyenne to
Sherman, Wyoming, in
spite of the Union Pacific's
powerful 4–8–4s. Nos 809
and 823 are leaving
Cheyenne with the
California 'Fast Mail.'

Left: Preserved Union Pacific
4–8–4 No 8444 makes a
run-past between Denver
and Cheyenne for the
benefit of photographers on
an enthusiasts' special.

comment at the time, but it is less well known that older locomotives of this wheel arrangement also figured in the general speed-up in the 1930s. When the 'Hiawatha' was introduced, the 'Detroit Arrow' of the Pennsylvania Railroad, a Chicago–Detroit Service, was already covering the 64.2 miles (103.3 km) from Plymouth to Fort Wayne in 51 minutes, achieving an average speed of 75.5 mph (121.5 kph) and the locomotives used at first were Pennsylvania Atlantics dating from 1915. In Europe the Paris, Lyons & Mediterranean Railway in 1935 rebuilt an even older Atlantic, dating from 1906–07, for working an experimental streamlined train between Paris and Lyons. At that period the speed limit in France was 75 mph (120 kph) but on a trial run the streamlined four-cylinder compound hauling three coaches and a dynamometer car reached 97 mph (156 kph).

One of the best known 'families' of Hudsons ran on the New York Central, where the 1930s saw accelerations of long-established trains which were as demanding on the steam locomotive as the new high-speed services. There were several series of NYC Hudsons, going back to 1927. The earlier types were classified J–1a to J–1e; all had certain differences of detail but common features included two outside cylinders, 25 by 28 inches (635 by 711 mm), 6-foot 7-inch (2007-mm) diameter coupled wheels, 225 lb per square inch (15.8 kg/sq cm) boiler pressure, and a booster driving the rear axle of the training truck. Because of the booster, the diameter of the rear wheels in the truck, 4 feet 3 inches (1295 mm), was greater than that of the leading pair, 3 feet (914 mm).

All these locomotives performed well on heavy trains at high speeds and were associated in particular with the crack New York–Chicago express, the 'Twentieth Century Limited,' on which they began to replace Pacifics from 1927. When the J–1e series came out in 1932 the previous 20-hour schedule of this train had been cut to 18 hours for the 926 miles (1490.2 km). The train left Grand Central Terminal, New York, behind an electric locomotive and steam took over at Harmon, 33 miles (53.1 km) out. At Syracuse it ran for 1.3 miles (2.1 km) along a main thoroughfare, Washington Street, the locomotive bell tolling continuously. This procedure continued until the street section was by-passed in 1936, when the journey time was reduced to 16.5 hours, including seven intermediate stops.

The railway travel market in the 1930s was demanding. To meet growing expectations for comfort and service, operators called for new rolling stock which imposed an extra load on the locomotives not only in increased weight but also in power required for air-conditioning and other electrically based amenities. A more powerful version of the Hudson type had been planned as early as 1931. It materialized in 40 locomotives delivered by the American Locomotive Company (Alco) late in 1937, forming the J–3a series. The engines had a new boiler of greater evaporative capacity, working at 275 lb per square inch (19.3 kg/ sq cm), although this was later reduced to 265 lb per square inch (18.6 kg/sq cm). Cylinder dimensions were changed as well to 22.5 by 29 inches (571 by 737 mm). The first 40 engines were followed in 1938 by ten of a streamlined version.

These were not the first NYC streamliners, however. Responding to the growing fashion of the day, one of the J–1e series had been streamlined in 1934 and named *Commodore Vanderbilt*. It was often to be seen on the famous 'Twentieth Century Limited' between Chicago and Toledo, a run of 233 miles (375 km). Toledo was a locomotive changing point; changes were also made at Harmon (from electric traction as already noted) and Buffalo. Trains calling at Cleveland, where reversal was necessary in the Union Terminal station, also changed engines there, but the terminal could be by-passed and the 'Twentieth Century Limited' did not call there after the 1920s. In the later Hudsons some of the changes were omitted and the engines made very long through-runs such as from Harmon to Toledo, 693 miles (1115.3 km); or right through from Harmon to Chicago, 925 miles (1488.6 km).

The style of streamlining chosen for the J–3a engines was different from that originally adopted for *Commodore Vanderbilt* and soon became the accepted public image of the New York Central. In 1939 *Commodore Vanderbilt* was reclad in the new style. Two more of the J–3a series were streamlined for working the 'Empire State Express' after it acquired new stainless-steel stock. With the introduction of the J–3a engines the timing of the 'Twentieth Century Limited' was reduced to 16 hours, and it remained thus until the United States entered World War II in December 1941. With the return of peacetime conditions the schedule was resumed, but was cut to 15.5 hours from 1 April 1947. In the immediate postwar period the Hudsons yielded their heavier duties to new 4–8–4s but steam was nearing its end and by the time of the 1947 acceleration, multiple-unit diesel locomotives were becoming the normal power for the 'Twentieth Century Limited.' This famous express ceased to run on 13 March 1967 in the twilight of the long-distance American express passenger train.

The rival of the 'Twentieth Century Limited' for the New York–Chicago traffic was the 'Broadway Limited' of the Pennsylvania Railroad. This company had electrified its main line from New York to Philadelphia and Washington in 1933 and, with further electrification in mind, was not actively engaged in developing new steam locomotive designs. Its staple main-line power up to World War II consisted of a series of Pacifics of a class first seen in a single example in 1914. Series production began three years later and continued until 1928, by which time 425 had been built, including the prototype. The whole series was classified K4. There were differences between various production models but basically the locomotive was a two-cylinder simple with cylinders 27 by 28 inches (686 by 711 mm), 205 lb per square inch (14.4 kg/ sq cm) boiler pressure, and 6-foot 8-inch (2032-mm) diameter coupled wheels. Walschaerts valve gear was fitted to all engines as built but there were later experiments with poppet valves when double-heading was found necessary on the fastest and heaviest trains. Tests showed that the existing steam circuit would not meet the requirement of 100 mph (161 kph) on the level with 1000 US tons/893 UK tons/907 tonnes – the standard being sought by the Association of American Railroads.

No further development of the class took place, however, for the Pennsylvania decided to go in a completely new direction. In 1929–30, on the threshold of the speed and load revolution, two slightly larger Pacifics known as Class K5 were built but there was no follow-up here either. They are proof that the Locomotive Department was looking ahead even though the management may have been

Left: CNR streamlined
4–8–4 No 6401 at work on
a Toronto–Windsor service.

Below: A rebuilt 4–8–4 of
the Canadian National
passes Lachine with the
Ottawan evening business
express from Montreal.

Above: A Canadian
National 4–8–4 on the
turntable at Glen Yards,
Montreal.

inhibited from further investment in steam locomotives by thoughts of future electrification.

By the late 1930s there was a sudden change. Electrification extensions were only a long-term prospect and discussions took place with locomotive manufacturers on how best to meet current needs. It was decided that the answer would be a 'duplex' locomotive of the type favored by the Baldwin Locomotive Works. Essentially a 'duplex' meant having two two-cylinder steam engines in one nonarticulated frame, each pair of cylinders driving its own set of coupled wheels.

The first Pennsylvania 'duplex' was the one and only locomotive of the S–1 class, the largest rigid frame passenger locomotive ever built. Wheel arrangement was 6–4–4–6, the six-wheel bogies fore and aft being necessary to share in the support of a boiler no less than 62 feet 4 inches (18.9 m) long from firebox backplate to smokebox door. The diameter of the leading bogie wheels was 3 feet 6 inches (1118 mm), and that of the trailing wheels 4 feet 2 inches (1270 mm). Coupled wheel diameter was 7 feet (2134 mm) and the rigid driving wheelbase 64 feet 4 inches (19.6 m). A 16-wheel double-bogie tender contributed to an overall length of the whole locomotive of 140 feet 2.5 inches (42.7 m).

This gigantic locomotive ran on the main line only briefly before being put on exhibition at the New York World Fair in 1939 where it was the centerpiece of a joint 'American Railroad' display. Nearly a year

Below: Somewhat naturally the big coal-carrying road, the Norfolk & Western, was one of the last North American railroads to use steam. Its engines as well as its trains were huge and heavy, like this 2–8–8–2 at Shenendoah, Virginia, in 1956.
Right: The Union Pacific has left one of its last-built express steam locomotives for use on fan specials. This loco, No 8444, a massive 4–8–4 with headlights aglow takes a special Centennial excursion from Salt Lake City to Ogden and back.

Bottom: Another Norfolk & Western giant, this time a class A 2–6–6–4, heads a passenger train eastbound near River Gorge, Ripplemead, Virginia.

later it went into service on the Chicago–New York main line but was restricted by its weight to the section between Chicago and Crestline, 283 miles (455.4 km) long. Here it worked the principal trains and could average 66 mph (106 kph) westbound or 63 mph (101 kph) eastbound with a load of 1350 US tons/1205 UK tons/1224 tonnes, reaching 100 mph (161 kph) on slight downgrades. But its appetite for fuel was voracious; it was retired from active service about 1944 and scrapped in 1949.

If not wholly satisfied with its first essay in the duplex field, the Pennsylvania nonetheless went ahead with the principle and in 1940 ordered two 4–4–4–4s, built to more modest dimensions than the S–1 prototype but again with a boiler pressure of 300 lb per square inch (21.1 kg/sq cm). Coupled wheel diameter was slightly less at 6 feet 8 inches (2032 mm). These were followed in 1945 by 50 production engines, sufficiently similar to the first two for the whole series to be classified T–1. The external 'air-smoothed' design was created by Raymond Loewy, who had also been responsible for the S–1, but in the 4–4–4–4s he substituted a jutting 'prow' for the bulbous contours of the earlier design, foreshadowing the 'nose' of later diesels. Various changes in the shaping and extent of the exterior casing took place during the life of the locomotives.

Right: Two CNR 4–8–4s at rest in Brockville Yard, Ontario. No 6258, on the right, worked the Royal Train in Canada in 1938 and carries a special plate below the headlight.
Below: Dormant power at Sherbrooke, Quebec, as a CNR Pacific waits to leave with a night train for Montreal.

Below: One of the Norfolk & Western's magnificent class J streamlined 4–8–4s with a westbound passenger train at Bluefield.
Left: Pennsylvania Railroad 2–10–0s descending the Horseshoe Curve, Altoona, Pennsylvania, after banking a heavy freight.
Below left: Big Boy: the Union Pacifics giant at rest at Steamtown Museum, Bellows Falls.

Left: CPR 4–8–4 No 5908 heads the second portion of the Dominion transcontinental express at the top of the Kicking Horse Pass.
Right: Semistreamlined 4–4–4 locomotives were introduced by the CPR in 1936 for light main-line stopping trains with fast point-to-point timings. An example of this wheel arrangement is seen at Toronto.
Below: Semistreamlined booster-fitted Canadian Pacific 2–10–4 No 5929 acts as pilot to a train in the Rockies near Field, on the border between Alberta and British Columbia.

The T–1s worked as far east as Harrisburg on the Chicago–New York main line and worked on all the crack trains, some of them making start-to-stop runs of between 120 and 140 miles (193 and 225 km) at speeds over 70 mph (113 kph). On many occasions they were recorded as running at 100 mph (161 kph) with a load of 1000 US tons/893 UK tons/907 tonnes. However, they were heavy on fuel and overshadowed from the first by the challenge of the diesel. By 1949 most of them had been retired. Scrapping began in 1951.

Duplex locomotives were also built for fast freight work on the Pennsylvania in the 1940s; the first was a 4–6–4–4 completed in 1942. In this prototype design, class Q–1, the first three-coupled axles were driven by cylinders in the usual position under the smokebox, but the cylinders for the rear pair were behind them, below the firebox and drove 'forward.' It was not a satisfactory arrangement because of heat, abrasive dirt, awkward steampipe connections and poor support for the slidebars. Surprisingly in a freight locomotive, the coupled wheel diameter was 6 feet 5 inches (1956 mm). The next move was to a freight duplex production series, class Q–2. Here the wheel arrangement was reversed; the four-coupled engine was in the front and the six-coupler at the rear. The coupled wheel diameter of this 4–4–6–4 was reduced to 5 feet 9 inches (1753 mm). The second pair of cylinders was arranged in front of its coupled axle group in the usual way. Deliveries of 26 Q–2 class locomotives were made in 1944 and 1945. Some of them outlived the T–1 passenger engines, continuing to work until 1951, but the Pennsylvania's leap forward from conventional Pacifics to the duplex system could not be judged a success by any standards.

In seeking higher power many railways in North America chose the 4–8–4 wheel arrangement. The name 'Niagara' adopted for this type of locomotive by the New York Central did not enjoy general usage. It has been mentioned already that the NYC began replacing its Hudsons with 4–8–4s in the mid-1940s, but there were many earlier examples. The Southern Pacific introduced eight classes between 1930 and 1943, all oil-fired and with boosters. Best remembered of them is class GS3 ordered in 1937 for working the 'Daylight' express (San Francisco–Los Angeles), the first of five classes with 6-foot 8-inch (2032-mm) diameter driving wheels. When inaugurated in the 1920s the 'Daylight' was allowed 12 hours for its journey of 471 miles (758 km), which abounded in long gradients of 1-in-100, short stretches as steep as 1-in-46, and severe curvatures. The new motive power was needed for an accelerated schedule in 1938 which cut the time to 9 hours 45 minutes. With the GS3s the train no longer needed piloting up the long 756-foot (230.4-m) climb of 16.5 miles (26.5 km) between San Luis Obispo and Santa Margarita. The locomotives were air-smoothed and finished in an orange, red and black color scheme which matched the special 'Daylight' rolling stock. At peak traffic periods the train consisted of 14 cars weighing 650 US tons/580 UK tons/590 tonnes. It was not a route for high speeds, the maximum rarely exceeding 80 mph (129 kph).

In 1938 the Association of American Railroads carried out tests with existing locomotive classes to establish principles for future design which it was hoped would enable a train of 1000 US tons/893 UK tons/907 tonnes to be accelerated to 100 mph (161 kph) and held at that speed on level track. The types tested were a Chicago & North Western 4–6–4, a pair of Pennsylvania K4 Pacifics and a Union Pacific 4–8–4. The UP engine came closest to target, accelerating 1005 US tons/897 UK tons/912 tonnes to 89 mph (143 kph) up 1-in-660 and touching 102.4 mph (164.8 kph) on a 1-in-500 downgrade. An

improved version of the UP 4–6–4 followed, designed specifically for 100 mph (161 kph) running and a top speed of 110 mph (177 kph). Driving-wheel diameter was increased from 6 feet 5 inches (1956 mm) to 6 feet 8 inches (2032 mm). Engines of this new series ran without change over the 1026 miles (1651.1 km) between Omaha and Salt Lake City, and the 1394 miles (2243.4 km) between Omaha and Huntington, Oregon.

By this time large American locomotives were being fitted with roller bearings throughout, a working application of the low rolling resistance qualities which had been demonstrated in an unusual manner by the Timken company in 1930. Timken had a 4–8–4 locomotive specially built by Alco as a demonstration unit, with tapered rolling bearings in all axleboxes and motion points. A photograph of the period shows it being pulled along by three men heaving on a rope (although it has been suggested that there may have been hidden manpower at the rear to get it on the move). This locomotive made lengthy demonstration tours and was eventually bought by the Northern Pacific Railroad, which used it for years in ordinary traffic.

The Norfolk & Western introduced its streamlined J class 4–8–4 in 1941. One of the class is claimed to have achieved 110 mph (177 kph) on the level during a special test on the Pennsylvania Railroad near Crestline, although the coupled wheels were of relatively small diameter – 5 feet 9 inches (1753 mm). In daily running on their own system the Js handled trains of 14 or 15 cars over gradients between 1-in-100 and 1-in-200 and regularly achieved 90 mph (145 kph).

The Canadian National Railways were consistent users of 4–8–4s over a long period, beginning in 1927, and finally had a fleet of 150, not counting those built for its Grand Trunk Western subsidiary. Many of them lasted to the end of steam in 1960. Construction of the 4–8–4s continued until 1942. Although they formed ten different classes, certain features were common throughout. Only the air-smoothed engines built in 1936 and a batch for the Grand Trunk Western of the same year interrupted the basic 25.5 by 30-inch (648 by 762-mm) cylinders and 6-foot 1-inch (1854-mm) diameter coupled wheels. The two batches of 1936, ten locomotives in all, had cylinders measuring 24 by 30 inches (610 by 762 mm) and 6-foot 5-inch (1956-mm) diameter coupled wheels.

The Canadian National was not the first of Canada's great railways and indeed was not planned as a nationwide system. Those distinctions fell to the Canadian Pacific Railway, which was incorporated in February 1881 after extensive survey work by parties of explorers who ventured into wild country to seek out a transcontinental route. By the end of the century the CPR had taken over many small railway companies which had existed in the provinces of Quebec and Ontario since the 1850s.

The task of building the line was a daunting one for the route traversed rocky outcrops, swamps, mountain passes, ravines, cliff edges, hundreds of miles of prairie and the great chain of the Rocky Mountains. Nevertheless, the new company, supported by the government, pushed the line east and west from Winnipeg so rapidly that in four years the line from Vancouver in British Columbia to Montreal on the St Lawrence River was completed, in spite of the fact that William Van Horne, the general manager,

Below: A Union Pacific 4–8–4 heads a northbound evening passenger train at Denver, Colorado.

Right: New York Central Railroad Westbound freight at Dunkirk, New York, behind 4–8–2 No 3113.
Below right: Southern Pacific Railroad 4–8–4 No 4436 at San Francisco, California.

Below: A Union Pacific 'Challenger' class 4–6–6–4 Mallet storms through the Weber Canyon with a heavy freight.
Above: Union Pacific 4–12–2 No 9044 leads 47 cars at an estimated 30 mph near Sherman in 1947.
Above left: An eastbound extra freight of 64 cars is headed near Sherman, Wyoming, by 4–6–6–4 No 3993.

Left: UP 4–6–6–4 No 3967 has a spell of passenger work as it pulls out of Denver for Cheyenne with the Denver Post Frontier Days Special, a promotional exercise by the local Denver Newspaper taking guests free of charge and with meals and refreshments 'on the house' to an annual rodeo.

Above: A red Canadian
Pacific Railway Pacific No
2471 with an evening
commuter train leaving
Windsor station, Montreal.
Right: Canadian Pacific
4–6–2 No 2413 takes an
eastbound passenger train
out of Toronto.

Above: A Canadian
National Railway 4–6–4
No 5700 at Toronto depot.

79

described one section – the north-shore stretch – as 200 miles of engineering impossibilities.

James Coughlin, a roadmaster on that section, later described conditions:

> 'We had to ride six or seven miles from the boarding cars to the track-laying machine on open flatcars when the thermometer registered 40 to 50° F below zero (40 to 46° C below zero). We would stand together in close groups and when the front men could not stand it any longer they would go round to the opposite side of the gang, and thus we kept moving until we reached work. . . . We had to use a tin stove and a piece of heavy zinc to heat the spikes sufficiently to prevent frozen heads from snapping off when they were being driven into the ties. We often found that the ties would split from end to end, so intense was the cold, if the spike turned on striking the sap.'

The first regular passenger train did not run from the east into Vancouver until 23 May 1887 (the intervening period was used to improve the track). In succeeding years as the company became more profitable, many of the original 'temporary' structures such as the dramatic timber-trestle viaducts, built from wood from nearby forests, were replaced with permanent steel constructions.

Canadian National was officially created in 1923 though the name had been used since 1919. Its formation took place in stages which involved the acquisition of several small railways and the Canadian Northern Railway (CNoR), the publicly owned Canadian Government Railway (CGR) and the British-owned Grand Trunk Railway (GTR), which was the oldest of these three and included the country's first railway, the Champlain & St Lawrence, built to a 5-foot 6-inch (1.67-m) gauge and opened on 21 July 1836.

Left: A formidable sight
confronts any motorist or
pedestrian venturing over
this rudimentary crossing
as Union Pacific 4–6–6–4
No 3999 bears down with
an express freight.
Right: One of Union Pacific's
'Big Boy' 4–8–8–4s blasts
through a cutting near
Hermosa Tunnel,
Wyoming, with a train of
mixed freight.

Left: A pair of 2–8–8–2s of
the Denver & Rio Grande
Western lend their muscle
at the rear of a freight
train climbing a bank.
Below left: One of the
Southern Pacific's 4–8–8–
2s built in 1937 with the
boiler 'turned round' so
that the cab is at the front,
heads 61 cars near Lang,
California. The 'cab-at-
front' layout improved
conditions for the crew in
tunnels.

The Canadian Pacific used 4–8–4s to a smaller
extent than the CNR but began early with two locomotives built in its own works in 1928. Both companies used 4–6–4s during their period of intense
competition in 1932 between Montreal and Toronto,
when for a time they displaced the 'Cheltenham
Flyer' from its place as 'the fastest train in the world.'
The CPR 4–6–4s on this service were built in 1929
and were characterized by huge boilers and fireboxes
designed for continuous heavy steaming. The 'Cheltenham Flyer' soon reasserted itself, but in fairness
to the Canadians it should be mentioned that they
were working much heavier trains – 672 US tons/
600 UK tons/610 tonnes compared with the Flyer's
usual 280 US tons/250 UK tons/254 tonnes.

Canadian Pacific steam is best remembered for its
mountain-climbing ability on the transcontinental
route. From Calgary the line climbs into the mountains
for 120 miles (193 km) to reach the Kicking Horse
Pass. The stiffest gradients are in the last four miles
(6.4 km) to the summit where they steepen to 1-in-40
on sharp curves. Here the line crosses the Continental
Divide between Alberta and British Columbia and then
descends for 13 miles (21 km) to Field with an average
gradient of 1-in-52. This was the home of the 5800
series of 2–10–2s employed on banking trains over
the 'hill,' and they were sometimes joined on these
duties by the celebrated 2–10–4s of the 'Selkirk' class,
although both also worked the head. A pair of 'Sel-
kirks' or a 2–10–2 and a 'Selkirk' hauling a heavy passenger train through the mountain section was a sight
expressive of steam power in its ultimate development.
Lighter trains were worked by the G4a class passenger
Pacifics, and freight was generally in charge of 2–8–2s
assisted by a 2–10–2 or 2–10–4.

A train such as the eastbound 'Dominion' would be
divided to run through the mountain section in two
parts, separated by an interval of about ten minutes,

and each part might be heavy enough to be double-
headed. Up they would go with the engines in full gear
and full regulator, shooting their exhaust 100 feet
high up into the sky. The mountains would rever-
berate with the noise and then suddenly, mysteriously,
fall silent, for just as the leading portion entered the
upper of the two spiral tunnels on the section the
second part would be entering the lower tunnel. After
a brief pause the exhausts hammered out again as the
trains wound their way to the summit, speed barely
exceeding 10 mph (16 kph). Westbound trains crawled
down the hill at about the same speed with great
caution, the bells on the locomotives clanging continuously. At night the spectacle had a new fascination.
Watchers on the mountain slopes could follow the
progress of a train as a string of lights crawling along
the rock face. They would disappear into the first spiral
tunnel, then be glimpsed again higher up and moving
in the opposite direction as the train emerged. Another
blackout followed as it was swallowed by the upper
tunnel, then the lights were seen again, higher still and
having changed direction a second time.

North America had its 12-coupled rigid-frame locomotives on the Union Pacific, built for working fast
freight between Ogden, Idaho and Cheyenne, Wyoming, a distance of 483 miles (777.3 km). The first
appeared in 1926 and four years later the railway had
a fleet of 86. Ogden-Cheyenne is a mountain section
with a long climb of 1-in-88 going east. After the summit there is easier going to Laramie with a ruling
gradient of 1-in-125, but from there to Cheyenne most
of the way is down a continuous gradient averaging
1-in-83 with two steep sections at 1-in-66. Westbound
trains starting out of Cheyenne were faced with a climb
of this severity extending for 31 miles (50 km). The UP
had some Mallet articulated compounds in service, but
their speed over the easier sections of the route was too
low to maintain the necessary flow of traffic without

Above: East Broad Top Railroad 2–8–2 No 17 working for her living with a coal train before the line became part of the leisure industry.
Above left: The pull-out regulator and brake controller in a typical US steam locomotive cab layout. Note the engineer's gauntlets.
Left: Accelerating after picking up cars, a narrow-gauge Denver & Rio Grande Western freight train near Alamosa emits a sculptured plume of smoke.

impeding passenger trains. There were also some ten-coupled engines but axle-load limitations ruled out development of a more powerful design with this wheel arrangement. The railway therefore felt obliged to go to a 12-coupled design, and with the heavy piston thrust that would be necessary it had to be a three-cylinder engine with divided drive.

The UP 4–12–2s were the largest three-cylinder engines ever built. The coupled wheelbase was 30 feet 8 inches (9.35 m), which was 4 feet 5 inches (1.35 m) longer than that of the closest equivalent in this respect, the Bulgarian 2–12–4T. To get the engine safely around curves the leading single-axle truck had a controlled lateral movement of 6.25 inches (158 mm), while the first and sixth coupled axles were allowed a spring-cushioned sideplay of 1 inch (25.4 mm). The thickness and spacing of the driving wheel flanges varied; originally the fourth pair of driving wheels were flangeless but had wider treads than the others. Thin flanges were added later. The two outside cylinders measured 27 by 32 inches (686 by 813 mm) and the inside cylinder 27 by 31 inches (686 by 787 mm). Boiler pressure was 220 lb per square inch (15.5 kg/sq cm). As built the class had two sets of Walschaerts valve gear. The valve of the inside cylinder was originally driven by rocking levers on the Gresley principle, but this arrangment was removed and a third set of Walschaerts gear was fitted later.

In service the locomotives increased the traffic capacity of the section between Green River and Laramie by 44 percent compared with what the 2–10–0s could shift. They could take 4000 US tons/3571 UK tons/3628 tonnes from Ogden up the bank to Green River, cruising on level stretches at 35 to 40 mph (56 to 64 kph). Banking assistance was pro-

vided uphill when loads reached 125 cars. Coming west from Cheyenne trains were banked up the 31 miles (49.8 km) of continuous gradient whatever the head-end power. The 4–12–2s could take the same load as a Mallet on this section at a slightly higher speed. In the late 1930s, however, they were joined by a new family of UP articulated locomotives – the 4–6–6–4s of the 'Challenger' class – and some were transferred to the Idaho Division of the system.

As conceived by its inventor, Anatole Mallet, the locomotive named after him was a compound, but its distinctive feature was its articulated construction. Purists sometimes object that an articulated locomotive on Mallet's system but with simple propulsion is not a Mallet, but the objection is overruled by common usage. A locomotive built on the Mallet system actually comprises two steam engines, the rear one in a fixed frame and the leading one in a separate truck which can swing about a pivot at the rear and is coupled to the rear engine by an articulated joint through which the tractive effort is transmitted. The forward end of the boiler and smokebox is supported by a bearing surface on the leading truck. Basically this was the arrangement of the 'Challenger' class, plus leading and trailing guiding bogies, but the front and rear engines were three-cylinder simple-expansion machines, and developments in articulation and bearers had produced a Mallet-style locomotive suitable for speeds around 60 mph (97 kph), which was what the Union Pacific needed for its fastest freight services. Alco supplied UP with 105 of these locomotives. Others by the same builder went to Delaware & Hudson, Denver & Rio Grande Western, Western Pacific and the Clinchfield Railroad of Tennessee. The United States was an inveterate user of Mallets, both compound and simple-expansion, dating back to some Alco 0–6–6–0 units on the Baltimore & Ohio in 1903.

The 'Challengers' pointed ahead to the ultimate in the American Mallet, again produced for the Ogden–Green River section of the Union Pacific. These were the 4000 class 4–8–8–4s of 1942–44, better known as the 'Big Boys.' The nearest previous approaches to an articulated locomotive of comparable size had been the Northern Pacific 2–8–8–4 of 1927 and the Southern Pacific 4–8–8–2 of 1937, the latter built 'back-to-front' so that the cab and the four-wheel bogie were at the leading end, and the crew was less troubled by the exhaust in long single-line tunnels.

The 'Big Boys' were special-purpose machines, destined not only for a particular route but also for a particular traffic – fast fruit trains of 70 refrigerator cars. They were therefore designed for a top speed of 70 mph (113 kph). Appearing in 1941, however, they were soon plunged into wartime traffic conditions which made the 3200 US tons/2857 UK tons/2902 tonnes of the fruit trains seem relatively modest and soon loads were being hauled over the gradients at both ends of the Ogden–Cheyenne line that needed two 'Big Boys' in tandem. These were the largest and heaviest steam locomotives ever built, weighing 534 US tons/477 UK tons/484 tonnes with engine and tender and measuring 132 feet 11 inches (40.5 m) overall. The tender ran on 14 wheels, consisting of a leading four-wheel truck and a ten-wheel fixed wheelbase, and carried 25 US tons/22 UK tons/23 tonnes of coal and 25,000 US gallons/20,817 UK gallons/94,635 liters of water. Majestic in every respect, the 'Big Boys' were a worthy finale to the international cavalcade of Mallet articulated locomotives.

4. Standardization in Germany

Political events did much to shape the development of the steam locomotive in Germany. When the German Empire was founded in 1871, the various state systems found themselves working alongside a host of private companies which were supplied with locomotives by a highly competitive industry whose member firms were more interested in stamping their products with their own individuality than in moving toward any measure of uniformity. The Prussian State Railways were the first to tackle the problem of deciding which classes to retain and what should be built in the future.

Although the lack of standardization had been severely felt in military transport during the war of 1870, most of the state systems failed to learn the lesson and continued building locomotives in rich variety. In Prussia, however, two standard types were introduced as early as 1877 – a 2–4–0 for passenger traffic and a 2–6–0 for freight traffic – and in the next five years 11 more designs were approved for construction. Nonetheless Germany entered the 1914–1918 war with a locomotive stock almost as variegated as before, although this time the consequences were more serious. A demand for standardization in 1917 came too late.

Political changes after 1918 brought amalgamation of the state systems into the Deutsche Reichsbahn

in 1920. The new organization took over more than 350 different types of steam locomotive but as a result of wartime losses, reparations and serious arrears of repairs the stock of serviceable motive power was much depleted. Quick action was necessary. First the well-proven types of the former individual state railways were reviewed and it was proposed to select a limited number for further building using standard components. This idea was later discarded, however, and it was decided to build a completely new range of standard types. For this purpose the newly formed Transport Ministry set up a committee of specialists from the railways and the locomotive manufacturing industry to lay down essential guidelines for developing a new fleet of steam locomotives, and to decide on the types to be built.

Eventually the committee created a Standardization Office to which was entrusted the task not simply of agreeing on principles but of producing complete designs for the new locomotives, working in collaboration with the manufacturers who would produce them. By 1922 the Office had approved 14 designs, including two Pacifics with 6-foot 3-inch (1905 mm) wheels for express passenger traffic, one of which (class 01) was a two-cylinder simple, and the other (class 02) a four-cylinder compound. Although opinion generally favored simple propulsion it was

Left: Ex-Prussian P8 class 4–6–0s continued to be built after grouping of the individual State Railways into the Reichsbahn. No 038 772–0 leaves Wolfrach, now in Western Germany, with a local train. Right: Another view of 038 772–0 at Wolfrach.

decided to make a practical comparison between the two systems before completing the program. No overall advantage was found in compounding, however, and the 02s were converted to class 01 simple Pacifics between 1938 and 1942.

The first of the standard locomotives to appear was 02 compound Pacific No 02.001 which Henschel completed in time for it to be shown at the German Transport Exhibition in Munich in September 1925. Later in the same year the first 01 class locomotives were ready, while 1926 saw the two 2–10–0 goods (or freight) locomotive classes, 43 and 44. In all, locomotives of 29 standard classes were built between 1925 and 1945, both tender and tank engines to cover all types of duty – the range was extended to cover changing circumstances first in peacetime conditions and then in war.

In the early years of the plan deliveries of certain

Left: A prewar Reichsbahn 01 as rebuilt by the present Reichsbahn in East Germany and reclassified 01[5]. The train is at Honebach and is a Paris–Warsaw express. Below: Standard 01 class Pacific No 001 150–2 climbs the 1-in-40 bank between Neuenmarkt Wirsberg and Marktschorgast (the *Schiefe Ebene*) with the 06.04 Wurzburg-Hof on 17 May 1973.

classes of locomotives which had been operated by the former individual state railways continued while others were modified to improve their performance. Among the latter was the ex-Prussian State Railways P8 class 4–6–0 which, although dating from 1906 and of obsolescent design, remained a versatile and economical locomotive and a favorite with the staff. One reason for keeping the older designs in service was that the two Pacific classes were built with an axle-load of 22 US tons/20 UK tons/20 tonnes, which was too heavy for some of the main lines, and some time elapsed before all important routes could be brought up to the 20-ton standard. Soon, however, a new light Pacific with the same wheel diameter as the 01s but 20 US-ton/18 UK-ton/18-tonne axle-load was added to the standard classes. A preproduction series of three locomotives was turned out by Borsig in 1930. Full production began in the following year and continued until 1938. These engines were class 03. The class 44 2–10–0 was a three-cylinder simple, and as the transport requirements of the expanding Reich grew, other three-cylinder classes were introduced: the 05 streamlined 4–6–4, the 06 4–8–4, the class 45 2–10–2 and the heavy freight 2–10–2 tank locomotives of classes 84 and 85. There were also variations of earlier two-cylinder designs in three-cylinder form, such as the 01[10] streamlined Pacific class on which construction began in 1939. Orders had been placed for 250 of these locomotives but only 55 were completed when building was halted in 1940 to allow manufacturers to concentrate on wartime 'austerity' 2–10–0s.

Certain features ran through all the standard classes. Working pressure in the principal types rose from previous levels to 227 lb per square inch (16 kg/sq cm). Simple expansion with long-travel piston valves was general after the rejection of compounding. All locomotives had bar frames. In classes with a wide firebox, the trailing truck was set well back from the rear coupled axle to obtain optimum air inlet and ash removal conditions. A row of fitments lent interest to the top of the boiler, including a pump-operated feedwater heater, two domes (one covering the top feed arrangement from the feedwater heater) and one or, on ten-coupled engines, two large-capacity sandboxes. There were no splashers and the driving wheels revolved fully exposed beneath high running plates. Smoke deflector plates extended downward to the running plate but after the war these were replaced by a shallower version supported from the smokebox with its lower edge well above running-plate level. All engines had to pass through a loading gauge 13 feet 9.5 inches (4.2 m) high, which meant a very low chimney on large-boilered locomotives. However, detachable extensions were provided and these were virtually a permanent fixture on locomotives allocated to the principal main lines where a height of 14 feet 11 inches (4.5 m) was permitted. Commentators have noted how closely the general appearance of the standard locomotives approximated to that of the Prussian State Railway designs.

New locomotives were tested on the road with a special test train consisting of a dynamometer car and brake locomotives which was based at Grüne-wald. At that time the General Manager of the Reichsbahn was Dr Julius Dorpmüller, an engineer by training, who would often appear unannounced at Grünewald to accompany the train when important tests were afoot. These were pleasant occasions, much appreciated by the staff, concluding with a repast of smoked ham and the best champagne thoughtfully provided by the general manager himself. Grünewald was equipped with a roller test plant for express locomotives on which two-cylinder types could 'run' at 50 mph (81 kph) and three- or four-cylinder types at 62 mph (100 kph). A Prussian P8 was once pushed up to 74 mph (119 kph). However, it was difficult to keep slidebars and crossheads cool without the normal draft caused by motion and the slidebars of the P8 became red hot after 20 minutes. The 03 Pacifics could not be tested on the plant.

'Design by committee' seems unlikely to bring individual personalities to the fore, but the guiding spirit of Reichsbahn design, Dr R P Wagner, was well known throughout the locomotive world. He had been associated with the work from its inception and from his appointment as Chief of Motive Power Construction for the Reichsbahn in July 1923 he presided over its progress for two decades. Wagner's writings, and his technical papers delivered to institutions and learned societies both within and outside Germany earned him international recognition; it was his particular pride to have been elected an Honorary Member of the British Institution of Locomotive Engineers and to be the only German Member of the Royal Society. A British railway engineer who met him in the 1930s remembered him as 'a great bear of a man' and noted that his observance of the salutes and greetings which had become mandatory among German officialdom was somewhat perfunctory compared with that of certain of his colleagues. This independence of mind and behavior had its effect on his career in the war years. In contemporary pictures Wagner is unmistakable, usually being the tallest member of any group.

Experiment proceeded in parallel with standardization. In 1928 a Pacific was built with a Löffler high-pressure boiler in which steam was generated at 120 atmospheres in a special drum and fed to the high-pressure cylinders. The exhaust, at 18 atmospheres, passed through a heat-exchanger and the condensate was returned to the drum. The central low-pressure cylinder took steam from the boiler at 15 atmospheres, which was exhausted into the atmosphere and provided the draft for the fire. A very high degree of super-heat was used.

The trials, mostly between Potsdam, Burg and Magdeburg, were not without incident. A colleague of Wagner's recalls an occasion when one of the tubes in the high-pressure section of the firebox burst. Steam escaped into the inner firebox with a deafening noise, forcing red-hot coals through the grate into the ashpan. Luckily the firedoor was closed, but it was distorted by the pressure and the cab was filled with a cloud of coal dust. The crew and observers on the footplate emerged from the incident unharmed but as black as chimney sweeps. A representative of the builders, Schwartzkopff, accompanied the locomotive on its trials, and the same source recalls that despite this and other less dramatic mishaps his confidence was never shaken. Some of the Reichsbahn officers were less sure. It was so often necessary to take the locomotive off the train at Kirchmoser, where there was a repair facility, that the place became known as 'Schwartzkopff's Rest.' The locomotive was never taken over by the Reichsbahn. After lying idle for a few years at the builder's works it was finally cut up. A clause in the contract required Schwartzkopff to replace the high-pressure locomotive with a standard class 01 Pacific should the former prove unsuitable

for service but, in the end, a class 03 Pacific was supplied to settle the affair.

Krupp and Maffei each built a 4–6–2 turbine locomotive for the Reichsbahn in the 1920s and both were taken into the railway's stock with the numbers T 18 1001 and T 18 1002 respectively. The Krupp locomotive was damaged by bombing and taken out of service in 1940 but during its working life had yielded very favorable fuel consumption results. The Maffei locomotive was less successful in this respect. It was withdrawn and broken up in the war years.

The 1930s saw the zenith of the steam locomotive in Germany, spurred on by the demand for faster trains between the principal cities in the country and the revised Reichsbahn timetable of 1924. Competition from electric and diesel motive power was also beginning to be felt, particularly in the proliferation of fast railcar services. Early in the decade Borsig had experimented with streamlining Pacifics Nos

03.154 and 03.193 (lighter versions of the 01 class). Although the results did not fulfill expectations, the tests led to the building of the fully streamlined class 05 4–6–4s, designed specifically for working non-stop supplementary-fare trains between Berlin and Hamburg. They were required to run continuously on the level with a 280-US-ton/250-UK-ton/254-tonne train at 93 mph (150 kph) – the normal maximum for steam locomotives – but to be capable of 109 mph (175 kph) if necessary to regain time. They departed from the standard classes in various respects, for example the 7-foot 6.5-inch (2300-mm) driving wheels and the 284 lb per square inch (20 kg/sq cm) boiler pressure. Nos 05.001 and 05.002 appeared in the German railway centenary year, 1935, and earned Wagner a Gold Medal from the British Institution of Locomotive Engineers, an honor which had not been conferred for some time previously. A third member of the class produced in 1938 was equipped to burn pulverized coal and had the cab at the front.

Above: East Germany left some of the 01s in their original condition, among them 01036, seen leaving Bebra, the border station, with a Frankfurt–Cottbus train on 20 May 1967.

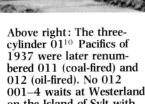

Above right: The three-cylinder 01[10] Pacifics of 1937 were later renumbered 011 (coal-fired) and 012 (oil-fired). No 012 001—4 waits at Westerland on the Island of Sylt with a train for Hamburg.

In 1936 No 05.002 achieved a world-record speed for steam of 124.5 mph (200.4 kph) with a special 336-US-ton/300-UK-ton/305-tonne test train. It was a triumph for the design team, heightened by the current rivalry with the high-speed diesel railcars. A humorous drawing showed No 05.002, which had an exterior somewhat like a whale, opening its stream-lined smokebox casing like a pair of jaws to swallow what was apparently the 'Flying Hamburger.' Wagner had a print of the drawing on the wall of his office behind his desk. When the British Institution of Loco-motive Engineers held its summer meeting in Germany in 1936, No 05.002 worked a special train for the delegates from Berlin to Hamburg and back. The load, with four coaches and a dynamometer car, was 158 US ton/141 UK tons/143 tonnes. After stopping at Wittenberge the train ran the next 27.4 miles (44 km) to Ludwigslust in 20 minutes 58 seconds, averaging 111.6 mph (179.6 kph) for 4.7 miles (7.5 km) and reaching a maximum of 118 mph (190 kph).

On the return trip a broken water connection between engine and tender necessitated an emergency stop which was made good from a speed of nearly 100 mph (161 kph) in exactly 60 seconds. After temporary repairs at Wittenberge the 70.1 miles (112.8 km) to a signal stop 13.9 miles (22.4 km) outside Berlin were run at an average speed of 86.7 mph (139.5 kph) with a top speed of 103.5 mph (166.6 kph). Steam trains on the Berlin–Hamburg route at this period were normally restricted to a maximum of 93 mph (150 kph) but were required to average 74.2 mph (119.4 kph) from Berlin to Hamburg and 73.7 mph (118.6 kph) in the reverse direction. The 03 Pacifics of the standard series, but streamlined, performed equally well on this route.

Wagner's reaction to the *Mallard* speed record of 1938 seems to have lacked enthusiasm. In a speech on one occasion he could not resist commenting that it had been achieved down a gradient of 1-in-200 (the 05.002 record had been on the level) and he

quoted a comment attributed to Charles S Lake, technical editor of the British journal *The Railway Gazette*, that there might justifiably be doubts as to whether the Blue Ribbon of speed for steam had in fact been wrested from Germany.

Compounding reappeared briefly in 1932 in con-nection with experiments with a 'medium-pressure' boiler working at 25 atmospheres ('medium' in rela-tion to the 120 atmospheres high-pressure boiler in the Schwartzkopff experiment). The 25 atmospheres pressure was considered too high for expansion in a single stage and so orders were placed for two com-pound Pacifics and a compound 2–10–0 freight locomotive; also for a 4–6–0 on the Stumpf/Wagner system. Professor Stumpf had devised a system based on stationary engine practice at the beginning of the century in which expanded steam was exhausted half-way through the piston stroke through a ring of orifices at the middle of the cylinder. The main ports therefore only passed live steam at high temperature and condensation on the cylinder walls was reduced. The experiments were short-lived but the Pacifics were rebuilt with a normal-pressure boiler and re-numbered 02.101/2. In this form they worked alongside other 02s on the Leipzig-Hof-Regensburg section of the important north-south express route from Berlin to Munich. The Berlin–Leipzig section was the province of 01s and 03s as well as former Prussian P10s and S10[1]s.

Although the streamlining of the two 03s by Borsig was not followed up at once, more of these engines (built in 1939) were streamlined and classi-fied 03[10]. A contemporary of the 05 class streamlined 4–6–4s was a high-speed streamlined tank engine of the same wheel arrangement, No 61.001, which, after trials and demonstration runs, went into service between Berlin and Dresden with a train of special coaches designed by the Wegmann Company. A similar tank engine, but with an additional axle in the trailing truck, giving it the unusual 4–6–6 wheel arrangement, followed in 1939.

Wagner's career reached its climax in the middle

1930s. In the second half of the decade there were signs that his star was setting. His powers were diminished by a new organization at Reichsbahn headquarters, and his future was not helped by his attitude to the Nazi Party. He once described the Rome–Berlin axis as 'a cheap tin tube for blowing hot air across the Alps' and he was less than complimentary about the eagle symbols in aluminum with which the Reichsbahn proposed to adorn its locomotives. In this tense atmosphere criticism of some

mountain retreat, a young engineer approached the Doctor and asked to take his photograph standing in front of the engine. Wagner shook his head. 'No,' he said, 'the return crank arm's too short.' He already showed signs of nervous strain, and when a crash program of locomotive building for the war effort was launched under the direction of Albert Speer, Minister for Armaments and Munitions, it was clear that the future lay with younger men. Wagner retired on health grounds on 1 October 1942.

Above: A postwar Reichsbahn light Pacific of the prewar Reichsbahn's 03 class is studied with interest by an observer in Leipzig Hbf.

aspects of his standard locomotive policy flourished, and centered particularly on the development of a large streamlined three-cylinder 4–8–4 for duties which were beyond the capacity of the 03 Pacifics. A feature of the design was that by adjustment of the weight on the bogies, the driving axle-load could be set at either 20 or 22 US tons/18 or 20 UK tons/18 or 20 tonnes. This was class 06 of 1939. Only two engines were built. The international crisis and the outbreak of war imposed a complete revision of locomotive building policy in which Wagner played a diminishing part.

Seeing his precepts set aside while he was still in office was a bitter experience for Wagner. There is a memory of him at Berchtesgarden in 1942 during trials of a new 2–6–2 for secondary passenger service for which he was responsible. During a stop in the newly built Berchtesgarden station with its platforms for receiving special trains conveying Party leaders, Ministers and deputations to visit the Führer in his

After the war Wagner's reputation outside Germany as a locomotive engineer earned him an appointment through the British occupation authorities to the Reichsbahn management in Bielfeld where he headed a group concerned with the ordering and distribution of materials and acted as a liaison officer between the railroads and the Allies until a second retirement. Thereafter he continued to serve as an Honorary Member of the Locomotive Committee of the Bundesbahn, interesting himself particularly in questions of metallurgy and filing patents on this subject when in his seventies. In 1952, to his great pleasure, his membership of the Institution of Locomotive Engineers and of the Royal Society, suspended during the war, was restored. He died after a short illness on 14 February 1953.

Up to the war the German locomotive building firms pursued their individual development programs and, indeed, once orders for standard locomotives had been placed, by the later 1930s they were intro-

Above: The class 65 2–8–4 tanks were a Bundesbahn design, appearing in 1951, but were soon displaced by diesels. No 065 001–0 sails through leafy setting at Laudenbach.

ducing detail features of their own as construction proceeded. One product of this period was overtaken by the war – a Henschel locomotive with its four driving axles individually powered by two-cylinder vee-form steam engines which was not completed until 1941. The birth of the idea, however can be traced back to 1937 when two Henschel engineers had discussions with the Reichsbahn on the steam railcars they were developing, with the emphasis on burning cheaper fuel. This project was running into problems and seemed liable to be cancelled. Henschel had to find something new to interest the steam partisans in the Reichsbahn, who already saw themselves challenged in some areas by the success of the high-speed diesel railcars. A small two-cylinder steam engine had been developed as a blower and feed pump drive for one of the Henschel steam railcars and it was decided that this could be developed for traction. The outcome was the construction of the Reichsbahn's 1–Do–1 locomotive No 19.001. In

appearance the high-speed steam engines, with their two cylinders forming a 90-degree vee, were similar to an internal combustion engine. They were mounted alternately on the right-hand and left-hand sides of the main frames and drove the axles directly through flexible couplings. Although designed for a top speed of 110 mph (177 kph) the driving wheels were only of 4 feet 1.25 inches (1251 mm) in diameter which gave locomotives a very high maximum tractive effort. The valve gear and piston valves were enclosed in an oil-tight casing forming a unit with the crankcase. The locomotive was fully streamlined although the casing was slightly raised along the driving wheelbase.

From the first trials it was evident that there would be no question of early introduction of the locomotive in regular express service. The boiler did not steam well, the drawgear lacked strength, and there was some leakage of steam past the piston rings. This may have contributed to an exceptionally high steam consumption which limited the radius of action of the

Above: Class 23 No 23 047 threads the intricacies of the layout through the yards at Saarbrücken. Previous page: A postwar DB class 23 mixed traffic 2–6–2 leaves Bullay with the 17.00 to Trier on 28 August 1969.

locomotive in spite of its high-capacity tender. Tractive effort did not remain constant for a particular setting of the controls but was found to increase although no alteration had been made. All these and other problems required investigation on a scale which was not practical in wartime. No 19.001 went into retreat near Hamburg until the end of the war, when it was sent to the United States for further study of its possibilities. However, steam-locomotive building in the United States was already in decline and in 1952 the locomotive was scrapped.

The war brought a four-year plan of locomotive construction, reorganization of the locomotive industry on mass-production lines, and an end to individual initiative by the locomotive building firms. Construction continued of the 2–10–0 standard freight 50 class locomotive which had been introduced in 1938. The design was soon simplified in some respects and the later engines reclassified 50UK (*Ubergangs-kriegslokomotiv*). As more territories became occupied in Europe the demand for motive power grew continuously, and after control of production was taken over by the Ministry of Armaments and Munitions in 1942 a new design of 2–10–0 was introduced. It was generally similar to the 50 class but planned to economize in man-hours for construction and in scarce materials. It was called

class 52. Over 6000 were built, many of them coming from works outside Germany.

The war in Russia took German locomotives deep into a territory with meager provision for watering. Further class 52s were therefore built with condensing tenders and classified 52KON. Their equipment differed from that of the rest of the class, for as the exhaust steam was led back to the condensing tender the draft had to be supplied by a fan in the smokebox driven by an exhaust turbine. Further exhaust turbines drove the fans in the tender that drew air through the cooling elements. The flow was regulated by adjustable shutters which could be closed altogether in severe weather. With this equipment the locomotives could run 625 miles (1005.8 km) without rewatering, an ability which proved valuable during the withdrawal from Russia when water supplies were destroyed by Soviet troops or partisans, as well as during the initial advance.

All these classes had axle-loads between 17 and 18 US tons/15 and 16 UK tons/15 and 16 tonnes. A heavier locomotive was proposed in 1942 and materialized a year later as the class 42 2–10–0. Maximum axle-load for most of the class was 20 US tons/18 tons/18 tonnes but a series for the Austrian railways was modified in various ways to reduce this figure to 19 US tons/17 UK tons/17 tonnes.

Cylinder bore in class 42 was increased by 1.18 inches (29.9 mm) to take advantage of the higher adhesive weight. Classes 50, 52 and 42 were known collectively as the *Kriegslokomotiven* War locomotives); over 8000 were built between 1941 and 1945 and many of them found widespread use in the postwar years.

The long survival of main-line steam in Western and Eastern Germany after the war may seem surprising considering the development of long-distance electric traction in the country. As the European crisis deepened in the late 1930s, however, strategic considerations imposed too great a commitment for any motive power with its range of action limited by an electrical supply system which, moreover, was vulnerable to attack. In the immediate aftermath of the war locomotive building in Germany was not permitted but the ban was lifted in 1950. After the division of the country, West Germany had about 17,700 steam locomotives, a total which far exceeded its requirements. A wave of scrapping began, in which survivors of the pre-Reichsbahn State systems suffered most. Seven new classes were proposed embodying developments in construction and practice which had taken place since the '1925 Standard,' but in the end only five were built, and in limited quantities. At the same time existing classes

which were suitable for retention were modernized. New boilers with combustion chambers were designed for the Pacific Classes 01, 03, and their three-cylinder variants, 01^{10} and 03^{10}. The three-cylinder 01s had been put into store toward the end of the war but were returned to traffic after 1945 with their steamlining removed. Troubles developed in the all-welded boilers, however, and they went back into store until the middle 1950s. In its final years this series was reclassified 011 or, if fitted for oil-burning, 012.

The first postwar locomotives were class 82, a 0–10–0 design for the West German Bundesbahn Class 94 of the former Prussian State Railways. The first of 41 engines in this series appeared in 1950. Class 82 was employed on heavy shunting and slow passenger duties but had mechanical weaknesses in the arrangement for allowing radial movement of the leading and trailing pairs of coupled axles which led to frequent renewal of components. The last of the class was scrapped in the spring of 1972 at which time 24 of the ex-Prussian class 94 veterans they were intended to replace were still in service.

Class 23 also appeared in 1950. This was a mixed traffic 2–6–2 similar to the wartime locomotives of the same class. Only two of the originals were built, however, and they both remained in East Germany

Above: Class 44, a three-cylinder simple 2–10–0, was one of the early standard classes. A postwar survivor heads a freight train near Singen on the Swiss border.

Left: One of the *Kriegslo-komotiven.* a 2–10–0 of class 52 on postwar passenger duty.

after the war. The Bundesbahn class 23s were virtually a new design and differed appreciably from the forerunners in appearance with the removal of the top feed dome and sandboxes from the top of the boiler, while a wide-diameter chimney encircled the exhaust outlets of the air and feedwater pumps as well as the main exhaust from the cylinders. There were some superheater troubles with these engines and some were rebuilt for saturated steam. Riding was poor – a British commentator has written of 'a fore and aft shuttling motion' which could be felt in the train – and the weight distribution between the axles was the cause of other problems. Nonetheless, this was a numerous class, comprising 105 locomotives, and for some years worked international expresses between the Dutch border and Cologne.

In 1951 the first 2–8–4 tank engines of class 65 appeared but the class was soon outdated by the V100 diesels. Its maximum speed in passenger traffic of only 53 mph (85 kph) did not compare favorably with the ex-Prussian class 78 4–6–4 tanks, and although a powerful machine its usefulness in freight traffic was limited by its fuel capacity. Its axle-load of 19 US tons/17 UK tons/17 tonnes also restricted its employment on secondary lines. Only 18 of the class were built. The most successful postwar Bundesbahn design was the three-cylinder class 10 Pacific of 1958, but only two were built. With their good riding qualities at speed and economy in fuel consumption they would have had a distinguished future had they not been overtaken by the rapid development of electric and diesel traction.

In all the postwar steam locomotive designs special attention was given to the comfort of the crew. Cabs had large skylights in the roof, improved ventilation and footwarmers for winter use. Instruments were grouped together and all controls arranged so as to be accessible while seated. At the same time many locomotives of the East German Reichsbahn were modernized in various ways: roller bearings were fitted, equipment for oil-firing installed and so on. In the last days of steam in Western Germany the best-known locomotives to foreign visitors were the 01 and 03 Pacifics and survivors of the *Kriegslokomotiven.*

Pockets of main-line steam lasted until the 1970s. One result of the partition of Germany was that the importance of the town of Hof in northeast Bavaria as a junction of several principal north-south routes was diminished. The proximity of the new frontier virtually deprived it of a direct outlet to the north and as a result the lines through Hof were not electrified. The service from Hof westward to Lichtenfels remained almost 100 percent steam-worked until the end. (Some of the steam locomotives ran to and from Bamberg on the electrified line.) Tank locomotives of classes 64 and 86 continued to work branch lines in the Hof–Nürnberg–Schwandorf triangle. On the Lichtenfels line there is a five-mile gradient at 1-in-40 (the Schiefe Ebene) between Neuenmarkt–Wirsberg and Marktschorgast and it was here that (until 1973) 01 Pacifics could be seen and heard in the manner that delights the steam enthusiast. The last main-line steam workings in Western Germany were in the north of the country on the line from Rheine to Emden where 0 42s, 0 43s, 0 44s and 0 50s worked heavy mineral trains right into 1977.

Steam motive power in East Germany, where the Reichsbahn name has survived, was inherited from the West and remained virtually unchanged for ten years. Thereafter some of the older types were rebuilt,

including 01 Pacifics, which in their revised form presented a considerably altered appearance. The Reichsbahn administration introduced its own 2–6–2 design, classified 023[10], to replace the Prussian P8. The prewar 4–6–6 tank, already noted as the one used on the Berlin–Dresden one-class trains before the war, was rebuilt in 1961 as a 4–6–2 tender locomotive. Here, too, electric and diesel power made rapid inroads but steam lingered on a number of narrow-gauge lines.

In West Germany a renumbering system suitable for data processing by computer was introduced in 1968–69. Class 01, for example, became 001, the additional 0 representing a steam locomotive, and a seventh figure was added as a check digit. A typical number of an 01 Pacific would, therefore, be 001.088–4. The first three digits show motive power and class, the next three are the individual locomotive number, and the digit after the hyphen is derived from the others for checking purposes.

Before leaving the German railway scene it is worth recalling that Germany's school of locomotive design not only took ideas from other countries but also contributed a great deal to the design of others and exported a considerable number of ideas as well as locomotives.

Possibly the greatest advance in design since the earliest days of George Stephenson himself was the high-degree superheater developed by Wilhelm Schmidt. It was, indeed, one of the few locomotive features to be adopted on a truly worldwide basis. Its purpose was to reduce heat loss in the cylinders by eliminating condensation during admission and expansion and re-evaporation at exhaust. The incoming steam from the regulator was divided into a number of small tube elements each leading into an enlarged flue tube in the boiler. The result in the original design of 1902 was a gain of 20 to 30 percent in steam consumption. Its success was such that by 1914 it had become an almost universal feature on locomotives in many countries.

The work of Wagner and Professor Nordmann to establish the ideal relationship between boiler and tube dimensions and the flow of hot gases to obtain maximum steaming capacity and efficiency also established a formula which was applied universally in locomotive design. Many of the engines designed for the Reichsbahn after 1918 were subsequently to be seen in other countries, either in their original form or adapted to a particular country's needs. In France the Est was so impressed by the German G12 class 2–10–0s, it had acquired in 1919 as reparation for World War I damage that it built 195 similar engines under license from 1926. At the same time, Belgium received some 1960 German locomotives of 43 different types and many of these were still in service when the Nazis overran that country again in 1940 – and indeed were still being used for a decade after World War II. Poland, Bulgaria, Yugoslavia and Turkey also received large numbers of German locomotives or built them themselves. For Bulgaria, German manufacturers improved on their designs to produce locomotives suited to that country's needs.

Thus, it was by way of intentional exports and foreign manufacture under license, and by enforced dispersal as reparation after two world wars that the typically Teutonic locomotives – by no means beautiful but well-proportioned and thoroughly designed – had their influence on the steam railroads of many countries.

5. The Steam Locomotive in France

There still exists in some corners of the world the mistaken belief that the French are insensible to the fascination of the steam locomotive. To realize its falseness one has only to look at railway scenes painted by the French Impressionists of the 19th century, or preserved in words of such great novels as Emile Zola's *La Bête Humaine*.

To a generation that remembers the late 1930s, *La Bête Humaine* was a superb railway film, its action set in that period. Jean Renoir's film updated the novel, which ends in 1870 with a driverless troop train bound for the front in the Franco–Prussian war careering to inevitable destruction, filled with inebriated soldiers singing and shouting, unconscious of their doom. It is a curious book, its central character an engine driver who sees his locomotive as a living creature. On an early page there is a descriptive passage vibrant with the atmosphere of the steam railway, seen through the eyes of Rouband at Le Havre station:

'A powerful express engine with a single pair of huge driving wheels for eating up the miles, stood alone with smoke billowing from its chimney and climbing slowly straight upwards in the still air. But his attention was focused on the 3.25 to Caen, already loaded and waiting for its engine. He could not see the engine, for it was on the other side of the bridge, but he could hear it whistling impatiently for the road in a series of short, sharp blasts. An order was shouted, and acknowledged by an answering screech from the whistle. Then, before the engine moved off, there was a moment of

silence, suddenly broken by the opening of the cylinder drain cocks and the deafening hiss of escaping steam sweeping along the tracks. He saw a great white cloud emerging from under the bridge, swirling and eddying like snow and climbing up through the girders. Half the scene before him was blotted out with white, while the thickening smoke from the other engine spread an ever-growing veil of black. Beyond the obscurity, the sound of shunters' horns, men's shouts and the clatter of turntables were half muffled. Part of the cloud thinned and was rent, and through the gap he saw two trains passing each other, one from Versailles which was running into the station and one on its way out to Auteuil.'

Such was the scene from the Pont de l'Europe, outside the Gare St Lazare, where now the electric trains pass with a sigh and a swish of the pantograph on the contact wire that are scarcely heard above the roar of the road traffic. There is a similar scene in a painting by Monet. One wonders which came first — whether Zola's words inspired Monet's brush or were a verbal interpretation of the canvas. The two men belonged to the same circle. They can be seen together in a group portrait in the Galérie du Jeu de Paume in Paris surrounded by other literary and artistic figures of the day.

In another passage Zola describes the work of an engine crew on the footplate with a precision and detail that must surely have come from personal observation. The central character of the novel, the driver Jacques Lantier, and his fireman, Pecqueux,

Left: Calais Maritime about 1904 with a de Glehn–du Bousquet 4–4–0 compound on a boat-train. Right: Crampton locomotive No 80, *Le Continent*, built for the Paris to Strasbourg Railway (later part of the Est system) in 1852, is displayed at the Gare de l'Est in Paris in 1939. The 'single pair of huge driving wheels' on the locomotive of the Ouest system which impressed Zola some 20 years later is already in evidence.

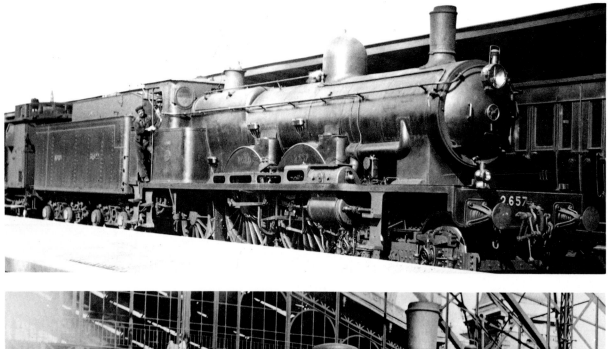

Top: De Glehn–du Bousquet
compound Atlantic No
221.2657 of the Nord at
Boulogne-sur-Mer Ville.
Above: Introduced in 1908,
the Nord four-cylinder
compound 4–6–0s of class
3500 remained in service
until the mid-1960s. No
3586 is at Calais in August
1935.

are working an express from Paris to Le Havre.

In analyzing Jacques Lantier's affection for his engine, Zola considers the mystery of how inanimate materials can come together to build not simply a machine but a personality:

'Like the other engines of the *Compagnie de l'Ouest* it bore the name as well as a number – *Lison*, a station in the Cotentin. But Jacques' affection had made a woman's name out of it, *La Lison*, and on his lips the name became a caress.

'For it was true. In the five years that he had driven *La Lison* he had come to love her. . . . She was gentle, obedient, easy to handle when starting a train, and a steady runner because she steamed well. People liked to say that if she started so easily it was something to do with the tires and, above all, the precise setting of the slide valves; similarly, if she was a good steamer and burned little fuel, that was due to the quality of the copper in the tubes and good design of the boiler. But he knew there was something else, for other engines built to exactly the same plans and assembled with equal care showed none of these qualities. Here there was a spirit, a mystery of manufacture, something hammered

into the metal by forging, diffused into every part by the workman's hands; the personality of the locomotive, its very life.'

This same elusive quality remained with the steam locomotive to the end. The engines Zola knew were simple-expansion machines, for compounding did not begin in France until later in the century. Compounding is a system for extracting maximum energy from the steam by expanding it down to a low pressure, much below that at which it normally escapes from the locomotive blastpipe. This has to be done in two stages; the high-pressure cylinders take steam direct from the boiler in the usual way, but instead of the steam being exhausted direct to the atmosphere it is fed to the steamchests of the low-pressure cylinders (or cylinder) and does more work in those cylinders before reaching the blastpipe.

The history of the French compound, which culminated after World War II, began with a 4–2–2–0 built for the Chemins de fer du Nord in 1885. Its design was a joint venture by Alfred de Glehn, Chief Engineer of the builders, the Société Alsacienne des Constructions Mécaniques (SACM), and Gaston du Bousquet, Chief Mechanical Engineer of the Nord. The wheel arrangement, with two uncoupled driving axles

powered individually by the high-pressure and low-pressure cylinders, was the same as that of one of the compound classes designed by Francis Webb for the London & North Western Railway in England, and a Webb compound of that type had in fact been bought by the Chemins de fer de l'Ouest in 1884. Both designs showed a tendency to slip when starting trains, but it was far more acute in the Webb engines, which were no more than a passing phase in the development of the British steam locomotive whereas the de Glehn-du Bousquet compound was the beginning of an era in France. Later compounds for the Nord, however, were 4–4–0s with coupled axles, and in 1900 the railway introduced a series of compound Atlantics which soon acquired widespread fame. Engines of the same design were bought by other railways in France, and one went to the Great Western Railway in England.

Soon the same compounding principle was applied in France to 4–6–0 locomotives, but the Nord Atlantics had a long and distinguished career. Various changes took place over the years. In later engines of the series the bogies wheelbase was lengthened and in 1912 they were superheated and the diameter of the high-pressure cylinders was increased. From 1930 some of the class were fitted with high-capacity tenders for making nonstop runs, such as Paris–Brussels. Up to World War II they could be seen on moderately loaded trains such as the 'Oiseau Bleu' and the 'Nord Express.' The Atlantics which finally worked these services were equipped with smoke deflectors and Lemaître blastpipes, somewhat to the detriment of their appearance. The engines could maintain 75 mph (120 kph) on the level with 448 US tons/400 UK tons/406 tonnes and on through services between Calais and the Mediterranean coast were known to recover as much as a 40-minute delay in leaving Calais with loads of between 180 and 225 US tons.

Like the other lines, the Nord advanced to the 4–6–0, putting its 3500 class with this wheel arrangement into traffic between 1908 and 1912. In January 1938, by which time they had become class 230D, there were still 149 in service. These were very versatile machines, and to this fact they owed their long lives, for when they were stepped down from the crack trains such as the 'Nord Express,' which they worked regularly before 1914, they acquitted themselves well on duties ranging from perishable freight running at express speed to the

Above: An earlier du Bousquet 4–6–0, class 230A, was also long-lived, No 3.181 having been photographed at the Gare du Nord in 1939.

humblest miscellaneous goods. They could run at 75 mph (120 kph) with trains of 560 US tons or climb a 1-in-200 gradient with a load of between 1000 and 1120 US tons. The only material modification made to them was in their exhaust arrangements. Otherwise there were mainly changes in detail, such as the fitting of turbo-generators for lighting, lengthening of the cab roof, and alterations in the lateral control of the bogie. Schmidt superheaters and piston valves were fitted in the 1930s. Du Bousquet had thought of a mechanical stoker but did not put the idea into practice. The floor of the tender coal space was inclined, however, to feed the fuel forward toward the fireman. With coupled wheels of only 5 feet 9 inches (1753 mm) in diameter, the 3500s anticipated the later general-purpose locomotive at a time when classes for different types of traffic were still proliferating, and they survived into the period when the ability of small-wheeled engines to run at high speeds was becoming generally accepted. Du Bousquet had allowed for the high-piston speeds necessary with 5-foot 9-inch (1753-mm) wheels by an increase in the cross-section of the steam passages of 25 percent on the high pressure side and 30 percent on the low pressure compared with the Atlantics.

In 1912 the Nord went ahead to compound Pacifics. They had been preceded by two compound 4–6–4s which had been planned by du Bousquet to cope with heavier trains than the 4–6–0s but did not appear until after his death. For this reason they were sometimes called 'the two orphans' and no more were built. The design was aimed at hauling trains of 448 US tons/400 UK tons/406 tonnes on the level at 75 mph (120 kph) and to maintain 60 mph (97 kph) up gradients of 1-in-200, but they were long and cumbersome engines and it soon became apparent that the same performance could be obtained from a 4–6–2. Motive power shortage after World War I made it necessary to keep the 4–6–4s in service, but with restricted route availability. In 1937 one of them was sectioned for display at an exhibition in Paris and in this condition actually survived World War II.

The first Nord Pacifics were the 20 engines of 1912. They immediately showed their advantage over the Atlantics in pulling power and speed. Before World War I, one of them was recorded as accelerating a 37-US-ton/33-UK-ton/34-tonne train from 35 to 64.5 mph (56 to 103.8 kph) up ten miles (16.1 km) of 1-in-200, another maintained 72–73 mph (116–118 kph) on the level with 414 US tons/370 UK tons/376 tonnes, and a third climbed the 1-in-200 of Survilliers bank with the 'Nord Express' weighing 594 US tons/530 UK tons/538 tonnes at a minimum of 50 mph (81 kph), afterward maintaining 64.5 mph (103.8 kph) along the level.

Even while the first 20 Pacifics were under construction, however, designers were thinking of something larger for the future, when the axle-load restriction of 19 US tons/17 UK tons/17 tonnes might be lifted. Action in this direction was delayed by the war and it was 1923/4 before a new series appeared. By this time the main lines had been relaid and could take an axle-load of 20.7 US tons/18.5 UK tons/18.8 tonnes. This new batch of 40 engines soon earned the name of Les Supers and did notable work on express trains of between 675 and 785 US tons. Their employment on boat trains between Paris and the Channel ports of Boulogne and Calais made them familiar to many travellers outside France. Cylinders were larger than in the first Pacifics and there was ten percent more adhesion weight. Working pressure was 227 lb per square inch (15.9 kg/sq cm) as before but grate area was increased from 34.7 to 37.7 square feet (3.2 to 3.5 sq m). One of these engines hauled the 'Golden Arrow' on its inaugural run on 11 September 1926 when the load of nine Pullman cars and a van totalled 608 US tons/543 UK tons/552 tonnes. Other services at this period loaded regularly up to between 675 and 725 US tons and on occasions the Calais–Mediterranean Express with 14 vehicles weighed even more. With loads of this order the Supers ran easily on the level at the official maximum speed of 75 mph (120 kph) and were little perturbed by gradients. On one occasion a special train of 851 US tons/760 UK tons/772 tonnes was taken up the 1-in-200 of Survilliers bank at 53 mph (85 kph). But still better was to come from later developments of steam motive power.

The success of the French compound locomotive

Above: The Nord Pacifics built between 1922 and 1931 were known as Les Supers. No 3.1255, of the batch built in 1930/31, waits to leave the Gare du Nord with an express to Boulogne and Calais in 1939.
Left: The Etat also developed Pacifics and improved the breed by rebuilding in the 1930s. The 231D class No 606 heads an express to Le Havre near Bonnières sur Seine in SNCF days.
Right: Packages in the van appeal mutely for attention while the crew of 231D755 enjoy a chat after arrival at Cherbourg.

in the de Glehn/du Bousquet tradition is a tribute to the competence of the crews and the standard of technical training they received. The de Glehn compound had two regulators, one controlling the high-pressure and one the low-pressure cylinders, and an intercepting valve. For starting a train it was usual to open both regulators but to leave the intercepting valve shut. Live steam then entered all four cylinders.

The high- or low-pressure regulators could also be used alone with the intercepting valve shut; the engine then worked as a two-cylinder simple with one or the other pair of cylinders in action. This arrangement was suitable for maneuvering a light locomotive.

In normal running the driver closed the low-pressure regulator and opened the intercepting valve controlling the engine with the high-pressure regulator. In this condition the engine worked as a four-cylinder compound, the steam exhausted from the high-pressure cylinders passing to the low-pressure cylinders. If the low-pressure regulator was opened in this condition, live steam was admitted to the low-pressure steamchests raising the pressure there to a

Below: Impressed by
Chapelon's rebuilding of a
PO Pacific, the Nord ordered
20 rebuilds from the PO
and had more locomotives
built on similar lines by
outside industry. These
were the Chapelons Nords,
class 231E. No 231E17
climbs out of Boulogne with
a Paris–Calais train.
Above: Chapelon Nord No
231E44 waits at Calais
Maritime to take the
'Golden Arrow' to Paris.
Above right: No 231E27
on shed at La Chapelle
Depot, Paris.

Left: The 4—8—0 class, 240P, was another conversion on Chapelon principles from earlier PLM locomotives and was carried out in wartime in 1940. The engine illustrated is 240P12.

Below: K class Pacific No 231K37 is about to leave Brussels Midi with the 18.57 express to Paris Nord.

limit set by a safety valve. This was called 'reinforced compound' working and could be used to boost the effort for short periods when accelerating a train or climbing a gradient.

Added to the above possibilities was the fact that the driver had separate sets of valve gear for the high-pressure and low-pressure cylinders under his control. Getting the best out of such a locomotive required skill and judgment, with quick interpretation of the readings given by the instruments in the cab. All this was forthcoming in full measure. It meant, of course, that the engine crews had to be supported by expertise and dedication on the part of the maintenance staff.

The Paris, Lyons & Mediterranean Railway (PLM) was another early and ardent supporter of compounding. In fact its curious 4–4–0s of 1894, the Machines à bec with their wedge-shaped smokebox doors intended to reduce wind resistance, were of the same type. Compounding on the PLM did not follow the de Glehn/du Bousquet pattern. There was no separate adjustment of the high- and low-pressure valve gear and no provision for simple working. When starting, however, the driver could operate a valve which increased the pressure in the low-pressure cylinders.

In 1909 the PLM introduced two Pacifics, one a saturated steam simple and the other a superheated compound. Comparative trials showed the superiority of the compound in fuel consumption so that arrangement was adopted for the future. By the early 1930s the PLM had 371 engines of substantially the same Pacific design in service and had converted a number of simple Pacifics to compound working.

A series of improvements was made in the PLM Pacifics over the years. Rebuilding of one machine with an improved steam circuit laid the foundation for the PLM 231 class, the most powerful of the PLM Pacifics, capable of 3200 indicated horsepower at 75 mph (120 kph). Similar modifications were made in other earlier Pacifics, producing classes 231G and 231K.

In the 1920s the Pacifics were having difficulty in accelerating quickly with heavy trains if delayed on severe gradients. A 4–8–2 design was therefore introduced to provide greater adhesion, the prototype appearing in 1925. The first of the production series appeared in 1927 and by 1932 the class totalled 145. Their work was mainly on the Laroche–Dijon and Marseilles–Nice sections of the PLM main line.

A similar step was taken by the Chemins de fer de l'Est when it needed more power for working heavier trains over the 1-in-167 gradients of the main line from Paris to Belfort. The first Est 4–8–2, in fact, came out a month or so before the PLM prototype and was the first locomotive with the 4–8–2 (Mountain) wheel arrangement in Europe. It had a long trial period during which changes were made in cylinder dimensions and grate area, and experiments with smoke deflectors were carried out. In 1930 it was on show at the Liège exhibition and it was not until a year later that deliveries of the production version began. These 40 new engines were similar to the prototype except that they had a shorter smokebox and a further increase in grate area. The class worked on the Paris–Nancy line as well as the Paris–Belfort, tackling its long gradients at 1-in-125, one of which extends for over eight miles (12.8 km). After further modifications in 1933 which included an improved steam circuit, higher superheat and feedwater heating, the Est 'Mountains' showed themselves able to

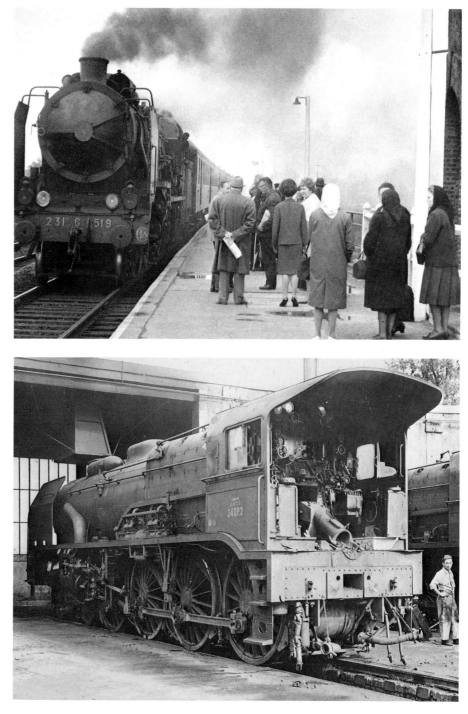

haul a 728 US tons/650 UK tons/660 tonnes train on the level at 56 mph (90.1 kph) and to take 616 US tons/550 UK tons/559 tonnes up 1-in-125 at 37 mph (60 kph).

In the 1930s the Chemins de fer de l'Etat, once a somewhat somnolent concern, underwent vigorous modernization. In updating its motive power it acquired some 4–8–2s similar to those on the Est but also rebuilt some of its Pacifics. Rebuilding was much in the air in those days. It had begun with the work of André Chapelon on the Paris–Orleans (later PO–Midi) Railway in 1929. A Pacific locomotive had been built for the company in 1907 to work over the heavily graded lines in the Massif Central, and other PO Pacifics followed, but their performance proved little better than that of the Atlantics which had preceded them.

Chapelon set out to find the reason why. This was no mere juggling with dimensions in the hope of hitting on a magic formula but a thoroughgoing application of thermodynamic principles to which he

Top: Modification and modernization of earlier PLM Pacifics produced classes G and K, both of which in course of time worked over all Regions of the SNCF. Pacific 231G519 arrives at Yvetot with a morning express from Le Havre to Paris in May 1964. Above: This footplate view of a 240P shows the pipe through which coal was fed by a rotating screw into the mechanical stoker.

Above: The PLM introduced 4–8–2s in 1927 for duties which were getting beyond the capabilities of the Pacifics in some respects, and by 1932 had 145 of the type in service. A PLM 4–8–2 enters Toulon with a train from Marseilles in 1938.

Below: More 4–8–2s were built by the SNCF between 1948 and 1952 for the main line from Paris to Marseilles, but were confined to the Dijon–Marseilles section because of electrification between Paris and Dijon. Their territory diminished as 'the wires' extended southward, and they were later sent to other Regions. One of this impressive series is caught by the camera at speed.

had devoted deep thought. The result was a complete redesign of the steam circuit of Pacific No 3566, involving enlarged and 'streamlined' steam passages, better steam flow through the valves, higher superheat and improved draft arrangements. Tested in heavy express traffic after this treatment, No 3556 showed an increase in maximum output of no less than 50 percent and better thermal efficiency. On one occasion the locomotive took a train of 635 US tons/567 UK tons/576 tonnes over the 70.1 miles (112.8 km) from Poitiers to Angoulême in 62.75 minutes. Similar success attended Chapelon's rebuilding of PO 4–8–0 locomotives.

Chapelon's philosophy of steam locomotive design can be studied in his book, *La Locomotive à Vapeur*, first published in 1938. It is a solid work of 900 pages and it is more often referred to with reverence than it is actually read or quoted. Much of it is highly detailed discussion of advanced physics which is usually preceded by a simple statement of what the author is about to demonstrate. Here is his introduction to the all-important subject of the steam circuit:

'The flow of the driving fluid results in simul-

taneous displacement of the products of combustion. These fluids are in frictional contact with the surfaces that guide them, but while the energy so expended is useful in the case of the combustion gases, since the coefficient of transmission of heat by convection depends on the intensity of this friction, the same is not the case with steam. Any loss of pressure therein which does not produce external work, that is, which does not act on the pistons, constitutes a loss, by irreversibility which is inadmissible in the Carnot cycle.'

Among the best known products of Chapelon's work outside the PO Railway were the Pacifics on the Chemins de fer du Nord known as the Chapelons Nords. In 1933 the Nord tested a rebuilt PO Pacific against one of its own Pacifics and certain other locomotives on the main line between Paris and Calais. Chapelon's product proved so superior in power output to the Nord Pacific that the Nord ordered 20 rebuilt Pacifics from the PO company and had 28 similar locomotives built by the locomotive industry. The first were in service in 1934, inaugurating the famous 231E class. Many exploits of the Chapelons Nords have been recorded but one which is little known occurred as late as 1965 during tests of the overhead contact system for the Paris–Lille electrification. A test train was made up consisting of an electric locomotive which was propelled 'dead,' but with pantograph raised, by a 231E Pacific. A laboratory vehicle and an ordinary vehicle behind the steam locomotive made up a load of 252 US tons/225 UK tons/229 tonnes. Three Pacifics were involved and more than 70 return trips were made between Aulnoye and Valenciennes, in the course of which maximum speeds of between 100 and 105 mph (161 and 169 kph) were reached at Le Quesnoy.

A correspondent of the English technical weekly *The Engineer* described a number of runs he made on class 231E Pacifics in the 1960s. He was impressed by the equipment of the cabs:

'Everything necessary for efficient and economical operation is there; the numerous gauges which are for use, not ornament – they are

watched closely and the engine is handled accordingly. They indicate superheater temperature, steamchest and receiver pressure, exhaust pressure, smokebox vacuum, pyrometer. They tell the crew what is happening all over the engine – there is no guesswork about anything.'

Although the high-pressure and low-pressure valve gears were independently adjustable it became the usual practice to lock the controls together and operate them as one. Separate adjustment might be used in special circumstances such as maintaining speed with a heavy train on a rising gradient. At one time there had been a theory among the crews that engines would run better with a long low-pressure cut-off. Chapelon discouraged the practice in the section of his book dealing with driving practice, characteristically by drawing attention to the message of the cab instruments. If the driver watched their readings while running with a long low-pressure cut-off, he would see a higher exhaust pressure and smokebox vacuum, two infallible indications of more steam entering the cylinders. But this was an artificial way of getting more steam in. He should try the experiment of lengthening the high-pressure cut-off while keeping the low-pressure cut-off short. Then he would find similar readings to before, but with the engine running still better. Chapelon advocated keeping the two cut-offs approximately the same, especially on locomotives with an improved circuit and therefore an in-built safeguard against wiredrawing. Ill-considered use of the valve gear controls could undo all the designer's work in planning the machine proportions and dimensions.

On his passenger train journeys with 231Es the correspondent of *The Engineer* noticed no use of the facility for admitting live steam to the low-pressure cylinders for boosting effort. This was done, however, when working freights on steeply graded routes at speeds in the 10- to 15-mph (16- to 24-kph) range, when it might continue for half-an-hour or more. The same commentator noted the smooth operation of the two regulators, which he considered contributed to the rarity of slipping, for during all the thousands of miles he had travelled on French railways he had seen this occur less than half a dozen times. The smooth riding of the 231Es impressed him in particular: 'It is delightful to ride them and feel their sewing machine smoothness noting the nonexistent opposing action between engine and tender – at times I have observed this less than an inch . . . engine and tender might have been glued together.'

These comments were made in the last years of French steam and in very different circumstances from those in which Chapelon had begun his work. On 1 January 1938 the French main-line railways had come together in the Société Nationale des Chemins de fer Français (SNCF).

A step toward rationalizing the motive power and rolling-stock policy of the French railways had been taken as early as 1919 by setting up the Office Central d'Etudes de Matériel (OCEM), but limited finance restricted its powers. It was to the OCEM, however, that the Nord turned in the 1930s for new designs of heavy passenger locomotives as successors to the Chapelons Nords, stipulating that they should follow the Chapelon doctrines that had proved so successful in that case. The result was a series of 4–6–4 express passenger engines comprising an experimental turbine design, three three-cylinder simples and four four-cylinder compounds (SNCF classes 232Q, 232R and 232S respectively). Monsieur de Caso of OCEM was responsible for the design and he was imbued with the Chapelon principles. The class appeared at the beginning of World War II.

Chapelon's last design for the PO Railway before it merged with the SNCF was an experimental 2–12–0 compound for heavy freight with four low-pressure and two high-pressure cylinders. Nominally a conversion of an existing 2–10–0, it was so completely rebuilt as to be really a new locomotive. The design first took shape in 1936 and was inherited by the SNCF on its formation two years later. Work was delayed by the war and locomotive trials did not begin until 1948. By that time steam on the SNCF was in eclipse. Chapelon retired in 1953 and his 12-coupler was scrapped in 1955. It had been a

Below: It is June 1939 and already the troop trains are rolling. Est 4–8–2 No 241–008 waits at the Gare de l'Est for departure to 'somewhere on the frontier.'

Left: De Caso's 4–6–4 compound 232U–1 has arrived at the Gare du Nord with an evening express from Belgium. This locomotive was built as a replacement for a 4–6–4 turbine locomotive which was scrapped after the war. Right: The eight 4–6–4s sanctioned before the war by the SNCF comprised the turbine 232Q1, three three-cylinder simples of class 232R, and four four-cylinder compounds of class 232S, built in the war years. No 002 of the 232S class is seen in this picture.

radical departure from the conventional compound layout. To provide the high tractive effort required for heavy goods working, the high-pressure cylinders had to be of large diameter, which meant that the low-pressure cylinders were larger than anything used before, too big in fact to go between the frames. Two were therefore placed outside, and two inside the frames, one pair driving the second and the other the third coupled axle. This arrangement is not readily apparent in photographs of the locomotive because of the steam jacketing of the cylinders (which included the high-pressure pair) to reduce losses by compensation. The high-pressure cylinders were between the frames near the center of the locomotive and drove the fourth coupled axle.

In the war years utility had to be the watchword. At first, construction of existing types continued, but from 1942 the SNCF began placing in service a series of general-purpose 2–8–2s (class 141P) designed for a top speed of 65 mph (105 kph) and of low adhesive weight for wide route availability. They were four cylinder compounds with linked high-pressure and low-pressure valve gears of the type favored by the PLM (now the Région Sud-Est) and performed well on the types of duty for which they were intended. Compounding was adopted for its proved economy in fuel consumption, which was foreseen as becoming a critical factor in the war years, but at the same time the relatively complicated mechanism of a compound was not an ideal choice for war conditions from the point of view of maintenance.

Had wartime destruction in France been less severe, the 141P class might have formed the nucleus of a large postwar standard general purpose fleet, with a new generation of locomotives for the fastest express duties. With the return of peace the turbine 4–6–4 of de Caso's prewar design was scrapped and replaced by a compound of the same wheel arrangement classified 232–U1. Here de Caso used PLM compounding practice, but with refinements. The locomotive started as a simple with 75 percent cut-off in the high-pressure cylinders and the low-pressure

cut-off advanced by a servo mechanism to 90 percent. The driver notched up in the usual way, with a partly opened regulator to reduce the risk of slipping, and when the high-pressure cylinders were cutting off at 55 percent the servo system notched up the low-pressure valve gear to the same extent; the locomotive then worked as a compound with the two sets of valve gear controlled together.

Chapelon had continued to work on designs for larger and more efficient steam locomotives. The opportunity to put his plans into practice came in 1946 when the SNCF sanctioned conversion of an Etat 4–8–2, which had been designed by the OCEM and was a somewhat doubtful performer, into a 4–8–4 on Chapelon's principles. This was the classic 242–A1, a three-cylinder compound capable of a maximum output of 5500 indicated horsepower. On trial runs it climbed the steep gradients to Blaisy Bas summit, north of Dijon, at between 60 and 70 mph (97 and 113 kph) with loads of over 896 US tons/ 800 UK tons/813 tonnes, and on one occasion on the Nord accelerated 874 US tons/780 UK tons/793 tonnes from a start at Creil to 72 mph (116 kph) at the summit of the 1-in-200 Survilliers bank. However plans for electrification of the former PLM and Nord main lines were already advanced. No 242–A1 was returned to the Etat (now the Region Ouest) where it had made its undistinguished start as a 4–8–2, and little further use was made of its new potential until it was withdrawn in 1960.

To return to the immediate postwar scene, the French locomotive works were in no condition to produce locomotives on the scale required in the period of reconstruction. Re-equipment of the SNCF after the war had to come partly from outside and so one saw the influx of the American built 2–8–2s of class 141R under the Marshall Plan. These were simple expansion engines, robust and easy to maintain; 1340 were ordered, but 16 went down in the transport ship Bel Pamela and one was lost during unloading in France. By 1947 the 1323 engines safely delivered could be seen at work all over France

Above: The 2–8–2 wheel arrangement was also used in tank locomotives for suburban services from St Lazare. Two three-cylinder locomotives of class 141T are on a spur line outside the terminus, with the Pont de l'Europe in the background, setting of the scene described by Zola and quoted at the beginning of this chapter.

on the widest possible variety of duties, from steel and coal trains in northeast France to the Blue Train on the Riviera. The last 141R 'dropped its fire' for the last time in 1974. Some of the class had run more than 1,240,000 miles (1,995,160 km) on the SNCF by the time they were withdrawn.

De Caso's 4–6–4 232–U1 survived to work the last steam train into the Gare du Nord on 30 September 1961. Train No 144 from Jeumont to Paris was also the last trip for the driver, Leprêtre. Crowds awaited the arrival and two bouquets were handed up to the footplate, one for Leprêtre and one for the locomotive, which, like him, was going into retirement. The occasion was recalled by Monsieur Jacques Vincent, shedmaster at the famous La Chapelle depot, who wrote to a friend:

'This memorable day was the end of steam at La Chapelle, the end of 116 years of coal, smoke, steam, very clean engines and a superb staff of men who were at one with their own beautiful machines. It was the March of Time, the Triumph of Progress, but for men such as ourselves it was not a wonderful day but a very sad one, and our hearts were heavy. We drank

champagne as if at a funeral rather than a baptism. If our lips smiled, our hearts were full of tears. We had lost the best of ourselves.'

The case for the displacement of steam was simple and had little to do with the capacity of the steam locomotive, which Chapelon had amply proved to be still capable of improvement. One crew per locomotive had been the rule. 'How these men know, love and nurse their engines!' wrote one enthusiastic observer. 'They often remain with an engine for years, getting to know it inside out and all its little tricks and whimsies, glad to do their own running repairs and working on them when general repairs are in hand.' But therein lay a weakness. The postwar authorities may have been doubtful over the continuing supply of men with such dedication. Even when they were to be had, the practice of *titularization* (the allocation of a crew to a particular engine) meant that the working hours of crew and engine were linked. Crewmen had 70 minutes preparatory work in the depot before taking their engine out, and another half-hour attending to it on their return.

The motive power departments were fully conscious of the problem and in some places the crew

rosters were planned to give very high mileages. At Tours in 1934 some Pacific crews were running 254 miles (408.8 km) a day in a 12-day stint which included a rest period at Bordeaux followed by a duty of 338 miles (543.9 km) which landed them up at Nantes for another rest period away from home. Sometimes two crews were allotted to an engine, which could thus be kept on the road while either crew was off duty, but the benefits in utilization were small. Only a few classes of locomotive in those days were suitable for full common use, and that practice did not become general until the arrival of the postwar 141Rs. It was then extended to certain other classes, and the average daily engine-miles averaged over the whole steam fleet, which had long hovered between 50 and 60 miles (80.4 and 96.5 km) eventually reached 75 miles (120.7 km).

Chapelon's arguments for steam in his book were the arguments of an engineer rather than an operator. He quotes better sustained tractive effort at speed in a steam locomotive than in the diesel. In fact, he does not wholly concede the role of the diesel even as a shunting unit, but envisages a completely automatic oil-fired steam shunter which could be driven by one

man. He calculates load hauled per indicated horse-power and shows that while for the private car and the truck the figures are 46.3 lb and 90.4 lb (21 kg and 41 kg) respectively, for the passenger train they are 881.8 lb (400 kg) and for the freight train 1411 lb (640 kg).

In a reference to his own initial success with the PO rebuilds, he quotes an increase in power/weight ratio measured at the cylinders from 23.7 hp/ton to 36 hp/ton, for an increase in locomotive weight of less than ten UK tons. He was optimistic about the future of the high-speed train, foreseeing average speeds 'between 80 and 90 mph (129 and 145 kph) or even more' which he thought, given the comfort, safety and convenience of rail travel, would be enough to outweigh the advantages of the private car or even the airplane.

It has been claimed that Chapelon's final 4−8−4 was quietly pushed into a corner because its prowess was embarrassing to the authorities when they had decided on far-reaching main-line electrification. But power *per se* had become a quality of less significance to the operators than availability. Addressing a conference in 1952 Monsieur Louis Armand, General

Above: The 2−8−2s of class 141E were rebuilds of Est locomotives by the SNCF. Nos 141E566 and 430 leave St Cecile with a heavy train.

Left: A DB rebuilt class 001 4–6–2 No 001 133–8 arrives at Cochem with a stopping train from Koblenz to Trier.
Right: German State Railways class 038 4–6–0 (Prussian P8) climbs past Ehlenbogen with a passenger train for Freudenstapt.
Below: East German steam. One of the DR's fine 01 class Pacifics, beautifully polished with a Hamburg–Berlin express in 1970.

Manager of the SNCF, crystallized current thinking when he remarked that the American manufacturers of diesels were basing their publicity not on maximum speed or engine horsepower, but simply on the fact that their machines would be more productive than anything known previously and would run the greatest number of miles a day. In France electric locomotives were already covering 436 miles (701.7 km) a day on the Paris–Dijon section of the PLM main line and some had reached 620 miles (997.8 km) hauling trains of 896 US tons/800 UK tons/813 tonnes. Chapelon himself had stressed the need for research, urging that the railway should not be allowed to become like an old house which its owners neglected because they disliked change, or were skeptical of proposed improvements. Now the period of change had begun, and with it the running down of the form of traction to which he had devoted his career.

The Chapelon principles remained to the last, with some modifications. The final Chapelon was the famous 241P 4–8–2 of 1948 of which 35 were built. This had driving wheels of 6 feet 6.75 inches (2000 mm), a grate area of 53.8 square feet (5.0 sq m), axle-load of 22 US tons/20 UK tons/20 tonnes, total weight 144 US tons/129 UK tons/132 tonnes and capable of developing nearly 5000 horsepower. Though a few other locomotive designs and modifications appeared afterward, the 241Ps provided a suitable memorial to Chapelon and enabled the curtains to be drawn slowly on French steam to justified applause.

Below left: The class 141P 2–8–2 four-cylinder compounds were built between 1942 and 1949. No 141P 198 is the background to a conversation piece at Quimper in the last few moments before the 'off.'
Below right: The postwar SNCF was re-equipped with 2–8–2s built in the United States, the very numerous class 141R, to be seen all over the system on duties of all kinds. No 141R772, an oil-burner, waits to move off shed at Sotteville Depot, Rouen.

Right: The whole world of steam, glowing in the twilight that was well advanced by 1960, lives in this picture of a 141R restarting a heavy fright near St Gerand-Mogret.

Left: French Railways No
141P198 2–8–2 at
Quimper with an express
for Paris in 1963.
Below left: East meets West.
Czech State Railways
2–10–0 No 556 arrives at
Schirning in West Germany
with the Prague–Paris
'Zpadni Express.' The
2–10–0 has only come
across the border from Cheb.
Right: Historic train. Swiss
Central Bahn Engerth type
0–4–6T No 28 *Genf*
(built in 1858) climbs the
old Hauenstein line on the
120th Anniversary of the
opening, August 1978.

6. Southern European Steam

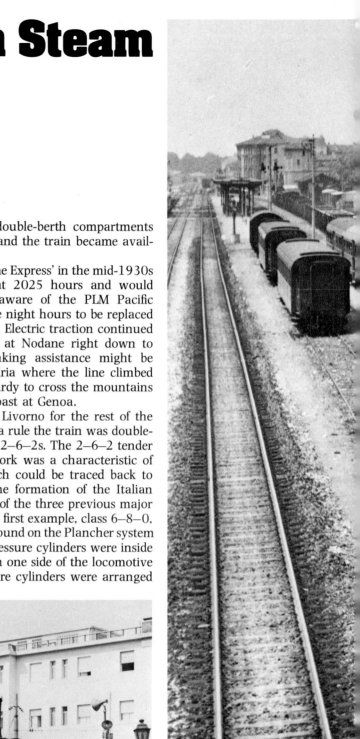

In the 1930s the 'Rome Express' ranked second only to the 'Orient' and the 'Simplon–Orient' in its appeal to writers of fiction and producers of films. Its route from France into Italy was historic. The Romans built a military road across the Mont Cenis pass, and when the Emperor Constantine had to hasten south from Gaul to suppress a usurper at home, that was the route he took, leading his troops 'with such active diligence that he descended into the Plain of Piedmont before the court of Maxilenus had received any certain intelligence of his departure from the banks of the Rhine.' Centuries later a railway climbed through the Maurienne Alps on the French side and burrowed under the pass in the Mont Cenis Tunnel.

The 'Rome Express' ran for the first time in 1897 as a through train from Calais. Later it started from Paris, where a portion from Calais was attached. In the middle 1930s the Calais portion consisted of through coaches for Rome and Florence which were worked to Paris Gare du Nord on an ordinary train and then taken round by the Ceinture to the Gare de Lyon. For many years the 'Rome Express' was first class only and remained so when new rolling stock was introduced in 1930. The new sleeping cars provided six double-berth and four single-berth compartments each. A year later the double-berth compartments were made second class and the train became available to both classes.

A traveller on the 'Rome Express' in the mid-1930s left the Gare de Lyon at 2025 hours and would probably have been unaware of the PLM Pacific coming off at Culoz in the night hours to be replaced by an electric locomotive. Electric traction continued from the Italian frontier at Nodane right down to Livorno, but steam banking assistance might be provided out of Alessandria where the line climbed out of the Plain of Lombardy to cross the mountains between there and the coast at Genoa.

Steam took charge at Livorno for the rest of the journey to Rome, and as a rule the train was double-headed by two class 685 2–6–2s. The 2–6–2 tender locomotive for express work was a characteristic of the Italian railways which could be traced back to 1907, two years after the formation of the Italian State Railways by fusion of the three previous major independent systems. The first example, class 6–8–0, was a four-cylinder compound on the Plancher system in which the two high-pressure cylinders were inside and outside the frames on one side of the locomotive while the two low-pressure cylinders were arranged

Left: The class 625 2–6–0, dating from the first decade of the century, exhibits the typical Italian feature of inside cylinders with outside valve gear.

Above: The characteristic
Italian main line 2–6–2.
FS No 685.172 leaves
Cremona with the 12.56
train for Milan on 31
May 1967.

similarly on the other side. Both cylinders in each group had a common steamchest with one piston valve admitting steam to both cylinders. The valves were driven by outside Walschaerts gear. On the first movement of the regulator, live steam was admitted to all cylinders, but as it was opened further the locomotive worked as a compound.

As built, the class 680 locomotives were not superheated, but after a trial of superheating in two of them, 36 of the class were converted similarly and reclassified as class 681. In seven locomotives the ratio of the high-pressure to the low-pressure cylinder dimensions was altered and these became class 682.

In the next new design of 2–6–2s, class 685, the State Railways dropped compounding and chose a four-cylinder simple with superheated steam. There was much in common with the superheated 680s, and the same arrangement of a common steamchest

and piston valve for the two cylinders on each side of the locomotive was retained in the simple locomotive. The first of the class were supplied by Breda in 1912. Four locomotives were equipped with Caprotti valve gear in 1924 and reclassified as class 686. Results were satisfactory and 30 new Caprotti engines of class 686 were built in 1926/27. In 1930, however, all the Caprotti engines, rebuilds and new, were taken back into class 685. Five of them were rebuilt in 1940 with Franco–Crosti boilers, their numbers at first taking a letter 'S' prefix but they were later designated class 683.

The Italian 2–8–2s underwent numerous changes during their working life, the most fundamental being the rebuilding of 680 class No 110 as a turbine locomotive in 1930. An early experiment with turbine propulsion had been made in Italy in 1908 with the conversion of an 0–6–0 shunting locomotive to

Right: Italian State Railways 2–6–2 locomotive at Táranto.
Below: Italian branch line. Steam is spasmodic in Italy with very little on the active list. This class 625 2–6–0 is one of those still in use, some with Crosti boilers. This is No 625.042 with an enthusiasts' excursion in 1974.
Bottom: Once the pride of Calais Depot, this SNCF class 231K Pacific is now part of the collection of preserved steam engines at Steamtown Museum, Carnforth.

geared turbine drive to the design of Professor Guisseppe Belluzzo. No condenser was used, the object being to test the mechanical suitability of a turbine drive rather than its economics. This pioneer machine worked for some 12 years. The 1930 conversion, however, did not get beyond a few trial runs on which a speed of 80 mph (129 kph) was reached. The experiment was not judged a success and the locomotive was restored to its original form, remaining in service until 1969.

Professor Belluzzo was still interested in turbine locomotives in the 1930s and was behind the building by Breda in 1931 of an experimental 2–8–2 with turbine drive and a condenser. In contrast with previous condensing turbine locomotives have a separate tender, in this design all the equipment – turbines, condenser and heat exchanger – was carried on the engine itself. The turbine group, consisting of high – and intermediate – pressure turbines on one side of the locomotive and two low-pressure turbines on the other side, was positioned between the second

and third coupled axles, leaving the area in front of the smokebox free for the heat-exchanger. The condenser was between the smokebox and the first coupled axle. The drive from the turbine shafts was taken through gears and a jackshaft to the coupling rods. After a few trial runs the project was abandoned.

The visitor to Italy in the 1930s who saw one of the turbine locomotives would have been fortunate, but he might well have been surprised to see one of the cab-at-front 4–6–0s of class 670 which dated from 1900 but were still at work in 1936. They were built for the Rede Adriatica system and taken over by the State Railways. At first sight one would have thought that a class 670 was an 0–6–4 tank engine running bunker first and towing a small tank wagon but closer inspection would show the 'bunker' to be a cab and the tank wagon a tender carrying water supplies. Coal was carried in two bunkers alongside the firebox which had the appearance of the water tanks in a conventional side-tank engine. Early tests were carried out on a section of the PLM in France,

Above: Class 940 2–8–2T, No 940.050, leaves a wayside station with an evening local train from Lecco to Como. This class was a tank version of the class 740 2–6–0 of 1911.
Above right: Class 625 No 625.042 heads an enthusiasts' special at Lagonegro. These engines worked some of the last regular steam passenger trains in Italy, between Verona and Modena.
Right: An enthusiasts' special headed by a class 625 2–6–0 winds its way through a hilly landscape.

124

using a French dynamometer car, and a maximum speed of 78.3 mph (126 kph) was recorded with a train weighing 146 US tons/130 UK tons/132 tonnes. In their early days they had been regarded as an express locomotive and the cab had a rounded front to reduce wind resistance at speed. The class numbered 43 locomotives, the last of which were delivered after the formation of the State Railways. At the end of their days they could be seen working local passenger trains out of Milan and shunting in the carriage sidings; by that time they looked extremely shabby but were still apparently capable of useful work.

To return to the 2–6–2s, their axle-load was 15 or 16 UK tons, according to class, which enabled them to be used on nearly all the main routes. For the most part, however, they worked on the less hilly lines in central and northern Italy. The last survivors were members of class 685, which ended their days from the middle 1960s on local passenger and freight duties on secondary lines, some of them going to Sicily.

Those who watched the twilight of Italian steam will also remember the inside-cylinder 2–6–0s with outside valves and Walschaerts valve gear. Some of the 2–8–0s were similar. Pacifics were built from 1911 but were sluggish performers. A project for a more modern three-cylinder simple Pacific with three sets of valve gear was mooted in the 1920s but did not come to fruition. At the same period a series of large 2–8–2s was introduced. These were four-cylinder compounds with a conventional cylinder arrangement, the low-pressure cylinders being out-

Above far left: Italian State Railways class 940 2–8–2T No 940.050 heads a Lecco-to-Como train between Civate and Sala al Barro Galbiate.

Above left: A southbound freight double headed by RENFE 241F 4–8–2s climbs toward Bujedo on the Miranda de Ebro-to-Burgos line.

Above: Portugal's CP 4–6–0 No 281 arrives at Tua with a freight bound for Porto.

Below: Spanish local. RENFE 4–8–2 No 241F 4065 approaches San Felices beside the river Ebro with a stopping train from Logrno to Miranda de Ebro.

side and the high-pressure inside. As in the Pacifics, the steam circuit was not conducive to free flow and the engines gradually retired to the south of the country where less arduous duties were to be found.

Perhaps Italy's most important contribution to the steam locomotive was the Caprotti valve gear, but even here the native product did not progress to the same extent as the corresponding gear built abroad under license. Main-line electrification came early to Italy, which had ample water power but no coal of its own. In these circumstances less effort was devoted to steam locomotives development than might otherwise have been the case. Even so, the apparent neglect of lessons to be learned from the steam practice in neighboring countries remains a surprising and not wholly explained aspect of Italian railway history.

The late 1970s saw the restoration of a little-known direct rail link between Italy and France. The first move came from the Italian side with the proposal for a line from Cuneo to Ventimiglia, serving Nice by a branch from Breil. By 1900 they had built a line across the Col di Tenda and reached Vievola on its southern slope. Long discussions with France followed, for the next stage of construction down the valley would cross and recross the frontier. It was finally agreed that the Italians should continue their line from Vievola, via Breil, to Ventimiglia, while the French would build a connecting line from Nice to Breil.

Work was delayed by World War I, and although the section from Ventimiglia to Breil was completed in 1921, the Nice–Breil branch was not ready until 1928. On 30 October 1928 the work was completed and there was through communication from Nice to Cuneo. French and Italian inaugural trains, bedecked with flags, met in Breil station.

A few international services were instituted over the new route, which reduced the distance by rail from Nice to Turin from 180.2 miles (290 km) via Savona to 137.3 miles (220.9 km). The Italians worked their services at first with 0–10–0 locomotives of class 471 but replaced them later with the more powerful 2–8–2 tank engines of class 940. The PLM began its services with the few 4–6–0s of class 230C–1 to 230C–170 which were shed at Nice Saint Roch. Some 4–8–0s were sent specially from Alès later and worked on the line for a few months, to be followed by 4–6–4 tanks of the classes working coastal services. From 1930 the workings were largely in the hands of 4–8–4 tanks class 242T–1 to 242T–120, and these continued to be employed on the Nice–Breil section of the line until 1956–57, when they were succeeded by the 2–8–2s of class 141R. Between 1930 and 1935 the Italians electrified the route from Cuneo to Ventimiglia.

When Italy entered World War II in 1940 some of the works at the southern end of the line were destroyed by the French Army but were later restored and freight traffic to Italy and Germany continued. After the Allied landing in Provence on 15 August 1944 there was further bomb damage but the major destruction occurred in April 1945 during the German retreat and put the section from Breil to Vievola completely out of action. It remained derelict for many years and reconstruction was not put in hand until 1976. On 19 January 1979 the last fish-

Right: As late as 1975 the class 835 0–6–0Ts were widely dispersed over Italy on shunting duties, although replacement with diesels was beginning. No 835.234 shunts at Cremona in May 1967.

Below: Another development of class 740 was its rebuild with a Franco–Crosti boiler, forming class 743. This view of No 460 at Cremona shows the two rear exhausts in action. Below right: RENFE 4–8–0 No 240F2274 leaves Salamanca with a local train.

plate was bolted home in Breil station, re-establishing a through route from Italy to France via the Col di Tenda.

Spain, like Italy, acquired new rail links with France in the 1920s, although the 5-foot 6-inch (1.6-m) gauge of the Spanish Railways prevented through running. One of these lesser-known routes was opened in 1928 from Bedous on the French side of the Pyrenees to Jaca in Spain, giving a shorter journey from Pau to Zaragoza. It was a formidable line for the steam locomotives employed by both administrations, rising 2662 feet (811.4 m) from Bedous into the mountains in a distance of about 18 miles (29 km). The average gradient was around 1-in-35 and the steepest section was 1-in-23. The frontier was crossed in the Somport Tunnel, five miles (eight km) long; the line emerged at Canfranc, three miles (five km) inside Spain. From here a new line some 16 miles (25.7 km) long was built to Jaca on the existing Spanish network, dropping through 1300 feet (396 m) with an average gradient of 1-in-65. The section from Bedous is now closed and a bus service has been substituted, but RENFE railcars run between Canfranc and Zaragoza.

The other new link between France and Spain,

Above: Even the massive
'Mountains' were some-
times dominated by the
craggy Spanish landscape,
as in this scene near
Pancorbo in 1968.
Above left: The 'Mountain'
(4—8—2) wheel arrange-
ment was first seen in
Spain in the 1920s, following several 4—8—0 classes.
It lasted until the end of
steam. A 'Mountain' of
class 241F No 2087 heads
a passenger train in arid
surroundings near
Salamanca.
Left: Front-end assistance is
provided by a 2—8—2 for a
'Mountain' leaving
Pancorbo.

opened in 1929, provided a more direct journey from
Toulouse to Barcelona than by the main line via Port
Bou and Cerbère. New construction was necessary
on the Spanish side from Ripoll to the frontier near
Puigcerda. The frontier station was at La Tour de Carol
on the French side, 33 miles (53.1 km) from Ripoll.
Again the French section was the steeper, climbing
from 4035 feet (1230 m) at La Tour de Carol to a
summit of 5200 feet (1585 m) in the Puymorens
Tunnel, 3.25 miles (5.23 km) long. Onward to a
junction with an existing line at Ax les Thermes the
new line descended steadily, and on the final section
of 13 miles (21 km) from L'Hospitalet to Ax passed
through 11 tunnels, one of them a spiral tunnel which
dropped the line 200 feet (61 m) at an average
gradient of 1-in-25. The route remains rail-operated
throughout. First- and second-class sleeping cars are
operated between Paris and La Tour de Carol by the
SNCF.

In the period of maximum steam development
elsewhere, Spain was in the midst of a civil war.
When normal travel hours and tourism resumed after
World War II visitors were impressed by the massive
steam locomotives still coming into service in spite
of much electrification work in parts of the country.

As in other countries of Europe, the 'big engine' era
in Spain began in the latter half of the 1920s, although
eight-coupled designs had long been in use because
of the steeply graded main lines. Earlier in the century
locomotives had been ordered from foreign builders
but by 1920 a Spanish-built version of the Northern
(*Norte*) Railway's 4—8—0 of 1912 was being produced.

The next step was to the Mountain (4—8—2) wheel
arrangement, first seen in six passenger locomotives
with eight-wheel bogie tenders built in Germany for
the *Norte* in 1925. They were four-cylinder compounds of the de Glehn/du Bousquet type, but the
width between the frames enabled all cylinders to be
almost in line. Driving wheels were of just under
5 feet 9 inches (1753 mm) in diameter and the
nominal top speed was 68.35 mph (110 kph). Later
engines of the same class were built in Spain. One of
these *Norte* 4—8—2s was rebuilt with a steam circuit
incorporating Chapelon features. As a result of its
improved performances 28 more locomotives incorporating similar modifications to the original design
were built in the 1946—48 period.

The Madrid, Zaragoza & Alicante Railway (MZA)
also introduced a 4—8—2 class in the middle 1920s

Right: A class of standard
2–8–2s was introduced by
RENFE as late as 1953.
One of these locomotives is
on a passenger-working
near San Felice.
Below: Huge and elusive as
the Abominable Snowman,
the RENFE 4–8–4s of class
242F became almost a
legend in the last days of
Spanish steam. The camera
has caught and fixed No
2009 for all time in this
scene near Bujedo in 1968.

Above: Class 141F 2–8–2
No 2327 approaches Haro
with the 18.15 Miranda de
Ebro-to-Casetas train on
15 May 1968.
Above right: RENFE used
the boiler of its 4–8–2s in a
2–10–2 heavy freight series.
No 151.3112 of this class
heads a southbound freight
through Palencia, on the
Northern main line from
Oveido and Leon to Madrid.

Above: A short freight on the Portuguese Railways near San Mameda de Tua is headed by an outside-cylinder locomotive characterized by a simplicity of line rarely seen on the Continent.
Right: Another 4–6–0 of the same class is on a freight working near Tua.
Above far right: A Portuguese example of the classic inside-cylinder 4–6–0 outline.
Far right: Broad-gauge 2–8–4T No 0181 arrives at Regua with a freight train from Porto in May 1968.

but these were two-cylinder simples and were built in Spain from the outset. Driving-wheel diameter was the same as in the *Norte* class. In 1939 the MZA ventured into streamlining with a further batch of generally similar 4–8–2s but with the high boiler pressure of 295 lb per square inch (20.74 kg/sq cm), which involved some novelties in the design of the cylinder and piston-rod packing. Streamlining seems to have been adopted for ostentation rather than utility for no speeds at which aerodynamics needed to be seriously considered were in prospect.

The Spanish National Railways (RENFE) were formed in 1941 and continued the construction of 4–8–2s using a larger boiler. The same larger boiler was used in a class of three-cylinder simple 2–10–2s for heavy coal traffic in the north of the country. As late as 1953 a standard design of 2–8–2 mixed traffic locomotive was introduced, of which the first 25 came from the works of the North British Locomotive Company Limited in Scotland. Further construction followed in Spain and eventually 232 of these reliable and versatile locomotives were in service. Ten 4–8–4s built in the country in 1955–56 were the climax of Spanish steam design, although the last steam locomotives built in Spain were Beyer-Garratts under license. The 4–8–4s were still at work in 1974, ending their days on heavy freight duties. Like all the Spanish eight-coupled classes they were of majestic build but these stood out from the others by reason of their green livery. Deceptively, they had that air of permanence peculiar to the steam locomotive, looking as if they would last as long as the rocky terrain through which they moved with massive dignity. Against those towering smokeboxes the waves of time must surely dash themselves in vain. Yet all this was an illusion.

Spain was the only country in Europe to use Garratts regularly in passenger service. They were of a 4–6–2- and 2–6–4-type built under license by Spanish firms for the Central of Aragon Railway and six were delivered in 1931, together with six of a 2–8–2+2–8–2 class for freight. The passenger engine was designed for the steeply graded main line from Zaragoza to Valencia via Caminreal, where it was required to haul trains of 336 US tons/300 UK tons/305 tonnes at up to 62 mph (100 kph) on the level and at up to 25 mph (40 kph) up gradients of 1-in-46, with curvature of 984 feet (300 m) radius. These engines remained on their home ground for some ten years after RENFE was formed and then were put on the coastal line between Taragona and Valencia for working the Barcelona–Sevilla express. The Garratts coped single-handed with 17-coach trains which had previously required double-heading on this section, where the train made frequent stops and faced gradients as steep as 1-in-75. They remained on this duty until diesels came on the scene in 1966–67.

The freight Garratts were of smaller proportions than the passenger class. They remained on the Old Central of Aragon line until it was dieselized in 1966–67 but under RENFE also worked from Valencia to La Encina. In 1961 the original half-dozen were supplemented by ten more, generally similar but built for oil-burning. The others were all converted to oil fuel in the course of their lives.

Another type of articulated locomotive seen in Spain was the Mallet. A number of 0–6–6–0 Mallets were built between 1906 and 1928 for work on heavily graded lines and were still active around

and involving frequent stops.

The creation of Czechoslovakia in 1918 resulted in a railway system equipped with a varied assortment of locomotives from different sources, counting nearly 200 different types in all. Works in Prague (CKD) and Pilsen (Skoda) took part in a standardization program based at first on Austrian practice but moving gradually towards a distinctive national locomotive identity. In World War II these factories had to build German *Kriegslokomotiven*. Most of those from Skoda remained in Czechoslovakia after the war as class 555.3. They were still to be seen at work around Breclav in 1977.

In the immediate postwar years Czechoslovakian builders produced over 500 2–10–0s based on the prewar 534.0 class and classified 534.03. Standardization began again with an express passenger 4–8–2 produced in 1946 and classified 498.0. It has much in common with the 486.0 class, a three-cylinder design built between 1934 and 1938. The same wheel arrangement was used for the mixed-traffic class 475.1 which followed but this two-cylinder series introduced more recent practice such

as a taper boiler, combustion chamber and thermic siphon, and roller bearings throughout. In a short series with smaller wheels and higher boiler pressure which followed there was a reversion to three cylinders but this time with compound working, surprisingly in view of the fact that earlier Czech three-cylinder compounds had all been converted to simples.

A further development from the prewar 486.0 class was a new express passenger 4–8–2 which came out in 1954. This was Czechoslovakia's final contribution to the steam express passenger engine; it was again a three-cylinder simple design but it incorporated many refinements and had an impressive appearance.

The most numerous class of locomotives still operating in the 1970s were the class 556.0 freight 2–10–0s, of which over 500 were built between 1952 and 1957. Steam fanciers who visited Czechoslovakia in the final years still speak of the staccato crackle of their double-Kylchap exhaust, perhaps the most characteristic steam sound in Czechoslovakia. These engines were known to work 560-US-ton/500-UK-ton/508-tonne trains single-handed and coped with 336 US tons/300 UK tons/305 tonnes even on steeply graded routes, although double-heading was common and sometimes heavy freights could be seen being urged westward out of Puchov by three, or sometimes four engines of the class.

A highly characteristic Czech locomotive class was the 4–8–4 passenger tank manufactured from 1951 onward. The first 38 were similar to a solitary engine of that wheel arrangement built in 1935 in that coal and water supplies were carried behind the cab. In later builds from 1955 onward some of the water was carried in small side tanks. These were well for-

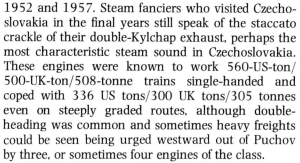

Far left: Class 477.0 was the larger of two 4–8–4 tank engine classes of post-1945 construction. No 477.036 approaches Nezamyslice with the 13.55 Brno–Prerov train on 9 June 1969.
Far left below: One of the 4–8–0s built in Hungary for the Yugoslav railways follows a winding track through the mountains with a train of mixed freight and passenger stock. On the left is the 2ft 6in narrow gauge.
Below left: A Yugoslav Pacific at Belgrade in 1969 carries the national flag on its smoke deflectors.
Left: A 2–10–2T of the Bulgarian State Railways (narrow-gauge section) on a Cerven/Breg to Orjahovo train.

ward of the cab and the intervening space was filled by a false tank to give continuity of line. In later years the original engines were equipped with similar tanks but the false tank was omitted, leaving the former isolated and conspicuous. If there was discontinuity here, however, amends were made by the neat continuous enclosure of the boiler mountings, giving the locomotives an uninterrupted 'skyline.' The modified engines and those built later constituted class 477.0.

Yugoslavia was another complex political and geographical creation with inherited motive power. At first, construction of classes originating in Serbia was continued but in 1930 three designs specific to the new Yugoslav requirements were delivered. They were a Pacific for express service, a mixed traffic 2–8–2 and a standard freight 2–10–0. In the later 1930s a number of 2–4–2 tanks of Hungarian design were acquired, some of which were built in Yugoslavia. World War II brought Deutsche Reichsbahn 2–10–0s of class 52 into the country, some of which were retained afterward and joined by over 200 more. American standard

Top left: Bulgarian Monster: One of Europe's most powerful tank locomotives ran over the BDZ (Bulgarian State Railways) metals. Used to head heavy freights up the grades out of Sofia to Pernick, these grand monsters were gone from active service by 1966. Today some are still in evidence dumped at a loco graveyard to Valkerel near Sofia.

Top center: Hungary still uses steam today but even though it is kept in first-class condition, it is dying fast. One of the most ubiquitous classes (still in use) is the 424 class 4–8–0 used, as the British class 5 was, on almost any type of train. No 424.339 was at Budapest West in 1975 ready to work a push-and-pull suburban train.

Top right: Czech express: CSD class 475 4–8–2 No 475.1125 threads the Svitava Valley near Bilovice with a Semlly-to-Brno fast.
Right: A German built (Prussian P8) 4–6–0 heads a northbound local through the Fin Gorge, Rumania.

Center: A 2–10–0 of the Hellenic State Railways 'belches black smoke' (perhaps the very 'vast, unkempt 2–10–0' of the traveller's tale in this chapter).

Below: The 'Orient Express,' looking rather less than romantic at the end of its lengthy journey, creaks to a halt near the steam shed before the change to electric traction for the last stage of the run to Istanbul.

Top right: Trains passing at Plovdin station in Bulgaria are both headed by 2–10–0 locomotives with a distinctive type of smoke deflector perched on top of the smokebox.

Bottom right: A train from the meter-gauge section of the Greek railways west of Athens arrives in Athens station behind an American-built 2–8–2 in 1964.

Left: Bulgarian State Railways double-headed freight train close to Sofia.
Below: A German abroad. An ex-German State Railways *Kriegslok* 2–10–0 with a passenger train in southern Turkey in 1977.

types made up immediate postwar motive power shortages, and Yugoslavia took the largest number of the 'Liberation' class 2–8–0s built in Great Britain for countries hard hit by wartime destruction or depletion of motive power.

The postwar locomotives in Yugoslavia with the most interesting history were the 4–8–0s of the Hungarian 424 class, some of which remained in Yugoslavia after the war. In 1947–48 a further 49 were delivered from Hungary, but as Hungary was now under the aegis of Josef Stalin and as the political 'coldness' developed between the USSR and Yugoslavia, the supply dried up. By 1955, however, there was a change of heart in high places and ten more of these engines were delivered.

Visitors to Orahovia, some 31 miles (50 km) north of Slavonski Brod, can see a diminutive 0–12–0 tank engine that worked for over 25 years on a meter-gauge mineral railway in Yugoslavia and is now preserved. The locomotive was built by Krauss Maffei in 1939 for the S H Gutmann Company in Belsice. This concern had its own railway to serve a quarry. In a distance of 2.75 miles (4.43 km) the line climbed 738 feet (225 m), equivalent to an average gradient of 1-in-20, and much of it was on curvature of 98 feet 5 inches (30 m) radius. For a quarter of the distance the gradient was between 1-in-13.3 and 1-in-12.5. Trains of empty wagons weighing 4032 lb (1829 kg) each had to be hauled up the hill to a quarry at the top, returning to the valley with a payload of 157 US tons/140 UK tons/142 tonnes. These conditions were more severe than faced by any rack locomotive of similar wheel arrangement.

Wheel diameter was as small as practicable at 2 feet 3.5 inches (698 mm), and with a minimum spacing of 2 feet 6.37 inches (771 mm) between coupled axles the total wheelbase was 13 feet 7 inches (4.14 m). Overall length of the locomotive was 27 feet 1 inch (8.26 m). The leading and trailing pairs of coupled axis were carried in pivoted subframes which also allowed some sideways displacement of individual axles, and the coupling rods had ball-and-socket joints for the same purpose. Outside cylinders drove the third coupled axle which, with the fourth axle, had bearings in the main frames. In the absence of trailing wheels, bunker capacity was limited and the locomotive usually operated coupled to a wagon carrying a reserve fuel supply.

The mountainous Balkans provided a natural home for the long coupled wheelbase. Bulgaria had two 12-coupled classes – an 0–12–0T and a 2–12–4T – both for freight. The 0–12–0 had been ordered on the eve of World War I but could not be delivered until 1922. It was designed for coal traffic on the section of 21 miles (33.8 km) between Sofia and the mining center of Pernik, where an average gradient of 1-in-38 extends for 6.8 miles (10.9 km) and there is a curvature of 902 feet (275 m) radius. There were ten engines in the class, two-cylinder compounds with a low-pressure cylinder no less than 15.75 cubic feet (445 liters) in volume, which was the biggest in Europe. At first the locomotives were not superheated, but superheaters were fitted later and the piston valves replaced with Lentz poppet valves. The first of the class were not withdrawn until 1973. Originally class 40, the locomotives became class 47 after superheating and conversion to poppet-valve gear.

The second 12-coupler for Bulgaria was a 2–12–4T intended primarily for the Pernik–Sofia coal traffic

as a successor to the 0–12–0s. (The latter had proved so satisfactory, particularly since being superheated, that they continued working side by side with the larger engines after deliveries began in 1931.) The first batch of 2–12–4s came from a Polish builder who supplied 14 in all. These were two-cylinder simples with superheaters. During World War I more locomotives of the same type were needed and were built in Germany by Schwartzkopff, but these final eight units of the class were three-cylinder machines with divided drive, the outside cylinders driving the third axle as before but the inside cylinder drove the second axle. The fuel capacity of these locomotives was greater than that of many tender engines and in their later years they were moved to longer-distance runs on the new west–east direct line from Sofia through Karlovo to Kazanlik and on to the Black Sea at Burgas. Here they worked trains of up to 1030 US tons/920 UK tons/935 tonnes over the 1-in-62.5 gradients which face trains crossing the watershed between Sofia and Kazanlik in either direction. As diesel and electric traction in Bulgaria was extended, withdrawals of the 2-12-4s began and they had gone by 1973.

Development in locomotives of more conventional wheel arrangements in Bulgaria took a new turn early in the 1930s when the maximum permitted axle-load was increased from 16 to 20 US tons. German design influence was strong, and classes with eight- or ten-coupled wheels were often favored both for passenger and freight traffic. At first two-cylinder types predominated but in 1935 three-cylinder propulsion was chosen for some new 2–8–2s. Early in World War II a similar design with a leading bogie was produced (4–8–2) together with a generally similar 4–10–0 for mixed traffic. By this time the latter were the only locomotives in the world with that wheel arrangement.

The traveller across Europe by one of the Orient Express services in the 1930s could enjoy an interesting panorama of steam motive power in some of the less visited countries. One who used the through coaches of the Arlberg-Orient Express recorded his impressions in lively style. He arrived at Athens by sea from Egypt on his way home to England and on going to the station was surprised to find that the Hellenic State Railways still followed the practice in 1939 of locking passengers in the waiting room until their train was at the platform. He was released on the arrival of nine coaches for various destinations, the rear two being resplendent blue Wagons-Lits cars labelled for Paris, one by the Simplon-Orient service and the other by the Arlberg-Orient. In due course 'a vast, unkempt 2–10–0 appeared, belching black smoke.' No doubt this was one of the 40 locomotives of Austrian parentage ordered in the 1920s which remained the principal Greek main-line class for two decades, supplemented later by some more engines of the same wheel arrangement loaned to Greece by Austria.

The journey to Salonika was exciting for its scenery rather than for speed, the train groaning its way round fearsome hairpin bends and threading breathtaking gorges and chasms; then smoother running, followed by reversal in Salonika and departure after a wait of half-an-hour behind 'another vast and sluggish 2–10–0' bound for the Yugoslav frontier.

The Yugoslav 2–6–2 which took over at the frontier station of Devedelija was viewed more ap-

Above: Pt47 class 2–8–2 No Pt47–13 looms over the evening rush-hour scene at Lublin station. This class was a postwar development of class Pt31, which was based on a German design.
Right: Polish State Railways 4–6–0 of class OK22, a Polish development of the Prussian P8. The locomotive is at Choszczno shed.

Below: Turkish State Railways 2–8–0 – one of the LMS Stanier-design locomotives supplied to the Middle East during World War II and still at work in 1979.

Far right: Arrival of the Mail. The daily Victoria Falls-to-Bulwayo passenger train – the mail, at Bulawayo in 1973. The engine is a 4–6–4+4–6–4 Garratt. This was an overnight train with full dining and sleeping-car facilities.

Right: South African Railways GMA class Garratt with a freight train taking water before climbing over the Lootsberg Pass.
Center right: South African Railways 4–8–2 locomotive at Port Elizabeth.

provingly as 'shapely and sprightly-looking' but this did not save it from running short of breath from time to time. A glance at the tender supplied the reason: 'the coal would not have been accepted at a slag heap in Lancashire.' Engines were changed (another 2–6–2) at Skolpje and the journey continued to Nis where a portion from Istanbul was attached. The 2–6–2, probably inherited from the Serbian Railways or one of the batch of 120 built in 1922–23, was now replaced by 'a rousing great Pacific of obvious German parentage.' Forty two-cylinder Pacifics were built for Yugoslavia by Schwartzkopff and were mainly used in the flatter territory between Nis and Beograd (Belgrade).

The Pacific steamed away from Nis with a train now composed entirely of Wagons-Lits stock, half Arlberg-Orient and half Simplon-Orient. From Beograd, where there was much splitting up and shunting in the night hours, the two services took different routes and the Arlberg coaches were taken on to the Hungarian frontier by 'a Yugoslav 4–6–0 of startling appearance, as hung-about with gadgets as a wartime soldier.' It was exchanged for 'an equally gaunt Hungarian sister, also a 4–6–0 and equally hideous with excrescences' (one of which was probably the horizontal drum of the Brotan boiler). And so to Budapest and more shunting, the Arlberg-Orient coaches from Bucharest being attached during various interesting early-morning maneuvers. The despised Hungarian 4–6–0 rolled away to its depot and an electric locomotive backed on to the train. The perspicacious recorder of this epic journey thought he detected a difficulty in cornering as the train rolled on to Hegyeshalom across the Great Hungarian Plain, ceremonially saluted at its passage through every station by the station staff lined up on the platform. He suggested that the problem might be the centrifugal effect of 'the immense revolving armature inside.' He may have been right, for not only would there have been the single massive traction motor for the side-rod drive but also the machine which converted the 50Hz single-phase supply in the contact wire into three-phase current. Electric locomotives were more impressive in the days before almost everything which revolves was tucked away in the bogies or hung below the underframe.

Steam resumed control at the Austrian frontier and the journey continued behind a 2–6–2 'of modest dimensions' as far as Vienna. Here the substitution of a 4–6–4 tank engine caused the traveller some misgivings for its small wheels made him think at first that it was a shunter. But he need not have worried, for 'in spite of our 5-feet 5-inch wheels we scuttled along with the great abandon and arrived at Linz panting for water, to find that we had run 118 miles in 133 minutes, including the long haul through the Wiener Wald.' The engine would have been one of A Lehner's 4–6–4Ts of class 729, introduced in 1931 and much used both on the Arlberg-Orient and the Orient Express when these formations were fairly light.

Electricity took over at Salzburg for the run through the Arlberg Tunnel to the Swiss frontier at Buchs, and on through Switzerland to Basle. An Alsace Pacific worked the train on to Belfort, followed by an Est Mountain. By this time our commentator had moved into a through coach for Boulogne which had joined the cavalcade earlier and noted that at Chaumont it was detached from the rest of the train, which proceeded to Paris. A restaurant

car and brake were added and the Boulogne coach, now part of a miniature train, was worked forward to Laon by an Est 4–6–0. A Nord Pacific completed the journey to the English channel. The whole run of 2200 miles (3540 km) had taken 67 hours, and 17 different types of locomotive had been involved. Such an experience cannot be repeated unless one were to fall asleep over an old *Continental Bradshaw* and dream.

Although Poland put a large electrification program in hand after World War II, by the end of the 1970s it was still operating the largest fleet of steam locomotives in Europe. During the nineteenth century period of railroad development Poland was divided between Prussia, Russia and Austria and its railroad system was operated as parts of the system of those countries. The railroads in the Russian sector were broad gauge, but most were converted to standard gauge during World War I, when the whole country was occupied by Germany and Austria. Today the Polish main line network is wholly standard gauge. The Polish State Railways also operate some local lines of various narrow gauges.

As a result of frontier changes after 1918, East Prussia was separated from the rest of Germany by a strip of Polish territory extending to the Baltic coast. This was the Polish Corridor, a name which became all too familiar in the critical years leading up to 1939. Several railroad routes from Germany to East Prussia traversed it, the most important being the main line from Berlin to Marienburg and Konigsberg which crossed the corridor from Firschau on the west to Dirschau on the east, a distance of about 60 miles (96 km), followed by the short stretch of 11 miles (18 km) to Marienburg which crossed territory belonging to the Free City of Danzig. Through trains between Germany and East Prussia by this route were hauled across the corridor by Polish locomotives, and passengers not holding Polish passports or visas were not allowed to alight. Among the corridor services was the Riga portion of the 'Nord Express.'

The line from Stettin to Dirschau via Gdynia and Danzig entered the corridor at the German frontier station of Gross Boschpol, and trains by this route were worked under arrangements similar to those of the main corridor crossing. Various less important lines were severed completely when the corridor was created, and the situation as a whole was a source of considerable bitterness in Germany.

Because of the history of the country, German and

Above: A JS class 2–8–4 passenger locomotive of the Soviet Union Railways at Voronesh.
Right: Class TKt 2–8–2T No 184 arrives at Nasielsk with the 13.29 from Ilawa on 2 October 1975.
Below right: US-built 2–10–0 Ty246.30 passes Tarnowskie Gory with a coal train on 10 August 1975.

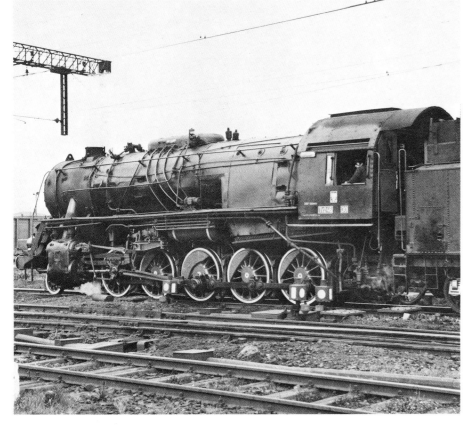

Austrian locomotive designs were numerous in Poland after World War I, some being received as reparations. Certain classes of Polish design were built, and some German designs were developed by the Poles, such as the Polish Ok22 class 4–6–0 based on the Prussian P8 but with a bigger firebox and higher-pitched boiler, giving the class a quite different appearance from the original. One of the most numerous types was the Ty23 class 2–10–0 of which 610 were built from 1923 onwards. In the next decade the more modern Ty37s of the same wheel arrangement were introduced, followed after World War II by the class Ty45 2–10–0s. Also in Poland at this time were large numbers of both German *Kriegslokomotiven* which had been built for Poland during the German occupation, and the British built 2–8–0 'Liberation' locomotives which in Poland were classified Tr202. The United States contributed 2–8–0s and 2–10–0s to ease the postwar motive power shortage, and the Poles built more 2–8–2s developed from the Reichsbahn 19–101 class, and classified Pt47 by the Polish State Railways.

Poland continued to be visited by steam enthusiasts from Western Europe up to the end of the 1970s and at this period it was described as 'without doubt the steamiest country this side of the Bosphorous.' One visitor in 1978 recorded over a thousand steam locomotives of 15 different types seen during a single week.

177

9. The Wider World

The starting point for this last look round the world of steam is the African continent. Here some of the largest steam locomotives in the world worked out their final years. Africa saw the ultimate development of the Beyer-Garratt articulated locomotive, a design developed for countries where increasing traffic had to be worked over lines which had been laid originally with light rails for reasons of economy. The tractive effort that can be usefully developed by a locomotive is limited by the weight on the axles. If the effort exceeds a certain proportion of that weight, adhesion is lost and the wheels slip on the rails. The permanent way restricts the load that can be placed on an axle, and so to haul heavy trains it may be necessary to spread the locomotive weight over a large number of driving axles, each contributing a relatively small proportion of the total tractive effort. In a conventional locomotive this would involve a long rigid wheelbase and consequent difficulties in negotiating curves, particularly the sharp curvature of many lines in the less-developed countries where heavy engineering works were kept to the practicable minimum. Various types of articulated locomotives have been designed for such conditions. One of the best-known and longest-lasting articulation systems is the Beyer-Garratt, a name associated in particular with very powerful locomotives on narrow-gauge lines in Africa.

The Garratt system of construction was devised by H W Garratt, a British engineer, who patented it in 1908. The manufacturing rights were taken up by the Manchester firm of Beyer Peacock & Co Ltd, so that locomotives built on Garratt's principle are often referred to as Beyer-Garratts. A Beyer-Garratt consists in effect of two bogie-mounted steam engines taking steam from a common boiler which is carried on a cradle slung between them. With no machinery below the boiler itself, the usual constraints on the side of firebox and grate are removed. The 'power' bogies at each end of the machine usually carry guiding as well as driving axles but the overall wheelbase of each is short and the locomotive adapts itself well to severe curvature.

Typical Garratt territory is found in East Africa, where the prewar Kenya and Uganda Railways used the type very extensively on their meter-gauge system. This system began using Garratts in 1926. The permanent way on its main line from Mombasa

Left: A Stanier 2–8–0 of LMS origin works out its years to retirement in Asiatic Turkey, near Ankara.
Right: A German-built 4–6–4T of the Turkish State Railways makes ready to emerge from Haydarpasa shed on the eastern shore of the Bosphorus opposite Istanbul.

Above: Rhodesia Railways
16A class Garratt (2–6–2+
2–6–2) at work in 1975.
Above left: A Rhodesia
Railways Garratt at Soma-
bula, 4638 feet above sea
level, on the main line from
Bulawayo to Salisbury.
Left: Egyptian State Rail-
ways 2–6–0 No 597 at
Cairo Main Shed in 1946.
This locomotive was built
in 1928 by Armstrong
Whitworth.

to Kampala restricted axleloads to 13.16 US tons/
11.75 UK tons/12 tonnes, but the EC3 class Garratt
introduced in 1939 produced a tractive effort of
46,100 lb (20,910 kg). These were the first Garratts
with the 4–8–4+ 4–8–4 wheel arrangement and the
largest and heaviest engines built up to that time to
work over rails weighing only 50 lb (22.7 kg) per
yard. They were employed on the section between
Nairobi and Kampala, a distance of 550 miles
(885.1 km), on which the line climbs to a summit of
9000 feet (2743 m) at Timbora, shortly after crossing
the equator, and there are long stretches with a
ruling gradient as steep as 1-in-50.

After World War II, when the system merged into
the East African Railways, a still larger Garratt was
introduced for working between Mombasa and
Nairobi, on which heavier rails had by that time been
laid, permitting an axle-load of 23 US tons/21 UK
tons/21.3 tonnes. This was the class 59 4–8–2+
2–8–4, weighing 282 US tons/252 UK tons/256

tonnes and developing a tractive effort 83,350 lb
(37,807 kg). With these locomotives schedules between Mombasa and Nairobi were accelerated by
33 percent. Train loads up to 1120 US tons/1000
UK tons/1016 tonnes were worked over 1-in-50
gradients and around curvatures so severe that sometimes the driver could see the tail end of his train
running parallel with him but in the opposite
direction. When the 'Big Boy' Mallets in the United
States were withdrawn in the late 1950s, the EAR
class 59 Garratts became the world's largest steam
locomotives.

On the 3-foot 6-inch (1.067-m) gauge Rhodesia
Railways the Garratt locomotive was the principal
motive power for both freight and passenger services
up to dieselization, and returned to service when oil
supplies became difficult. In the final design for this
system coupled wheels of 4 feet 9 inches (1448 mm)
diameter gave the locomotives a useful turn of speed
and 55 mph (88.5 kph) was easily obtained. An

Below left: A South African Railways 4–8–2+2–8–4 Garratt of class GMAM pauses at Koloniesplaas with a Mossel Bay-to-Johannesburg express.
Below: A 58th class (4–8–2+2–8–4) Garratt of the East African Railways crosses a viaduct near Fort Ternan on the Kisumu branch.

Above: The age of the clerestory lives on in 1965 in this passenger train of the Victorian Railways, seen passing Woodend.

observer who has ridden on the footplate of these locomotives has commented on their very smooth negotiation of curves at speeds of this order, free from lurching or oscillation, and considered them an object lesson in the design of the steam locomotive as a vehicle. These 15th class locomotives, of 4—6—4+ 4—6—4 wheel arrangement, used to work through between Bulawayo and Mafeking, a distance of 484 miles (778.9 km). Two crews took turns driving and thus made the round trip of twice that distance. The engines were hand-fired and worked by a three-man crew, one man helping with bringing coal forward from the bunker ready for the fireman, and undertaking other duties. The 15th class locomotives developed a tractive effort of 47,496 lb (21,544 kg). For still heavier duties, principally freight, on the Northern main line the 20th class 4—8—2+ 2—8—4 was introduced, equipped with mechanical stoker and developing 69,330 lb (31,448 kg) tractive effort. This class could take loads of 1792—1904 US tons/ 1600—1700 UK tons/1626—1727 tonnes over the severely curved and steeply graded line from Thompson Junction, Bulawayo, to Victoria Falls on the border with Zambia, where on one section the line climbs for 20 miles (32.2 km) at an uninterrupted 1-in-150, curving continuously all the way.

The South African Railways, of the same gauge as

the Rhodesian system, began testing Garratt locomotives as early as 1921 and found them preferable in South African conditions to the Mallet type of articulation. Beginning with a modest 2—6—2+ 2—6—2, by 1929 the railways were using the massive GL class 4—8—2+ 2—8—4 with a tractive effort of 89,130 lb (40,430 kg). For more general service the GM class of the same wheel arrangement was introduced in 1938. On the 1-in-40 gradients of the line from Johannesburg to Zeerust the GMs handled loads of 784—840 US tons/700—750 UK tons/711— 762 tonnes to the same schedules as previous locomotives which had been restricted to 504—560 US tons/450—500 UK tons/457—508 tonnes. The Garratt was the type of steam locomotive with the greatest potential for development in the last days of steam and might well have exceeded the performance of the largest actually built.

In conventional locomotives the South African Railways long favored the 4—8—2 and ultimately about half of the railways' steam stock was of this wheel arrangement. Between 1935 and 1939 the 4—8—2 locomotives of classes 15E, 15F and 23 were reaching the practicable limits of size without a four-wheel trailing truck to support a larger boiler and firebox. The next step was to a 4—8—4, ordered in 1951 and delivered between 1953 and 1955.

The Leprechaun's Gold

It was Lady Day and everyone who had worked on the harvest had a holiday. The sun shone brightly, and there was a pleasant breeze, so Tom Fitzpatrick decided to go for a walk across the fields. He had been strolling for a while, when he heard a high-pitched noise, "Clickety-click, clickety-click," like the sound of a small bird chirruping.

Tom wondered what creature could be making this noise, so he crept quietly towards the sound. As he peered through some bushes, the noise stopped suddenly, and what did Tom see but a tiny old man, with a leather apron, sitting on a little wooden stool. Next to the old man was a large brown jar. The little man seemed to be repairing a miniature shoe, just large enough for his own feet. Tom could not believe what he saw.

All the stories Tom had heard about the fantastic riches of the little people came back into his mind. "If I'm careful," he said to himself, "I've got it made." And Tom remembered that you should never take your eyes away from one of the little people, otherwise they disappear.

"Good day to you," said Tom. "Would you mind telling me what's in your jar?"

"Beer, some of the best there is," said the little man.

"And where did you get it from?"

"I made it myself. You'll never guess what I made it from."

"I suppose you made it from malt," said Tom.

"Wrong!" said the leprechaun. "I made it from heather!"

"You never did! You can't make beer from heather!"

"Don't you know about the Vikings? When they were here in Ireland they told my ancestors how to make beer from heather, and the secret has been in my family ever since. But you shouldn't be wasting time asking me pointless questions. Look over there where the cows have broken into the corn field and are trampling all over the corn."

Tom started to turn round, but remembered just in time that it was a trick to make him look away from the little man. He lunged at the leprechaun, knocking over the jar of beer, and

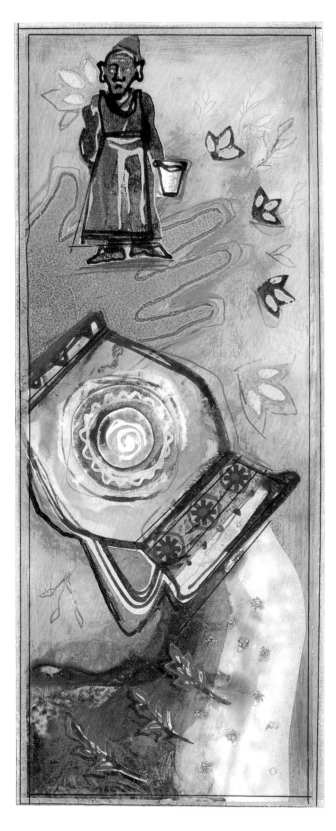

grasped the little man in his hand. Tom was angry at being tricked, and was sad to have knocked over the beer, which he had wanted to taste. But he had the creature safe in his hand.

"That's enough of your tricks!" shouted Tom. "Show me where you keep your gold, or I'll squeeze the life out of you before you can blink!"

And Tom put on such a fearsome expression that the leprechaun began to quake with fright, and to worry that Tom might truly hurt him. So he said to Tom, "You just carry me through the next couple of fields, and I'll show you the biggest crock of gold you could imagine."

So off they went. Tom held the leprechaun tightly in his fist, so that, no matter how much he wriggled and slithered, the little man could not escape. And Tom looked straight at the tiny creature, never changing his gaze, so that the leprechaun had no chance to disappear.

They walked on and on, over fields, across ditches, and through hedges. They even had to cross a crooked patch of bog, but somehow Tom managed to get through it without once looking away from the leprechaun. Finally they arrived at a field that was full of hundreds and hundreds of turnips. The leprechaun told Tom to walk towards the middle of the field, where he pointed towards a large turnip. "You just dig under that one," said the leprechaun, "and you'll find a crock full to the brim with gold coins."

Tom had nothing to dig with. He realised that he would have to go home and get his spade. But how would he find the right turnip when he returned? Quickly, he bent down to remove one of the red ribbons holding up his gaiters, and tied the ribbon around the turnip. "Now you swear to me," he said to the little creature, "that you won't take the ribbon from that turnip before I return."

The leprechaun swore that he would not remove the ribbon,

and Tom ran home to get his spade. He ran as fast as he could, because he could not wait to unearth the leprechaun's gold.

By the time Tom ran back to the turnip field, he was quite breathless. But when he opened the gate into the field he could not believe his eyes. Across the entire field a mass of red ribbons was blowing in the breeze. The leprechaun had kept his promise. He had not taken away Tom's ribbon. Instead he had tied an identical ribbon to every single turnip in the field. Now Tom knew he would never find the leprechaun's gold. His dream of fabulous riches was over.

Tom walked sulkily back home, cursing the leprechaun as he went. And every time he passed a turnip field, he gave one of the turnips a mighty wallop with his spade.

The Horned Women

It happened five hundred or more years ago, when all well-to-do women learned how to prepare and card their wool and spin it to make yarn. One evening, a rich lady sat up late in her chamber, carding a new batch of wool. The rest of the family and all the servants had gone to bed, and the house was silent. Suddenly, the lady heard a loud knocking at the door, together with a loud, high-pitched voice shouting "Open the door! Open the door!".

The lady of the house, who did not recognise the voice, was puzzled. "Who is it?" she called.

"I am the Witch of One Horn," came the reply.

The lady, who could not hear very clearly through the thick oak door, thought that it was one of her neighbours who needed help, or one of the servants in a panic, so she rushed across the room and threw open the door. The lady was quite astonished to see a tall woman, with a single horn growing in the middle of her head. The newcomer, who was carrying a pair of carders, strode across the room, sat down, and set to work carding some of the lady's wool. She worked in silence,

but all of a sudden, she looked around the room and said, "Where are all the others? They should be here by now."

Straight away, there was another knock on the door. Although she was by now rather frightened, the lady of the house could not stop herself from crossing the room and opening the door once more. To her surprise another witch came into the room, this time with a pair of horns and carrying a spinning wheel.

"Make room for me," she said. "I am the Witch of Two Horns." And no sooner had she said this than she started to spin, producing fine woollen yarn faster than anyone the lady had seen before.

Again and again, there came knocks on the door, and again and again the lady felt she had to get and up and let in the newcomers. This went on until there were twelve women in the room, and each had one horn more than the previous witch. They all sat around the fire, carding and spinning and weaving, and the lady of the house did not know what to do. She wanted to get up and run away, but her legs would not let her; she wanted to scream for help, but her mouth would not open. She began to realise that she was under the spell of the horned women.

As she sat watching them, wondering what she could do, one of the witches called to her: "Don't just sit there. Get up and bake us all a cake."

Suddenly, the lady found she could stand up. She looked around for a pot to take to the well to get some water for the cake mixture, but there was nothing that she could use. One of the hags saw her looking and said to her, "Here, take this sieve and collect some water in that."

The lady knew that a sieve could not hold water, but the witches' spell made her powerless to do anything else but walk off to the well and try to fill the sieve. As the water poured through the sieve, the lady sat down and cried.

Through her sobs, the lady heard a voice. It seemed as if the spirit of the well was talking to her. "There is some clay and moss behind the well-shaft. Take them, mix them together, and make a lining for the sieve. Then it will hold water."

The lady did as she was told, and the voice spoke again. "Go back to the house, and when you come to the corner, scream three times and shout these words as loud as you can: 'The mountain of the Fenian women is all aflame.'"

Straight away the lady's screams were echoed by the cries of the horned women. All twelve witches dashed out of the house and flew away at high speed to their mountain, Slievenamon, and the lady was released from the spell. She sighed a huge sigh of relief, but she saw quickly that the witches had made their own cake and poisoned the rest of her family. The lady turned to the well, asking the spirit "How can I help my children and servants? And what shall I do if they return here again?"

So the spirit of the well taught the lady how to protect herself if the witches should return. First she had to sprinkle on her threshold some water in which she had washed her child's feet. Next she was to take pieces of the witches' cake and place a piece in the mouth of each member of her household, to bring them back to life. Then the spirit told her to take the cloth woven by the witches, and put it into her chest. And finally she was to place a heavy oak crossbeam across the door. The lady did all these things, and waited.

Soon the twelve witches returned, screaming and howling, for they had arrived at their mountain and found no fire, and were mad for vengeance.

"Open the door! Open, foot-water!" they yelled, and their cries made people tremble in the next village.

"I cannot open," called the water, "I am all scattered on the ground."

"Open the door! Open wood and beam!" they shouted, and their noise could be heard far over the hills.

"I cannot open," said the door. "For I am fastened with a stout crossbeam."

"Open the door! Open cake that we made with our enemies'

blood!" they screamed, and their screams could be heard by the sea.

"I cannot open," said the cake. "For I am broken in pieces."

And then the witches knew that they were defeated, and flew back to their mountain, cursing the spirit of the well as they went.

The lady of the house was finally left in peace. When she went outside to see that the coast was clear, she found a cloak that one of the witches had dropped. She hung the cloak up in her room, and it was kept in her family for five hundred years, in memory of her victory over the twelve horned women.

Hudden and Dudden and Donald O'Neary

Once upon a time there were two farmers, called Hudden and Dudden. They each had a huge farm, with lush pastures by the river for their herds of cows, and hillside fields for their sheep. Their beasts always brought good prices at the market. But no matter how well they did, they always wanted more.

Between Hudden's and Dudden's land was a little field with a tiny old cottage in the middle, and in this house lived a poor man named Donald O'Neary. Donald only had one cow, called Daisy, and barely enough grass to feed her.

Although he was only poor and had but a narrow strip of farmland, Hudden and Dudden were jealous of Donald. They wanted to turf him out and divide his land between them, so that they could make their farms even bigger. And whenever the two rich farmers met up, their talk would always turn to how they could get rid of poor Donald.

One day, they were talking about this and Hudden suddenly said, "Let's kill Daisy. If he has no cow, he'll soon clear out." So, Hudden and Dudden crept quietly into Donald's cow-shed, fed some poison to Daisy, and made off with all speed.

At nightfall, Donald went to the shed to check that Daisy was comfortable. The cow turned to her master, licked his hand affectionately, collapsed on to the floor, and died.

Donald was saddened at Daisy's death. But, because he was a poor fellow, he had learned long ago how to cope with hardship, and he soon began to think whether he could turn his misfortune to good use. "At least I can get some money for Daisy's hide," he thought. And then he had an idea.

The next day, Donald marched off to the fair in the nearby town, with the hide slung over his shoulder. Before he got to the fair, he stopped in a quiet spot, made some slits in the hide,

and put a penny in each of the slits. Then he chose the town's best inn, strode through the door, hung up the hide on a nail, and ordered a glass of the best whisky.

The landlord looked suspiciously at Donald's ragged clothes. "Don't worry that I can't pay you," said Donald. "I may look poor, but this hide gives me all the money I want." Donald walked over to the hide, hit it with his stick, and out fell a penny. The landlord was flabbergasted.

"What can I give you for that hide?" he asked.

"It's not for sale," replied Donald. "Me and my family have lived off that hide for years. I'm not going to sell it now." And Donald whacked the hide again, producing another penny.

Eventually, after the hide had produced several more pennies, the landlord could stand it no longer. "I'll give you a whole bag of gold for that hide!" he shouted. Donald, who could not believe his good fortune, gave in, and the deal was struck.

When Donald got home, he called on his neighbour Hudden. "Would you lend me your scales? I sold a hide at the fair today and want to work out how much I have made."

Hudden could not believe his eyes as Donald tipped the gold into his scales. "You got all that for one hide?" he asked. And as soon as Donald had gone home, he raced round to Dudden's, to tell him what had happened. Dudden could not believe that poor Donald had sold Daisy's hide for a whole bagful of gold,

so Hudden took his neighbour to Donald's hovel, so that he could see for himself. They walked straight into Donald's cottage without knocking on the door, and there was Donald sitting at the table, counting his gold.

"Good evening Hudden; good evening Dudden. You thought you were so clever, playing your tricks on me. But you did me a good turn. I took Daisy's skin to the fair, where hides are fetching their weight in gold."

The next day, Hudden and Dudden slaughtered all their cattle, every single cow and calf in their fine herds. They loaded the hides on to Hudden's cart and set off to the fair.

When they arrived, Hudden and Dudden each took one of the largest hides, and walked up and down the market square

shouting "Fine hides! Fine hides! Who'll buy our fine hides?"
Soon a tanner went up to Hudden and Dudden.

"How much are you charging for your hides?"

"Just their weight in gold."

"You must have been in the tavern all morning if you think
I'll fall for that one," said the tanner, shaking his head.

Then a cobbler came up to them.

"How much are you charging for your hides?"

"Just their weight in gold."

"What sort of a fool do you take me for?" shouted the
cobbler, and landed Hudden a punch in the belly that made
him stagger backwards. People heard this commotion and

came running from all over the fair ground. One of the crowd was the innkeeper. "What's going on?" he shouted.

"A pair of villains trying to sell hides for their weight in gold," replied the cobbler.

"Grab them! They're probably friends of the con-man who cheated me out of a bag of gold pieces yesterday," said the innkeeper. But Hudden and Dudden took to their heels. They got a few more punches, and some nips from the dogs of the town, and some tears in their clothes, but the innkeeper did not catch them, and eventually they ran all the way home.

Donald O'Neary saw them coming, and could not resist laughing at them. But Hudden and Dudden were not laughing. They were determined to punish Donald. Before the poor

man knew what was happening, Hudden had grabbed a sack, and Dudden had forced Donald into it and tied up the opening. "We'll carry him off to the Brown Lake and throw him in!" said Dudden.

But Hudden and Dudden were tired, with running from the town and carrying Donald, so they stopped for a drink on the way, leaving Donald, in his sack, on the inn doorstep.

Once more, Donald began to think how he could gain from his problem, and he started to scream and shout inside the sack: "I won't have her. I won't have her I tell you!" He repeated this on and on until a farmer, who had just arrived with a drove of cattle, took notice.

"What do you mean?" asked the farmer.

"The king's daughter. They are forcing me to marry the king's daughter, but I won't have her."

The farmer thought how fine it would be to marry the king's daughter, to be dressed in velvet and jewels, and never again to get up at dawn to milk the cows.

"I'll swap places with you," said the farmer. "You

can take my herd, and I will get into the sack and be taken to marry the king's daughter."

So the farmer untied the sack and let out Donald O'Neary. "Don't mind the shaking, it's just the steep palace steps. And don't worry if they curse you or call you a rogue. They are angry because I have been shouting that I don't want to marry the princess," said Donald.

Quickly, the farmer got into the sack, and Donald tied up the cord and drove away the herd of cattle. He was long gone when Hudden and Dudden came out of the inn and picked up their burden. Refreshed with their whisky, they soon arrived at the lake, threw in the sack, and returned home.

Hudden and Dudden could not believe their eyes when they arrived. There was Donald O'Neary, as large as life, with a large new herd of fine fat cattle.

Donald said, "There's lots of fine cattle down at the bottom of the lake. Why shouldn't I take some for myself? Come along with me and I will show you." When they got to the lake, Donald pointed to the reflections of the clouds in the water. "Don't you see the cattle?" he said. Greedy to own a rich herd like their neighbour, the two farmers dived headfirst into the waters of the lake. And they have never been seen since.

Munachar and Manachar

There were once two little fellows called Munachar and Manachar. They liked to pick raspberries, but Manachar always ate them all. Munachar got so fed up with this that he said he would look for a rod to make a gibbet to hang Manachar.

Soon, Munachar came to a rod. "What do you want?" said the rod. "A rod, to make a gibbet," replied Munachar.

"You won't get me," said the rod, "unless you can get an axe to cut me." So Munachar went to find an axe. "What do you want?" said the axe. "I am looking for an axe, to cut a rod, to make a gibbet," replied Munachar.

"You won't get me," said the axe, "unless you can get a stone to sharpen me." So Munachar went to find a stone. "What do you want?" said the stone. "I am looking for a stone, to sharpen an axe, to cut a rod, to make a gibbet," replied Munachar.

"You won't get me," said the stone, "unless you can get water to wet me." So Munachar went to find water. "What do you want?" said the water. "I am looking for water to wet a stone, to sharpen an axe, to cut a rod, to make a gibbet," replied Munachar.

"You won't get me," said the water, "unless you can get a deer who will swim me." So Munachar went to look for a deer. "What do you want?" said the deer. "I am looking for a deer, to swim some water, to wet a stone, to sharpen an axe, to cut a rod, to make a gibbet," replied Munachar.

"You won't get me," said the deer, "unless you can get a hound who will hunt me." So Munachar went to look for a hound. "What do you want?" said the hound. "I am looking for a hound, to hunt a deer, to swim some water, to wet a stone, to sharpen an axe, to cut a rod, to make a gibbet," replied Munachar.

"You won't get me," said the hound, "unless you can get some butter to put in my claw." So Munachar went to look for some butter. "What do you want?" said the butter. "I am looking for some butter to put in the claw of a hound, to hunt a deer, to swim some water, to wet a stone, to sharpen an axe, to cut a rod, to make a gibbet," replied Munachar.

"You won't get me," said the butter, "unless you can get a cat who can scrape me." So Munachar went to look for a cat.

"What do you want?" said the cat. "I am looking for a cat to scrape some butter, to put in the claw of a hound, to hunt a deer, to swim some water, to wet a stone, to sharpen an axe, to cut a rod, to make a gibbet, " replied Munachar.

"You won't get me," said the cat, "unless you can get some milk to feed me." So Munachar went to get some milk. "What do you want?" said the milk. "I am looking for some milk, to feed a cat, to scrape some butter, to put in the claw of a hound, to hunt a deer, to swim some water, to wet a stone, to sharpen an axe, to cut a rod, to make a gibbet," replied Munachar.

"You won't get me," said the milk, "unless you can bring me some straw from those threshers over there." So Munachar went to ask the threshers. "What do you want?" said the threshers. "I am looking for some straw, to give to the milk, to feed a cat, to scrape some butter, to put in the claw of a hound, to hunt a deer, to swim some water, to wet a stone, to sharpen an axe, to cut a rod, to make a gibbet," replied Munachar.

"You won't get any straw," said the threshers, "unless you

bring some flour to bake a cake from the miller next door." So Munachar went to ask the miller. "What do you want?" said the miller. "I am looking for some flour to bake a cake, to give to the threshers, to get some straw, to give to the milk, to feed a cat, to scrape some butter, to put in the claw of a hound, to hunt a deer, to swim some water, to wet a stone, to sharpen an axe, to cut a rod, to make a gibbet," replied Munachar.

"You'll get no flour ," said the miller, "unless you fill this sieve with water." Some crows flew over crying "Daub! Daub!" So Munachar daubed some clay on the sieve, so it would hold water.

And he took the water to the miller, who gave him the flour; he gave the flour to the threshers, who gave him some straw; he took the straw to the cow, who gave him some milk; he took the milk to the cat, who scraped some butter; he gave the butter to the hound, who hunted the deer; the deer swam the water; the water wet the stone; the stone sharpened the axe; the axe cut the rod; the rod made a gibbet – and when Munachar was ready to hang Manachar, he found that Manachar had BURST!

King O'Toole and his Goose

Many years ago lived a king called O'Toole. He was a great king, with a large and prosperous kingdom, and he loved to ride the length and breadth of his realm, through the woods and across the fields, hunting deer.

But as time went by the king grew old and infirm, and he could no longer ride and hunt. He became sad and bored, and did not know what to do. Then one day he saw a flock of geese flying across the sky. O'Toole admired the birds' graceful flight, and decided that he would buy his own goose, to amuse himself. The king loved to watch the goose flying around his lake, and every Friday, the bird dived into the water and caught a trout for O'Toole to eat.

The graceful flight of the goose, and the tasty fish she caught, made O'Toole happy. But one day the goose grew old like her master, and could no longer amuse the king or catch fish for him. Once more O'Toole became sad, and even thought of drowning himself in his own lake.

Then O'Toole was out walking and he saw a young man he had not met before.

"God save you, King O'Toole," said the young man.

"Good day to you," said the king. "I am King O'Toole, ruler of these parts, but how did you know my name?"

"Oh, never mind," said Saint Kavin, for it was he. "I know more than that. How is your goose today?"

"But however did you know about my goose?" said the king.

"Oh, never mind, I must have heard about it somewhere."

King O'Toole was fascinated that a total stranger should know so much about him, so he started to talk with the young man. Eventually, O'Toole asked Kavin what he did for a living.

"I make old things as good as new," said Kavin.

"So are you some sort of tinker or magician?" asked O'Toole.

"No, my trade is better than those. What would you think if I made your old goose as good as new?"

At this, the king's eyes nearly popped out of his head. He whistled loudly and the goose came waddling slowly up to her master. It seemed impossible that the young man would be able to restore the crippled creature to health.

Kavin looked at the goose. "I can help her," he said. "But I don't work for nothing. What will you give me if I can make her fly again?"

The king looked around him, thinking of the great lands and riches of his kingdom, and looked at the poor old goose. He wanted nothing more in the world than to see this creature

hale and hearty once more. Even his kingdom seemed paltry by comparison. "I will give you anything that you ask for," replied King O'Toole.

"That's the way to do business. Will you give me all the land that the goose flies over on her first flight after I make her better?"

"I will," said the king.

"Then it's a bargain," said
Saint Kavin.

And with that, the saint
beckoned, and the goose
waddled heavily towards him,
and looked up to his face, as
if she was asking him what
he would do next. Saint
Kavin picked up the goose
by her two wings, and made
the sign of the cross on her
back. Then he threw her into
the air, saying "Whoosh!", as if he was producing a gust of
wind to help her up into the sky. As soon as Kavin had thrown
her up, the goose soared up into the air, beat her wings gently,
and was flying, high and fast, just as she had when the king
first saw her.

King O'Toole could not believe his eyes. He stared up into
the sky, with his mouth open in amazement, his eyes following
every beat of the goose's wings and every turn of her flight.
She seemed to be flying further, and higher, and more grace-
fully than ever before. Then the goose made a final turn and
swooped down, to land at the king's feet, where he patted her
gently on the head.

"And what do you say to me," said Saint Kavin, "for making her fly again?"

"It goes to show that nothing beats the art of man," said O'Toole.

"Anything else?" said Kavin.

"And that I am beholden to you."

"But remember your promise," went on Kavin. "Will you give me every patch of ground, every field and every forest, that she has flown over on her first flight?"

King O'Toole paused and looked at the young man. "Yes, I will," he said. "Even though she has flown over every acre of my kingdom. Even if I lose all my lands."

"That is well spoken, King O'Toole," said the young man. "For your goose would not have flown again if you had gone back on your word."

So the king showed the young man all the lands of which he was now master. He called his scribes to draw up documents to prove that the kingdom had been passed from one man to the other. And so it was that Saint Kavin made himself known at last to King O'Toole. "I am Saint Kavin in disguise. I have done all this to test you, and you have not failed the test. You have done well, King O'Toole, and I will support you and give you food, drink, and somewhere to live now that you have given up your kingdom."

"Do you **mean** all this time I have been talking to the greatest of the saints, while I just took you for a young lad?" said the flabbergasted O'Toole.

"You know the difference now," replied Kavin.

And Kavin was good as his word, and looked after O'Toole in his old age. But neither the king nor the goose lived long. The goose was killed by an eel when she was diving for trout, and the old king perished soon afterwards. He refused to eat his dead goose, for he said that he would not eat what Saint Kavin had touched with his holy hands.

The Story of Deirdre

Long ago in Ireland lived a man by the name of Malcolm Harper. He was a good man, with a wife, and a house, and lands of his own, but no family. One day, a soothsayer called on Malcolm, and when Malcolm found out that his visitor could see into the future, he asked if the soothsayer could foretell what the future held in store for him. The soothsayer paused, went out of the house for a few minutes to collect his thoughts and look into the future, and returned to face Malcolm.

"When I looked into the future I saw that you will have a daughter who will bring great trouble to many men in Ireland. Much blood will be spilled on her account, and three of the country's bravest heroes with lose their lives because of her."

A few years later a fine daughter was born to Malcolm's wife, and they called the girl Deirdre. Malcolm and his wife were afraid of the trouble she might bring them, so they decided to find a foster mother, who would agree to keep Deirdre away from the sight of men.

When they found a suitable foster-mother, they went to a far country and raised a mound of earth, and built inside a house, which could hardly be seen from outside. And there Deirdre and her foster-mother lived, unknown to the world, until the girl was sixteen years of age.

The foster-mother passed on all her knowledge to Deirdre, so soon the girl could sew and spin and cook, and knew all about the plants and flowers that grew around their hidden home.

Then one foul night, when a gale was blowing and black clouds filled the sky, a hunter passed the mound where Deirdre lived. He had lost the scent of his quarry, and found himself far away from his companions. Tired and lost, he settled down by the side of the grassy hillock to rest, and soon, with his tiredness

and the oncoming dark, he fell into a deep sleep.

As he slept, the hunter dreamed that he had come upon a place where the fairies lived. It seemed that he could hear the little creatures playing their music, and he began to shout out loud, "Let me in! I am a hunter far from home, and I need warmth and shelter."

Snug inside her house, Deirdre heard the huntsman's cry. "What noise is that? It sounds as if some poor creature needs our help."

Deirdre's foster-mother realised what they had heard, and tried to keep her ward away from the man outside. "Just some bird or beast looking for its mate," she replied. "Leave well alone, and it will disappear into the woods."

But Deirdre had heard the hunter asking to be let in, and, kind-hearted as she was, she would not turn away a creature in peril. "Foster-mother, you have taught me to be kind and considerate to others. I will let the poor creature in and give it shelter." And Deirdre unbolted the door to their house, and let the hunter come in.

When the hunter saw Deirdre, he realised that there were many men at King Connachar's court who would be over-whelmed by her beauty. He mentioned especially the great hero, Naois, son of Uisnech, who would be glad of such a wife. Although Deirdre's foster-mother tried to persuade the

hunter to tell no-one about the girl, he would make no such promise, and soon left, heading towards the royal palace.

As soon as he arrived at the court, he asked leave to speak to the king. "What is it you want?" asked Connachar.

"I came to tell you about the fairest woman I ever saw," replied the hunter. "Surely she must be the most beautiful in all of Ireland."

The king questioned the hunter about Deirdre, and promised him rich rewards if he would tell the king how to find her dwelling-place. Then King Connachar called for his kinsmen, and they rode off to find the place where Deirdre lived. When the king knocked at the door, the foster-mother, little thinking

who it was, called out that she would only open if the king commanded her.

"This is King Connachar himself," he called, and they could do nothing but obey his command and open the door. As soon as Connachar saw Deirdre he wanted to carry her away and marry her forthwith. But Deirdre hesitated, asking the king to wait for a year and a day before their marriage. Connachar said he would wait, so long as she promised solemnly that she would marry him at the end of that time. Deirdre promised, and Connachar took her to his palace, where there were ladies-in-waiting to look after her every wish.

One day, Deirdre was out

walking with her ladies, when a group of men came past. When she saw them, Deirdre was struck with their handsome appearance, and thought that they must be Naois, son of Uisnech, and his two brothers. Deirdre could not take her eyes from Naois as he passed, and realised that she was falling in love with the young lord. Suddenly, she gathered her gown about her and began to run after the young men, leaving her ladies-in-waiting behind. "Naois, son of Uisnech," she called. "Will you leave me behind?"

When he heard Deirdre calling, Naois turned back, saw the girl, and was smitten with love himself. Swiftly, he decided to take the girl with him, and they rode away together, Naois' brothers with them, never stopping until they reached Scotland.

Naois and his brothers Allen and Arden lived in their tower, and Deirdre was happy with them, until the time came when Deirdre had promised to marry Connachar. The king began to think how he might get Deirdre back, and he decided on this plan. He would hold a great feast, inviting all the lords from his kingdom and thereabouts, including Naois and his brothers. And Connachar sent his uncle, Ferchar Mac Ro, together with Ferchar's three sons, to Scotland, to invite Naois.

Deirdre was worried when she heard Ferchar tell Naois about the king's invitation. "Do not go," she begged. "It is a

trick. I had a dream, in which I saw three hawks coming to Scotland and hovering above your tower. Their beaks were stained with red blood. They were coming for you."

But Naois insisted. "It will be bad luck for us if we do not accept the king's invitation," he said. And Ferchar Mac Ro agreed, saying, "If the king is kind to you, be kind to him in return. But if he is violent towards you, treat him in the same way. I and my three strong sons will stand by you." So Ferchar and his sons returned with Naois and his brothers. And although she was unwilling, and wept and trembled with fear, Deirdre went with them.

Once they had arrived at the palace of Connachar, Ferchar sent a message that he was back, and that Naois, Allen, Arden, and Deirdre were with him. Connachar was surprised, since he had thought that Naois would not have dared return. Because he was not yet ready to receive his guests, Connachar asked his servants to show them to a small house he kept for visitors, some way from the palace.

Connachar grew impatient and anxious about Deirdre, so he sent his kinsman Gelban Grednach down to the house to see how they fared. "Tell me whether Deirdre looks well, and whether she is still as beautiful as she was," he ordered. Gelban crept down to the house and looked in at the spy hole in the door. There was Deirdre, together with Naois

and his brothers, who were playing dice. Deirdre blushed, as she always did when someone looked at her, and Naois noticed her reddening face at once. Naois, maddened that someone should be spying on Deirdre, grabbed one of the dice and hurled it straight at the spy hole. Gelban reeled back in pain. The dice had taken out his eye. He scrambled back to the king, his hand clasped to his bleeding face.

Gelban told the king what had happened, adding that Deirdre was so beautiful he almost risked losing the sight in his other eye.

Connachar realised that he should lose no time, if Naois would ruin the sight of any man who even looked at Deirdre.

So straight away he gathered together his three hundred bravest men, and they vowed to take Deirdre and kill her captors.

When Connachar and his men arrived, Ferchar's sons came to the aid of Naois, as they had promised. Never before was there such a fearsome sight, as the sons of Ferchar fought all comers, slashing left and right with their swords, and killing every one of Connachar's men. The king could hardly control his wrath as Naois, his brothers, and Deirdre made their escape, and the sons of Ferchar left to tell their father all about their great deeds of heroism.

Connachar had almost given up hope when he remembered his best magician, Duanan Gacha Druid. "You are supposed to be the most powerful magician in Ireland," the king said. "I have spent sacks of gold on books of spells for you and on ingredients for your magic potions, yet still my enemies escape from me. What can you do?"

"I will find a way to stop them," replied the wizard, lifting up his arms and pointing towards the middle distance. Suddenly a vast, dense forest appeared, with trees, briars, and underbrush

blocking the way of the sons of Uisnech. But Naois and Allen and Arden hacked their way through the middle of the trees, and Deirdre followed, holding Naois' hand.

"It's hopeless," said Connachar. "They can get through the trees with hardly a moment's hesitation. Surely we are powerless to stop them escaping."

"Then I will find another way to stop them," proclaimed the magician, lifting his arms once more. This time, instead of a grass-covered plain in front of the sons of Uisnech, there was a grey sea. But Naois and Allen and Arden took off their outer clothes and each man tied them in a bundle on his back. Naois lifted Deirdre and put her on his shoulders. Then the three men began to wade steadily through the great grey sea, walking further and further away from Connachar.

"They are still getting away," moaned the king. "Have you no other powers to stop them in their tracks?"

"I have yet one more way to stop them," cried the druid, gesturing with his arms yet again. And no sooner had the druid raised his arms than the sea began to freeze. Each wave was as sharp as a sword on one side, and the other side was coated with deadly poison. It seemed that no living thing would be able to pass through.

Arden was the first to be overcome. Naois lifted him above the frozen waves, but Arden was already dying. Soon Allen too was feeling faint, and perished before Naois could do anything to help him. When he saw his two beloved brothers dead beside him, Naois too gave up hope. With his brothers gone he little cared whether he was alive or dead, and soon he was overcome by the deadly frozen sea.

"All the sons of Uisnech are gone," said the druid. "You may take your rightful wife."

But hard as he looked, Connachar could no longer see Deirdre. "Take away the frozen waves, so that I can see if she still lives," commanded the king. The druid's magic took away the sea, and there was the green plain once more. In the centre were the three dead sons of Uisnech, and by their side was Deirdre, her head bowed in mourning for the death of Naois, the man she truly loved.

Connachar ordered graves to be dug for the three brothers, and Deirdre followed them, still sorrowing, to the burial place. When she arrived, she told the gravediggers to make the grave larger and wider, until she jumped into the grave beside the body of Naois, and died by his side.

The king told his men to take her body out of the grave and buried it well away, on the opposite shore of the loch. But as time went by, a fir tree grew above the grave of Naois, and another over Deirdre's grave. Slowly, the two trees grew together, until their branches met above the loch's waters. Connachar did not like to be reminded of the love of Naois and Deirdre, so ordered the branches to be cut. Again, the branches grew, and again they were removed. But the time came when Connachar took a new wife, and she told him to let the branches grow over the waters as they would, and to leave the dead to lie in peace.

Stuck for a Story

There was once a king of Leinster whose favourite pastime was listening to stories. Every evening, before the king went to sleep, he called his best story-teller to him, and the story-teller told him a story, a different one each night. And whatever problems or worries had troubled the king during the day, they were eased away by the skill of the story-teller, and the king always had a good night's sleep. In return, the king granted his story-teller a large estate, with a big house and acres of land, for he thought that the story-teller was one of the most important men in his entire kingdom.

Each morning, when the story-teller got up, he went for a walk around his estate before breakfast and thought up his story for the evening. But one morning, after walking around his whole estate, he found it impossible to think of a new tale. He seemed to be unable to get beyond "There was once a king of Ireland" or "In olden times there was a great king with three sons".

His wife called the story-teller in to breakfast, but he said he would not come in until he had thought of a story. Then, as she was calling him again, he saw an old, lame beggarman in the distance, and went up to talk to him.

"Good morning to you. Who might you be, and what are you doing here?" asked the story-teller.

"Never mind who I am," replied the old man. "I was resting awhile, for my leg is painful and I am tired, wondering who would play a game of dice with me."

The story-teller thought that a poor old man would have little money to gamble with. But the beggar said he had a hundred gold pieces, and the story-teller's wife said, "Why don't you play with him? A story might come to you afterwards." And so the two men began to throw.

Things did not go well for the story-teller. Soon he had lost all his money, but the old man still asked him to play another game. "I have no money left," said the story-teller.

"Then play for your chariot and horses and hounds," said the old man. The story-teller was unwilling to gamble away his possessions, but his wife encouraged him to take the risk.

"Go on, play another game, you might win. And anyway I don't mind walking." So they threw the dice, and again the story-teller lost the game.

"Will you play again," said the old man.

"Don't make fun of me," said the story-teller. "I have nothing to stake."

"Then play for your wife," said the beggar. Once again, the story-teller was unwilling, and turned his back on the beggar, but again his wife encouraged him, so they played and the story-teller lost once more.

The story-teller's wife went to join the beggar.

"Have you anything else to stake?" asked the old man. When the story-teller remained silent, the old man said simply, "Stake yourself."

They rolled the dice for the final time, and yet again the story-teller was the loser. "You have won me," said the story-teller. "Now what will you do with me?"

"What kind of animal would you prefer to be, a fox, a deer, or a hare?"

The story-teller thought, and decided that he would rather be a hare, for at least he would be able to run away from danger. So the old man took a wand out of his pocket and turned the story-teller into a hare. Then his wife called her hounds, and they chased the hare, round and round the field, and all along the high stone wall that ran around it. And all the while the beggar and the story-teller's wife laughed and laughed to see the hare twist, turn, and double back on his path to try to avoid the hounds. The hare tried to hide behind the wife, but

she just kicked him back into the field. The hounds were about to catch him when the beggar waved his wand, the hounds fell back, and the story-teller reappeared in the hare's place.

When the beggar asked the story-teller how he liked the hunt, the story-teller said he wished he was a hundred miles away. Suddenly, the beggar waved his wand, and the story-teller found himself in a different part of the country, at the castle of the lord Hugh O'Donnell. What was more, the story-teller realised quickly that he was invisible – he could see all about him, but no-one could see him.

Soon the beggar arrived at O'Donnell's castle.

"Where have you come from and what do you do?" asked the lord.

"I am a great traveller and magician," said the beggar.

Soon, the beggar was playing tricks on O'Donnell's men. "Give me six pieces of silver and I will show you that I can move one of my ears without moving the other."

"Done," said one of O'Donnell's men. "You'll never move one ear without moving the other, even great ears like yours!"

The beggarman then put one hand to one of his ears, and gave it a sharp pull.

O'Donnell roared with laughter, and paid the beggar six pieces of silver for the joke. But his man was less pleased.

"What sort of trick do you call that?" he said. "Any fool could move his ear that way." And the man gave his own ear a mighty pull – and off came ear and head together.

Everyone in the castle was dumbstruck, except for the beggar, who said, "Now I'll show you an even better trick." He took out of his bag a ball of silk, unrolled it, and threw it up into the air, where it turned into a thick rope. Then he sent a hare racing up the rope, followed by a hound to chase it.

"Who will catch the hound and stop it eating my hare?" challenged the beggar. Sure enough, one of O'Donnell's men ran up the rope, and everyone below waited. When nothing had happened for a while, the beggar said, "It looks as if he has fallen asleep and let the dog eat the hare."

The beggar began to wind up the rope, and sure enough,

there was the man fast asleep and the hound polishing off the hare. The old beggar looked angry that the man had failed in his task, drew his sword, and beheaded both man and hound.

O'Donnell was enraged that two of his men, and one of his best hounds, had been beheaded in his own castle. He went to seize the beggar, but the old man put up his hand. "Give me ten pieces of silver for each of them, and they shall be cured."

No sooner had O'Donnell paid over the silver, than men and hound were restored to their former health. As for the beggar, he had vanished, taking the invisible story-teller with him.

To the story-teller's relief he

found himself back at the court of the King of Leinster, with the beggar beside him. But his relief did not last long. The king was looking for his story-teller, and instead here was the old beggar, who started to insult the royal harpers. "Their noise is worse than a cat purring over its food, or buzzing honey-bees," said the beggar.

"Hang the man who insults my harpers," shouted the king.

But when the king's guards took him off to be hanged, the beggar escaped, and they found that the king's favourite brother was mysteriously hanged in his place.

"Hang the right man this time!" bawled the king.

But this time the king's best harper was found on the gibbet.

"Do you want to try hanging me again?" grinned the beggar.

"Get out!" roared the king.

But before he went, the beggar made the story-teller visible again, and gave him back his chariot, his horses, his hounds – and his wife. "I had heard you were in difficulties," he said to the story-teller. "Now you have the story of your adventures to tell the king." Sure enough, the king thought the new story was the best he had ever heard. From that day on, it was the tale the king always wanted to hear, and the story-teller never had to think up a new story again.

The Legend of Knockgrafton

By the Galtee mountains long ago lived a poor basket-maker. He always wore a sprig of foxglove in his straw hat, so everyone called him Lusmore, an old Irish name for the foxglove. The most noticeable thing about Lusmore was that he had a huge hump on his back. This hump was so large that his head pressed down and his chin rested on his chest.

When they first saw Lusmore, most people were scared of him. But when they got to know him, they realised that he was one of the most charming and helpful of people. People were surprised that he was so sweet-tempered, since he had to bear such a deformity.

One day, Lusmore had been to a nearby town to sell some baskets, and he was walking back home. He could only go quite slowly, and found himself by the ancient mound at Knockgrafton as it got dark. He still had a way to travel, so decided to sit down beside the mound and rest for a while.

As soon as he sat down, Lusmore began to hear the most beautiful, unearthly music. He had never heard anything so

56

melodious before, with many voices singing different words, but blending in perfect harmony. Stranger still, the sound seemed to be coming from within the mound.

Lusmore was enchanted with the music which came from the mound, and eventually started to sing along with it, adding his own strain which blended beautifully with the music, making it sound even better than before. Suddenly, Lusmore found himself picked up at lightning speed, and before he knew what had happened, he was inside the mound. All around Lusmore danced tiny fairies, obviously delighted that he had liked their singing and added his own voice to their song.

Round and round they danced, in constant movement in time to the melodious song, and Lusmore smiled in amazement and enjoyment.

When the song was finally over, Lusmore watched the group of fairies start to talk among themselves, occasionally glancing up at him before going back to their conversation. He felt rather frightened, wondering what they would do to him now that he had seen inside their secret home. Then one fairy stepped out from the group and came towards him, chanting, "Lusmore, Lusmore, The hump that you bore, You shall have it no more, See it fall to the floor, Lusmore, Lusmore!".

Lusmore felt lighter, and he seemed to be able to move more easily. In fact, he felt as if he could jump to the Moon and back. Slowly, he started to lift his head, and, yes, he could stand up straight, straighter than he had ever stood before. It was true! The hump was gone!

As he looked around him, noticing again the strange beauty of the fairies who had been so kind to him, Lusmore began to feel dizzy. Then a tiredness came upon him and he fell asleep amongst the fairies.

When Lusmore awoke, he found himself outside the mound at Knockgrafton, and the morning sun was shining brightly. He said his prayers, then moved his hand gingerly towards his back. There was still no hump, and Lusmore stood proudly up,

standing his full height for the first time. To his delight he also noticed that the fairies had left him dressed in a smart new suit of clothes. So off he went home, with a spring in his step that he had never had before.

To begin with, none of his neighbours recognized Lusmore. But when they realised that he had lost his hump, word spread quickly, and soon everyone was talking about Lusmore's amazing good fortune.

One day, Lusmore was sitting by his door working away at a new basket, when an old woman appeared.

"Good day," she said. "I am looking for a man called

Lusmore, who had his hump removed by the fairies. For my best friend's son has such a hump, and if he could visit the fairies just as Lusmore did, perhaps he too could be cured."

The basket-maker told the old woman that she had found Lusmore, and explained the story of how he had heard the fairies singing, how he had joined in their song, how his hump had been taken away, and how he had been given a new suit of clothes. And the old woman thanked Lusmore, and went back to tell her friend what her son, Jack Madden, should do to rid himself of his hump.

Straight away Jack Madden set off for the old mound at Knockgrafton, and sat down beside it. Soon he began to hear the bewitching sound of the fairies singing. In fact, the music was even sweeter than before, because the fairies had added Lusmore's part to their song. Jack Madden was in a hurry to be rid of his hump, and started joining in straightaway. Unlike Lusmore, he was a greedy fellow, who thought that if he sung louder, he might get two new suits of clothes instead of Lusmore's one. And unlike Lusmore, Jack did not listen carefully to the song, and make his own voice blend with the fairies. He bawled away as loudly as he could, almost shouting out the fairies in his eagerness to be heard.

Just as he expected, Jack Madden was taken inside the mound and surrounded by fairies. But the fairies were angry with Jack

Madden. "Who was spoiling our song?" they cried. And one of the fairies started to chant at Jack Madden:

"Jack Madden, Jack Madden,
You are such a bad'un, Your life we will sadden, Two humps for Jack Madden!"

And a group of fairies took Lusmore's old hump and stuck it on Jack's back.

When Jack Madden's mother and her friend came to the mound to look for Jack, they found him with his two humps. Although they pulled and pulled at the new hump, they could not remove it. They went home cursing the fairies and anyone who dared to go and listen to fairy music. And poor Jack Madden had two humps for the rest of his life.

A Donegal Fairy

There was once an old woman who lived in Donegal, and she was boiling a large pot of water over the fire. The water was just starting to boil when suddenly, one of the little people slid down the chimney and fell with one leg in the hot water.

He screamed a piercing scream, and the old lady looked on in wonder as dozens of tiny fairies quickly appeared around the fireplace and pulled him out of the water.

One of the rescuers pointed suspiciously towards the old woman. "Did the old wife scald you?" said the tiny figure, with a menacing tone in his voice.

"No, no, it was my own fault. I scalded myself," replied the first fairy.

"Ah, just as well for her," said the rescuer. "If she had scalded you, we would have made her squeal."

The Giant's Causeway

In ancient times, when giants lived in Ireland, there were two who were the strongest and most famous giants of them all, Fin M'Coul and Cucullin. Cucullin rampaged all over Ireland, fighting with every giant he met, and always coming out the winner. People said that Cucullin could make an earthquake by stamping on the ground, and that he once flattened a thunderbolt into a pancake, and carried it around in his pocket. They said that his strength lay in the middle finger of his right hand. Fin was strong too, but he was secretly afraid of Cucullin, and whenever he heard that the other giant was coming near, Fin found some excuse to move on.

It happened at one time that Fin and his relatives were away working on the Giant's Causeway, a great road that they were building over the sea to link Ireland and Scotland. As they worked, word reached Fin that Cucullin was on his way. "I think I'll be off home for a while to see my wife Oonagh," said Fin. "She misses me when I go away to work."

So Fin set off to his home on top of the hill at Knockmany. Many people wondered why Fin and Oonagh lived there. It

was a long climb up and they had to carry their water to the top. Fin said he chose the place because he liked the view. In truth, he lived there so that he could see whether Cucullin was coming. And Knockmany was the best lookout for miles around, higher than any hill in the region except for the nearby hill of Cullamore, where Oonagh's sister Granua lived.

As Fin embraced Oonagh, she asked him, "What brought you home so early, Fin?"

"I came home to see you, my love," said Fin, and the couple went in happily to eat.

Oonagh had not been long with her husband when she realised that he was worried, and she guessed that there was some other reason for his return.

"It's this Cucullin that's troubling me," admitted Fin. "He can make the earth shake by stamping his foot, and he can squash thunderbolts into pancakes. The beast is coming to get me. If I run away, I will be disgraced; if I stay, he'll squash me like a pancake. I don't know what I'm going to do."

"Well, don't despair," said his wife. "Maybe I can get you out of this scrape." And Fin wondered what she was going to do.

First of all, Oonagh called across to her sister Granua, on the neighbouring hill of Cullamore. "Sister, what can you see?" she shouted.

"I can see the greatest giant I ever saw. He is coming this way and has just walked through Dungannon. I will call him up my hill and offer him refreshment. That may give you and Fin some more time to prepare for him."

Meanwhile, Fin was getting more and more nervous. All he could think of was the thunderbolt, flattened like a pancake in Cucullin's pocket, and he trembled with fear at what might become of them.

"Be easy, Fin," said Oonagh. "Your talk of pancakes has given me an idea. I am going to bake some bread."

"What's the point of baking bread at a time like this?" wailed Fin. But Oonagh ignored him, and started mixing the dough,

singing quietly to herself, as if she had not a care in the world. She then went out to visit her neighbours, something that made Fin even more anxious. She did not seem to be giving a thought to the giant Cucullin.

When Oonagh returned, she was carrying twenty-one iron griddles, which she had borrowed from her neighbours. She went back to her work and kneaded each iron griddle into a portion of the dough, to make twenty-one bread cakes, each with a hard iron griddle in the centre. Oonagh baked the bread cakes in the fire, and put them away in her cupboard when they were done. Then she sat down to rest, and smiled contentedly.

On the following day, they finally spied Cucullin coming up the hill towards their house. "Jump into bed," said Oonagh to Fin. "You must pretend to be your own child. Don't say anything, but listen to what I say, and be guided by me."

At two o'clock, as they expected, Cucullin arrived. "Is this the house of Fin M'Coul?" he asked. "I have heard talk that he says he is the strongest giant in all Ireland, but I want to put him to the test."

"Yes, this is his house, but he is not here. He left suddenly in great anger because someone told him that a great beast of a giant called Cucullin was in the neighbourhood, and he set out at once to catch him. I hope he doesn't catch the poor wretch,

for if he does, Fin will surely knock the stuffing out of him."

"Well I am that Cucullin," replied the giant. "And I have been searching for him. He will be sorry when I find him, for I shall squash him like a pancake."

Fin began to tremble when he heard the dreaded word "pancake", but Oonagh simply laughed.

"You can't have seen Fin," she said. "For if you had, you would think differently. But since you are here, perhaps you could help me. You'll notice that the wind is blowing at the door and making a terrible draught. Turn the house round for me, as Fin would have done if he were here."

Cucullin could harldy believe that Fin had the strength to turn the whole house around. But he went outside, grasped the building in his hand, pulled hard, and moved it around, so that the wind no longer blew at the door.

"Now, Fin was telling me that he was going to crack those cliffs on the hill down below, to make a spring come up and bring us water. Will you do that for me, since Fin is not here to do it himself?" Again, Cucullin was astonished at Fin's strength, and went outside to make a crack in the rocks for the water to come through.

Oonagh thanked him for the trouble he had taken, and offered him some food for his pains. And out with the meat and cabbage, she brought one of the bread cakes she had baked. When Cucullin bit on the bread, he cried out in pain, "Aagh! That's two of my best teeth broken!" he wailed.

"But that's the only bread that my husband will eat," said Oonagh. "Try another cake. It may not be so hard."

The hungry giant grabbed another, but his hand flew to his mouth in horror: "The Devil take your bread, or I'll have no teeth left!" he roared.

Oonagh pretended to be surprised. "Even our son eats this bread," she said, passing Fin a bread cake with no iron inside.

By now Cucullin was shaking in terror. If the young lad was so strong he could eat bread like this, what would his father be like? Cucullin decided he would be off before Fin came home. But he could not resist asking to look at the teeth of the child that could eat bread with iron inside.

"It's the back teeth that are the strongest," said Oonagh. "Put your finger into the child's mouth, and feel for yourself."

Cucullin slipped his middle finger into Fin's mouth, and Fin knew his chance had come. Fin bit hard on the giant's finger, and when Cucullin pulled his hand away in surprise, the middle finger was gone. Cucullin was crushed. He knew his strength was gone with his finger, and he ran from the house, screaming and roaring, and they never saw him again.

Fair, Brown, and Trembling

Once upon a time long ago lived King Hugh Curucha, and he had three daughters called Fair, Brown, and Trembling. Fair and Brown were his favourite daughters. They were always given new dresses and were allowed to go to church every Sunday. But Trembling, who was the most beautiful of the three, had to stay at home, where she did the cooking and housework. The other two forced Trembling to stay at home like this because they were jealous of her beauty, and feared that she might attract a husband before them.

After Trembling had been kept at home like this for seven years, the Prince of Emania met Fair, the eldest of the sisters, and fell in love with her. Just after this had happened, Fair and Brown went off to church as usual and Trembling stayed at home to cook dinner. As she worked, she talked to the old Henwife, the woman who kept the chickens on the royal farm, who had called at the kitchen. "Why haven't you gone to church too?" asked the Henwife.

"I cannot go to church," replied Trembling. "All my clothes are in tatters. Besides, if I dared to go to church, my sisters would beat me for leaving the house."

"If you could have a new dress," said the Henwife, "what sort of dress would you choose?"

"I would like a dress as white as the snow, with a pair of bright green shoes to go with it," replied Trembling.

Then the Henwife put on her cloak, snipped a tiny piece of cloth from the dress Trembling was wearing, and asked for the most beautiful white dress, and a brand new pair of green shoes. Straight away, a long white dress appeared in the old woman's hands, and a pair of green shoes, and she gave them to Trembling, who put them on. Then the Henwife gave the girl a honey-bird to put on her shoulder, and led her to the door. There stood a fine white horse, with a saddle and bridle

richly decorated with gold.

"Off you go to church," said the Henwife. "But when you get there, do not go inside, be sure to stand just outside the church door. As soon as the people start to leave at the end of Mass, be ready to ride off as quickly as you can."

So Trembling rode to church, and stayed by the door as the old woman had told her. Even though she remained outside, many people within caught a glimpse of her, and began to wonder who she was. At the end of Mass, several people ran out to get a better look at her, but she turned her horse and galloped away at great speed, so no one could catch her.

As she entered the kitchen, Trembling began to worry that no one had finished cooking dinner for her sisters. But she saw straight away that the Henwife had cooked the meal, and Trembling put on her old dress as quickly as she could.

When Fair and Brown returned, they were full of talk about the mysterious lady in white whom they had seen outside the church door. They demanded that their father buy them fine white dresses like the lady's, and next Sunday, they wore their new dresses to church.

Again, the Henwife appeared in the kitchen, and asked Trembling if she wanted to go to church. This time the old woman produced a black satin dress, with red shoes for Trembling's feet. With the honey-bird on her shoulder, she rode on a black mare

with a silver saddle, and stayed quietly by the door of the church.

The people in the church were even more amazed when they saw the strange lady by the door. Everyone wondered who she could be, but Trembling gave them no chance to find out, and rode away as soon as Mass was over.

Back home, Trembling removed her fine robe as she had before, and put the finishing touches to the meal prepared by the Henwife. When Fair and Brown arrived home from church, they were full of talk about the fine lady and her black satin dress. "No one even noticed our fine dresses," complained Fair. "They were too busy admiring the lady by the church

door and wondering who she might be. Everyone was staring at her with their mouths open, and none of the men even glanced at us!"

Fair and Brown would give their father no peace until he bought them fine black satin dresses, just like the one they had seen their sister wearing, and red shoes to go with them. Of course, Fair and Brown's dresses were not as elegant nor as finely made as Trembling's gown. They could not find one to match it anywhere in Ireland.

Off went Fair and Brown next Sunday in their new black dresses, and yet again the Henwife turned to Trembling and asked her what she wanted to wear to church. "I would dearly like a rose-red dress, a green cape, a hat with feathers of red, white and green, and shoes of the same colours."

The Henwife smiled to think of the fantastic mixture of colours that Trembling had chosen, but once more did her magic, and quickly Trembling was dressed in the garments of her choice, and mounted on a mare with diamond-shaped spots of white, blue, and gold over her body. The honey-bird began to sing as Trembling rode off to church, to wait outside the door.

By this time, news had spread all over Ireland about the beautiful lady who waited outside the church every Sunday, and many lords and princes had come to see her for themselves. Amongst them was the Prince of Emania, who, once he had seen Trembling, forgot all about her elder sister, and vowed to catch the strange lady before she could ride away. At the end of Mass, the prince sprinted out of church, and ran behind Trembling's mare. He was just able to grab hold of one of her shoes, before she galloped away into the distance.

The Prince of Emania vowed that he would search the length and breadth of Ireland until he found the woman whose foot would fit the shoe in his hand. The other princes joined him, as they too were curious, and they searched in every town and village until they came to the house of Fair, Brown, and Trembling. Both Fair and Brown tried to force their feet into

the shoe, but it was too small for them. The prince asked if there was any other woman in the house. Trembling began to speak up, but Fair and Brown tried to stop her.

"Oh, she is just a serving-girl we keep to clean the house," said Fair. But the prince insisted that every woman should have the chance to try on the shoe.

When the shoe fitted exactly the prince was overjoyed. He was about to declare his love, when Trembling begged him to wait. She ran very quickly to the house of the Henwife, who helped Trembling on with her white dress; then she returned home to show everyone that she was truly the mysterious lady. She then did the same thing with the other dresses, amazing her sisters more and more each time. The princes were just as surprised, and before she had put on the third dress, they were all challenging the Prince of Emania to fight for her hand.

The Prince of Emania fought bravely, defeating the Prince of Lochlin, who fought him for nine hours, the Prince of Spain, who fought for eight hours, and the Prince of Greece, who fought for seven hours. And at the end no one would fight the Prince of Emania, for they knew he would be the winner. So the Prince of Emania married Trembling, and the celebrations lasted for a year and a day.

All seemed to be going happily, but Fair was still very jealous of her sister. So one day, she called on her sister, and the two walked by the coast. When they came to the sea, Fair waited until there was no-one to see her, then pushed Trembling into the water. Just as it seemed Trembling would drown, a great whale came and swallowed her up. When Fair returned to the prince she put on her sister's clothes and pretended to be Trembling. But even though the two were as alike as could be, the Prince was not fooled by her trick.

Now Fair thought that no one had seen her push her sister into the sea, but a young cow-boy had watched the two sisters from a nearby field. Next day he was again in the field when he saw the whale swim by and throw Trembling out upon the sand.

Then Trembling spoke to the cow-boy, saying "Run home and tell the prince my husband what has happened. If he does not come and shoot the whale, it will carry on swallowing me, and casting me out, while keeping me under a spell. I will never be able to leave the beach and come home."

The cow-boy ran to tell the Prince what had happened, but the elder sister stopped him in his tracks, and gave him a potion to drink. The drink made him forgetful, and he said nothing about what he had seen. The next day the cow-boy returned to the sea, and once more saw the whale cast out Trembling on the shore. Trembling asked the boy if he had taken her message to the Prince and the boy admitted that he had forgotten. Shamefully, he ran to tell the prince, and again Fair gave him the potion. On the third day, when the cow-boy was by the sea and saw Trembling cast out yet again, the girl guessed what had happened and spoke to him, saying "Do not let her give you any drink when you go home. She is using a potion to make you forget what has happened."

And so it was that the prince was finally brought news of his wife. He ran to the shore, loaded his gun, and shot the whale, releasing Trembling from the creature's spell. From then on the cow-boy lived in the Prince's household, and when he came of age, he married Trembling's daughter. They all lived happily, for many years, until the Prince and Trembling died, contented, of old age.

The Haughty Princess

There was once a king who had a daughter. She was very beautiful and many dukes, earls, princes, and even kings came from all around to ask for her hand in marriage. But the princess was a proud, haughty creature who would have none of them. As each suitor approached her, she would find fault with him, and send him packing, usually with a rude remark which meant that the suitor was sure to have nothing more to do with her.

One of her suitors was plump, and to him she said, "I shall not marry you, Beer Belly." Another had a pale face, and to him she said, "I shall not marry you, Death-Mask." A third suitor was tall and thin, and to him she said, "I shall not marry you, Ramrod." Yet another prince had a red complexion, and to him she said, "I shall not marry you, Beetroot." And so it went on, until every unmarried duke and earl and prince, and even king, for miles around had been rejected, and her father thought she would never find a man she liked.

Then one day a prince arrived who was so handsome, and so polite, that she found it hard to find any fault with him at all.

But still the princess's pride got the better of her, and in the end, she looked at the brown curling hairs under his chin and said, somewhat reluctantly, "I shall not marry you, Whiskers".

The poor king was at his wit's end with his daughter, and finally lost his temper with her. "I'm sick of your rudeness. Soon no one will come to visit me for fear of what you will say to them. I shall give you to the first beggar who calls at our door for alms, and good riddance to you!"

Soon a poor beggar knocked at the door. His clothes were tattered and torn, his hair dirty and matted, and his beard long and straggling. Sure enough, the king called for the priest, and married his daughter to the bearded beggar. She cried and

screamed and tried to run away, but there was nothing for it.

After the ceremony, the beggar led his bride off into a wood. When she asked where they were going, he told her that the wood and all the land around belonged to the king she had called Whiskers. The princess was even sadder that she had rejected the handsome king, and hung her head in shame when she saw the poor, tumble-down shack where the beggar lived. The place was dirty and untidy, and there was no fire burning in the grate. So the princess had to put on a plain cotton dress, help her husband make the fire, clean the place, and prepare them a meal.

Meanwhile, the beggar gathered some twigs of willow, and after they had eaten, the two sat together making baskets. But the twigs bruised the princess's fingers, and she cried out with the pain. The beggar was not a cruel man, and saw that he must find some other work for her to do, so he gave her some cloth and thread, and set her to sewing. But although the princess tried hard, the needle made her fingers bleed, and

again tears came to her eyes. So
the beggar bought a basket full
of cheap earthenware pots and
sent her to market to sell them.

   The princess did well at market on the first day, and
returned with a profit. But the
next morning, just after she had
set out her wares, a drunken
huntsman came riding through
the market place, and his
mount kicked its way through
all the princess's pots. She returned to her husband in tears.

   In the end, the beggar spoke to the cook at the palace of
King Whiskers, and persuaded her to give his wife a job as a
kitchen maid. The princess worked hard, and every day the
cook gave her leftovers from the table to take home for her
husband. The princess liked the cook, and got on quite well in
the kitchen, but she was still sorry she had rejected King
Whiskers.

   A while later, the palace suddenly got busier. It turned out
that King Whiskers was getting married. "Who is going to
marry the king?" asked the princess. But no one knew who
the bride was going to be.

Because they were curious, the princess and the cook decided to go and see what was going on in the great hall of the palace. Perhaps they would catch a glimpse of the mysterious bride. The princess opened the door quietly and the two of them peeped in.

King Whiskers himself was in the room, and strode over when he saw the door begin to open. "Spying on the king?" he said, looking hard at the princess. "You must pay for your nosiness by dancing a jig with me." The king took her hand, led her into the room, and all the musicians began to play. But as they whirled around, puddings and portions of meat began to fly out of her pockets, and everyone in the room roared with laughter. The princess began to run to the door, but the king caught her by the hand and took her to one side.

"Do you not realise who I am?" he asked her, smiling kindly. "I am King Whiskers, and your husband the beggar, *and* the drunken huntsman who broke your pots in the market place. Your father knew who I was when he let me marry you, and we arranged all this to rid you of your pride."

The princess was so confused she did not know what to say or do. All sorts of emotions, from joy to embarrassment, welled up inside her, but the strongest of all these feelings was love for her husband, King Whiskers. She laid her head on his shoulder, and began to cry.

When she had recovered, some of the palace maids led her away and helped her put on a fine dress fit for a queen. She went back to join her husband, and none of the guests realised that the new queen was the poor kitchen maid who had danced a jig with the king.

The Man Who Never Knew Fear

There were once two brothers, called Lawrence and Carrol. Lawrence was known as the bravest boy in the village and nothing made him afraid. Carrol, on the other hand, was fearful of the least thing, and would not even go out at night.

When their mother died, they had to decide who would watch her grave. In those days it was the tradition that when a person had died, their relatives would take it in turns to stand guard over the grave, to protect it from robbers.

Carrol, who did not want to watch his mother's grave at night, made a bet with his brother. "You say that nothing makes you afraid, but I bet you will not watch our mother's tomb tonight."

Lawrence replied, "I have the courage to stay there all night." He put on his sword and marched boldly to the graveyard, where he sat down on a gravestone next to his mother's tomb.

At first, all went well, but as the night went on, the young man became drowsy. He was almost dropping off to sleep, when he saw the most awesome sight. A huge black head was coming towards him. It seemed to float through the air, and Lawrence realised that there was no body attached to it. Without taking his eye from the head, Lawrence quickly drew his sword and held it out in front of him, ready to strike if the thing came any closer. But it did not, and Lawrence stayed, looking straight at the head, until dawn.

When he got home, Lawrence told Carrol what he had seen. "Were you afraid?" asked Carrol.

"Of course I wasn't," replied Lawrence. "You know very well that nothing in the world will frighten me."

"I bet you will not watch another night," taunted Carrol.

"I would, but I have missed a whole night's sleep. You go tonight, and I will watch the third night."

But Carrol would not go, so Lawrence slept in the afternoon, and went off to the graveyard at dusk. Around midnight, a huge black monster appeared and started to scratch about near his mother's grave. Lawrence drew his sword and chopped the monster up. The graveyard was peaceful until daybreak.

Carrol was waiting for his brother to come home. "Did the great head come again?" he asked.

"No, but a monster came and tried to dig up mother's body," said Lawrence.

When the third and final night of watching came, a strange white creature appeared, with a man's head and long fangs. Again, Lawrence reached for his sword, but the ghost began to speak: "Do not strike. You have protected your mother's grave and shown yourself the bravest man in Ireland. Great wealth awaits one as brave as you. Go and seek it."

The next day Lawrence took the fifty pounds he had won from his brother in the bet, and set out to seek his riches. On his way he met a baker, and told him the story of his adventures in the graveyard. "I'll bet you another fifty pounds you'll be scared by the graveyard near here," said the baker. "Go there tonight, and bring me the goblet on the altar of the old

church." The baker had heard that the church was haunted, and that no one ever came out of the building alive.

In the dead of night, Lawrence strode up to the door of the church and hit it firmly with his sword. Straight out of the door charged an enormous black ram, with horns as long and sharp as scythes. In a flash, Lawrence struck out at the creature, and it fled, scattering its blood all around the church doorway. Then Lawrence took the goblet, and went to the baker.

The baker was astounded that Lawrence had returned in one piece, and they went to see the priest to tell him the news. The priest was overcome with joy. He paid the young man still more money, and straight away prepared to say Mass in the church. And Lawrence continued his journey, searching for something that would make him afraid.

Lawrence travelled a long way through lonely countryside, and hardly saw a house all day, when he came to valley where a crowd of people were gathered. They were watching two men playing a ball game, but they seemed to be frightened. Suddenly, one of the players hurled the ball towards Lawrence, and it hit him straight in the chest. Lawrence reached to catch it, and saw that it was the head of a man. As Lawrence took hold of it, the head screeched, "Are you not afraid?"

"No I am not!" said Lawrence, and straight away the head, and the crowd of people, vanished from sight.

Lawrence carried on until he came to a town, by which time he was weary and in need of lodgings. When he explained his quest to a young man, his acquaintance pointed to a large house across the road. "If you will stay the night in there, you will find something to put fear in you. If you can stand it, I will give you fifty pounds more."

So Lawrence found himself making his lodgings inside a cold, dark cellar, waiting to see what would happen. The first night, a bull and a stallion came into the room with a fearful neighing and bellowing, and began to fight for all they were worth. The next night two great black rams fought in the room, with such screeching and howling that Lawrence thought they would wake the whole town. But still he did not feel fear.

On his third night in the old house the ghost of an old, grey

man appeared. "You are truly the bravest man in Ireland," he said. "Never, since I died twenty years ago, have I found such a hero as you. Do one thing for me, and I will lead you to your riches." The old man went on to tell Lawrence how he had once wronged an old woman called Mary Kerrigan, and how he wanted Lawrence to go to Mary and beg her forgiveness. If he did this he could buy the old house and marry the old man's daughter.

Lawrence went to Mary Kerrigan and won her forgiveness. He bought the house, and all the land around it, and married the old man's daughter. They lived happily in the house, and the ghosts never returned.

The Enchantment of Earl Gerald

Earl Gerald was one of the bravest leaders in Ireland long ago. He lived in a castle at Mullaghmast with his lady and his knights, and whenever Ireland was attacked, Earl Gerald was among the first to join the fight to defend his homeland.

As well as being a great fighter, Gerald was also a magician who could change himself into any shape or form that he wanted. His wife was fascinated by this, but had never seen Gerald change his shape, although she had often asked him to show her how he could transform himself into the shape of some strange beast. Gerald always put her off with some excuse, until one day her pleading got too much for him.

"Very well," said Earl Gerald. "I will do what you ask. But you must promise not to show any fear when I change my shape. If you are frightened, I will not be able to change myself back again for hundreds of years."

She protested that the wife of such a noble warrior, who had seen him ride into battle against fearsome enemies, would not be frightened by such a small thing, so Gerald agreed to change his shape.

They were sitting quietly in the great chamber of the castle when suddenly Gerald vanished and a beautiful goldfinch was flying around the room. His wife was shocked by the sudden change, but did her best to stay calm and keep her side of the bargain. All went well, and she watched the little bird fly out into the garden, return, and perch in her lap. Gerald's wife was delighted with the bird, and smiled merrily, when suddenly and without warning, a great hawk swooped through the open windows, diving towards the finch. The lady screamed, even though the hawk missed Gerald and crashed into the table top, where its sharp beak stuck into the wood.

The damage was done. Gerald's wife had shown her fear. As she looked down to where the goldfinch had perched, she realised that the tiny bird had vanished. She never saw either the goldfinch or Earl Gerald again.

Many hundreds of years have passed by since Earl Gerald disappeared, and his poor wife is long dead. But occasionally, Gerald may be seen. Once in seven years, he mounts his steed and is seen riding around the Curragh of Kildare. Those few who have glimpsed him say that his horse has shoes made of silver, and the story goes that when these shoes are finally worn away, Gerald will return, fight a great battle, and rule as King of Ireland for forty years.

Meanwhile, in a great cavern beneath the old castle of Mullaghmast, Gerald and his knights sleep their long sleep. They are dressed in full armour and sit around a long table with the Earl at the head. Their horses, saddled and bridled, stand ready. When the right moment comes, a young lad with six fingers on each hand will blow a trumpet to awaken them.

Once, almost one hundred years ago, Earl Gerald was on one of his seven-yearly rides and an old horse-dealer was passing the cavern where Gerald's knights were still sleeping. There were lights in the cavern, and the horse-dealer went in to have a look. He was amazed to see the knights in their armour, all slumped on the table fast asleep, and the fine horses waiting there. He was looking at their steeds, and thinking whether he might lead one of the beasts away to market, when he dropped

the bridle he was holding. The clattering of the falling bridle echoed in the cavern and one of the knights stirred in his slumber.

"Has the time come?" groaned the knight, his voice husky with sleep. The horse-dealer was struck dumb for a moment, as the knight's voice echoed in the cave. Finally he replied.

"No, the time has not come yet. But it soon will."

The knight slumped back on to the table, his helmet giving a heavy clank on the board. The horse-dealer ran away home with all the speed he could manage. And Earl Gerald's knights slept on.

The Story of the Little Bird

Once long ago in a monastery in Ireland there lived a holy man. He was walking one day in the garden of his monastery, when he decided to kneel down and pray, to give thanks to God for the beauty of all the flowers and plants and herbs around him. As he did so, he heard a small bird singing, and never before had he heard any song as sweet. When his prayers, were finished, the monk stood up and listened to the bird, and

when the creature flew away from the garden, singing as it went, he followed it.

In a while they came to a small grove of trees outside the monastery grounds, and there the bird continued its song. As the bird hopped from tree to tree, still singing all the while, the monk carried on following the little creature, until they had gone a great distance. The more the bird sang, the more the monk was enchanted by the music it made.

Eventually, the two had travelled far away from the monastery, and the monk realised that it would soon be night-time. So reluctantly, he left the bird behind and retraced his steps, arriving back home as the sun was going down in the west. As the sun set, it lit up the sky with all the colours of the rainbow, and the monk thought that the sight was almost as beautiful and heavenly as the song of the little bird he had been listening to all afternoon long.

But the glorious sunset was not the only sight that surprised the monk. As he entered the abbey gates, everything around him seemed changed from before. In the garden grew different plants, in the courtyard the brothers had different faces, and even the abbey buildings seemed to have altered. He knew he was in the right place, yet how could all these changes have taken place in a single afternoon?

The holy man walked across the courtyard and greeted the

first monk he saw. "Brother, how is it that our abbey has changed so much since this morning? There are fresh plants in the garden, new faces amongst the brothers, and even the stones of the church seem different."

The second monk looked at the holy man carefully. "Why do you ask these questions, brother? There have been no changes. Our church and gardens have not altered since morning, and we have no new brothers here – except for yourself, for though you wear the habit of our order, I have not seen you before." And the two monks looked at each other in wonder. Neither could understand what had happened.

When he saw that the

brother was puzzled, the holy man started to tell his story. He told his companion how he had gone to walk in the monastery garden, how he had heard the little bird, and how he had followed the creature far into the countryside to listen to its song.

As the holy man spoke, the expression on the second monk's face turned from puzzlement to surprise. He said, "There is a story in our order about a brother like you who went missing one day after a bird was heard singing. He never returned to the abbey, and no one knew what befell him, and all this happened two hundred years ago."

The holy man looked at his companion and replied, "That is indeed my story. The time of my death has finally arrived. Praised be the Lord for his mercies to me." And the holy man begged the second monk to take his confession and give him absolution, for the hour of his death was near. All this was done, the holy man died before midnight, and he was buried with great solemnity in the abbey church.

Ever since, the monks of the abbey have told this story. They say that the little bird was an angel of the Lord, and that this was God's way of taking the soul of a man who was known for his holiness and his love of the beauties of nature.

The Demon Cat

In Connemara there lived a woman who was very fond of fish. She married a fisherman, and on most days he brought home a good catch. They had enough fish to sell in the market and plenty for the wife to eat. But every night a large black cat would break into their house and steal the best fish.

To begin with, the cat came only at night, and the woman could never catch it. But one day, dark storm clouds came, and the beast arrived during the daytime, as the woman and her friends were spinning. The woman's daughter looked at the cat. "That great beast must be the devil," she said. Straight away the cat scratched the girl's arm, and stood by the door to stop them escaping. "I'll teach you how to behave to a gentleman," he said.

The women began to scream, and a passing man heard them, and pushed at the door. The cat held the door closed, but the passer-by managed to get his stick through and gave the cat a hefty blow. The beast would have none of this, and jumped up to scratch the man's face. Blood flew everywhere, and the man ran off, scared out of his wits.

"Now I'll have my dinner," said the cat, once more taking the biggest fish. And when the women tried to hit it, it scratched and tore at them, and they ran away in terror.

When she had got her breath back, the fisherman's wife decided on a new plan. She went to the priest, asked for some holy water, and returned home. Walking on tiptoe, she entered her house, and there was the cat, helping himself to more fish. Silently she sprinkled holy water on to the beast, and thick black smoke rose up from its fur. Soon the cat began to shrivel up, and only the animal's two red eyes could be seen, staring through the blackness. Then the animal's remains disappeared, and the smoke began to clear away. The woman knew that the demon cat would trouble her no more.

The Maiden from the Lake

There was once a shepherd who lived in Myddvai, by the mountains of Caermarthen. A great lake was near his pastures, and one day he was watching his sheep near its shores when he saw three beautiful maidens rise from the waters. The young women came to the shore, shook the water from their hair, and walked around among the sheep.

The shepherd was overcome by the beauty of the maiden who came nearest to him, and he offered her some bread from his pack. The girl took the bread, tried a little, and said to the shepherd, "Your bread's too hard. You won't catch me." Then she ran back to the lake with the others.

The shepherd wondered whether he would see the maidens again, but just in case, on the next day, he brought some bread that was not so well baked. To his delight, the maidens appeared again, and he offered the softer bread. But this time the girl said, "Your bread's not baked. You won't catch me." Once more, she returned to the water.

On the third day, the shepherd waited for the young woman. When she came, he offered her some bread that had been

floating on the water. This she liked, and the couple talked for a long while. Finally, the maiden agreed to marry the shepherd, but gave this warning: she would be a good wife to him, as good as any ordinary Welsh woman, unless he struck her three times without reason. The shepherd vowed that he would never do this, and the couple were soon married.

The shepherd and his bride were happy, and in time had three fine sons. It happened that they were going to christen one of the children when the wife said that it was too far to walk to church.

"Then go and get the horses," said the shepherd, "and we will ride all the way."

"While I get the horses, will you fetch my gloves from the house?" asked his wife.

But when the shepherd returned with the gloves he found that she had not fetched the horses, and he tapped her gently on the shoulder to remind her.

"That's one strike," said his wife.

A little while later, the pair were at a friend's wedding. The shepherd found his wife crying and again he tapped her on the shoulder as he asked her what was wrong.

"Trouble is coming for you," she replied. "That is the second time you have struck me without reason. Take care to avoid the third time."

From then on, the shepherd was careful not so much as to tap his wife, until one day the couple were at a funeral. All of a sudden, the wife began to laugh loudly. The shepherd was amazed. He could not understand why anyone should laugh at such a sad time, so, touching her rather roughly, he said, "Wife, why are you laughing when all around you are sad?"

"I am laughing because people who die leave their troubles behind them. But your troubles have just begun. You have struck me for a third time. Now I must make an end to our marriage and bid you farewell."

The shepherd knew that the time had come for his wife to leave him, and he was sad to the bottom of his heart. But he was still more surprised when he heard his wife calling all the cattle around her, bidding them follow her to her home

beneath the waters of the lake. He saw all his cattle, even a black calf that had recently been slaughtered and a team of oxen that were ploughing a field, get up and follow her away. The oxen even took their plough with them, cutting a deep furrow all the way to the shore.

The mark left by the plough can still be seen running across the pastures by the lake. But the lady has only been seen once more. When her sons had grown up, she returned to visit them. She gave them miraculous gifts of healing. And ever since, the Doctors of Myddvai have been famous throughout the land of Wales.

The Wooing of Olwen

Long ago lived Kilhuch, son of King Kilyth. Kilhuch was brought up by his stepmother, because his own mother died when he was a baby. And his stepmother foretold that when Kilhuch was a man he would marry a young woman named Olwen, great in beauty but difficult to win.

When Kilhuch came of age, none of his family knew Olwen. His father told him to go to the court of his cousin, King Arthur, in the hope that the king would know the lady's whereabouts, and grant his consent for Kilhuch to marry.

Kilhuch looked a brave young knight as he set off on his journey, riding a fine steed with bridle and saddle of gold and cloth of richest purple. Kilhuch carried spears of silver and a gold-hilted sword, and two greyhounds, their collars studded with rubies, followed him along the road.

Arthur gave Kilhuch a royal welcome when he arrived, and straightaway offered the young man board and lodgings with his knights. But Kilhuch explained that he had come to ask a favour of the king, not to stay at court. When Arthur heard what Kilhuch wanted, he replied, "Young man, I have never heard of Olwen, and do not know her family. But I will send my messengers out to find her." So Kilhuch remained at Arthur's court while messengers went to every part of the kingdom in search of the mysterious Olwen.

The messengers returned after a year, and none had any news of Olwen. Kilhuch, full of sadness, was preparing to leave Arthur's court, when one of the knights, Kay, came up to him. "Do not go alone," he said. "I will come with you and we will search the whole of Britain until either we find Olwen, or find that she does not exist."

Arthur saw that the two men were serious in their quest and chose a number of his knights to go with them. Bedwyr,

swiftest of the knights and firm friend of Kay, Kynthelig, the best guide of all, Gwrhyr, who knew many languages, and Menw, gifted with powers of enchantment – all these went with them, and they journeyed far until they found a castle on a broad, open plain.

They asked a shepherd and his wife about Olwen, and the woman told them that Olwen lived nearby, and after a while the maiden arrived. She was dressed in a robe of red silk with a collar of gold, studded with rubies and emeralds. She had the fairest, most golden hair that Kilhuch had seen, the clearest skin, and the rosiest cheeks. When Kilhuch saw her, he knew that he was in love.

Kilhuch declared his love to Olwen, and she said that to win her, he would have to do whatever her father asked. So Kilhuch and his knights asked to talk with Yspathaden Penkawr, Olwen's father.

When they met him, Yspathaden lifted up his eyebrows, which had fallen right over his eyes, using a forked twig. "Now I can see the man who wants to be my son-in-law," he said, promising to tell them in the morning whether he would give his consent to the marriage. Then he picked up a poison dart from beside him and hurled it at Bedwyr. Quick as a flash, the knight caught the dart and threw it back to Yspathaden, hitting him in the knee. "So much the worse for my son-in-law," snarled Yspathaden.

Next day, when they came again to see Yspathaden, the old man said he should ask Olwen's grandparents before giving his consent. As they were leaving, Yspathaden again picked up a dart, throwing it at Menw. Like Bedwyr, Menw caught the dart and cast it back to the old man, hitting him in the back. "So much the worse for my son-in-law," he said again.

The following day Yspathaden threw a dart at Kilhuch, who caught it yet again. When Kilhuch threw the dart back, it caught Yspathaden in the eye. "So it is you who seek my daughter?" he said.

"Yes, it is I," replied Kilhuch.

"Then this is what I want you to do." And Yspathaden went on to describe a series of quests that Kilhuch was to undertake before he could win the hand of Olwen. He was to find the razor, comb, and scissors belonging to boar Truith, the only ones that would tame Yspathaden's unruly hair. He was to find the huntsman Mabon, who would help him on the quest. And he would track down Mabon's kinsman Eidoel, said to be as difficult to find as Mabon. When he had done all these things, Yspathaden would allow him to marry his daughter.

The knights spoke to Arthur about their quest, and he agreed to go with them. They soon found Eidoel imprisoned in the

castle of Glivi, who let them take his prisoner when he heard of their quest. But no one knew where they might find Mabon, although they asked every man they met. Then Gwrhyr began to talk to the birds and beasts. He searched out the Ousel of Cilgwri, one of the oldest of birds, and asked him about Mabon. "Many years have I been here," said the Ousel.

"But I have heard nothing of Mabon. But there is one family of animals that has been here longer than me. Search out the Stag of Redynvre."

When they found the Stag, he said "I have been here many years. I have seen yonder oak tree grow from a sapling and wither away to a stump. And in all that time I have heard nothing of Mabon." The Stag told them to ask the Owl of Cwm Cawlwyd, who was older still.

When they found the Owl, he said "Long have I been here. I have watched entire woodlands grow, men fell them, and new woods grow in their place. But in all that time I have not heard tell of Mabon. Seek out the Eagle of Gwern Abwy, the oldest bird of all."

So they went to find the Eagle, who told them "When first I came here, this rock was a tall cliff. Now it has worn away. But in all this time I have not heard of Mabon. Once, when I was flying above a river, I tried to catch a Salmon at Llyn Llyw. Instead, the fish caught me,

and tried to pull me under the water. It was a narrow escape.
That creature swims up and down the River Severn, hearing
news of all men and creatures. Seek out the Salmon and tell
him of your quest."

Finally they found the Salmon, who told them about his
travels. "When I swim down the river to Gloucester, there I see
a strong walled city with a great prison. Go there and you may
find the man you seek."

So Arthur, his knights, and the birds and beasts they had met
travelled to Gloucester and stood outside the prison walls.
Inside they could here a terrible wailing.

"Who is within?" asked Gwrhyr.

"It is Mabon, imprisoned here," came the reply, and they knew their quest was almost at an end. Arthur stormed the prison, and then Kay and Bedwyr broke into the dungeon and rescued Mabon. It remained only for them to find the razor, comb and scissors of the boar Truith.

When they found the boar, they had to chase him all across the land of Wales. The creature and his seven young piglets made a brave stand, and Arthur's men had to kill them one by one, until only Truith remained. At last, they cornered the boar, and Mabon and Kay managed to seize his razor and scissors. But the boar would not give up his comb, until they chased him into the sea and he disappeared beneath the waves.

Kilhuch, Arthur, Mabon, Eidoel, and all the knights returned to seek Yspathaden and Olwen. Yspathaden was shaved with the razor of Truith, and then he turned to Kilhuch.

"You shall have my daughter," he said, grudgingly. "For you have won her, although you could not have done it without the help of Arthur. I give her to you, even though it grieves me to lose her."

So Kilhuch, son of King Kilyth, finally married his Olwen, and Arthur and his knights returned to their round table.

Beth Gellert

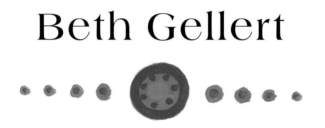

More than anything in the world, Prince Llewelyn loved to hunt. When he was ready for the chase he would stop by the castle gate and blow his hunting horn. All his hounds would come running, and fastest and keenest of all was his favourite hound, Gellert. This hound had been a gift from the prince's father-in-law, King John. The prince loved the hound because, although he was brave as a lion when hunting, he was the gentlest creature at home, and was especially fond of the prince's young son, still a babe in arms.

The dog would always come to his master's bidding and was usually the first to scent a deer and lead the huntsmen to their quarry. Few were the days when they returned home without venison for the prince's table when Llewelyn went hunting with Gellert.

One morning Llewelyn waited by the castle gatehouse and blew his horn to call his hounds as usual. All the hounds came running to the call except for Gellert. Llewelyn was surprised, for this rarely happened, so he sounded the horn once more, but still Gellert did not appear. In the end, they gave up their

wait and Llewelyn rode off
without his favourite hound.

That day they had poor
hunting. They rode far, but
the few deer they sighted
managed to escape, and
Llewelyn and his men
went home empty-handed.
The prince felt that it was
because he did not have his
best hound with him, and he
was angry when he returned
to the castle. As he
approached the gatehouse,
who should come running
towards him but his favourite
hound? At first Llewelyn was
overjoyed. But then, as the
dog grew near him, he saw
that the animal's muzzle was
dripping with blood.

The prince was mystified,
but a horrible suspicion came
to him. He thought of his

young son, just one year old, and how Gellert loved to play with the child. Could it be that the dog had harmed the child? Quickly, the prince bounded up the stairs to the nursery.

   When he got to the room, his fears were confirmed. The baby's basket lay upset on the floor, and there was no sign anywhere of Llewelyn's son. He looked more closely, and there was blood on the cradle. Surely the dog had murdered his child. Frantically, the prince searched for his son, but he could only find more patches of blood and signs of a struggle. He turned to Gellert, saying, "Monster! You have killed and eaten my son." And without further ado, the prince drew his sword and plunged it into the greyhound's side. The dog howled in pain and expired, gazing, as if in wonder, at his master's face.

As Gellert howled, a small, plaintive cry came from somewhere on the other side of the room. Straight away, Llewelyn realised his fatal mistake. He strode across the room, and looked beneath the baby's basket. Sure enough, there was his baby son, unharmed, and waking from sleep. Beside the child was the body of a great wolf, its flesh torn and bloodied. Gellert had not killed the boy, but had stood guard and protected him from the wolf. The prince hung his head in regret and shame.

Llewelyn knew he could do nothing to bring his faithful hound back to life. He took Gellert's body out of the castle walls, and carried him to a spot where the peak of Snowdon could be seen. Here they made his grave, and when the hound had been buried with due ceremony, the prince piled a cairn of stones over the burial so that all would know the spot.

Ever since, the place of the hound's burial has been called Beth Gellert, the Grave of Gellert. If a passer-by asks about the grave, the locals always tell this story, so that every visitor shares a little of the prince's grief for his hound. As for Llewelyn, it was a long time before he relished the hunt once more.

The Emperor's Dream

Macsen Wledig was emperor of Rome and his empire was so great that twenty kings were his subjects. He took the kings out hunting from time to time, and on one of these hunts the emperor grew tired. So his servants made a comfortable place for him and before long, Macsen Wledig was fast asleep, and dreaming.

Macsen dreamed that he was going on a long journey. He crossed fields and rivers, hills and mountains, until at last he came to a harbour. Macsen dreamed that he stepped aboard the finest ship, which was built of gold, silver, and ivory, and set sail across the ocean. He sailed until he came to a beautiful island, where there was a castle, bigger than any he had seen in his life. The castle was decorated all over with gold, and in his dream the emperor entered the building and met the people who lived there. There was an aged man, who seemed to be a king, two fine young princes, and the most beautiful maiden that Macsen had ever seen. When she saw Macsen, the maiden stood up and embraced him, and Macsen felt greater happiness than he had ever known.

It was at this point that the emperor awoke, to realise that this vision was nothing but a dream. The beauty of the maiden, her white and gold garments, the jewellery of rubies and pearls that she wore, the gold decoration of the castle, all had seemed so real – and now Macsen's heart was filled with sadness that everything had been an illusion.

The emperor returned to Rome, and nothing would rouse him from his sadness. He no longer wanted to hunt, and he neglected his duties of state. Fine food, music and dancing meant nothing to him. Eventually one of his advisers spoke quietly to Macsen, "My lord, your men are worried. They can get no answer from you about questions of state, and you no longer enjoy anything in your life."

And so it was that Macsen explained about his dream and why he was so sad. Quickly the servant called all the wise men of the empire together, and they listened to Macsen's story. One of the wise men said, "This beautiful maiden may yet live in the world. Send out your men to the four corners of the empire; they may find her and bring her to you."

So the emperor's men set out, travelling far and wide. But after a while, they began to return. None had found the fair maiden of Macsen's dream, and the emperor seemed even sadder than before.

Then another of the wise men spoke up. "My lord, I suggest that you go yourself to the place where you had your dream. Then set out from that spot and see if you can find the places that you saw when you slept." Macsen thought that this was a good idea, and he and his men set off.

When they got to the place where the emperor had rested, they looked around them, and Macsen began to look towards a distant range of mountains. "This looks like the way I saw in my dream," he said. And the emperor sent his men off in the direction that he thought he had travelled in his dream.

Far they rode, the messengers of the

emperor. They crossed fields and rivers, climbed hills and mountains, until they had made their way across France and found a fine ship of silver, gold, and ivory. "Truly, this must be the ship," they said. They spoke to the captain and set sail across the sea until they came to Britain. Here they travelled still further, retracing the steps of Macsen's dream until they came to a great castle decorated in gold. And there, within the castle, they met the old man, his two sons, and the fairest maiden they had seen. They returned at once to Rome and brought Macsen to the place. And when they arrived, they hailed the maiden, Elen, as empress of Rome, and Macsen and she were married. The emperor grew friendly with Elen's brothers, Cynan and Adeon, and their father, Eudaf, and he stayed many years in their castle. Meanwhile, the people of Rome thought that Macsen had left them for good and chose another to be their emperor.

The new emperor wanted to make sure that Macsen would

not return to claim his throne, so he sent word to Macsen that he would be killed if he should return. "How dare he take my rightful place?" said Macsen. And straight away he called his men together and left Britain for Rome.

Swiftly they rode across France and Burgundy, conquering as they went. Soon all the empire in the west was under Macsen's rule – except for Rome itself, where the new emperor held out. Macsen lay siege to the city, but the new emperor would not give in. So Macsen's army surrounded the city for a whole year, and still the emperor stood his ground. He would not surrender.

Towards the end of this year,

word came to Britain of Macsen's difficulty, and Cynan and Adeon decided to go to Rome to help him. Elen recognized them as soon as they arrived, and they came forward to greet their sister and to see how Macsen was faring.

"Truly Macsen's soldiers are brave," said Adeon to his brother, "but we have greater cunning." Cynan suggested that they attack when the rival emperors were eating dinner, when no fighting normally took place and everyone was off their guard. They had their carpenters make ladders for everyone, and then, when the food was served, the Welsh soldiers scaled the walls and took the city by surprise. Soon the gates were opened, Macsen entered Rome, and the new emperor fled in confusion. Macsen was grateful for the help given him by Cynan and Adeon and spoke to them in thanks: "Thanks to you, my empire is my own once more. Take command now of my army and conquer what lands you will."

So Cynan and Adeon marched westwards with their army, conquering fine kingdoms for themselves in Britain and Brittany while Macsen and Elen ruled in Rome. And as long as they were on the throne there was peace between Rome and the lands of the west.

King Lludd and the Plagues of Britain

One of the greatest of all kings of Britain was king Lludd. When he came to the throne as a young man he found the greatest city in his kingdom in disrepair. He ordered it to be restored with fine stones of many colours and when it was finished, he spent most of his time in his castle in his city, which became known as Caer Lludd, or Lludd's fortress, the origin of the name London.

Lludd's favourite relative was his youngest brother, Llefelys, and the two were close companions. One day, when Lludd had been king for some seven years, Llefelys came to his brother. "Brother, the king of France has a beautiful daughter. We love each other dearly and I wish to marry her."

Lludd was pleased that the two young people loved each other, and gave his consent right away. Their joy was tinged with sorrow, however, for, just before the wedding, the king of France died, and Llefelys became ruler of his new country from his wedding day onward.

All went well for another seven years. The two realms were at peace and Caer Lludd prospered as never before. Then one day came a series of misfortunes to Lludd's kingdom.

First came a wicked band of mischief-makers, a people known as the Coranieid. They seemed to get everywhere, hearing all Lludd's plans and keeping one step ahead of him whenever he tried to expel them from the island. They listened in to every private conversation, and could cause ill-will between friends by telling lies about what people had said.

Second was a mysterious piercing scream, which was heard every May Day. In every house in the land, this

scream could be heard, and anyone who was unlucky enough to hear its full blast suffered soon afterwards. The young lost their energy and beauty, the old lost their sense, even crops and trees became diseased and died when the scream made itself heard. And yet no one in the kingdom knew where the scream came from or what creature could be making it.

The final terror of the land of Britain was a terrible famine at the king's court. Now Lludd had always been a generous king, who stocked his larders well and was hospitable to all comers. But when this plague struck, no matter how full his grain bins or how many bottles of wine or barrels of ale he kept in his store-rooms, all the food and drink seemed to disappear.

Lludd was baffled about how to stop the second and third

plagues, but he supposed he could fight the wicked people who caused the first, and set sail to France, to ask his brother for help. Lludd explained his difficulty to his brother, and Llefelys produced a special bronze speaking horn, so that they could talk into each other's ears, without being overheard.

At first, they found it difficult to make themselves heard through the horn, and Llefelys said "There is a demon in this speaking horn. Bring me wine, and we will flush the demon out." Sure enough, when they poured wine down the tube, out came a tiny demon, holding his nose so as not to drown in the liquid.

Lludd first explained to his brother about the Coranieid. "Take some of these insects," said Llefelys. "Grind them up and

dissolve the pieces in water.
When you have done this, call
everyone in your kingdom
together, both British and
Coranieid. Sprinkle this water
over all of them – it will kill
only your enemies."

Next, Lludd told his brother
about the mysterious scream.
"Surely that is the sound of
two dragons fighting," said
Llefelys. "You must measure
your kingdom and find the
precise centre. Here, dig a pit,
fill it with gallons of your
finest mead, and cover it with
a great cloth. Then wait for
the dragons to come. When
they are tired of their fight,
they will turn into two pigs,
and will rest, exhausted, on
the cloth. They will fall into
the mead and you must bury
them quickly."

Finally Lludd told his brother about the famine at court. "A great magician with unstoppable hunger and thirst is stealing your food and drink," said Llefelys. "Keep watch for him, with a tub of ice-cold water nearby. He will try to send you to sleep, so when you feel tired, jump into the water to keep yourself awake. Then you will be able to fight the magician."

Lludd thanked his brother and returned to his kingdom, where he began to do what Llefelys had advised.

Sure enough, when he sprinkled the water over everyone, only the Coranieid dropped down dead; the Britons were all hale and hearty. Next he dug his pit and killed the dragons.

Then Lludd lay in wait for the magician, jumping into the cold water when he started to feel drowsy. "Leave my meat and drink alone!" shouted Lludd, when the magician started to fill his huge basket. At once, the two men began to fight. They hit out and slashed with their swords until the weapons were blunt. They battered each other with their shields. They even fought with their fists. In the end, Lludd pinned the magician against the ground and the thief begged for mercy.

"Spare me, and I will right all the wrongs I have done you."

Lludd paused and looked at his opponent. Ever a generous man, Lludd was merciful, and the magician served him all his life. The plagues of Britain were banished, and Lludd is still remembered as a great and merciful king.

The Boy Who Went to Fairyland

Many years ago in southern Wales lived a boy called Elidor. He was a bright lad and his mother wanted him to become a priest, so she sent him to study with a good, but strict, teacher.

By the time he was twelve, Elidor was doing well in all his lessons, but he could not bear the beatings he got from his master. So one day, he ran away and hid near a river, where the waters had hollowed out a cave by its banks.

The lad stayed in his hollow for two days, and had nothing to eat while he was there. He was just about to give in and go back hungry to his teacher when he turned and found himself looking down on two tiny men. Elidor's jaw dropped and he looked silently at the two small creatures, for in truth he did not know what to do or say. Then one of the men spoke to him: "If you come with us, we will take you to a place where there is play and pleasure all day long."

Elidor thought of the hard work and harsh punishment that awaited him at home, and agreed to follow the little men. They took him deep down into the cave, which turned into a dark underground tunnel, before opening out into a landscape of rivers, fields, woodlands, and plains. This land was more beautiful than the countryside around Elidor's home, but darker, because no sun shone there. As he looked around him, Elidor's eyes got used to the dark, and he could make out woods and streams, plains and meadows, the latter growing with beautiful flowers, the like of which he had not seen before.

Elidor paused to look at the beauty around him, but the two men hurried him along. He soon realised that the men were taking him to their leader. The king, who was much taller than his subjects, sat with all his court around

him, and looked at Elidor curiously. The king's courtiers, most of whom were pale-skinned with long, flowing, shoulder-length hair, also stared at Elidor, for they had never been so close to a mortal before. Finally, when everyone had looked at him and marvelled at him for some time, the king led Elidor to a young creature, who turned out to be his son.

When the fairy prince and Elidor had introduced themselves, and the prince had heard how the two little men had found Elidor near the cave, the prince turned to the young boy, "You must be hungry after all this time without food. Come with me." And they went off to a banqueting hall, where Elidor ate the first of many amazing meals. He quickly saw that the food of fairyland was unlike the fare he was used to. There was no meat or fish, and the little people normally ate foods that looked like milky puddings, made with all sorts of different fruits and flavoured with spices. When he had eaten his fill, the prince told Elidor about the ways of the fairy kingdom.

The fairies, it seemed, were a gentle, peace-loving people, who came and went often between their land and the world of humans. But because the fairies were small and silent, rarely did any mortal see them or even suspect that they were there. So it was that, while humans knew little of the ways of the fairies, the little people knew a great deal about mortals – their farms and their towns, their people and kings, their beliefs and their wars.

In turn, Elidor learned much about the fairies. He found that they travelled between their world and the human world through a variety of different routes. But he could never remember the ways through their passages, so baffling were their twists and turns, and he realised now why no human being had ever found their strange world before.

The little people had no gods or churches, but they held one thing sacred above all else – the truth. They acted peacefully and honestly with each other at all times, and were rather scornful of humans, with their jealousies, arguments, and wars.

As Elidor won the trust of the little people, they allowed him

to visit his own world and return to fairyland. When he first told his mother where he had been, she did not believe him. She still listened, fascinated, to his stories of the little people and their ways. But Elidor felt she was listening in the way that a person listens to a good story, rather than one who is hearing the truth. So he wondered what he could do to convince her that what he was saying was true.

He had often told his mother that gold, although precious in the mortal world, was a commonplace metal in fairyland. He and the king's son even played games of catch with a golden ball. So Elidor decided that he would bring back the golden ball to show his mother.

Next time Elidor and the prince finished their game of

catch, Elidor stealthily picked up the golden ball. Then he made his way quietly up the dark passage into the cave and out towards the mortal world. He did not realise until too late that the little people were running after him. As he reached his mother's house, he ran faster in his excitement, tripping as he raced through the front door. The ball slipped from his hands, just as his two tiny followers burst into the room after him. The first of them scooped up the ball, then they turned on their heels and dashed off, glaring at Elidor, who realised how stupid and selfish he had been.

Immediately he ran the way he had come, intending to return and apologize to the little people. He reached the river, and found the place where the bank overhung the water. But when he entered the cave, he realised that everything had changed. There was no longer a dark passageway inside the cave. Elidor came out of the darkness, and walked up and down the river bank, thinking that he had mistaken the place. He even went back several times, in the hope that he had been mistaken and would find the passage. But try as he did, Elidor never again found the entrance to fairyland. His time with the little people was over.

Arthur's Resting Place

There was once a cattle drover who had to drive a herd of fine cattle all the way from Wales to sell them in London. He knew that he needed a good staff to carry as he walked, and to prod any cattle who wandered from the road, so he stopped by a hazel tree to cut himself a branch.

The young man drove the cattle all the way to London, found the market, and sold them for his master. He had made good time and had not visited the great city before, so he decided to rest awhile there and see some of the sights before returning to Wales. The drover stood on London Bridge admiring the view, when an old man came up to him.

"That's a fine staff you are carrying," said the old man. "I would like to see the tree that it came from, and it would be worth your while to show me."

"Then you will have to come with me all the way to Wales," answered the drover. "For that is where I cut the staff."

So, once the drover had paid for his board and lodgings, the two set off, back down the long road to Wales. When they arrived, the drover led the old man straight to the hazel tree, and the old man pointed to a narrow passage at the foot of the tree, which the drover had not noticed before.

"Come with me down this passage," said the old man. One after the other, they squeezed through the narrow opening. They walked for a few minutes and the passage began to widen. A large bell hung from the ceiling, and next to the bell was the entrance to a cave. The two men eased their way around the bell, into the cave, and what they saw next quite

took the drover's breath away.

A group of knights lay sleeping, and at their head was a noble figure, crowned and robed, who looked to the drover like a king. The glinting of their metal armour lit up the cave. "It is King Arthur and his knights," whispered the old man. "They sleep until the kingdom needs them, when Arthur will rise up and reign over a golden age."

As the old man said the words "golden age", the drover noticed something even more amazing. Next to the king were two great heaps of gold and silver. "You may take as much as you want," said the old man, "as long as you do not wake

Arthur or his men." The old man explained that if any of the knights stirred, they would ask "Is it day?" and the drover must reply "No, sleep on." Above all, the drover must not touch the great bell, which would give Arthur the warning signal to arise and kill his enemies.

The drover started to gather his first load of gold, and he was surprised to see that the old man was not taking any himself. "It is not gold and silver that makes me wise," said the old man knowingly.

The drover started as he dropped a gold coin on the floor of the cave. One of the knights stirred.

"Is it day?" groaned the knight.

"No, sleep on," said the drover. And he tiptoed out of the cave, just squeezing past the bell with his heavy load.

A second time the drover entered the cave. Again, one of the knights seemed to be waking.

"Is it day?"

"No, sleep on."

And even though his heap of coins was large and bulky, the drover managed again to get past the bell without touching it.

But the third time he entered the cave, the drover, more confident than before, was also more careless. As he was leaving, he brushed the bell, and its deep ring echoed all around. Before he could move, knights began to leap up and circle him.

The drover was surrounded by clanking armour and shouting knights. The noise, in the echoing cave, was awesome, and the drover dropped his load of gold and silver in terror, and began to run. But one of the knights caught him, and several started to give him a beating. Somewhere in the fray he heard several of the knights yelling, "Wales is in danger! The hour is come!"

But suddenly, a louder voice rang out above the others. "Enough! Lay down your arms! Would you rise from your sleep for *him*?" Then the cave was silent, for it was Arthur himself who spoke. Only a single knight, Kay, held on to the drover, and when the king glanced at

Kay, he threw his captive roughly against the hard wall of the cave. Picking himself up, the drover ran down the passage and out into the light, thinking only of escaping with his life. Behind him, he heard a loud rumbling as a great stone was pushed to seal the entrance of the cave. But the drover thought little of this as he ran home, thankful that he had escaped with a few wounds and bruises.

The drover's friends and relatives asked him how he came by his wounds, but it was a long time before he told his story. Finally, though, he described the passage, the cave, and the sleeping king to a group of friends, and they decided to arm themselves and return to see if they could recover some more gold and silver from Arthur's cave.

Together they went to the place where the hazel tree grew. But they could no longer find any tree growing there, nor was there any stone, nor any passage to the cave. The drover's friends looked suspiciously at their companion. It seemed that he had made up the whole story, and they rounded on him, calling him a fool and a liar.

They went on and on with their taunts, until the drover could stand it no more. So he left home, and since has not been seen. By now he must be long dead, and no one expects him to come back. But people still talk of the return of Arthur, who one day will wake from his slumber under the hills.

Brewery of Eggshells

A shepherd and his wife lived among the hills at Treneglwys. The shepherd won respect for his care for his sheep, which always produced fine lambs. The wife kept a tidy home and cooked good food. The two lived in happiness, and one day their joy was crowned with twins, a boy and a girl.

All went well until a messenger arrived at the shepherd's cottage. A neighbour, some distance away across the hills, was ill, and the messenger asked the woman if she would go to the aid of her friend.

The woman was unwilling to leave the babies, but finally decided that she must help her neighbour. So she tucked the infants up in their cot, and set off to see what she could do. She walked as quickly as she could, for she had heard that the little people had been seen in the neighbourhood. But it was the middle of the day, and she thought it unlikely that the fairies would be about in broad daylight. Sure enough, when she returned she found her twins safe where she had left them.

Everything seemed to be well, but after a month or two, both parents sensed that there was something wrong with the twins.

Neither of them seemed to be growing at all.

The shepherd looked at his wife, and at his son and daughter. "They cannot be our children," he said.

"But they must be ours," objected his wife. "Whose else could they be?"

And so it was that the shepherd and his wife argued day and night, and their happiness seemed to be at an end. Meanwhile, the twins showed no signs of growing. The woman thought once more of the fairy people, and worried that they had interfered with her children.

The shepherd's wife had heard tell that in the town of Llanidloes there lived an old man, famous for his wisdom. She decided that she would visit him and ask his advice, both about the children and the strife between her and her husband.

She was tired when she reached Llanidloes, for the journey was long, but she went straight to the wise man's house. It would soon be harvest time and she did not want to delay. The wise man listened patiently to the woman's story, and then told her what she should do.

"It is soon harvest time and you will be making food for the reapers. Take a hen's egg and clean out the shell. Put some of the reapers' broth in the shell and take it to your door. Listen carefully to see if the twins say anything. If you hear them talking in a way that is beyond the normal understanding of children, you must take them up in your arms, carry them to Lake Elvyn, and throw them into the water. If you hear them say nothing unusual, then leave them be and do them no harm."

The woman thanked the wise man and returned home, and soon the first day of the harvest was come. The shepherd's wife made a broth to take to the reapers in the fields. She cleaned out an eggshell, filled it with broth, and took it to the door. As she listened, she heard the piping voice of one of her children recite these words:

Acorn before oak I knew,
An egg before a hen,
But I never heard of an eggshell brew
As a dinner for harvest men.

The woman looked sadly at the two children. She knew now that they were children of the little people and that she must throw them into the lake, yet she found it hard to be so cruel. But she took a deep breath and, remembering the words of the wise man, gathered the twins up in her arms and made off towards Lake Elvyn. When she got to the shore she threw them into the water. Immediately, lots of small, goblin-like creatures wearing blue trousers appeared and caught the babies.

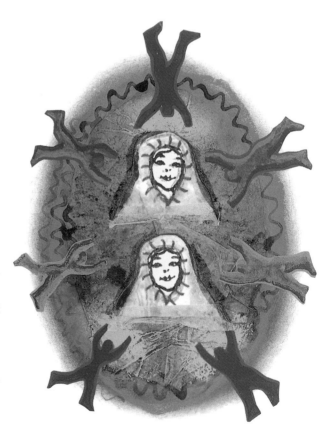

When she returned to her house, the woman was overjoyed to see two healthy children in the cot from which she had taken the changelings. Her own children were returned, and her strife with her husband was over.

The Lost Kingdom

In former times, the best land in Wales lay towards the West. The fertile plains and lush grasslands were fine country for farming, and all who worked these fields grew rich. But there was one problem with the country in the West. The ground lay so low that it was often flooded by the sea. So the kings of the West built a great wall, with strong sluice gates, to hold back the sea. For many years the people of the West enjoyed a life without floods, and they became the envy of all Wales.

One of the greatest of all the western kings was Gwyddno. Sixteen beautiful cities grew up in his kingdom while he reigned, and the lands of the West became more prosperous

than before. After the king, the most important person in the kingdom of the West was a man called Seithennin, whom Gwyddno appointed as the keeper of the sluices. Whenever a storm brewed, and the sea threatened to overwhelm the kingdom, Seithennin would close the great sluice gates, and the lands of the West would be safe.

Seithennin was a big, strong man, chosen because he could easily turn the handles to close the heavy oak sluice gates. But there was a problem. Seithennin was a drunkard. Sometimes, when he had had too much to drink, he would be late to close the gates, and there would be some slight flooding. But the kingdom would recover, and no great harm was done.

One day, King Gwyddno ordered a great banquet in his hall. All the lords and ladies of the kingdom were there, as well as other men of importance such as Seithennin. The banquet went on long into the night, and the sluice-keeper got more

and more drunk. There was singing and harping, and everyone was enjoying themselves to the full. But because of all the noise of the revelling, no-one could hear that a great storm was brewing up outside. Even when people did start to notice, they assumed that Seithennin had closed the sluice gates and that they would be safe from flooding, as they had been for years now. But no one saw that the sluice-keeper, who had drunk more than anyone else at the banquet, was fast asleep.

Outside, the waters of the sea were pouring through the sluice gates. Soon the fields were flooded and the streets of the towns were awash. But still the banquet went on, until the flood waters poured through the doors of Gwyddno's hall. There had been floods in this part of Wales in earlier years, before the sea wall was built. Then people had lost their lives and good farm land had been spoiled.

But this time it was worse. The water poured in with such speed that it was unstoppable. Men, women, and children, lords and servants alike, were swept under the flood. Even those who knew the sea, including many fishermen who were excellent swimmers, lost their lives. Sheep and cattle went the same way. Soon the whole great kingdom of the West, every field and every town, was deep under the water. And all were drowned apart from one man, the poet Taliesin, who survived to tell the tale. They say that the sigh that Gwyddno let out as he was lost

under the waves was the saddest sound ever heard.

The sea now covers Gwyddno's former kingdom, in the place now called Cardigan Bay. Occasionally, at low tide, wooden posts and fragments of stone wall are revealed among the sand, and men say that these are the last remaining parts of one of Gwyddno's cities. Sailors and fishermen who cross the bay say that they can sometimes hear the bells of the sixteen cities, sounding beneath the waves, reminding them of the terrible power of the sea. Some even say that on a quiet, still day they can hear the echoing sound of Gwyddno's final sigh.

Where Time Stood Still

The countryside in eastern Glamorgan used to be famous for sightings of the mischievous little people. They were said to use their singing to tempt people away from their path, so that many a traveller ended up in a pond or marsh; they were also well known for their habit of stealing children.

This last thing worried one woman more than most. She was a young widow, who had a small farm and a three-year-old son. She was the best of mothers, and her son was seldom out of her sight. But sometimes, she would have to leave her son indoors when she went out to check the beasts in the cow-house, and she worried that the fairies would get in while she was gone.

One day, while she was cooking, she heard a noise in the cow-house and went to investigate. When she had finished, she ran back to her house as usual. Panic filled her heart as she saw that her child had gone. She searched the house and all the farm buildings, calling "Rhoddri! Rhoddri!" But nowhere could she find the boy.

It began to grow dark, and the widow, despairing at ever

finding her child, sat down in her kitchen and wept. Suddenly she heard a noise, and looked up to see a small figure standing by the door. "Mother," it said.

The widow looked at the child curiously. He did not look at all like Rhoddri. "You cannot be my Rhoddri," she said.

"Yes, it's me," replied the child.

Confused, she ushered the child into the room and gave it food. The boy was thankful for his food, and seemed to behave like Rhoddri used to. So the little child stayed with the widow, and she looked after him just as carefully as she had looked after Rhoddri. And yet a mother knows her children, and the woman could not believe that it was he.

As the months went on, the boy did not seem to grow as her true son had done. The widow was convinced he was a changeling, left by fairies who had taken Rhoddri. She decided to consult a wise man, to see if she could find the truth.

The wise man listened carefully to the woman's story, and gave her the recipe for a brew. She should make this brew and put some of it into half an eggshell, and listen to what the child said as she did this.

When the widow got home, she lost no time, and was soon pouring the brew into the eggshell. She heard the child speaking: "Great oaks from little acorns grow. I saw the acorn long ago." And as he recited the lines he looked uglier and more annoyed than ever before.

The widow returned to the wise man to ask the meaning of the child's words. "He is saying that he remembers the acorn before it was an oak tree," said the wise man. "He is an ancient infant and truly one of the little people. To get back your own

child you will have to do two more things, and I shall now tell you the first. In three days' time it will be full moon. Go to the crossroads at midnight, hide yourself and wait. You may see something which will make you cry, but keep quiet. If you make any noise, you will lose your child for ever. Then return to me and tell me what you have seen."

Trembling with fear, the widow made her way to the crossroads on the evening of full moon. There was a thorn bush nearby, so she hid herself behind and waited. After a while she heard music and voices, and as the music got nearer, she felt more and more sleepy. But she fought to keep herself awake, and through the leaves she saw a group of little people, the men with red hats, the women with blue and green skirts, dancing along and singing. Amongst them was Rhoddri, and the fairies seemed to be guarding the boy. At once, she felt a cry welling up inside her, but, remembering the words of the wise man, she stifled the cry, let the fairy procession pass,

and returned to her cottage. Her relief at seeing her child alive and well was tainted with sadness because she had let him go, but she trusted the wise man.

"It is as I thought," said the wise man, when the widow told the story of the fairy procession. Then he told her the second thing she should do. "Find a black hen and kill her, but do not pluck her feathers. Let the changeling see what you are doing, but do not make any remark to him. Next close all your doors and windows, and roast the hen. Then, as the feathers fall from the roasting fowl, watch the fairy child carefully."

The widow left the wise man and went to carry out his bidding. There was no black hen among the widow's own fowls, so she called on each of her neighbours.

At the last house in the village she met a woman carrying a sieve. "I can't carry any sunlight into my house using this sieve," said the woman. "I don't know what to do."

"Why, open your shutters," replied the widow. "That will bring the sun into your house."

The woman saw that this was good advice, and happily gave the widow a black hen in thanks. So the widow took the hen, and roasted it as she had been told. As the feathers began to fall from the bird, she heard music playing outside her house. She concentrated on what she was doing, and watched the feathers falling off the hen. As the last feather fell, there was a loud blast of music outside. She looked around and the fairy child had vanished. Now she had no child at all. She sat in despair, looking at the remains of the roast fowl, and wondering what to do next. Suddenly, she heard a cry coming from outside the house. She rushed out, saw her own lost Rhoddri, and swept him into her arms.

The child seemed mystified at his mother's joy, especially when she asked him where he had been for the past year.

"But I have not been away a year," said the child. "I only stayed a few minutes, to listen to the music."

The Cry of Vengeance

Long ago in the ancient town of Bala lived a wicked prince called Tegid Foel. All his people feared him, for if anyone got in his way, or disagreed with him, the prince had them killed.

Some men plotted to dethrone the prince, but none of them succeeded, for Tegid Foel surrounded himself with guards and henchmen who were almost as ruthless as himself. One day, the prince heard a small voice, whispering in his ear, "Vengeance will come, vengeance will come!" Tegid took no

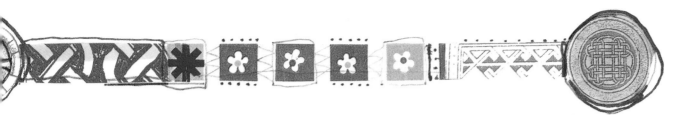

notice of the voice, even though he heard it again, and soon he heard it every day. And the prince's rule carried on for many years of cruelty, until his three sons were grown up and his first son was married.

Tegid Foel's castle was usually a quiet, sombre place, but one day there was noise of rejoicing there. The wife of Tegid's first son had given birth to her first child, a grandson for the prince, and a great feast was ordered. Everyone in the kingdom was invited – and woe betide anyone who did not attend.

One of those who did not want to come was a young, peace-loving harper from the hills near Bala. He was known as the best musician for miles around, and Tegid wanted him to play at his feast. The harper knew that there would be trouble if he did not go, so he took his harp and strode to the castle.

When the harper arrived, the banquet was already beginning, so he took his place as quickly as he could and began to tune his instrument. When the prince saw him, he roared "Waste no time! Play, harper!" in a voice that sent a chill through all who heard. So the harper sang and played, to the delight of everyone in the hall. It seemed as if his music had brought some tranquillity and beauty to the place, where the atmosphere was usually brooding and evil.

At around midnight, there was an interval, and the harper strolled outside in the courtyard to relax for a while. As he did so, a voice whispered in his ear, "Vengeance has come, vengeance has come." Then he saw a small bird that seemed to be beckoning to him with its beak. The creature seemed to be telling him to leave the castle.

At first, the harper was doubtful, and he wondered what would become of him if he left the banquet now. But he had always listened to the sounds of nature, so he decided to obey the call, slipping through the castle gates and making for the hills. When he had walked for a while, the harper paused. He realized in horror that he had left his harp behind him in the hall. At once he was in turmoil. His harp was his livelihood. But the guards had probably already noticed that he had gone. If he returned – either to play or to take the harp – he risked losing his head. So he decided to continue on his way.

Far the harper climbed into the hills, leaving the sounds of revelling behind him, until he began to tire and could walk no more. He felt that he was far enough away to be out of reach of the castle guards, who were anyway too intent on revelling to chase him tonight. So he lay down and fell asleep.

At dawn, the harper awoke and stretched and rubbed his eyes. As he looked down to the valley he saw an astounding sight. The town and castle of Bala were no more. In their place was a gigantic lake. The only sign of the previous night's feast was his harp, floating unharmed. As the ripples of the water brought the instrument back to him, the harper sighed with relief that he had listened to the quiet, sweet voice of the bird instead of the harsh, ugly voice of the prince's command.

A Rare Quarry

Two friends were out hunting otters and they walked beside a stream, looking at the banks for holes where the creatures might be hiding. Suddenly, one of them saw a flash of red. The creature moved quickly, darting along the bank and vanishing into a hole near a tree.

One friend turned to the other: "What was that? It was too large for a squirrel, too small for a fox. Could it be a rare, red-furred otter?"

The two men had never seen such an otter before, but could not think what other sort of creature it might be, so decided to try to catch it. They looked carefully at the burrow and saw that it had two entrances, one on either side of the tree. "We'll need a sack," said the first man, and he ran off to a nearby farm to borrow one.

When he returned, he held the sack over one end of the burrow, while his friend stood at the other end and made a noise to frighten the creature out. Sure enough, there was a mighty plop as the creature jumped into the sack. Holding the end closed, the two men made off for home, very pleased with their rare quarry.

The pair walked home across the fields, and had not gone very far when they were amazed to hear a tiny voice inside the sack calling "I hear my mother calling me. I hear my mother calling me." The men dropped the sack in astonishment and watched as a tiny figure climbed out. On his head was a red hat, and he wore trousers and jacket and shoes that were also bright red. As he ran off towards the cover of some low bushes, again he looked like a streak of red, and the men saw how easy it had been to mistake him for an animal.

Looking at each other in alarm, the two hunters ran off towards home. They never hunted for otters again on that stretch of the river.

The Farmer and the Goat Girl

There was once a farmer called Cadwalader. Unlike all his neighbours, who were sheep farmers, Cadwalader had a large flock of goats. Of all his goats he had a special favourite that he called Jenny, and Jenny was the whitest and most beautiful of all his flock.

For many years Jenny was Cadwalader's best milk-producer, and she was always obedient, unlike some of the stubborn

creatures in his flock. Then, one day, Jenny bolted from the field and ran away. Up the nearest mountain she went, and seemed not to be stopping, so Cadwalader gave chase.

They climbed higher and higher, Jenny always slightly ahead. When it seemed as if the farmer would catch her, she jumped on to a nearby crag, leaving Cadwalader stranded.

Not only did the farmer feel stupid, stuck on the mountain like this, he also collected bruises and sprains as he clambered among the rocks. Finally, he had had enough, and he picked up a stone and hurled it at the goat in frustration as she was jumping another chasm.

The stone hit Jenny in the side, and, bleating loudly, she fell far down into the gap between the rocks. Straight away Cadwalader was full of remorse. It was only in a moment of frustration that he had wanted to hurt the animal, and now his only wish was to see that she was still alive. He clambered down to the rocky gap where she lay, and saw that, although she was still breathing, she was badly injured. He did his best to make her comfortable, and tears of sadness formed in his eyes as he saw how she was hurt.

It was now dark, but the moon appeared between the rocks and shed its light on the scene. As the moon rose, the goat turned into a beautiful young woman who was lying there before Cadwalader. He looked in bafflement at her brown eyes and soft hair, and found that not only was she beautiful, she was also well and looked pleased to see him. "So, my dear Cadwalader," she said. "At long last I can speak to you."

Cadwalader did not know what to make of all this. When the young woman spoke, there seemed to be a bleat in her voice; when she held his hand, it felt like a hoof. Was she goat or girl, or some strange mixture of the two?

As she led him towards an outcrop of rock, Cadwalader felt he was heading into danger. As they rounded a corner, they found themselves surrounded by a flock of goats – not the tame creatures Cadwalader was used to, but large wild goats,

many of which had long horns and beards. Jenny led him to the largest goat of all, and bowed, as if he were a king.

"Is this the man you want?" the goat asked Jenny.

"Yes, he is the one."

"Not a very fine specimen," said the goat-king. "I had hoped for something better."

"He will be better afterwards," replied Jenny.

Cadwalader wondered what was going to happen, and looked around him in fear. Then the goat-king turned to Cadwalader.

"Will you, Cadwalader, take this she-goat to be your wife?"

"No, my lord. I want nothing to do with goats ever again." And with that, Cadwalader turned and ran for his life. He was fast, but not fast enough for the great goat-king. Coming up behind Cadwalader, the huge billy goat gave the farmer such a tremendous butt that Cadwalader fell headlong down the crag, rolling and falling, falling and rolling, until he came to a stop, unconscious, right at the bottom of the mountain.

There Cadwalader lay for the rest of the night, until he woke, aching from head to toe, at dawn. He limped home to his farm, where his goats bleated in welcome. But Cadwalader wanted to be a goat farmer no more. He drove his goats to market, and bought a flock of sheep, just like his neighbours.

Jack and his Golden Snuff-Box

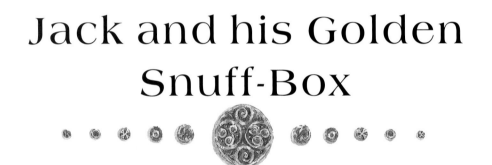

Long ago in the forests of Wales few people travelled very far. They grew their own food, built their houses and made their furniture from timber from the forests, and kept a few sheep or goats to provide milk and wool. So it was that there was once a couple, getting on in years, who never left the forest. They never saw any other people than their young son, Jack, and were happy with their own company.

They told Jack many old stories – about kings and princes, towns and villages – and Jack became curious to see the world beyond the forest. One day, when his father was out cutting wood, Jack turned to his mother. "Here I see nothing but trees, and the only difference is the changing seasons. Let me go away for a while and see the world, for I think I shall go mad with boredom if I stay here."

His mother paused, for she was sad to see him go. "Well, if you must, you must," she said. "And God go with you. But stay awhile before you go and I will bake you a cake. Would you like a small cake, with my blessings, or a large cake, with my curses?"

"I am going far and may be hungry. Bake me a large cake," replied Jack.

So Jack's mother baked him a large cake, and when he left, she went to the top of the house, and cursed her son as long as she could see him.

Soon Jack met his father, who asked him where he was going. Like his mother, Jack's father was sorry to see him go, but realised that it was what the boy wanted. The old man took from his pocket a small golden box and handed it to Jack. "Take this snuff-box, keep it in your pocket, and be sure not to open it until your death is near," said the father.

Jack tramped on for many miles. By the end of the long day he had finished his cake and was still hungry. He saw a large house, so he stopped there, and asked one of the maids if there was somewhere he could stay the night. In the kitchen, the servants gave Jack some food to eat and sat him down by the fire, and soon the daughter of the house came to have a look at the young visitor.

When Jack saw the young woman, he was stunned by her beauty, and the young woman was hardly less pleased with the sight of Jack. Before long, she had called her father to see him, and the master of the house asked Jack what he could do. Jack was so fascinated by the beauty of the man's daughter that he did not think before answering, "Why, I can do anything you like."

"If you can do anything, make me a great lake in front of my house, with a fleet of sailing ships. I want one of the ships to fire a salute, and the last round of the salute must break the leg of the bed where my daughter sleeps. If you can't achieve this, then prepare to meet your doom."

Jack went to bed in gloom. He knelt down to say his prayers, thinking that he would soon be dead. And that thought

brought to mind the golden snuff-box, which he should only open when death was near. Jack took out the box and lifted the lid. Out jumped three tiny men, all dressed in red, and one of them spoke to Jack: "What do you want us to do?"

Jack explained what had been asked of him, and the little man told him to go to sleep. Much later, Jack was woken by a loud banging. When he looked through the window he saw a great lake in front of the house, on which were sailing stately men-of-war. One of these was firing a salute.

When he went down to meet the master of the house, Jack felt proud that the little men in the snuff-box had done so much for him. He felt that now he really could do anything

that was asked of him. Over breakfast, he talked with the master, who asked him to perform two more magical feats. If Jack could do these, he would be rewarded with the hand of the daughter of the house.

First of all, Jack had to fell all the tall trees within several miles of the house; this was done, and the gentleman was pleased. Jack's second task seemed even more difficult. The gentleman asked for a huge castle standing on twelve golden pillars, guarded by regiments of soldiers. With the help of the little men in his box, Jack produced the castle and the soldiers. Then the gentleman placed his daughter's hand in Jack's, and the couple looked at each

other lovingly. It seemed that Jack's troubles were over. But they were only just beginning.

Jack lived happily with the gentleman and his family. He now had fine clothes and servants to do his bidding. One day, they were going out hunting. Jack's man-servant, tidying his master's clothes when Jack was out on the hunt, came across the golden snuff-box. The valet opened the box in curiosity, and nearly dropped it when the three small men popped out. "What do you want us to do?" asked the men. The valet saw his chance. "I want this castle to be moved far across the sea, and I want to go with it and become its lord."

There was confusion and turmoil when Jack and the others came back from the hunt. His father-in-law rounded on Jack, accusing him of sorcery. Jack stood in misery, wondering what he could do now both castle and snuff-box were gone. "Give me a year and a day," Jack pleaded. "I will travel the world and try to find your castle."

So Jack began his travels once more. Everywhere he went he asked people about the castle, but no one could tell him where it was. When it seemed that he had asked everyone he could, he sat down in despair.

As he sat, Jack saw a little mouse looking up at him. "I don't suppose you know where the castle could be?" said Jack, half jokingly. "I guard the palace of the king of the mice," said the little creature. "Let us ask him if he knows." So to his surprise, Jack found himself in front of the mouse-king.

The king of the mice called all the mice in his kingdom to his palace, and asked all of them if they had seen the fine castle with its twelve golden pillars. None knew of its whereabouts, but one mouse suggested, "Two creatures who travel far are the king of the frogs and the king of the birds. Go and see them, and they may have news for you."

Taking with him the little mouse he had first met, Jack went off to seek these two creatures. After a long walk, they found the place where the king of the frogs lived. A frog stood guard, and at first would not let them in, but Jack insisted that he must see the king, and soon the king of the frogs came out to

ask him what he wanted. The frog-king listened to Jack's story in silence, then made an enormous and extraordinary croak, the like of which Jack had never heard before. Gradually, the land and water all around them filled with frogs, as all the king's subjects came to his call. The king asked them if they had seen the castle with twelve golden pillars, and they all croaked "No".

Jack began his journey once more. This time, he took with him the frog who had stood guard, as well as the mouse. Together, they went to search for the ruler of the birds.

Again, Jack asked to meet the king, and again was admitted. The king called all the fowls of the air around him and asked if any had seen the castle with the twelve golden pillars. Although they had flown far and wide, none of the birds had seen the castle. Jack was downhearted. It seemed that his last hope had been dashed. Then the king spoke up. "Where is the great bird?" All the feathered creatures looked about them, and it became clear to Jack that one of their number was missing.

As they waited, there was a great whooshing of wings, and an eagle appeared in the sky above their heads. The king turned

to the eagle, and asked again about the castle. "Yes, I have seen it," said the eagle. "I will take Jack to its resting place."

Jack, the mouse, and the frog clambered aboard the eagle's back and they flew to where the castle stood. Jack was puzzled about how to move the castle, but he told the mouse about his snuff-box. When they landed, the little animal ran off in search of the box, and the others hid quietly on the battlements. Soon the mouse returned, clutching the box in its paws, and they all flew off again, to make their way back to the home of Jack's father-in-law. As they flew, the mouse and the frog argued about who had been most helpful in finding the box, and, in the squabble, the box slipped into the sea below.

Jack started to panic and curse the creatures, but the eagle swooped low over the sea, and the frog dived to look for the box. Twice the frog dived and came up with nothing. The third time the frog seemed to be under the water for hours. In the end he came up, grasping the box and croaking with glee.

And so it was that the four friends returned to the land of Jack's father-in-law. Jack opened his box, out stepped the tiny men, and the castle was returned to its rightful place. The father-in-law thanked Jack, and Jack's young wife was pleased and relieved to see her husband home again. By now, she had a fine young son, all the family lived happily, and the castle with the twelve golden pillars never moved again.

The Green Man of No Man's Land

Jack was a miller and a great gambler. One day, a gentleman was passing Jack's mill and stopped to talk. The two soon began to play cards and as the game went on the stakes got higher and Jack was winning as usual – no one seemed able to beat him. Then the stranger said, "What do you want to win next."

"I will have the great castle over the way," replied Jack, and they dealt the cards.

Sure enough, Jack won again. But when they dealt again, the gentleman was the winner. "Now you must find *my* castle," said the gentleman to Jack. "My name is the Green Man of No Man's Land. I'll give you a year and a day to find my castle. If you fail, I will cut off your head."

Jack set off on horseback, for he thought that his journey would be long. He travelled far until he came to a land where it was cold and the ground was covered in snow. Jack felt cold and hungry, and decided to stop at the next house he could find.

The next house was the cottage of an old woman, who asked

Jack to come to her fireside and offered him food. Straight away, Jack asked her about the castle of the Green Man. "I do not know it," said the old woman. "But I can ask one quarter of the world if they know."

Next morning, Jack was amazed to see the old woman climb up on to the roof of her house. She raised a horn to her lips and blew a tremendous blast, and soon people came running towards her house from all directions. Surely, thought Jack, some of these people would know the Green Man's castle.

But when the old woman asked them, they all shook their heads. None of them had heard of the castle of the Green Man of No Man's Land. So the old woman blew her horn once

more, and all the birds of the neighbourhood flew to her call. She asked the birds, who had travelled far and wide in their flight. But none even of these had heard of the castle. The old woman turned to Jack.

"I have a sister farther along this road. Take my horse and ride to her house. She may have heard of the Green Man's castle." And she gave Jack a ball of thread, which he was to leave trailing behind him as he rode.

Jack took the old woman's horse and rode away. When he came to the sister's house, she recognized the beast. "It is long since I have seen my sister's horse," she said. "What is your business with me?" Jack asked her about the castle of the Green Man. "I do not know it," said the sister. "But I can ask one half of the world if they know."

Next morning, Jack saw the woman climb up to the roof of her house with a horn, just as her sister had done. When she blew, an even greater crowd gathered around her house. Surely, thought Jack, some of these people would know the Green Man's castle. But once more, when the sister asked them, they all shook their heads. None of them had heard of the castle of the Green Man of No Man's Land. A second blast of the horn brought huge flocks of birds to the sky above the sister's house. But none of these had heard of the castle either.

Jack and the sister went back into the house. "I have another sister," she said. "If she does not know of this castle that you seek, then no other will know. Take my horse, and this ball of thread, and make your way to where she lives."

So Jack set off once again, trailing his thread behind him, until he came to the house of the eldest of the sisters.

At once the old woman recognized her sister's horse. Jack questioned her about the castle, but again the woman knew nothing of it. So Jack was not surprised when in the morning she blew her horn to bring still greater crowds to her house. Still no one knew, and when the woman summoned the birds, it seemed as if once more they had failed to find the castle. Then there was a whirring of wings in the sky and one last

bird, a noble eagle, appeared above their heads. "Where have you been all this long while?" asked the woman.

"I have been in the country of the Green Man of No Man's Land," said the eagle. And he told them where it was.

The eagle and the old woman told Jack to go to a place where there was a lake with three white swans. Jack was to hide by the shore until the swans came near him and shook out some of their feathers. Jack was to take these feathers and wait. "When one of the swans comes to ask for her feathers, do not give them back, but ask her to ferry you across the lake to her father's castle."

Jack set off, and did as he had been told. Sure enough, one of the swans came to Jack and asked him to return her feathers. At first, she refused to carry Jack over the lake, but Jack insisted. Then the swan said to Jack: "Very well, get up on my back. But do not tell my father that I helped you."

This was how Jack finally reached the castle of the Green Man of No Man's Land. "One of my daughters must have helped you to get here," said the Green Man.

"No," replied Jack. "I have not seen her."

"Then you must clean out my stables. And if you do not, I will cut off your head."

Jack saw no escape, so went to work. It soon became clear that the task was never ending. Every shovelful he cleared,

three more seemed to appear in its place. Then the youngest daughter appeared and offered Jack some food. While he was eating, the stable was miraculously cleared. Every bit of the filth had disappeared. Jack looked at the girl in gratitude, but she warned him: "Do not tell my father that I helped you."

When the Green Man saw the work done, he looked at Jack suspiciously. "One of my daughters must have helped you," he said.

"No," replied Jack. "I have not seen her."

"Then you must fell all the trees in my forest," said the Green Man.

Jack set to work, but the job seemed endless, with new trees springing up as soon as he cut one down. The second daughter appeared, and gave Jack some food. When Jack returned to his

task, all the trees were cut down. Again the girl warned Jack not to tell her father.

When the Green Man saw the work done, he looked at Jack once more. "One of my daughters must have helped you," he said. Jack denied that he had seen her.

"Then you must build me a new barn, and thatch it with birds' feathers."

Jack saw that this was another impossible task, and that again he would need the help of one of the daughters. Sure enough, the girl appeared and the job was completed.

Jack's next task was to collect an egg from a mountain by the lake. Before long, one of the daughters appeared and told Jack to take off his shoe. Before his eyes, it turned into

a boat, so that they could row across and pick up the egg. As they returned, the girl spoke to Jack: "Tomorrow my father will turn me and my two sisters into swans. Only the one that you choose will be saved. But if you choose all three, we will all escape."

The Green Man and Jack stood by the castle as the three swans flew overhead.

"Which one will you have," asked the Green Man. Jack chose the first of the three. Again the swans flew past, and this time Jack pointed to the second. The birds circled and passed once more, and finally Jack chose the third.

"Then she shall be your wife," said the Green Man. And so she and Jack were married, and lived happily, but the sisters were saved too. And as for the Green Man, he died soon afterwards, and he and his tricks were never heard of again.

Taliesin

Long ago in the middle of Lake Tegid lived a gentleman called Tegid Voel and his wife Caridwen. They had a daughter named Creirwy, and two sons, Morvran ab Tegid and Avagddu. The youngest child, Avagddu, was an ugly infant, and Caridwen feared that no one of noble birth would have anything to do with him. So she decided to brew him a magic potion that would give him the gifts of knowledge and shape-changing, so that he could make a better way in the world.

She added marvellous herbs and spices to her cauldron and set the mixture over the fire. To work properly, the brew had to boil for a year and a day, so Caridwen asked a young lad called Gwion to stir the cauldron, and a blind man called Morda to look after the fire.

Each day Caridwen added fresh herbs and recited spells over the pot, and the time grew near when the brew would be ready. As he was stirring, a few drops of the mixture splashed on to Gwion's finger. Automatically, Gwion licked his finger to make it clean, and straight away the young lad was blessed with the gift of seeing into the future and the ability to change his shape into whatever he liked. As he looked into the future, he saw that Caridwen planned to kill him, so straightaway he took to his feet and ran, knocking the cauldron, which split in two behind him.

Caridwen turned to Morda and cursed him, but the blind man pointed out that all was Gwion's fault, and the woman saw that she must chase the lad and stop him. Off she ran, and as he saw her, Gwion changed himself into a hare. But Caridwen transformed herself into a greyhound, and started to gain on him. Next Gwion turned himself into a fish, leaping into the river. But Caridwen transformed herself into an otter, and swam after

him. Gwion left the water behind, taking the shape of a bird. But Caridwen transformed herself into a hawk and flew up after him. Gwion landed on a heap of wheat and turned himself into one of the grains. But Caridwen transformed herself into a great black hen, and pecked away at all the grains until she had swallowed him.

Gwion stayed for nine months in Caridwen's belly, and then she fell into labour and gave birth to him, and he had once more the form of a baby. When she saw her child, Caridwen could not bear to kill him. So she put him in a leather bag, and threw him into the sea.

The place where Caridwen threw Gwion into the sea was

near the weir of Gwyddno. Here Gwyddno and his ill-favoured son Elphin often came to catch salmon, and it chanced that Elphin came to do just that, the day after Gwion had been abandoned.

Elphin found no fish at the weir, and was anxious that his father would be cross with him for returning empty-handed. But he found the leather bag, opened it, and was struck by the child's beauty. "Behold a radiant brow!" he said. "Let him be called Taliesin." And he set off to take the child to his father.

As they went, Taliesin startled Elphin by beginning to sing. He sang to Elphin that he should not despair, for good fortune would come to him. The song seemed to be consoling Elphin for returning home without any fish, and the man's mood began to improve. He looked at the child and asked him whether he was a human or a spirit. In reply, Taliesin sang another song, describing how he could change his shape, and how he had to change his shape to escape the clutches of Caridwen. As he sang, he embroidered his tale, imagining all the creatures he could have become:

> I have fled as a roe in a tangled thicket;
> I have fled as a wolf cub, and lived in the wilderness;
> I have fled as a thrush and sung of the future;
> I have fled as a fox, and lived by my cunning;
> I have fled as an iron in the glowing fire;
> I have fled as a spear-head, and woe to my enemies;

I have fled as a fierce bull bitterly fighting;

I have fled as white grain of pure wheat.

Into a dark leathern bag I was thrown;

On a boundless sea I was sent adrift;

And the Lord God then gave me my liberty.

When Taliesin's song was finished, they arrived at Gwyddno's court, and Elphin said, "I have something here that is better than fish – a bard."

"What use is a bard?" complained Gwyddno. But when he heard Taliesin sing, he thought that a bard might be more use than he had first believed. So he told Elphin to give Taliesin to his wife, and the woman brought up the child as lovingly as if he were her own.

Taliesin indeed seemed to bring good fortune to Elphin. Everything he did brought him either riches or favour with the king. And so it went on until Taliesin was just thirteen, when Elphin was invited to spend Christmas with his uncle, Maelgwyn Gwynedd, with all Maelgwyn's knights and squires at his castle of Dyganwy.

As knights did when they were assembled in their lord's house, the men all fell to praising Maelgwyn – his generosity, his bravery, the beauty of his queen, his fine horses, and the skill and wisdom of his bards. For bards were highly valued at this time, as they always have been in Wales, and Maelgwyn had some twenty-four bards, all skilled in poetry and music, and valuable to their lord because they could speak many languages and act as envoys and messengers for Maelgwyn.

When they had finished praising Maelgwyn and his bards, Elphin spoke up: "Far be it from me to vie with a king, but if Maelgwyn were not a king, I would say that my own wife is more beautiful and virtuous than his queen and that my bard Taliesin is more skilled than any of his bards."

Maelgwyn was full of anger at his nephew's boastfulness. "Better than the bards of the royal court?" he roared. "Clap him in irons and lock him in prison." And so Elphin found himself bundled off and locked in the castle dungeon.

When Elphin was locked away, Maelgwyn turned to his son Rhun, the most evil and graceless character in the whole court. He told Rhun to visit Elphin's wife and find out if she was indeed virtuous. The women of the court feared for Elphin's wife when they heard that Rhun proposed to call on her in her chamber.

Meanwhile Taliesin sped to Elphin's wife. "Madam, you are in danger," he said. "Change places with one of the kitchen maids. Dress her in your clothes, and give her your rings to wear." Elphin's wife did as the bard advised, and soon it was as if the maid was the noblewoman, and the noblewoman was the maid.

Sure enough, Rhun soon came to call upon Elphin's wife, and found the maid in her place. The maid invited Rhun to eat and drink, and the evil lord dropped a sleeping draught into her drink. He pulled at Elphin's ring, which the maid wore on her finger, but it would not come off. So he took his knife and cut away the finger, and returned to the king with the evidence that he had been with Elphin's wife.

Maelgwyn showed Elphin the ring, and told him that it proved his wife was lacking in virtue to let Rhun come close. But Elphin defended his wife stoutly. "My lord, I cannot deny

that this is my ring. But the finger with it never belonged to my wife, and I will tell you three reasons why. First, my wife's fingers are much more slender than this — the ring would have come off easily; second, my wife trims her nails often and carefully, whereas the nail on this finger is untrimmed; third, the hand from which this finger came has recently been kneading dough — see the traces here — and my wife has never kneaded dough since we have been married."

The king was not used to being challenged in this way, and grew mightily angry with Elphin. "Take him back to prison," roared the king. "He shall stay there until the wisdom of his

bard is also proved."

Taliesin consoled Elphin's wife. "I will free your lord from prison. I will silence the royal bards and the king will hear how I can sing." And with that, off he went to the king's hall.

Taliesin entered the hall quietly and sat in a corner where no one noticed him. As each of Maelgwyn's bards came in, Taliesin pursed his lips and made the noise "Blerm, blerm" at them as they passed. They took little notice of this until the first two bards rose to sing to the king. When they opened their lips all that would come out was "Blerm, blerm". The king thought they were drunk, and sent a servingman to tell them off, but when the bards began again, still all they could sing was "Blerm, blerm". This went on until one of the king's squires took a broom and dealt a great blow on the head to Heinin Vardd, the king's chief bard.

Heinin kneeled before the king. "Your majesty," he said. "We do not wish to mock you. The noise that comes from our mouths was put there by some spirit that lives in that youth sitting in the corner." And Heinin pointed accusingly at Taliesin. The king called Taliesin and ordered the young bard to give an account of himself, which he did in the most extra-ordinary song he had sung:

> Chief bard of Elphin am I;
> I come from the region of the summer stars;
> And every king will call me Taliesin.
> I was with my Lord in highest heaven,
> And was there when Lucifer fell from grace;
> I fought with the great Alexander,
> And know the names of all the stars;
> I was in Canaan when Absalom was slain;
> I was in the court of Don before the birth of Gwdion;
> I was instructor to Eli and Enoch;
> I was at the place of crucifixion of the merciful Son of God;
> I am a wonder whose origin no man knows.

And so the song went on, with the most beguiling of music, and the king and all his court were speechless.

193

When he heard that this was Elphin's bard, the king challenged his own singers to produce a better song. But as each of the king's twenty-four bards came up to the high table, still the only sound he could make was the "Blerm, blerm" noise that Taliesin had put on his lips. Then Taliesin sang again, claiming that the power of his voice would release his master Elphin from prison and that his words would tell of the virtue and beauty of Elphin's queen. The young bard's song got louder and louder, until it seemed to merge with the sound of a mighty wind that was howling around the castle battlements.

As the wind grew, Maelgwyn and his people began to be afraid that the very castle might blow down. So the king ordered Elphin to be brought from the dungeon. When the guards brought Elphin into the hall, Taliesin started to sing once more, and at his very first notes, the chain binding Elphin snapped and the young man stood free. Then the king called for Elphin's wife, and everyone could see that she still had all of her fingers. Truly she had both beauty and virtue.

Taliesin had one last trick for the cruel king. He told Elphin to bet that his horse could beat any of the king's horses in a race. Taliesin gave the youth who rode Elphin's horse twenty-four sprigs of holly, and the youth struck each of Maelgwyn's steeds with a holly sprig as he passed. Finally, when his own horse stumbled, the youth threw down his cap at the spot – but he still won the race.

After the challenge was over, Taliesin led his lord to the place where the rider had thrown down his cap. "Dig a hole here, and you will find a cauldron full of gold," declared Taliesin. It is a reward for rescuing me from the sea and taking me into your protection."

Elphin found the gold, and they all returned to the hall. The whole court listened to Taliesin's songs all night through. And though Taliesin cured the other bards so that they could sing again, none in Wales ever heard song as sweet as Taliesin sung that night.

The Sprightly Tailor

Long ago, in a castle called Sandell, lived a laird called the great MacDonald. MacDonald liked his comfort, and favoured garments called trews, which were a combination of vest and trousers in one piece. One day the laird needed some new trews, and called for the local tailor.

When the tailor arrived the great MacDonald told him what he wanted. "I'll pay you extra," promised the laird, "if you will make the trews in the church by night." For MacDonald had heard that the church was haunted by a fearful monster, and he

wanted to see how the tailor fared when faced with this beast.

The tailor had also heard stories about the monster. But he was a sprightly fellow who liked a challenge – especially if it was going to lead to some extra money. So that very night he walked up the glen, through the churchyard gate, and into

the dark church. Finding a
tombstone where he could sit,
he got to work on the trews,
and very soon the garment was
taking shape.

After a while, the tailor felt
the floor of the church begin
to shake beneath him. A hole
seemed to open up in the
stone floor and a large and
gruesome head appeared. "Do
you see this great head of mine?" a voice boomed.

"I see that, but I'll sew these," replied the tailor, holding up
the trews.

The head paused as the tailor was speaking, then began to
rise again, revealing a thick, muscular neck. "Do you see this
great neck of mine?" the monster asked.

"I see that, but I'll sew these," replied the tailor.

Next the creature's shoulders and trunk came into view. "Do
you see this great chest of mine?"

"I see that, but I'll sew these," said the tailor. And he carried
on sewing, although, to tell the truth, some of the stitches were
a little less neat than normal.

Now the beast was rising quickly, and the tailor could make

out its arms. Its voice echoed in the stone building: "Do you see these great arms of mine?"

"I see those, but I'll sew these," replied the tailor. He gritted his teeth and carried on with his work as before, for he wanted to finish by daybreak and claim his payment from the great MacDonald.

The tailor's needle was flying now, as the monster gave a great grunt and lifted his first leg out of the ground. "Do you see this great leg of mine?" he said, his voice getting even louder.

"I see that, but I'll sew these," replied the tailor, making his final stitches a little longer, so that he could finish his work before the monster could climb out of his hole.

As the creature began to raise its other leg, the tailor blew out his candle, gathered up his things, and bundled the completed trews under one arm. He made for the door as the monster was emerging, and the tailor could hear the creature's footsteps echoing on the stone floor as he ran out into the open air.

Now the tailor could see the glen stretching in front of him, and he ran for his life, faster than he had ever ran before, for all that he was a nimble man. The monster roared at him to stop, but the tailor hurried on, his feet hardly touching the ground, and finally the great MacDonald's castle loomed up ahead of him and the tailor knew he had a chance to reach its gates.

Quickly the gates opened, and quickly they closed behind the tailor – and not a moment too soon, for as the great wooden gates slammed shut, the monster crashed to a halt and struck a resounding blow on the wall to show how frustrated he was at missing his goal when he had got so near.

To this day, the monster's handprint can be seen on the wall of the castle at Sandell. MacDonald paid the sprightly tailor for his work, and gave him a handsome bonus for braving the haunted church. The laird liked his smart new trews, and never realised that some of the stitches were longer and less neat than the others.

Gold-Tree and Silver-Tree

There once lived a king who had a queen called Silver-Tree and a beautiful daughter called Gold-Tree. They all lived together happily until one day Silver-Tree and Gold-Tree were sitting by a pool and it took Silver-Tree's fancy to peer into the water and talk to the trout swimming there: "Silver trout in the pool, who is the most beautiful queen in the world?"

"Gold-Tree is the most beautiful," replied the fish.

Silver-Tree was mad with jealousy. She could not stand the fact that there was someone in the world – someone in her very family – who was more beautiful than she. She decided that she would get Gold-Tree killed, and to be sure the girl was dead, she would eat Gold-Tree's heart and liver. The queen was so mad with jealousy that she told her husband, begging him to kill their daughter and give her the heart and liver to eat.

At just this time it happened that a prince from a far country had come to ask for Gold-Tree's hand in marriage. The king, who was a good man, saw that the two young people loved each other, and saw his chance. He sent Gold-Tree away with the prince to be married. Then, when out hunting with his

men, he took a deer's heart and liver, and gave them to his wife. Once she had eaten these, Silver-Tree was cured of her jealousy.

All went well until the queen visited the pool and again asked the fish who was the most beautiful.

"Gold-Tree your daughter is the fairest," said the trout.

"But my daughter is long dead!" exclaimed the queen.

"Surely she is not. For she has married a fine prince in a far country."

When Silver-Tree asked her husband she found that what

the trout had said was true.

"Make ready the great ship, for I must visit my daughter," said Silver-Tree. And because she had seemed cured of her jealousy, the king let her go.

When Silver-Tree came to her destination, the prince was out hunting. Gold-Tree saw her mother arriving, and knew that her life was in danger. She called her servants, and they locked Gold-Tree in her room. But Silver-Tree was cunning. When she found her daughter locked in, she called sweetly, "Put your little finger through the keyhole, so your mother may kiss it."

As soon as Gold-Tree's finger appeared through the keyhole, the wicked queen took a dagger that she had dipped in poison and stuck it into Gold-Tree's finger. Straight away, the princess collapsed, and soon she was dead, the poisoned point still in her finger as she lay.

When Gold-Tree's husband came home, he was horrified at what had happened. He broke into the room and saw his young wife dead on the floor. So beautiful was the dead princess, that he had her body preserved, and locked in her room, and kept the key himself.

After some years had passed, the prince's grief faded a little, although he never smiled, and he decided to marry once again. He did not tell his second wife about Gold-Tree's body, but one day she found the key to the dead girl's room. She was curious to see the one part of her husband's castle that she had never entered, so, when no one was looking, she quietly opened the door and went in. When she saw the beautiful body laid out in the room, she realised at once that this must be Gold-Tree, the princess who had died so tragically, for she had heard the tale of the girl's death. As she approached the body she saw the poisoned dagger still sticking in the girl's finger. Yes, this must be Gold-Tree. Still curious, the second wife pulled at the dagger to remove it, and Gold-Tree rose, alive, just as she had been before her mother's visit.

The second wife went to the prince and said to him, "What would you give me if I could make you laugh again?"

"Truly, nothing could make me laugh, unless Gold-Tree was alive again," said the prince sadly.

"Then come to her room, and surely you will find her living."

They ran to the room together and the prince saw that it was true. The second wife was amazed at the change that came over her husband and knew that Gold-Tree was his true love.

"Now you have your true love back again," she said, "I must go away."

But the prince was so grateful to her that he would not let her go. He insisted that she remain in his household, alongside Gold-Tree.

Everything went well for them until Silver-Tree visited the pool once more. The queen was horrified when the fish told her that Gold-Tree was still the most beautiful woman in the world.

"But I stabbed Gold-Tree with poison and she is long dead," protested the queen.

"You stabbed her, but she is still alive," the fish replied.

And so Silver-Tree once more set sail to her daughter's home, and it happened that the prince was out hunting when she arrived. Gold-Tree saw her mother approaching, and quaked with fear at what she would do. "Let us go to meet her," said the second wife calmly, and they went together, as if to greet a welcome guest.

Silver-Tree held out a precious gold cup that she was carrying. "I bring a refreshing drink for my daughter," she said.

The second wife looked at her coldly. "In this country, it is the custom for the visitor to drink first," she said.

Silver-Tree raised the cup to her mouth, but hesitated, knowing that if she drank, she would kill herself. Just at that moment, the second wife's arm shot out and struck the cup, sending some of the deadly poison straight down Silver-Tree's throat. The wicked queen fell dead to the floor, and the servants took up her body to bury her. At last, Gold-Tree, the prince, and his second wife could live in peace.

The Frog

A widow was baking in her kitchen and asked her daughter to go down to the well to fetch some water. Off the daughter went, down to the well by the meadow, but when she came to the well she found that it was dry. She wondered what she and her mother would do without water, for it was high summer and there had not been a cloud in the sky for days. And the poor girl was so anxious that she sat down beside the well and began to cry.

Suddenly, through her sobbing, the girl heard a plop, and a frog jumped out of the well.

"What are you crying for?" asked the frog.

The girl explained that there was no water and she did not know what to do.

"Well," said the frog, "if you will be my wife, you shall have all the water you need."

The girl thought that the creature was making fun of her, so she went along with the joke, and agreed to be the frog's wife. She lowered her bucket into the well once more, and sure enough, when she pulled it up, the bucket was full of water.

The girl took the water back to her mother, and thought no more about the frog until it was evening. Then, as the girl and her mother were about to go to bed, they heard a small voice and a scratching sound at the door of their cottage: "Open the door, my own true love. Remember the promise you made to me, when fetching your water down at the well."

"Ugh, it's a filthy frog," said the girl.

"Open the door to the poor creature," said her mother, for she was a gentle woman who liked to be kind to animals. And so they opened the door.

"Give me my supper, my own true love. Remember the promise you made to me, when fetching your water down at the well," the frog went on.

"Ugh, I don't want to feed the filthy beast," said the daughter.

"Give the poor creature something to eat," insisted her mother. So they laid out some food and the frog ate it all up thankfully.

"Put me to bed, my own true love. Remember the promise you made to me, when fetching your water down at the well," said the frog.

"Ugh, we can't have that slimy thing in our bed," protested the daughter.

"Put the poor creature to bed and let it rest," said the mother. So they turned down the sheets and the frog climbed into bed.

Then the frog spoke again: "Bring me an axe, my own true love. Remember the promise you made to me, when fetching your water down at the well."

The widow and her daughter looked at each other in deep puzzlement. "What would the creature want with an axe?" asked the girl. "It is far too heavy for a frog to lift."

"Fetch him an axe," said the mother. "We shall see soon

enough." So the daughter went out to the woodshed and returned with the ax.

"Now chop off my head, my own true love. Remember the promise you made to me, when fetching your water down at the well," croaked the frog to the daughter.

Trembling, the girl turned to the frog, who stretched out his neck obligingly. She raised the ax high, just as she did when chopping wood for the fire, and brought it down on to the frog's neck. When she had done the deed, the girl looked away for a moment, scared to see the dead creature and its severed head. But when she heard her mother's shout of surprise she looked back quickly. And there stood the finest, most handsome young prince that either of them had ever seen.

"It was me you promised to marry," smiled the prince.

And the poor widow's daughter and the handsome prince *did* marry, and they lived in happiness for rest of their lives.

The Black Bull of Norway

Long ago in Norway there lived a woman, and she had three daughters. One day the eldest daughter went to her mother and said that she had decided to seek her fortune. So the girl went to see the old witch-washerwoman who could foretell people's futures. And the witch-washerwoman said to her, "Stand by my back door and see what you can see."

The first day, the girl could see nothing unusual outside the witch-washerwoman's back door, and nothing came on the second day. But on the third day, a fine coach pulled by six horses appeared in the road beyond the back door. The girl went to the witch-washerwoman and told her what she had seen. "That's for you," said the witch-washerwoman, and the girl got into the coach and rode away.

Soon the second daughter decided she too should seek her fortune, and went to the witch-washerwoman's house, as her sister had done. The first day, she could see nothing unusual outside the witch-washerwoman's back door, and nothing came on the second day. But on the third day, a fine coach appeared. "That's for you," said the witch-washerwoman, and the second daughter rode away.

Then the youngest daughter followed in her sisters' footsteps, going to the witch-washerwoman's house in her turn. The first

day, she could see nothing outside the witch-washerwoman's back door, and nothing came on the second day. But on the third day, a great black bull appeared, bellowing as it walked. "That's for you," said the witch-washerwoman.

The girl was fearful of the great black creature, but in the end she plucked up the courage to climb on to the beast's back, and they galloped away together. The bull seemed kind, and when the girl felt hungry and asked for refreshment, the bull said, "Eat from out my right ear, and take drink from my left." The girl did so, and felt wonderfully refreshed.

By and by they came to a fine castle, and the bull slowed down at its gate. "Here lives my eldest brother," said the bull, and the two rested for the night at the castle. In the morning, the lord of the castle took the girl into a fine chamber, and gave her an apple. "Do not break into this apple until you are in the greatest need," said the lord. "Then it will help you."

The girl and the bull rode on for many miles more, until they arrived at a second castle, bigger and fairer than the first. "Here lives my second brother," said the bull, and the two rested there for the night.

In the morning, the lord of the castle took the girl into a fine chamber, and presented her with a pear. And he spoke to her rather as the first lord had done. "Do not break into this pear until you are in need," said the lord. "Then it will help you."

Once again the two traveled on, over hill and dale, until they came to a third castle, still finer and larger than the others. "Here lives my youngest brother," said the bull, and the lord of the castle once more gave them lodgings for the night.

In the morning, the lord of the castle took the girl into a fine chamber, and presented her with a plum. "Do not break into this fruit until you are in the greatest need," said the lord. "Then it will help you."

Off they went again, and after another long ride, the bull came to a halt in a dark and lonely glen. "This is where you must get down," the bull said. "For the time has come when I must leave you to go and fight with the devil. Sit down on that stone and do not move from here, for if you move I shall not find you. Look around you, and if everything turns blue, I shall have won my fight with the devil; but if all turns red that will mean I have lost."

After a while everything in the glen turned blue, and the girl's heart was filled with joy that the bull had won his fight. So pleased she was that she moved one foot and crossed it over the other, quite forgetting the bull's instructions to stay absolutely still. So, no matter how long she sat, the bull could not find her again.

When the black bull did not return, the girl saw the reason, and she knew that she must complete her journey alone. So off she went along the glen, until she came to a great hill made all of glass. She walked around the hill, but could not climb it, for its glassy surface was so slippery. Finally she found a smith's house, and the smith told her that he would make her some metal shoes so that she could cross the hill in safety.

The girl climbed the glassy hill, and made her way carefully down the other side, and what should she see but the house of the old witch-washerwoman—her journey had brought her full circle. When she was talking to the washerwoman and her daughter, they told her of a handsome knight who had

brought some bloodstained shirts
to be washed. The blood had
almost ruined the shirts, so he had
promised to marry the woman
who could wash away the stains,
but neither the old washerwoman
nor her daughter could do this,
no matter how they rubbed and
scrubbed.

The girl took the shirts and
began to wash them, and both the
washerwoman and her daughter
turned green with envy as they
saw the bloodstains
disappearing. But when the
knight returned for his shirts,
the washerwoman told him
that it was her daughter who
had washed them. And so it
happened that the knight and
the washerwoman's daughter
prepared to get married.

The girl wondered what to
do, since she admired the

knight and desperately wanted the truth to be known. So she decided to break open the apple she had been given at the first castle. Out tumbled a heap of gold and jewels. "Delay your marriage for one day," said the girl to the washerwoman's daughter, "and you shall have these jewels."

The bride-to-be agreed, and the girl planned to go to the knight in the evening and explain the truth to him. But the washerwoman saw how things stood and gave the knight a sleeping-potion to drink. Through her tears, the girl sang a snatch of song:

The bloody shirt I washed for thee.
Will you not waken and turn to me?

Next day, the girl could think of nothing to do but break open her pear. Out came jewels even more precious than those that had come out of the apple. "Delay your marriage for one day," said the girl to the washerwoman's daughter, "and you shall have them all."

The washerwoman's daughter agreed, and the girl once more got ready to go to the knight. But once again the washerwoman gave him a sleeping-potion, so that the truth could not be told him. Again the girl sang through her tears of sadness:

> The bloody shirt I washed for thee.
>
> Will you not waken and turn to me?

The knight heard nothing of this song. But the next day, when he was out hunting, one of his men said to him, "What was that singing and moaning last night outside your chamber?" The knight, curious to find out what was going on, was determined that nothing should make him fall asleep the next night.

Meanwhile, the girl broke open the plum, and still richer jewels fell out. These she offered to the washerwoman's girl, who again accepted them. But this time, the knight, who by now suspected the washerwoman, only pretended to drink.

So it was that the knight came to hear the truth. The girl who had ridden the black bull, climbed the hill of glass, and washed the blood-stained shirt finally married her knight. And the washerwoman's daughter was content with her jewels.

The Well at the World's End

There was once a king, a widower, and he had a daughter who was beautiful and good-natured. The king married a queen, who was a widow, and she had a daughter who was as ugly and ill-natured as the king's daughter was fair and good. The queen detested the king's daughter, for no one would notice her own girl while this paragon was beside her, so she made a plan. She sent the king's daughter to the well at the world's end, with a bottle to get some water, thinking she would never come back.

The girl walked far and was beginning to tire when she came upon a pony tethered by the roadside. The pony looked at the girl and spoke: "Ride me, ride me, fair princess."

"Yes, I will ride you," replied the girl, and the pony carried her over a moor covered with prickly gorse and brambles.

Far she rode, and finally she came to the well at the world's end. She took her bottle and lowered it into the well, but the well was too deep and she could not fill the bottle. Then three old men came up to her, saying, "Wash us, wash us, fair maid, and dry us with your linen apron."

So she washed the men and in return they lowered her bottle into the well and filled it with water.

When they had finished, the three men looked at the girl and spoke her future. "If she was fair before, she will be ten times more beautiful," said the first.

"A diamond and a ruby and a pearl shall drop from her mouth every time she speaks," predicted the second.

"Gold and silver shall come from her hair when she combs it," said the third.

The king's daughter returned to court, and to everyone's amazement, these predictions came true.

All were happy with the girl's good fortune, except for the

queen and her daughter. The queen decided that she would send her own daughter to the well at the world's end, to get her the same gifts. After traveling far, the girl came to the pony, as the king's daughter had done before her. By now, the beast was tethered once more. But when the creature asked her to ride it, the queen's daughter replied, "Don't you see I am a queen's daughter? I will not ride you, you filthy beast."

The proud girl walked on, and she soon came to the moor covered with gorse and brambles. It was hard going for the girl, and the thorns cut her feet badly. Soon she could hardly walk with the pain.

After a long and painful walk across the moor, the queen's daughter came to the well at the world's end. She lowered her bottle, but like the king's daughter, found that it would not reach the water in the well. Then she heard the three old men speaking: "Wash us, wash us, fair maid, and dry us with your linen apron."

And the proud daughter replied, "You

nasty, filthy creatures, do you think a queen's daughter can be bothered to wash you, and dry your dirty faces with my fine clean clothes?"

So the old men refused to dip the girl's bottle into the well. Instead, they turned to her and began to predict her future: "If she was ugly before, she will be ten times uglier," said the first.

"Each time she speaks, a frog and a toad will jump from her mouth," predicted the second.

"When she combs her hair, lice and fleas will appear," said the third.

With these curses ringing in her ears, the unhappy girl returned home. Her mother was distraught when she saw her daughter, for she was indeed uglier than before, and frogs, toads, fleas, and lice, jumped from her. In the end, she left the king's court, and married a poor cobbler. The king's fair and good-natured daughter married a handsome prince, and was happy—and good-natured—for the rest of her long life.

The Princess of the Blue Mountains

There was a poor widow who had one son called Will. Because he was all she had in the world she always let him have his way, and he became lazy. In the end she said to him, "Son, you must make your own way in the world. Then you will know what it is to find your own work and earn your own living." So young Will went off to seek his fortune.

Will traveled until he came to a fast-flowing river, which he had to cross. When he saw the rapid current and the sharp rocks, he was afraid to go into the water, and waited for a while. As he was standing there, a lady on the opposite bank saw him, and waved at him to cross, which finally he did.

When Will got to the other side, the lady said she would give him food and drink if he would go into her garden and find the most beautiful flower. But Will, struck by the lady's beauty, said "You are the fairest flower in all the garden."

The lady, already charmed by Will, turned to him. "Will you be my husband?" she asked. "There will be many dangers in store for you, but I'll try to help you through them."

Will looked at the lady and it did not take him long to say "Yes, I will be your husband, whatever dangers I must face."

Then the lady explained her story to Will. She was the Princess of the Kingdom of the Blue Mountains, and had been stolen away from her father's land by a demon called Grimaldin. For three nights, the demon would send his legions to do battle with Will. The lady gave Will three black sticks, one for each legion of demons, and a pot of ointment, in case he should be injured. "Use these things well, for now I must leave you."

As soon as the lady had left, three legions of demons appeared. They were armed with fearsome clubs, which they

raised to beat Will. But the young man stopped their blows, and used the lady's sticks to beat them off. Soon they were gone.

The next morning, the lady returned, and was pleased to see Will hale and hearty. "Well done. Never before has any man fought off the demons with such skill and courage. Tonight, twice as many demons will come to challenge you, so I will give you six sticks to help you fight them off." And the lady left once more, this time giving Will a larger pot of ointment, in case he should be wounded.

Sure enough, six legions of demons arrived to do battle with Will and again he beat them off successfully.

The lady greeted Will with gladness the following morning. "This time, I must give you twelve sticks, for twelve legions will come tonight. Look out of Grimaldin, for he will certainly come too." She left more ointment, for no one had survived a fight with Grimaldin without being sorely wounded.

Quickly Grimaldin and his whole army of twelve legions arrived, and the chief demon spoke to Will: "What is your business here?"

"I come to rescue the Princess of the Blue Mountains."

"Then you shall die."

Straightaway, the demons attacked, and Will beat them off with the sticks as before. But this time, Grimaldin attacked, and

struck Will to the ground. The young man, sore and wounded all over, quickly applied the ointment. He was amazed to feel whole and well again, and stood up to face Grimaldin. This time, he beat off the chief demon, who went away, howling.

When the princess reappeared, she looked relieved. "Your greatest danger is over," she said to Will. "Take this book about the history of my family, and let no one distract you from reading it. If you know all that is in this book, you will be one of my father's favourites, and he will allow you to marry me."

Will started to read the book. He heard all sorts of voices trying to distract him, but he kept his eyes glued to the pages. Then he heard a woman coming by selling apples. Will liked nothing more than a ripe apple, so he looked up from the

book. No sooner had he done so than he felt himself thrown against the apple woman's basket with such force that he passed out.

A while later, Will came to. The apple woman was gone and the princess was nowhere to be seen. There was an old man sitting nearby on a bench and Will asked him if he knew how to get to the kingdom of the Blue Mountains. The old man did not know, so he asked the fishes of the sea, and no fish knew the whereabouts of the kingdom. The old man said "I have a brother, five hundred years older than me, who can talk to the birds of the air. He will know, or will find out from the birds."

They went to see the old

man's aged brother, and all the birds were called together. None knew where the kingdom of the Blue Mountains could be found, until the last bird, a great eagle, arrived. "I can take you to the kingdom," said the eagle. And Will climbed onto the great bird's back.

In the kingdom of the Blue Mountains, they landed near a house hung with black drapery. Will asked for lodgings, but the people at the house said that they could not help him. Their master was to be fed to a giant who terrorized the kingdom, asking for a human victim to eat every day. Anyone who could kill the giant would please the king, and would be given the hand of his daughter in marriage.

Will knew what he must do. He put on his armour, and strode out to challenge the giant. They fought long and hard, and Will was finally the winner. The princess recognized him and when the king learned that he had killed the giant, gave his permission for Will and the princess to marry. After the wedding, Will's mother came to live with them at the royal castle, and they were all happy together.

The Widow's Son and the King's Daughter

There was once a young lad called Jack, whose father died, leaving Jack and his mother without money. So, for the first time in his life, Jack had to go out to work. He had few useful skills, but he knew that he was no use to his mother at home, so set off one day to seek his fortune, whatever it might be.

After travelling a long way on the first day, Jack came across a house near a wood. He stopped and talked to the people of the house and, as he looked weak from his journey, they offered him food and a bed for the night. In the morning, the man of the house asked Jack if he needed work, and Jack replied that he did. "I have a herd of cattle that needs minding," said the man. "If you will do that job for me I should be pleased. But do not go into the field with the fruit trees. For a giant lives in that field and he will surely gobble you up if you go there. He may even carry off my cattle to eat."

Jack went to the field to mind the cattle, and he had not been there long when he started to admire the fruit on the trees in the neighbouring field. There were red apples and ripe pears, as well as all sorts of other strange fruit that Jack did not recognise. He peered through the hedge and no one seemed to be about. So Jack thought he would risk a quick dash into the giant's field to take some fruit.

As Jack was picking some of the fruit, an old woman passed along the lane that ran by the edge of the field. She was also admiring the fruit, and asked Jack if he would pick some for her. Looking around him cautiously to make sure the giant was not coming, Jack agreed, and soon both he and the old woman had some fine, succulent fruit to eat.

"I will give you something useful in return for your favour," the old woman said to Jack. "Here are three stout rods and a

sword. Whoever you stab with this sword, they will be sure to fall down dead. You need never fear your enemies."

Jack thanked the old woman with all his heart, for in truth he had been worried about the giant, and wondered whether the beast would stride over the hedge into his field and take his revenge for the stolen fruit.

Sure enough, it was not long before the giant appeared. Jack hastily climbed a tree, for he had not tried the sword and wondered whether it would work. This did not put off the giant, who stepped towards the tree, held out his hand, and heaved. The tree was torn up by the roots, and Jack fell to the ground. But as the giant did this, Jack's sword grazed his flesh, and the giant fell down dead.

The next day, Jack was guarding his master's cattle again, when another giant appeared by the trees. "Do you dare to slay my brother?" the beast bellowed. Jack drew his sword and ran at the giant, felling the beast with one blow. As he looked at the massive corpse, Jack wondered if there were any more in the giant's family.

On the third day, another giant appeared. Jack hid himself in the hollow of a tree, and heard the creature grunting that he must have one of Jack's beasts to eat. "You will have to ask me first," shouted Jack from inside the hollow tree.

"Oh, is it you, who killed my two brothers?" roared the giant. "I shall take my revenge on you before long." But as the giant drew near the tree, Jack leaped out and stabbed him. The last of the giants was dead.

When he had got his breath back, Jack decided to go to the giants' castle, which was not far off, and see what riches might be hidden there. When he arrived, he told the giant's steward, who looked after the castle, that he had conquered the giants, and the steward, amazed at Jack's strength, gave the lad the keys to the castle treasuries. Jack took some of the money he found there and travelled back home to see his own people.

Jack found his country in turmoil when he arrived. People were weeping, and they told him that a fire-breathing monster had come to the country and had demanded one young boy or girl to eat every day. Tomorrow, it was the turn of the king's daughter, who would be killed by the beast if no one could slay the monster or drive it away.

Jack put on his armour and took his faithful sword. Then he went to see the princess whom the monster was hoping to devour. He told her that he had come to save her, and asked if she would marry him if he was successful. To this she agreed, and in relief, Jack fell at her feet and was soon asleep with his head in the princess's lap. While Jack was asleep, the princess wove a ringlet of white stones in his hair, as a good-luck charm.

Suddenly, the monster crashed into the room. The princess started in fear and Jack woke up. In one movement he jumped up and drew his sword. Holding the weapon in front of him, he aimed many blows at the monster, but he could not get close enough to wound the beast because of the fire that came spurting from the creature's mouth. They carried on like this for some time, Jack waving his sword and the beast spitting fire, until the monster began to tire and slunk away.

The next day, the beast returned. The same thing happened,

with neither the beast nor Jack the winner, until the monster again grew tired and this time flapped its wings and flew away.

Jack thought hard. It was the creature's fire that caused the problem. So on the third day, Jack borrowed a camel, and made the animal drink several barrels of water. When the dragon appeared, Jack made the camel spit out its water to put out the fire. Then, before the monster could produce more flames, Jack went in for the kill, stabbing the beast and laying it low. At last the princess, and all her people, were saved.

Jack and the princess were betrothed, and Jack went away for some more adventures before his planned wedding day. After nine months, the princess had a baby, but no one knew who the father could be. The king was angry with his daughter, but she persuaded him to go with her to see a fairy, who might be able to give them the answer. The fairy placed a lemon in the child's hand and said, "Only the child's true father will be able to take this fruit from its hand."

The king then called all the men in his kingdom to the palace and every one of them tried to take away the lemon. But no matter how hard they tried, the fruit would not

come away from the baby's hand. Finally, Jack appeared, and as soon as he touched the baby, the lemon came away.

The king was filled with anger towards Jack and his daughter, and wanted them to leave the palace forthwith. So he put the princess and Jack in rags and set them in a rotten boat and cast them out to sea. Just as the couple thought that they were going to sink, a lady appeared. "I was the fairy who gave Jack his sword, and the one who protected the princess from the breath of the beast," she said. "Once more, I will help you." She repaired the boat, turned their rags to fine robes, and so they returned to the palace.

Now Jack explained to the king who he was. "I was the man who saved your daughter from becoming the victim of the monster," said Jack. And Jack produced the king's gold cup, which he had taken before, and the monster's head, to show he spoke true. As further proof, the princess showed them all the ringlet of stones in Jack's hair. Convinced of the truth, the king allowed the couple to marry. They lived in happiness, and eventually, Jack himself became king.

Kate Crackernuts

Long ago there lived a king and a queen and each had a daughter. The king's daughter, Kate, was fairer than the queen's daughter, and the queen grew jealous of her. Soon the queen was plotting to find a way to spoil Kate's beauty.

The queen went to see a witch, who asked her to keep Kate from her food and to send the girl to her. So the next morning the queen sent Kate to the witch, to ask for some eggs. But Kate managed to snatch a bite to eat before she left the house. When Kate arrived, the witch said, "Lift the lid off that pot over there," and Kate obeyed. But nothing happened. "Tell your mother to keep the larder locked," said the witch.

So the queen knew that Kate had had something to eat, and was more careful on the next morning. Again Kate went to the witch, but on her way she saw some country people picking peas. They gave the hungry girl some peas to eat, so once more nothing happened when the witch asked Kate to open the pot.

On the third day the queen herself went with Kate to the witch, watching the girl all the way. When Kate lifted the lid of the pot, out popped the head of a sheep, and this instantly changed places with Kate's own head. The queen was satisfied at last.

When the queen's daughter saw Kate, she was sorry for her half-sister. So she put a cloth over Kate's head and announced: "Let us go and seek our fortunes, and see if anyone in the world can cure you." The two girls travelled far until they came to a great castle. Kate's sister did not feel well, so they hoped to find lodgings in the castle. When they asked some passers-by, they found that it belonged to a king. They knocked on the door, and the guards let them in.

Once inside the castle courtyard, the girls told the people they were travellers far away from home and asked if they could have lodgings for

the night. They were soon granted their wish, as long as Kate would stay up at night to look after the king's sick son. A purse of silver was promised to Kate if she did this, and she readily agreed.

All went well until midnight. As the castle clock struck twelve, the prince began to climb out of bed. He put on his clothes, opened the door of his room, and went downstairs to the stables. Kate followed, but made sure that the prince did not see him, even when she jumped silently up on the horse behind him.

Off they rode through a forest, and as they went, Kate reached up into the trees and picked nuts from the branches, gathering them all in her apron. When they reached a green hill, the prince stopped his horse. "Open and let the prince enter," said the king's son. "And his lady too," said Kate, quietly.

One side of the green hill opened and they rode in. Kate saw

a fine hall, filled with lords and ladies who were dancing. Kate sat by the door, where she saw some fairies and a child playing with a wand. "Three strokes of the wand would make Kate's sister well," said one of the fairies. So Kate rolled nuts across the floor to the child until he forgot the wand, and Kate hid it in her apron.

Then a cock crew, the prince mounted his horse, and Kate jumped up behind. Together they rode back to the castle. As soon as she could, Kate tapped her sister three times with the fairy wand, bringing her back to health. Kate's sister then touched Kate with the wand. The sheep's head disappeared, and Kate's fair face returned. Then Kate sat by the fire, cracking her nuts, and eating them, as if nothing had happened. When the king asked her how she had fared with his son, she replied that he had had a good night. The king asked her to sit with him one night more, and he offered her a purse of gold

pieces in payment if she would.

So the next night saw Kate once more sitting by the prince's bedside, and, when the clock struck midnight, the prince went to his horse and rode again to the green hill, as before.

The king asked Kate to watch his son for one night more. "How shall I reward you this time?" asked the king.

"Let me marry your son if I look after him for a third night."

As on the two previous nights, the prince went to his horse at midnight and rode to the green hill. Kate sat quietly as the prince danced. Once more, she noticed the small child who had had the wand. This time, he was playing with a bird, and Kate heard one of the fairies say, "Three bites of that bird would cure the prince." So Kate rolled nuts across the floor to the child until he forgot the bird, and Kate hid it in her apron.

They returned to the castle, and instead of cracking her nuts as before, Kate plucked the bird and roasted it. When he smelled the bird, the prince said "That smells very fine. I would like to have some of that meat to eat." Kate gave him one bite, and the prince rose up, supporting his weight on his elbow; she gave him a second bite, and he sat up in bed; she gave him a third bite and he got up, and sat by the fire.

When the king and the others came into the room they found the prince and Kate cracking nuts and eating them together. The prince looked as well as could be, and soon they were married. Meanwhile, the king's other son married the queen's daughter. They all lived in happiness, and were never again troubled by royal jealousy.

The Son of the King of Ireland

One day the son of the King of Ireland was out hunting, and brought down a raven. He looked at the bird's black feathers and red blood, and he said to himself, "I will not marry until I find a woman with hair as black as the raven's feathers, and cheeks as red as the raven's blood."

When he got home he told his father, who replied, "You will not easily find such a woman."

The youth said, "I will travel the world until I find her."

So the son of the King of Ireland set off on his search. Everywhere he went, he asked people if they had seen a woman with hair as black as the raven's feathers, and cheeks as red as the raven's blood. And he was told that the King of the Great World had three daughters, and that the youngest was just such a woman. So the lad determined to find her.

On his way, the lad called on a smith, who was making a great needle. "You are in luck," said the smith. "This needle I am making is for the King of the Great World himself. His boat comes tomorrow to collect it, and I will ask his men to ferry you across to his castle."

In the morning the boat came and the lad jumped on board. When they arrived at the castle, the lad, dusty with travel as he was, went straight to the King of the Great World, to ask him for one of his daughters in marriage.

"If you want to marry my daughter, you must be of nobler birth than you look," said the king.

"I am the son of the King of Ireland," the boy replied.

The King of the Great World paused. "You shall win the hand of my daughter," he said. "But you must do three things. First, clear all the filth from my great barn, and make it so clean that a gold ball will run from one end of the floor to the other."

The youth began to clear the barn. But no matter how much

filth he removed, more came in its place. Just then, the king's three daughters came by. They could see that the lad was harassed and could not finish his task.

The eldest daughter said, "If I thought it was me you wanted, I would clear the barn for you." And the middle one said the same.

But the youngest daughter said, "Whether you have come for me or not, I will clear the barn." She said, "Clean, clean, pitch-fork, put out shovel." Straight away the whole floor of the barn was clean.

When the king returned, he said he was pleased with the boy's work and told him his next task. "Tomorrow you must thatch the barn with birds' feathers. I want the stem of every feather to point inwards and whole roof to be secured with a silk thread."

As soon as the lad got any feathers on the roof, a wind came and blew them away. Then, the king's three daughters came by. The eldest said, "If I thought it was me you wanted, I would thatch the barn for you." And the middle one said the same.

But the youngest daughter said, "Whether you have come for me or not, I will thatch the barn." She took out her whistle and blew. Straightaway, a beautiful, neat thatch of birds' feathers covered the roof of the barn, just as the king had ordered.

When the king saw the barn he said, "I am pleased with your

work. But I am not pleased with your teacher. You have more work to do tomorrow. You must mind my five swans. If you let any of them escape, you will be hanged, but if you keep them, you shall have my daughter."

The boy tried to herd the swans together, but they always escaped. Then, the king's three daughters came by. The eldest said, "If I thought it was me you wanted, I would find the swans for you." And the middle one said the same.

But the youngest daughter said, "Whether you have come for me or not, I will find my father's swans." And she blew her whistle, and the swans came home.

When the King of the Great World arrived, the lad said, "Shall I get your daughter now?"

"Not yet," replied the king. "Tomorrow I am going fishing, and you must clean and cook the fish that I catch."

The next day the son of the King of Ireland began to scrape the scales from the fish. But no matter how many he removed, more appeared in their place. At that very moment, the king's three daughters came by. The eldest said, "If I thought it was me you wanted, I would clean the fish for you." And the middle one said the same.

But the youngest daughter said, "Whether you have come for me or not, son of the King of Ireland, I will clean the fish." And she cleaned the fish, saying, "My father will kill us both when he wakens. We must take flight together." And the pair

took flight, and galloped off together as fast as their steed could carry them.

Soon the king leapt on his horse, and gave chase. The lad and the princess heard the hooves of the king's horse beating on the ground behind them. The king's daughter said, "Look and see what you can find in the horse's ear."

"Just a little bit of thorn," said the lad.

"Throw it behind you," said the girl. At once, the thorn grew into a dense wood seven miles long. The king could not get through, until he called for an axe and hacked himself a path.

Again the daughter urged the lad, "Look in the horse's ear."

"A tiny stone," he said.

"Throw it behind you," she replied. And when he did, the stone turned into a massive rock, seven miles long and one mile high, and the couple were on the top.

The king could not climb the rock, so he returned home, and the couple went on their way to Ireland. As they approached the palace of the King of Ireland, the girl said, "I will not come in now. When you go in, the dog will jump up to welcome you. Try to keep him away, for if the dog touches your face, you will forget me."

So the couple went their separate ways. The daughter put on men's clothes and went to lodge with a smith who wanted a new apprentice. She stayed with him a year, and was soon the

best apprentice he had ever had.

Then a messenger arrived at the smithy, inviting the smith to the wedding of the son of the King of Ireland and the daughter of the King of Farafohuinn, and he decided to take his apprentice. "Please let me use the smithy tonight," said the daughter. By the following morning, she had made a hen of gold and a silver cockerel.

On the day of the wedding, the smith and his apprentice set off, she with the golden hen and silver cockerel, he with some grains of wheat in his pocket. Everyone was pleased to see them, and someone asked what they could do to entertain the guests. So the apprentice put the golden hen and the silver cockerel on the floor and threw down three grains of wheat. The cockerel picked up two grains, the hen only one.

"Do you remember how I cleaned the great barn for you? If you remembered, you would not take two grains instead of one," said the hen.

Everyone laughed, and they threw down another three grains. The same thing happened. "Do you remember when I thatched the barn with birds' feathers?" asked the hen.

As they threw down more grains, the son of the King of Ireland began to remember what had happened to him.

"Do you remember how I found the swans for you? If you remembered, you would not take two grains instead of one."

Now the king's son was sure. "It must be you," he shouted, and they undid the apprentice's costume to show that she was indeed a woman.

The son of the King of Ireland turned to the princess of Farafohuinn, who he was going to marry, and said "This is truly the woman I went in search of. I passed through many tests and trials for her, and I will marry none but her. Stay and celebrate with us if you wish, but otherwise you may go."

So the princess of Farafohuinn left the castle, and the Son of the King of Ireland at last married his true love.

The Black Horse

There was a king who had three sons, and when he died the youngest son was left nothing except a horse, an old, white mare with a limp. The young son realised that he would get nothing more, so he decided to leave home.

Off he went, sometimes riding the mare, sometimes walking to rest her, when he met a man riding a black horse. The two greeted each other, and the man with the black horse spoke: "I have had enough of this black beast. Will you swap him for your horse? There is one great advantage to this black horse. Wherever in the world you wish to go, he will take you there."

The king's son thought of all the places that he wished to go, and could not resist the bargain. So he exchanged his old limping horse for the stranger's mount, and went on his way.

Now the king's son had long wanted to visit the Realm Underwaves, so he decided to see if the black horse would take him. Sure enough, before the sun had risen the next day, they were there. The King Underwaves was holding court, and trying to find someone who would go to Greece, for the Prince Underwaves wanted to marry the king's daughter.

The rider of the black horse stepped forward. "Will you go to Greece to fetch the king's daughter?" asked the King Underwaves. And before he knew what he was doing, the young rider of the black horse was on his way.

As he rode, the black horse spoke to him. He explained that no one in Greece had seen a horse before, and the princess would surely want a ride. "But beware. Tell her that no man except you may ride, for some rascal may try to steal me."

When they arrived in Greece, it was just as the black horse had said. The princess saw the horse out of one of the castle windows and straight away asked for a ride. When she tried to ride the steed with her own servant, the black horse

251

threw the man from his back. So the princess of Greece set off to the Realm Underwaves, and the only man to go with her was the horse's rightful rider.

Soon they arrived in the Realm Underwaves, where the prince was eager to arrange his wedding. But the Greek princess spoke up. "The wedding must not be so soon," she said. "I will not marry until I have the silver cup that my mother used at her wedding, and her mother before her."

The Prince Underwaves turned to the rider of the black horse. "Go back to Greece, and bring the silver cup to me before dawn tomorrow." So the black horse and his rider set off once more. As they travelled, the horse told his rider what he should do. "All the king's people will be around him tonight, and the silver cup will be passed among them. Go in with them, pretend to be one of the people of the place, and take the cup when it is handed to you. Then we will be away."

 It all happened as the horse had said, and they were soon back in the Realm Underwaves with the silver cup. But when the prince began to talk of his wedding, the Greek princess spoke up once more. "I will not marry until I have the silver ring that my mother wore at her wedding, and her mother before her."

The Prince Underwaves turned to the rider of the black horse. "Go back to Greece, and bring the silver ring to me

before dawn tomorrow." So the black horse and his rider set off. As they travelled, the black horse told his rider what to expect on the journey. "This is a difficult quest," said the horse. "Before we can get the ring, we will have to climb a mountain of snow, a mountain of ice, and a mountain of fire."

On they rode, and the young man was amazed at the great leaps the horse took to climb the mountains of snow and ice. Perished with cold, he clung on to the creature's mane as he made his third leap. This took them through the mountain of fire, and so fast they went that they hardly felt the heat from the flames. "Now," said the horse. "Go into that town and make an iron spike for the end of every bone in my body, and then stick the spikes into me as I tell you." The young man was puzzled, but he went to the smith and got the spikes made, and stuck them into the horse's body as he had been told.

"Near here there is a great loch," said the horse. "Watch the waters when I dive in, and you will see them covered in flames. If you see the flames go out, wait for me, and I will come to you with the ring."

The young man stood by as the horse disappeared beneath the water. Suddenly, the waters turned into bright orange flames. The young man waited and waited, but the flames still burned. He began to doubt whether he would see the black horse again. Then, just before dawn, the flames on the lake went out and the black horse appeared. There was one metal spike left, on the creature's head, and on this spike was the silver ring.

Without delay, they returned to the Realm Underwaves. Again the prince started to ask when the wedding might be, but the princess of Greece had yet one more demand. "I will not marry until you build a castle for me," she said.

The Prince Underwaves looked upset. A castle would take years to build. But the black horse said, "This is the easiest of all the tasks. Leave it to me." And before long an army of diggers, stone masons, carpenters, and metalworkers, were at work before them, until a fine castle was built before dawn the following day.

The rider of the black horse, the Prince Underwaves and the princess of Greece stood looking at the castle, which had its own deep well. "It is a fine castle," said the princess. "But there is still one problem with my wedding arrangements."

"What is that?" asked the prince.

"You," said the Greek princess, and pushed the prince into the well. "If I must be married, then, I want to marry the rider of the black horse, who has done deeds of craft and valour for me while the other man stood by."

And so it was that the young rider of the black horse married the princess of Greece, and lived in the new castle which the black horse had made for them.

Three years passed and the young rider, in his happiness, neglected the black horse. One day, as he saw the horse grazing where he had left him, the young man felt sorry for forgetting the beast that had given him so much help. "It seems as if you have someone that you prefer to me," said the horse.

"I am sorry that I forgot you," said the young man.

"It does not matter," said the horse. "Draw your sword and chop off my head, and that will be an end to it."

The young man protested,

but the horse would not take no for an answer, so the young man drew his sword and cut off the horse's head with one stroke. Straight away, the horse vanished, to be replaced by a handsome young man. "Good day to my brother-in-law," he said, and the rider of the black horse stared in puzzlement.

"You look sad to lose the horse," said the stranger. "But I hope you will be pleased to meet your brother-in-law. I was the black horse, and have been put under a spell. I used my knowledge of my father's house to help you. What is more, you kept me long and well, and, since I was put under the spell, I never met any other man who could keep me. Thank you for releasing me from the spell and giving me back my true shape." And the rider of the black horse was thankful. For now he had both a fine wife and a true friend.

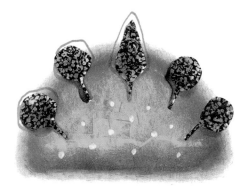

The Greek Princess and the Young Gardener

There was once an old king who had one daughter. When the king grew ill it seemed as if the end of his life was coming, but he discovered that the apples from the tree in his garden made him better. So the king became angry when a strange, brightly coloured bird flew into his garden one evening and began to steal the apples.

The king called his gardener. "You are not doing your job properly!" exclaimed the king. "You must guard my apple tree day and night, for a bird is coming into the garden and stealing all the fruit."

"It will not happen again, your majesty," replied the gardener. "I will set my three sons to guard the tree. And if the bird comes near, they will shoot it with their bows and arrows."

That night, the gardener's eldest son stood guard by the apple tree. As the night went on, the boy got drowsy, and soon he was asleep at the foot of the tree. At midnight, the bird flew into the garden and removed one of the fruit. The king heard the flapping of the bird's wings, for he was a light sleeper, and dashed to his window. When he looked out, the king saw the bird taking off with one of the finest fruits in his beak. "Wake up, you lazy good-for-nothing!" he shouted at the gardener's son. The lad grabbed his bow and arrow, but by the time he had taken aim it was too late. The bird had got away.

The next night, the gardener's second son was on guard. Again the lad fell asleep and again the bird came to steal an apple. The king roared at the gardener's boy, but by the time the lad had woken, the bird had flown away again, and another of the king's finest, most succulent apples was gone from the tree. The king began to despair.

On the third evening, the gardener's youngest son stood guard. He was determined to keep awake and do himself credit with the king. As usual the bird arrived and the boy was quick enough to let loose one arrow at the bird as it flew. He did not bring the bird down, but as his arrow fell to the ground, one of the creature's feathers fell with it.

The king was pleased, for the bird had not had the chance to steal an apple before it was frightened away by the young lad's arrow. But when he saw the feather, the king was fascinated. It was made of the finest beaten gold. As he looked at it, the king decided that he wanted to catch the bird with the golden feathers. So he sent out a message. He would give half his kingdom, plus the hand of his daughter in marriage, to any man who could bring back the bird to his palace.

All the young men of the king's household, including the gardener's three sons, wondered how they could find the bird. The gardener's first son was out one day when he met a fox. "If you want to find the golden bird," said the fox, "go along this road and take lodging with the poor man and his wife." So the boy went along the road, but when he came to the poor man's house, there was a house opposite where people were drinking and dancing, and the gardener's first son went there for his entertainment.

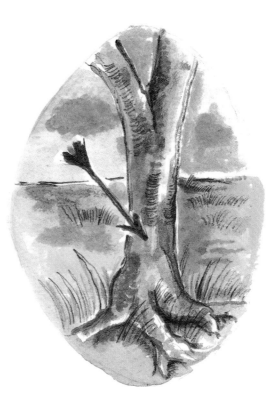

The same thing happened to the gardener's second son, who also met the fox and was given the same advice. But the drinking and dancing was of more interest to him, and he joined his brother.

When the third son met the fox, the animal gave him the same advice. Unlike his brothers, the young lad listened to what the fox had to say, and sought lodgings with the poor couple, and the next morning went on his way. Soon he met the fox once more. "Well done for taking my advice," said the fox. "Do you know where to find the golden bird?"

"I have no idea," said the young man.

"She is in the palace of the King of Spain, some two hundred miles from here," said the fox.

The gardener's son was sad to hear that the journey was to be so long.

"Do not despair," said the fox. "Hop up on my tail, and we shall soon be there."

So off they went, and to the young gardener's surprise, they soon got to the King of Spain's palace. The fox turned to the lad again and told him where in the palace to find the golden bird. "Get the bird out as quickly as you can, and do not stay looking for other treasure," said the fox. "Then you will be safe."

The youth entered the palace and found the bird in a dull iron cage. Next to it was a fine golden cage, and the lad thought that this would be a better home for the marvellous bird. So he tried to tempt the creature into the golden cage. But all that happened was that the bird let out a terrible squeal, and the palace guards came running. Soon, the boy found himself in front of the King of Spain himself.

"I should hang you for a thief," said the king. "But I will give you a chance to win your life, and the golden bird too if you succeed. Get me the bay filly belonging to the King of Morocco, a horse that can run faster than any other. Then you shall have the golden bird."

So the young gardener found his friend the fox, and they were soon on their way to the palace of the King of Morocco.

When they arrived the fox spoke to the lad again, more sternly than before. "When you get into the stables, do not touch a thing, not even the door or the door posts. Just lead out the bay filly, and you will be fine."

But when he entered the stable, the boy saw a fine golden saddle, much better than the leather one on the filly's back, so he decided to change it over. No sooner had he touched the golden saddle than palace guards appeared from every quarter. In a few moments, the King of Morocco himself had arrived.

"I should hang you for a thief," said the king. "But there is one thing that I want, and if you can help me, then I will let you go, and the bay filly with you." And the king explained that he wanted to marry Golden Locks, the daughter of the King of Greece, and asked the gardener's boy to go to Greece and bring back the princess.

Once again, the lad and the fox set off, and again the speed of the fox was such that by nightfall they arrived at the king's palace. "Do not let her touch anything or anyone as you come out," warned the fox.

The lad found the princess and quietly explained that he wanted to take her to Morocco. At first, she was unwilling to go on such a long journey to a husband she had never met, but as she looked at the young gardener, her heart began to melt and she agreed to go with him. "Only let me kiss my father goodbye," she said. The princess went to kiss her sleeping father, promising not to waken him. But as soon as her lips touched her father's he let out a great cry, and guards came running.

When he saw that his daughter was safe, he listened to the young gardener's story. He was sad to let his daughter go, for he had already lost his son, who had been spirited away by a wicked witch. "I will only let her go if you will clear up the great heap of clay in front of my palace," said the king. For no one had been able to clear the heap before, which got larger with every shovelful of clay that was removed.

To everyone's great astonishment, including that of the young

gardener, the pile of clay was cleared. The lad knew that the fox must have had something to do with it. So the young gardener, the princess and the fox went on their way.

By the time they reached the King of Morocco's palace, the young gardener and the princess were in love. When the king brought out his bay filly to exchange for the princess, the pair looked at each other with longing. "Please let me say farewell to the princess before I depart," said the lad. While the king was distracted, the pair jumped up on the horse and rode off at top speed, the bay filly galloping faster than the wind. When they reached the King of Spain's palace, the fox was there waiting for them.

The fox turned to them before they entered the palace.

"If you give the king the filly, I will have to carry you all home, and I doubt that I have the strength. When you are about to hand over the horse, go up to the creature and stroke it, as if you are saying farewell. Then, when the king is distracted, jump on the filly's back and ride away at top speed. Then we shall return in comfort."

The king brought out the golden bird, and handed it to the gardener's boy. Instead of giving the king the filly, as he expected, the boy rode out of the palace gates, leaving the king behind him in amazement. Soon he had met up with the fox and the princess once more, and the three returned to the homeland of the young gardener.

They finally reached the spot where the lad had first met the fox, and he turned to the creature to thank him for all his help. "Now will you help me?" asked the fox. "Take your sword and chop off my head and tail." The young man could not do this to his friend, but his eldest brother, who had come to meet them, knew nothing of how the fox had helped his brother, and dealt the two blows.

The head and tail vanished, and in place of the fox was a young man. Straight away, the Greek princess recognized her brother, who had been taken away and bewitched.

If they were happy before, the Greek princess and the young gardener were now overjoyed, and they longed to share their joy with the king. So the three of them went to see the old king and his daughter, gave the king his golden bird, and told them the whole story. The Greek princess married the young gardener, and the Greek prince married the daughter of the old king. The king himself was enchanted with his golden bird. He was so pleased with the creature, he even shared with it some of the apples from his favourite tree.

Canobie Dick

Canobie Dick was a horse trader who was well known for always getting the best deal. He did not care who he did business with, so long as he got more than he paid for every piece of horse-flesh that passed through his hands.

It happened one night that Dick was riding home across Bowden Moor by the Eildon Hills. He had with him two horses that he had not been able to sell that day. As he rode he saw a figure in the distance, coming towards him. As the man got nearer, Dick saw that he was an old fellow, wearing clothes that looked positively ancient. Dick was surprised when the old man wished him good day and asked if the horses were for sale. Soon they struck a deal, and the old man paid Dick a good price in ancient gold coins. Normally Dick would have refused old coins, but he knew that gold was valuable in whatever form it came, so he took the payment readily.

A few times more Dick met the man and sold him horses, the old man always asking that Dick come at night to make the sale. When this had happened several times, Dick decided that he should get to know this customer better, and he said to the man, "A bargain is always luckier when struck with a glass in hand."

So it was that the old man invited Dick to his home, but warned him, "Don't be afraid at what you see in my dwelling-place, for if you do you'll be sorry for the rest of your life."

Off they went along a narrow path up the hills until they came to a rocky outcrop. To Dick's surprise, the old man passed through a passage into the hillside. Although Dick had often passed this place, he had never noticed the passage before.

"You are sure you are not afraid?" said the old man.

"It is not too late to turn back."

Dick shook his head, for he did not wish to seem frightened. The passage was lit by flaming torches, and as they walked along, Dick saw a long row of stables, with a black horse in each. Next to each horse lay a knight in black armour. Nearby was an old table, and on it were a horn and a sword.

"The man that blows this horn and draws this sword shall become king of the whole of Britain," said the man.

Dick looked at the sword in fascination, lifted it briefly, but put it down again. For when he thought of the sleeping figures and the ghostly horses, he thought that drawing the sword might bring all the terrors of the mountain down upon him.

So he raised the horn to his lips and got ready to blow.

But Dick was shaking so much, and he was so breathless with fear, that all he could produce was a feeble, wavering note. Even so, this was enough to rouse the knights who were resting next to their horses. Great rumbles of thunder echoed through the rocky hall, the horses seemed to come to life and the knights rose up, their armour clanking and their swords glittering in the torch light. Once they saw the knights rise up, the horses began to neigh and stamp their hooves, tossing their heads in excitement.

The horse dealer looked at the growing army of knights and horses, coming to life around him, looking as if they were all about to launch an attack on him. Trembling, he dropped the horn, and made a grab for the great sword on the table. As he did so, a mighty voice spoke from among the knights:

> The coward shall rue the day he was born
>
> Who lay down the sword and blew on the horn.

As he heard these words, Dick was picked up by a mighty whirlwind that blew along the cavern and cast him out onto the open hillside. There he lay unconscious until a group of shepherds found him in the morning.

Dick told the shepherds his tale, but died soon afterwards. And no one found the passage into the hillside again.

The Knight of Riddles

Once there was a king called Ardan, king of all Albann, and his first wife died. Some time afterwards, he remarried, and the king had two sons, one from each queen. The two boys were very close, but the second queen was jealous of the king's first son, because she knew that her own boy would not inherit the kingdom. So she plotted to kill the elder son.

Twice the queen ordered her servant to put poison in the elder son's drink, and twice her own son overheard her giving the orders, and warned his brother. Then the elder son said to his brother, "I shall not live long if I stay in this house. It will be better for me if I leave home." And so the two brothers decided that they would leave together.

When they left, they took their mother's poisonous drink with them in a bottle, and before long, the eldest said, "It might not be poison after all. Let us try it on my horse." When they gave the poison to the beast, it keeled over and died.

"Well, she was a tired old nag anyway," said the elder brother. "Her time was up. Let's try the drink on your steed." So they gave the poison to the other horse, which fell down dead.

The brothers decided that at least they would skin the horse to make a blanket to keep themselves warm. While they were preparing the skin, twelve ravens flew down to feast on the carcass. But no sooner had they begun to eat than the birds fell dead from the poisoned meat.

The brothers took the dead birds with them, and when they reached the next town, they asked the baker to make twelve pies from the ravens' flesh. They packed up the pies and carried on with their journey. At night the brothers came to a dense, dark wood, and they were set upon by twenty-four robbers. "Give us your money!" demanded the thieves.

"We have no money," said the brothers. "All we have are

these meat pies."

"Food is as good as money. We will take the pies."

Greedily, the robbers began to eat the pies, and before long, they were falling down dead where they stood, for the poison was still in the meat. Relieved, the brothers went on with their journey, until they came to a fine house, which was the home of the Knight of Riddles. They decided to visit the knight, and the younger brother said that he would pretend to be the servant to the elder.

The Knight of Riddles had a beautiful daughter attended by twelve maidens. He would allow no one to marry the girl unless they could give him a riddle which he could not solve. When they heard this the brothers decided to put this riddle to him: "One killed two, and two killed twelve, and twelve killed twenty-four, and two got out of it."

The brothers stayed in the knight's house while he tried to think of an answer to the riddle, and meanwhile each of the maidens came to the younger brother and asked him what the answer to the riddle might be. They brought him gifts of cloth, but he would not tell them. "Only my brother may tell the answer," he said.

Then the knight's daughter went to the elder brother, and smiled winningly at him, and presented a gift of cloth to him, and he told her the answer to the riddle. Not long afterwards, the knight called the brothers to him and told them that he had solved the riddle.

"Your riddle was easy to solve," said the knight. "Your head will be chopped off in the morning."

"Before you behead me," said the elder brother, "I have another riddle for you. My servant and I were in the forest shooting. He shot twelve hares, skinned them, and let them go. Then came a hare finer than the rest. I shot her, skinned her, and let her go."

"That's not a difficult riddle," said the knight. And they all knew that the young man had discovered how the knight found the answers to his riddles.

The brothers had defeated the knight in their battle of the riddles, so the knight allowed the elder brother to marry his daughter. The elder prince was so full of joy that he told his brother to go home and inherit his kingdom; he would stay in the land of the Knight of the Riddles.

The elder brother did well in the country of the knight and lived there for many years. The local people were impressed at his bravery, especially when he killed three giants that were causing fear in the land. So the Knight of the Riddles gave his son-in-law his own title, the Hero of the White Shield.

The Hero of the White Shield became famed as the strongest and bravest man in the land. Many challenged him to a fight, but no one could beat the Hero. One day, a stranger came to challenge him and, after a long fight, the stranger sent the Hero jumping in alarm over a high stone wall.

"You must have some of my own fighting blood in your veins to be so strong," said the Hero of the White Shield.

"What is your family?"

"I am the son of Ardan, king of all Albann," replied the stranger. And the Hero of the White Shield knew that he had met his long-lost brother once more. The two stayed for years together in the land of the Knight of Riddles. But eventually the younger brother knew that he should return to his own kingdom, so the two parted.

On the way home, the younger brother stopped to watch twelve men playing at shinny by a tall palace. For a while he joined in, but soon the smallest of the twelve grappled with him and shook him as if he were no more than a child. "Whose sons are you, who are so strong?" he asked.

"We are the nephews of the Hero of the White Shield," they cried. And the younger brother knew that he had found his sons, and that all were alive and well. They went together to find his wife, and a great celebration was held. For hundreds of years, the kings of Albann were descended from their line.

The Humble-Bee

Two young men were out walking one summer's day and stopped by a tiny stream next to an old ruined house. They were admiring the place, and noticed how the stream turned into a miniature waterfall crossed by narrow blades of grass. One of the men was tired from the walk and the afternoon heat and sat down by the stream. Soon he was fast asleep, and the other sat quietly, watching the view.

Suddenly, a tiny creature, about the size of a humble-bee, flew out of the sleeper's mouth. It landed by the stream and crossed it by walking over some grass stalks which hung over the water at its narrowest point. The creature then approached the ruin and disappeared into one of the cracks in the wall.

The man who saw all this was shocked and decided to wake his friend to see if he was all right. As he shook his companion awake, he was astonished to see the tiny creature emerge from the ruin, fly across the stream and re-enter the sleeper's mouth, just as the young man was waking.

"What's the matter? Are you ill?" asked the watcher.

"I am well," replied the sleeper. "You have just interrupted the most wonderful dream, and I wish you had not woken me

with your shaking. I dreamed that I walked through a vast grassy plain and came to a wide river. I wanted to cross the river to see what was on the other side, and I found a place near a great waterfall where there was a bridge made of silver. I walked over the bridge and on the far bank was a beautiful palace built of stone. When I looked in, the chambers of the palace contained great mounds of gold and jewels. I was looking at all these fine things, wondering at the wealth of the person who left them there, and deciding which I would bring away with me. Then suddenly you woke me, and I could bring away none of the riches."

The Seal Woman

The was a farmer from Wastness who was not married. His friends used to tease him when he said he was not interested in women, but he took little notice. His only interest was his farm, which did well, and the good farmer grew rich.

One day the farmer was walking by the shore at the ebb tide, and he noticed a group of seal folk. Some were sunning themselves on a rock, others were swimming and playing in the sea. The seals were enjoying themselves and did not notice the farmer, so he crept closer and saw that they had all taken off their sealskins to reveal bodies which were as pale and white as his own.

The farmer thought what fun it would be to catch one of the naked seals, so he edged closer and then made a dash for the

seals. They grabbed their skins in alarm and jumped into the water, but the farmer managed to hold on to one of the skins.

He watched as the seals swam out to sea and then turned to walk homeward across the shore. As he went he heard a sound of sobbing behind him, and turned to see a seal-woman, weeping for her lost skin. "Oh, please give me back my skin," she cried. "I cannot join my family in the sea without it."

The farmer was filled with pity, but he was also smitten by the beauty of the seal woman, whom he thought far more attractive than any ordinary woman. So he talked to the seal woman, and told her his feelings, and soon he persuaded her to come ashore and live with him as his wife.

The seal-woman lived long with the farmer. She was as a good a farmer's wife as any normal woman, and bore him seven children, four boys and three girls. She seemed happy and people often heard her singing, but she would sometimes look with longing at the sea.

One day the farmer took his three eldest sons out in his boat to go fishing, as they often did. While they were at sea, the seal-woman sent out three of her other children to walk the shore gathering limpets and whelks. The youngest daughter stayed at home, with her mother, because the girl's foot was sore and she could not walk far.

Once they had all gone out the seal-woman started to search the house. At first she made as if she was tidying up, but her daughter realised that she was looking for something, and said to her mother, "What is it that you are looking for all around the house?"

"You must tell no one my dear," said the seal woman. "I am looking for a fine skin to make a dressing for your sore foot."

And the young girl replied, "I think I might know where you can find such a skin. One day when you were out and father thought we were asleep in bed, I saw him take a skin and look at it. Then he folded it carefully and hid it away up in the eaves above the bed."

Straight away the seal woman rushed to the place and took out the skin from under the eaves. "Farewell my little one," she said as she rushed out of the door and ran in the direction of the shore. There she put on her skin, dived into the sea, and swam quickly away. A male seal saw her coming and greeted her with excitement, for he recognized the seal he had loved

long ago.

As the farmer was returning to shore in his boat, he saw his wife diving into the sea and making for the male seal. "Farewell, dear husband," she called to him. "I liked you well and you treated me kindly. But it is time that I returned to my true love of the sea."

That was the last the farmer saw of the seal woman. He missed his seal-wife greatly, and it took him many years to recover from his sadness. And he often went for walks along the shore, hoping to catch sight of her again.

Rashen Coatie

There was a king whose queen died young, and after a time he remarried. His new queen was a widow, and both king and queen had a daughter from their first marriage. The king's daughter, Rashen Coatie, was good and beautiful, while the daughter of the queen was ill-featured and bad-tempered.

The queen treated the king's daughter badly in the hope that her own girl would gain. Her husband, anxious to keep the peace at home, turned a blind eye to this ill-treatment, and so it came about that Rashen Coatie ended up looking after the king's cattle, while the queen's daughter stayed at home and wallowed in luxury.

Every day the queen sent her own daughter with the worst food for Rashen Coatie to eat, in the hope that the girl would fall ill and die. But Rashen Coatie met a fairy, who taught her a spell. Whenever the girl said the magic words, a calf appeared, bringing her food as fine as any that was eaten in the king's palace. In this way, Rashen Coatie became stronger and more beautiful than ever, and the queen became angrier and angrier.

When it was clear that her plan was failing, the queen went to talk to a witch. The witch gave the queen the power to look into the unknown, and the envious woman quickly realised that it was the calf who was giving Rashen Coatie her food.

Straight away she went to her husband and asked him to have the calf killed, so that she might cook the animal for a banquet, and the king agreed. Rashen Coatie was distressed when she heard what was to happen, but the calf came to her and spoke in her ear. "If you do what I say you need not worry," said the calf. "When I am cooked and eaten, take my bones and bury them under this stone. Do this, and leave the palace

for a while, and you will be safe."

Rashen Coatie buried the bones beneath the stone, left the palace, and went into hiding. The calf came back to life and brought her food and so she was able to survive. Meanwhile, the queen was poisoned when she ate the calf's entrails and, after a long illness, finally died.

By this time, Rashen Coatie was grown into a fine young woman. She did not know how well she would be received at her father's court, so decided to return in disguise. But when she arrived she was thrown into confusion. Her father was so taken with her beauty that he wanted to marry her. She ran to the calf to ask him what to do.

"Ask the king for clothes made of the rushes that grow by the stream," said the calf. The king had just such a dress made, and still he wanted to marry Rashen Coatie.

"Ask the king for a dress of all the colours of the birds of the air," said the calf. The king gave her a dress with all the colours of the birds of the air, and still he wanted to marry her.

"Ask the king for a dress, with the colours of all the fish of the sea," said the calf. But again the king produced just such a dress, and still he wanted to marry Rashen Coatie.

So finally the girl felt she had used up all the possible excuses to delay, and the wedding day arrived. When she got to church, Rashen Coatie tried one last objection. "I must have

the ring my mother wore when she was married," she said. And then she put on her dress of rushes, and ran from her father's kingdom.

After long wandering, Rashen Coatie came to a hunting lodge which belonged to a prince. No one seemed to be there, so exhausted, she collapsed on to the prince's bed, and fell into a deep sleep. Later, the prince himself arrived and found Rashen Coatie asleep on his bed. He woke the girl and asked what she was doing there. "I meant no harm," she said. "I am far from home and was tired and lost. Is there some place near here where I might find work?" So the prince took Rashen Coatie home and she was put to work in the palace kitchens.

Soon it was Christmas and all the people in the palace, from the prince to his lowliest servants, went to church in the morning. Only Rashen Coatie was left in the kitchen to turn the roasting spits.

She too wanted to go to church, and decided to use a spell the calf had taught her so the spits would turn themselves:

Every spit turn on your way

Until I return on this yule day.

And with that, Rashen Coatie put on her finest dress and ran off to church.

In church, the prince was entranced by the beautiful young

woman who entered just as the service was beginning. Little did he guess that it was the kitchen maid Rashen Coatie. The prince decided to speak to her as she left the church, but she slipped out quickly and ran back to the palace, hoping that none would know that she had left the kitchen.

But as the girl flew along the path, one of her tiny golden shoes came off and she left it behind in her haste. The prince knew now what he should do. "The woman whose foot fits this shoe shall be my bride," he said.

Hundreds of women came to the palace, but no foot fitted the shoe perfectly. Then the witch's daughter appeared, and she had pared her nails and even rubbed some of the skin off her heels, so that she could squeeze on the shoe. The prince knew that she was not the woman he had seen, but he was true to his word, and announced that he would marry the girl. But a small bird fluttered over the prince's head, singing:

>Clipped the heel and pared the toe;
>
>In the kitchen the shoe will go.

The prince turned back and ran to the kitchen, finding Rashen Coatie, who had not tried on the shoe. When it fitted, the prince went to church with his rightful bride.

The Tale of Ivan

Ivan was a poor man who had no work. So one day he left his wife to look for a job. After a while he came to a farm and the farmer agreed to take Ivan on and give him lodgings.

Ivan worked on the farm for a year, and the master said, "Ivan, you have worked well this year. It is now time for you to be paid. Will you be paid in money or advice?"

"I would prefer to take my wages in money," said Ivan.

"I would prefer to give you advice," said the master. "Never leave the old road for the new one." So Ivan had to be content with this piece of advice, and worked for his master another year.

At the end of the second year, the same thing happened. This time, the master told Ivan, "Never lodge where an old man is married to a young woman." Again Ivan had to be content with the advice.

After a third year, the master gave Ivan a third piece of advice, "Honesty is the best policy." By now, Ivan saw that he would get no money from this master, so he decided to take his leave and return to his wife. Maybe there would be work

nearer home.

"Very well," said the master. "I will give you a cake to eat on your journey."

Ivan set off and soon he fell in with a group of merchants who were returning home from a fair. He got on well with the merchants, but when they came to a fork in the road, the men wanted to travel along the shorter, straighter, new road. Ivan remembered his master's first piece of advice. "I prefer the old road," said Ivan, and they parted company.

Before long, the merchants were set upon by robbers. Ivan

could see what was happening, for the new road was visible from the old. "Robbers! Stop thief!" he bellowed at the top of his voice. When the robbers heard this, they ran off, and the merchants kept hold of their money.

After many miles, the two roads joined again near a market town, and before long Ivan had met the merchants once more. "Thank you for saving us from the robbers," said one of them. "We will pay for your night's lodgings."

"I'll see the host first," said Ivan when they got to the inn. Ivan found out that the inn was owned by an old man with a young wife. He remembered his master's advice. "I'll not lodge here," he said, and while the merchants settled down to a meal of roast pork, Ivan took a room in the house next door.

Now it so happened that the young wife of the old landlord was plotting with a young monk to kill her husband and take over the inn. They saw that if they did the crime that night they could pin the blame on the merchants, who were the only guests. The pair were preparing to carry out their wicked plan in an upper room of the inn where the old man was sleeping. But they did not know that Ivan, getting ready to go to bed in his room next door, could hear them through the wall. There was a missing pine knot in the wall and Ivan looked through and saw them talking.

Suddenly, the young woman saw the hole in the wall. "We

must block that hole," she said, "or someone may see us." So
the monk stood hard against the hole while the wicked
woman stabbed her husband to death.

Ivan saw his chance. He took his knife and cut out a piece of
the monk's habit while he stood against the hole.

In the morning, the crime was discovered and the wife went
screaming to the justices. "It must have been that gang of
wicked merchants staying at the inn," she cried. The merchants
were marched off to prison, and Ivan saw them pass.

"Woe to us, Ivan!" they cried. "Our luck is running out. We
are taken for this murder, but we are all innocent."

"Tell them to find the real murderers," called Ivan.

"But no one knows who committed the crime," said one of the merchants.

"If I cannot bring them to justice," said Ivan, "let them hang *me* for the murder."

So Ivan went to the justices and told them everything he had heard. At first, the justices did not believe him, but when he showed them the piece of cloth he had cut from the monk's robe, they knew it must be true, and the young wife and the monk were arrested. The merchants were released, thanked Ivan for his trouble, and went on their way.

When Ivan got home to his wife she ran to greet him. "You come in the nick of time," she said. "I have just found a fine purse of gold. It has no name on it, but it must belong to the lord of the manor."

"Honesty is the best policy," said Ivan, remembering the third piece of advice. "Let us take it to the lord's house."

When they got to the lord's castle, they left the purse with the servant at the gatehouse.

One day, the lord passed Ivan's house, and his wife mentioned the purse to him. "I know of no purse returned to me," said the lord, in puzzlement. "Surely my servant must have kept it for himself."

Off they went to the castle and sought out the servant. As soon as the lord accused him, the servant saw that he was

found out, and gave up the purse. The lord frowned at his wicked servant. "I have no use for dishonest men. Be gone from my castle," he ordered.

Then the lord turned to Ivan. "Will you be my servant in his place?"

"Thank you," said Ivan. And he and his wife were given fine new quarters in the castle. When they were moving in, Ivan remembered the cake his old master had given him. They cut themselves a piece, and out fell three gold coins, Ivan's wages for his work for his old master. "Truly, honesty is the best policy," laughed Ivan. And his wife agreed.

Cherry of Zennor

Near the village of Zennor in Cornwall lived a man everyone called Old Honey. With him in his tiny two-room hut lived his wife and ten children. They managed with the little living space they had, and grew what food they could on the land around the hut, adding limpets and periwinkles, which they gathered from the shore.

Old Honey's favourite daughter was Cherry, who could run as fast as the wind. She was always mischievous, but had such a winning smile that everyone liked her. She loved to steal the horse of the miller's boy when he came into the village, and would ride out to the cliffs. If the miller's boy seemed to be catching up, she would leave the horse behind, and hide in the rocks or cairns that there were along the coast, and neither the miller's boy nor any other could catch her or find her.

Cherry was a sweet-natured child, but when she reached her teens she became discontented. She wanted so much to have a new dress, so that she could cut a fine figure at church or at the fair. But there was no money for dresses, so she had to mend the one she had. She thought it was not fit for her to go

to the fair and look for a sweetheart.

One day, Cherry decided that she would leave home and look for a job, so that she might have money of her own. So the next morning she wrapped her few possessions in a bundle and set off. On she trudged, but when she came to the cross roads at Lady Downs, she sat down on a stone and cried, for she felt tired, missed her family, and wished she had not set out on her own.

Just as she was drying her eyes and deciding that she would return to her family, a gentleman appeared. Cherry thought this was odd, since she had seen no one coming before, and on the Downs you could see for miles around. When the man bid her "Good morning," Cherry told him that she had left home to seek her fortune, but that she had lost heart and was going to return.

"I did not expect such good luck," said the man. "I am looking for a young woman to come and keep house for me, for I am recently a widower." So Cherry decided that she would go with the man, and they set off across the Downs together.

As they went, the gentleman told Cherry that she would have little to do but milk the cow and look after his small son. He did not live far away, he said, explaining that his home was in the "low country", the valley beyond the Downs. After a while they walked into an area where the lanes were sunk deep into the ground, with trees and bushes growing high on either side. Little sunlight reached the lane where they walked, but there was a rich scent of sweetbrier and honeysuckle, and these

pleasant scents reassured Cherry, who might otherwise have been afraid of the dark.

Next they came to a river, and the gentleman picked Cherry up around the waist and carried her across. On the other side, the lane seemed even darker, and Cherry held the man's arm.

Soon they came to the gentleman's home. When she saw the place, Cherry could not believe her eyes. The dark lane had not prepared her for a place of such beauty. The garden was full of flowers of every colour, fruit of all descriptions hung down from the trees, and birds sat in the branches, singing as if they were pleased that the master of the house had come home.

The garden was so unlike her own home that Cherry remembered how her grandmother had told her of places that had been enchanted by the little people. Could this be such a place?

Cherry looked up as a voice called "Papa!" and a small child, about two or three years old, came rushing towards the gentleman. But when Cherry looked at the child, although he was small, his faced seemed old and wrinkled. She was about to speak to the child when a haggard old woman appeared out of the house and came towards them.

"This is Aunt Prudence, my late wife's grandmother," said the gentleman. He explained that the old woman would stay until Cherry had learned her work, then she would leave.

When they went indoors, Cherry found that the house was even more beautiful than its garden. Aunt Prudence produced a large and tasty meal, and they all sat down to eat, after which the old woman showed Cherry to her room.

"When you are in bed, keep your eyes closed," said Aunt Prudence. "If you open your eyes, you may see things that frighten you." Then she explained what work Cherry would have to do the next day. She was to take the boy to the spring and wash him, after which she was to rub some ointment into his eyes. She would find the ointment in a box hidden in a gap in the rock by the spring. On no account should she put the ointment on her own eyes. Then she was to call the cow and milk her, and give the boy milk for his breakfast.

The following morning, Cherry rose early and began her work. She went with the little boy to the spring, where she washed him and put the ointment on his eyes. Then she looked around for the cow, but could see no beast anywhere. So Cherry made a clicking noise, which she had used when calling the cows in Zennor, and suddenly a fine cow appeared from among the trees, and Cherry sat down to milk her.

After breakfast, the old woman showed Cherry everything in

the kitchen. Then Aunt Prudence told Cherry that under no circumstances should she try to go into any of the locked rooms in the house. "You might see something that would frighten you," she repeated. After this warning, Cherry went out to help her master in the garden. She and the gentleman got on well, but Cherry did not like the old woman, who was often hovering around in the background, muttering, as if she did not like the girl and wanted her gone.

When Cherry seemed settled in her new home, Prudence said, "Now you shall see some parts of the house you have not seen before." One room had a floor that was polished like glass and around all the walls were figures of men, women, and

301

children, all made of stone. They looked to Cherry as if they were real people who had somehow been turned to stone, and she shivered with fear as she looked at them.

Poor Cherry thought she had come into a house of wicked conjurors, and looked at the old woman in fear. "I don't want to see any more," she said.

But the old woman laughed, and pushed Cherry into another room, where she was made to polish a large box that looked like a coffin on legs. "Rub harder, harder!" shouted the old woman, with a look of madness in her eyes, and as Cherry  rubbed, she heard an awful wailing sound, which chilled her to the bone. The girl fainted as she heard it, and the master burst into the room.

When he saw what had happened, the gentleman threw the old woman out of the house, shouting that she should never have shown Cherry the locked room. Then he gave Cherry a soothing drink to revive her. It made Cherry feel better, and it also made her forget exactly what she had seen. But she knew that she had been frightened, and that she did not want to go into that part of the house again.

Life was much better for Cherry with the old woman gone. She was happy in her master's house, but still curious about what was going on there. One day, when her master was out, she decided to try some of the child's ointment on her own

eyes. As she rubbed in the ointment, she felt a terrible burning and dashed to the pool under the rock to splash cool water on her eyelids. As she did so, she saw hundreds of tiny people at the bottom of the pool – and among them was her master!

The ointment had given Cherry the ability to see the little people, and when she looked, she could see them everywhere, hiding in the flowers, swinging in the trees, running around under blades of grass. Another time, she saw her master playing with a host of the little people. One of them, dressed up like a queen, was dancing on top of the coffin, and the master took her in his arms and kissed her.

Next day, when Cherry and her master were together in the garden, he bent to kiss her. This was enough for Cherry. "Kiss the little people like yourself, as you do when you go under the water," she cried, and slapped her master on the face. The gentleman knew that Cherry had used some of the ointment on her eyes. She would have to leave him for good.

Sadly, Cherry and her master parted. He gave her a bundle full of clothes and other fine things, picked up a lantern, and led her away from his garden, along the sunken lanes, and towards the Downs. Then he gave the girl a final kiss, and said with a hint of sadness in his voice that he was sorry, but that

she must be punished for her curiosity. Perhaps he would see her sometimes if she walked upon the Downs.

So Cherry returned to Zennor. Her people were surprised to see her, for she had been away for so long, without sending news of her whereabouts, that they had thought she was dead. When she told her story to her parents, they could not believe it at first, and thought she was telling it to cover up some mischief that she had been part of. But Cherry insisted that her story was true, and in time her family accepted what she said. Often she wandered on the Lady Downs, looking for her old master. But she never saw him again.

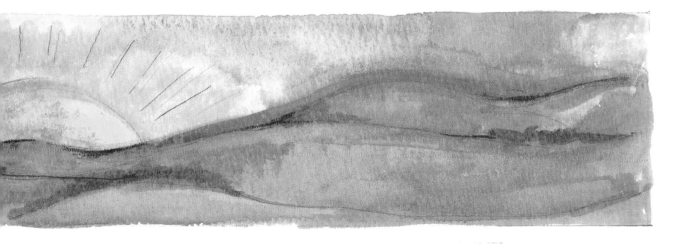

Skillywidden

A man was cutting furze on Trendreen Hill one fine day, and he saw one of the little people stretched out, fast asleep, on the heath. The man took off the thick cuff that he wore at his work, crept up quietly, and popped the little man into the cuff before he could wake up. Then he carried his find home with care, and let the creature out on to the hearth stone.

When he awoke, the fairy looked quite at home and soon began to enjoy himself playing with the children. They called him Bob of the Heath, and Bob told the man that he would show him where to find crocks of gold hidden on the hillside.

Several days later, the neighbours joined together to bring away the harvest of furze, and all came to the man's house to celebrate the end of their task with a hearty meal. To hide Bob away from prying eyes, the man locked him in the barn with the children.

But the fairy and his playmates were cunning, and soon found a way out of the barn. Before long they were playing a game of dancing and hide-and-seek all around the great heap of furze in the yard.

As they played, they saw a tiny man and woman searching round the furze. "Oh my poor Skillywidden," said the tiny woman. "Where can you be? Will I ever set eyes on you again?"

"Go back indoors," said Bob to the children. "My mother and father have come looking for me. I must go back with them now." Then he cried, "Here I am mummy!" And before the children knew what had happened, their playmate Bob had vanished with his parents, and they were left in the yard.

When they told their father what had happened, the man was angry, and gave them a beating for escaping from the locked barn.

After this the furze-cutter sometimes went to Trendreen Hill to look for fairies and crocks of gold. But he was never able to find either.

Tom and the Giant Blunderbuss

Long ago, when the world was ruled by giants, there was a young giant called Tom. Although he was young and strong, Tom was a lazy lad who spent most of the time mooching around with his hands in his pockets. Now and then, Tom would spring into action, and would move dozens of massive boulders to build a wall, just to show what he could do if he tried. But usually he was idle.

Tom's mother grew sick of her son's idleness, and after much nagging, persuaded him to take a job driving a brewer's wagon. Tom thought that if he had to have a job, this would be a good one, because at least he would be able to get plenty to drink. So off he went to live in the nearest market town, where he began to work for the brewer.

One day he was out with his wagon when he came across a group of men trying to lift a fallen tree. They seemed to be making a poor effort of it, so he stopped, helped them, and in a trice had lifted the tree where they wanted it. The men thanked him, and he set off again along the road to St Ives.

After a while, Tom came to a place where a wall blocked the
road. Tom knew that the lands behind the wall belonged to a
great giant known as Blunderbuss. Many years before, the road
had gone straight ahead, but now it was blocked by
Blunderbuss's wall. If the giant had not lived there, Tom could
have gone straight on in the direction of St Ives. But as it was,
he would have to go a long way round.

Tom looked at the giant's gate and wondered whether he
should take the short cut through. But the giant had a cruel
reputation. He had married several times, and people said that
he had killed each of his wives. Tom therefore thought better
of trespassing on the giant's land, and carried on his journey by

the normal road.

But on his way back, Tom was tired and full with the four gallons of beer he had drunk at St Ives, and he decided to take the shorter route home. So he drove his wagon through the giant's great gate and across the field where the giant's cattle grazed contentedly. When he had gone about a mile, he arrived at a gate in a high wall which surrounded the giant's castle.

The only way was forward, so Tom pushed open the gate and began to drive his oxen across the castle courtyard. As he went along, Tom heard some dogs barking loudly, and then the great giant himself emerged from his castle.

"What are you doing driving into my castle courtyard and disturbing my afternoon sleep?" roared the giant.

"I am on the right road," said Tom. "You have no right to stop me going home."

"I will not trouble myself to argue with a saucy young rascal like you," said Blunderbuss. "I shall fetch a twig and beat you to my gate."

The giant pulled up an elm tree taller than three men and began to strip the branches from the trunk. He still seemed to be half asleep, but he could do this without any effort at all. Tom saw what he was doing, and looked around for a weapon to defend himself. His eye lighted on his wagon, so he pulled out one of the axles, took one of the wooden wheels as a shield, and stood ready for the giant's blows.

Blunderbuss rushed at Tom, but Tom dodged quickly, the ground was slippery, and the giant squelched into the mud. Tom could have killed the giant easily when he was down, but the young lad thought that this was unfair. So he merely tickled Blunderbuss in the ribs with his axle, and said, "Up you get. Let's have another turn."

Quickly, Blunderbuss got up and rushed at Tom without warning. But Tom was ready for him, and held out his axle so that it pierced the giant's body right through. Blunderbuss gave out a dreadful roar.

"Stop bleating like a sheep!" said Tom. "I will pull out my

axle, then we can have another turn."

But when he withdrew his weapon, Tom saw that blood was pouring from the giant's wound. Tom cut some turf and gave this to the giant to plug the hole, and then Tom was ready to fight once more. But the giant Blunderbuss held up his hand. "No, I can fight no more. You have wounded me mortally. And you have done well, fighting bravely even when I tried to trick you by rushing at you when you were not prepared. I would like to do you some good, for you are the only one who has

been brave enough to stand up to me. Listen carefully. I have no near relations and I want you to have my wealth and my lands when I die. In my castle cellar, two dogs guard my gold.

The dogs are called Catchem and Tearem. If you go into the cellar they will attack you unless you call them by their names. Simply do this and you can take the gold."

Tom listened in silence as the giant told him of the wealth and lands that he would own. In the end he asked, "Did you kill your wives?"

"No. They died of natural causes. Please do not let people tell lies about me when I am dead."

And Tom was about to reassure the giant and tell him that his time was not yet come, when Blunderbuss closed his eyes, and all was over.

Tom went back home with his wagon, but returned to the giant's castle and found that all that Blunderbuss had told him was true. He also found the giant's young wife, who quickly got to know and love Tom. Soon the two were married, and they lived for many a long year in the castle by the road.

I Don't Know

Once there was a Duke who lived in Brittany, and he was riding home one day with his manservant when they saw a young child lying asleep and alone by the side of the road. The Duke was curious and sad to see a young boy, about five years old, left by the roadside, so he got down from his horse, went over to the boy, and woke him up.

"Who has left you here, my boy?" asked the Duke.

"I don't know."

"Who are your parents?"

"I don't know."

"Which town do you come form?"

"I don't know."

"What are you called?"

"I don't know."

"Well, no one seems to be taking care of you, so we will take you home and keep you safe." So the Duke took the child home to his castle, and called him N'oun-Doaré, which is the Breton for "I don't know."

N'oun-Doaré grew up in the family of the Duke and proved

to be a healthy, intelligent child. The Duke sent him to school and the lad grew into a handsome young man.

When N'oun-Doaré was eighteen, the Duke brought him back to live at the castle, and, to show N'oun-Doaré how pleased he was with his progress, took him to the local fair to buy him his own sword and his own horse.

First the Duke took N'oun-Doaré to look for a horse. There were many horse-dealers at the fair, but N'oun-Doaré could find no steed that suited him. Then they met a man leading an old mare and N'oun-Doaré shouted, "Yes! That is the horse I want!"

The Duke was surprised. "That old nag?" he said. But the boy insisted.

As the horse's owner was handing over the beast, he spoke quietly to N'oun-Doaré. "You have made a good choice, my boy. Look at these knots in the mare's mane. If you undo one of them, she will fly fifteen hundred leagues through the air."

Then the Duke and N'oun-Doaré went to see the armourer, and looked at many swords. But none was quite right for N'oun-Doaré. Then they came to a junk shop and saw an old, rusty sword. "That is the sword I would like."

"But it's an old, rusty thing," protested the Duke. "You deserve much better than that."

"Please buy it for me in any case, and I will put it to good use."

So they bought the old sword and the lad was pleased. He was even more excited when he looked closely at the weapon and saw that it had a faint inscription, almost covered by the rust. The words "I am invincible" were engraved on the sword.

When they got home, N'oun-Doaré could not wait to try a magical flight with his mare, and before long he was undoing one of the knots in her mane. Off they flew to Paris, where N'oun-Doaré marvelled at the sights of the great city. It chanced that the Duke was also there, for he had been called to attend the king. When he met the boy, they went to the royal palace together. The Duke introduced N'oun-Doaré to the king, and the lad was given a job looking after some of the

royal stables.

One night, N'oun-Doaré was passing a cross roads when he saw something glinting in the moonlight. He found that it was a crown, and that it was adorned with diamonds that shone in the dark. He picked up the crown when a voice said "Be on your guard if you take it." N'oun-Doaré did not know where the voice came from, but it was actually the voice of his old mare. It made N'oun-Doaré pause, but in the end he picked up the crown and took it with him.

He told no one about the crown and kept it secretly in the stables, but two of the other servants noticed it shining through the keyhole and went to tell the king. The king took the crown and called all his wise men about him. But none of them knew where the crown had come from. There was an inscription on the crown, but it was in a strange language and none of the wise men could read it.

Then a small child spoke up, saying that the crown belonged to the Princess of the Golden Fleece. The king turned to N'oun-Doaré: "Bring me the Princess of the Golden Fleece to be my wife, otherwise you will meet your death."

So the lad got on his mare and began his search for the princess, although in truth he had little idea about where to look. As he rode, he came to a beach, and N'oun-Doaré saw a fish stuck on the sand. The creature seemed to be breathing its last. "Put it back in the sea," said the mare, and N'oun-Doaré did so.

"Great thanks to you," said the fish. "You have saved the life of the king of the fish."

A while later they came to a place where a bird was trapped in a snare. "Let the creature go," said the mare, and N'oun-Doaré did so.

"Great thanks to you," said the bird. "You have saved the life of the king of the birds."

Further along on their journey they came to a great castle and nearby a man was chained to a tree. "Set him free," said the mare, and N'oun-Doaré did so.

"Great thanks to you," said the man. "You have saved the life of the Demon King."

"Whose castle is this?" asked N'oun-Doaré.

"It is the castle of the Princess of the Golden Fleece," replied the Demon King. They had reached their goal at last.

They entered the castle and N'oun-Doaré explained why he had come. The princess was unwilling to go at first, but N'oun-Doaré tricked her on to his horse, and away they flew before she could dismount. They quickly arrived back in Paris, where the king wanted to marry without delay.

"Before I marry, I must have my own ring," said the princess.

The king asked N'oun-Doaré to bring him the ring,

and N'oun-Doaré looked about in despair. How would he find it? Then the mare whispered to him, "Ask the king of the birds, who you saved. He will help you."

So they went to the king of the birds and explained that they needed the ring. The king of the birds called all the birds to him. He chose the smallest bird of all, the wren, and told her to bring the ring to the princess. "The wren is the best bird for this task," he explained. "She will be able to fly through the keyhole of the princess's chamber."

Soon the wren returned with the ring, and the king wanted to marry straight away. But the princess had another demand. "I must have my own castle brought to me," she said.

"How shall I ever achieve this?" said N'oun-Doaré in despair.

But the mare whispered to him, "Ask the Demon King, who you saved. He will help you."

So they went to the Demon King, and he called a whole army of demons, and they set to work moving the princess's castle, bit by bit, to Paris, until her wish had come true. The king, of course, wanted to marry straight away, but the princess had a final demand. "I do not have the key to my castle, for it was dropped into the sea when we flew here to Paris on N'oun-Doaré's mare."

N'oun-Doaré saw that this was a task for the king of the fish, who called all his subjects to him. Finally, a fish arrived with

the diamond-studded key in its mouth.

At last, the Princess agreed to marry the king. When the guests arrived they were amazed to see N'oun-Doaré leading his mare into the church. When the king and princess were pronounced man and wife, the mare's skin vanished, and there stood a beautiful young woman. "Please marry me, N'oun-Doaré," she said. "I am the daughter of the king of Tartary."

N'oun-Doaré and the princess set off arm in arm to Tartary. People say they lived happily ever after there, but they were never seen in Brittany again.

The Fenoderee

On the Isle of Man lived a fairy who had been sent out of fairyland because he had had a passion for a mortal girl. The fairy folk found out about his love for the girl when he was absent from one of their gatherings. They found him dancing with his love in the merry Glen of Rushen. When the other fairies heard what he was doing, they cast a spell, forcing him to live for ever on the Isle of Man, and making him ugly and hairy. This is why people called him the Fenoderee, which means "hairy one" in the Manx language.

Although his appearance frightened people when they saw him, the Fenoderee was usually kind to humans, for he never forgot the girl he loved, and wanted to do what he could for her people. Sometimes he even helped people with their work, and used what was left of his fairy magic to carry out tasks which would have been exhausting for the strongest of men.

One thing the Fenoderee liked to do was to help the farmers in their fields. On one occasion he mowed a meadow for a farmer. But instead of being grateful, the farmer complained that the Fenoderee had not cut the grass short enough.

The Fenoderee was still sad at losing his mortal love, and angry that the farmer was so ungrateful, so next year at mowing time, he let the farmer do the job him-self.

As the farmer walked along, swishing his scythe from side to side, the Fenoderee crept behind him, cutting up roots, and getting so close to the farmer that the man risked having his feet cut off.

When the farmer told this story, people knew that they should be grateful when the Fenoderee helped them with their work. So the custom arose of leaving the creature little gifts when he had been especially helpful.

On one occasion, a man was building himself a new house of stone. He found the stone he wanted on the cliffs by the beach, and paid some of the men of the parish to help him quarry it. There was one large block of fine marble which he especially wanted, but no matter how hard they tried, the block was too heavy to be moved, even if all the men of the parish tried to shift it.

Next day they were surprised to see that not only had the huge block of marble been carried to the building site, but all the other stone that the builder needed had been moved too.

At first, everyone wondered how the stone could have got there. But then someone said, "It must have been the Fenoderee who was working for us in the night." The builder

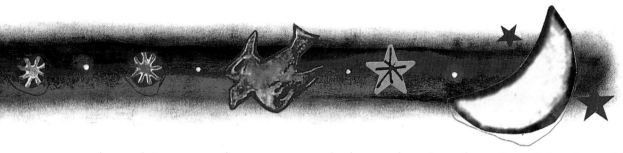

saw that this must be true, and thought that he should give the Fenoderee a handsome reward.

So he took some clothes of the right size for the creature, and left them in one of the places where he was sometimes seen. That night, the Fenoderee appeared and found the clothes. Those who watched him were surprised at his sadness as he lifted each item up in turn and said these words:

> Cap for the head, alas, poor head!
>
> Coat for the back, alas, poor back!
>
> Breeches for the breech, alas, poor breech!
>
> If these all be thine, thine cannot be the merry glen of Rushen.

With these words, the Fenoderee walked away, and has never been seen since in that neighbourhood.

A Bride and a Hero

Long ago the Irish believed that there was a faraway land called Tir na n-Og, the Land of Youth. Time went much more slowly there, and people stayed younger much longer. It was the law in Tir na n-Og that every seven years a race was held. All the strongest men of the land took part. The race began in front of the royal palace and finished at the top of a hill two miles away. At the summit of the hill was placed a chair, and the first runner to sit on the chair became king of Tir na n-Og for the next seven years.

There was once a king of Tir na n-Og who was worried that he would lose his kingdom in the next race, so he sent for his chief Druid.

"How long shall I win the race and rule this land before another reaches the chair before me?" he asked the druid.

"Have no fear," replied the druid. "You will rule for ever, unless your own son-in-law wins the race and takes the crown from you."

The king of Tir na n-Og had but one daughter, Niamh, and as yet she was not married. So the king decided that he would

326

keep his kingdom by making his daughter so ugly that no man would marry her. He borrowed his druid's staff, and struck the girl with it, and a pig's head appeared on her shoulders.

When the druid heard what had happened, he was very sorry that he had told the king to beware his son-in-law. He went to Niamh to talk to her.

"Shall I always be like this?" said Niamh to the druid.

"Yes," replied the druid. "You will always look like this unless you go to Ireland and marry one of the sons of Fin."

So Niamh set out for Ireland, hoping to meet one of Fin's sons, and wondering how she could persuade him to marry her. When Niamh had been in Ireland for a while she saw a handsome young man called Oisin, and she was overjoyed when she found out that his father was Fin himself.

It happened one day that Oisin was out hunting, and he and his men hunted further afield, and killed more game than they had ever done before. When Oisin turned to go home, his men were exhausted and hungry, and could carry none of the game home with them, so Oisin was left with his three dogs and a great pile of carcasses.

When the men left Oisin alone, Niamh went up to him and watched him look-ing at the game. When he saw her approach, the young man said "I shall be sorry to

leave behind some of the meat I have killed today."

"If you tie some of the game in a bundle, I will help you carry it," said Niamh. And off they walked together.

When they had talked for a while, it was clear to Oisin that Niamh was a fine young woman, caring and kind, and it struck the lad that she would probably be attractive too, if she did not have a pig's head on her shoulders. So Oisin asked her about the pig's head, and Niamh explained how she had been told that the only way to get back her own head was to come to Ireland marry one of the sons of Fin.

Oisin smiled. "If that is all it takes for you to get back your

beauty, then you shall not have a pig's head for long," he said.

So it was that Niamh married Oisin, son of Fin. As soon as the ceremony was over, the pig's head vanished, and Niamh's own beautiful face was revealed to her husband. And when he saw Niamh in her new beauty, he loved her deeply.

Soon it was clear that Niamh longed to return to the land of Tir na n-Og, and when she told Oisin of her wish, he was keen to go there with her. He knew that it was the land where people never grow old, and if he went there he would be young for ever. When they arrived at the castle of Niamh's

father, there was great celebration, for everyone had thought that the princess was lost for ever. So for a while the king lived happily with his daughter and son-in-law.

But after a while it was the time for the seven-yearly race to find who should be king. All the likely men in the kingdom, including the king and Oisin, gathered for the race. And before any other competitor was half way up the hill, Oisin was sitting in the seat at the top. No one could deny that it was Oisin's right to be king of Tir na n-Og.

Oisin ruled the Land of Youth for many years, and no one ever argued with his right to be king. He loved his wife dearly, and they were always seen together - in the palace, in the town, or riding their swift grey horse together. Oisin marvelled that he kept his youth, just as did anyone who had been born in Tir na n-Og and lived there all their years. But there was one sadness. Oisin missed his Irish homeland and longed to go back for a visit. He spoke of his wish to Niamh and she turned to him with a warning. "It will be dangerous for you if you return to Ireland," she said. "If you set foot on your native soil, you will lose your youth. You will become a blind old man and you will never come home to me."

Oisin could not believe that this would happen so easily.

"How long do you think you have lived with me in Tir na n–Og?" she asked.

"About three years," replied Oisin.

"But three of our years are like three hundred in Ireland."

Nothing that Niamh could say could change Oisin's mind. He insisted that he wanted to go back. So Niamh decided to help him, in the hope that her husband could hold on to his youth. "Ride to Ireland and do not dismount," she said. "You will only lose your youth if you put your own foot on Irish soil. But if you leave the saddle, the steed will come back to Tir na n-Og and you will be left, old and blind, in Ireland."

With this warning ringing in his ears, Oisin set off for his homeland. The beautiful white horse carried him across both land and sea, and he came at last to Ireland. It was rainy and

windy, but Oisin was happy to be home once more.

Soon he passed a girl and he asked her where he might find the house of Fin and his family. For the land and the buildings seemed changed from when Oisin had last been there. The girl looked at him with a puzzled expression. "I know of no such people," she said. "They do not live around here." And yet Oisin was sure that he was in the right neighbourhood.

He passed other people on his way, and asked each one about Fin and his household of mighty warriors. But no one seemed to know who he was talking about – which was strange, since Fin and his men had been among the most famous in Ireland.

Finally Oisin asked an old man if he knew the whereabouts

of Fin. "I remember my old grandfather talking about Fin and his warriors," said the old man. "They lived in these parts about three hundred years ago."

So Oisin's father and all his family were dead. Oisin could still not believe it. He found the fortress Fin had built, but it was in ruins. He began to believe that what the old man said was true, and that three years in the Land of Youth really were the same as three hundred mortal years.

Oisin decided to seek out the High King of Ireland himself, to tell him of his adventure. As he was riding along the road,

he came across a group of men who were trying to lift a stone. Since he had arrived in Ireland, Fin had noticed that the men seemed weak and feeble compared with those in Tir na n-Og, and these men were no exception. Six of them were tugging away at the stone, but they could not shift it, let alone lift it up into the cart that stood waiting nearby.

Riding up to the men, Oisin called that he would help them. He leaned over to pick up the stone and threw it into the cart, but the effort put Oisin off balance. As he reached out to stop himself falling, one of the stirrups broke and the hero tumbled off his horse and landed on the floor.

As he fell, all the warnings of Niamh ran through his mind.
And when he picked himself up from the ground he knew
that it was true, he was old, stiff, and blind. He heard Niamh's
horse trotting away, and knew that he would never return to
the land of Tir na n-Og.

It happened that Saint Patrick lived nearby, and the holy man
heard of what had happened. Soon Oisin was brought to
Patrick, who gave him a room in his own house, and asked his
cook to bring him food every day.

Oisin told Patrick all about his adventures, relating stories
about his father Fin and his band of warriors, as well as his
adventures in the land of youth, while the holy man listened
patiently. Although he was old and blind, Oisin still had a little
of his former strength, and sometimes, if Patrick prayed

devoutly, Oisin would regain enough energy to help the Saint build his church, and to help rid Patrick of a monster that came to destroy the building before it was finished. But Oisin's strength never lasted long, and soon he would be a weak old man again and it was all he could do to eat the food brought to him by Patrick's cook. And so, old and blind, Oisin lived out the last of his days, with only his memories of Tir na n-Og to console him.

The Lazy Beauty

Once upon a time there was a poor widow who had one daughter. The mother was the most hard-working of women. Her house was neat and clean, and she was especially good at using her spinning wheel to make the finest linen thread.

The daughter was a fine-looking girl, but the laziest creature in the town. She got up late every day, spent hours eating her breakfast, and dawdled around the house doing nothing all day. Whenever she tried to cook, she burned herself, and if she did any other work, she would straight away knock something over or break one of her mother's pots. The girl even drawled her speech, as if it took too much energy to get the words out of her mouth.

One day the widow was giving her daughter a good telling off when she heard the sound of hoof-beats on the road. It was the king's son riding by. When he heard the woman's voice he stopped to talk to her.

"What is the matter? Is your child so bad that you need to scold her so?"

"Oh no, your majesty," replied the old woman, for she saw a

chance to get rid of the girl. "I was telling my daughter that she works much too hard. Do you know, my lord, she can spin three whole pounds of flax in a single day? Then the next day, she will weave it into good linen cloth, and sew it all into shirts the following day!"

The prince reflected when he heard what the woman had to say. "That is amazing," he said. "Surely my mother, herself a great spinner, would be pleased with your daughter. Tell her to put her bonnet on and come with me. We might even make a fine princess of her, if she herself would like that."

The two women were thrown into confusion. Neither of them could have imagined that the old woman's trick would

have worked so well. But quickly enough, the girl had her outdoor clothes on and was lifted up to ride behind the prince. His majesty gave the mother a bulging purse in exchange for her daughter, and off they rode in the direction of the palace.

Now the girl did not know what to do. But it seemed to her that doing little and saying little had served her well to this day, so when she got to the palace she answered briefly and said but few words, in the hope that she would not show herself up as a lazy idiot.

By the evening, she and the prince seemed to be getting on well and the time came for them to show the girl her room. As she opened the door the queen showed her the work she was to do in the morning. "Here are three pounds of good flax. You may begin as soon as you like in the morning, and I shall expect to see them turned into thread by the end of the day."

The poor girl burst into tears as the queen closed the door behind her. She regretted now that she had not listened to everything her mother had told her about spinning, and that she had not taken all the opportunities she had had to learn the craft. She slept little that night with worry and vexation.

When the morning finally came, there was the great wooden spinning wheel waiting for her, and the girl started to spin. But her thread kept breaking, and one moment it was thick, the

next it was thin. She burst into tears as the thread broke again.

At that very moment, a little old woman with big feet appeared in the room. "What is the matter, my fair maiden?" asked the woman.

"I have all this flax to spin, and whatever I do, the thread seems to break," said the girl.

"Ah, if you invite the old woman with the big feet to your wedding with the prince, I will spin your thread for you," the woman offered.

"I will be glad for you to come to the wedding if you will do this work for me," said the girl. "I shall honour you for as long as I live."

"Very well. Stay in your room until evening, and tell the queen that her thread will be ready tomorrow," said the old woman.

And it was all as the old woman had said. The queen came, saw the beautiful thread, and told the girl to rest. "Tomorrow I shall bring you my fine wooden loom, and you can turn all this thread into cloth," she promised.

Of course, this made the girl more frightened than ever, for she was no better a weaver than a spinner. She sat in her room, trembling, waiting for the loom to be brought to her. When the loom was brought, she sat at it and cried once more.

Suddenly, another old woman appeared in the room, a woman with great hips and a small voice, and she asked why the girl was crying.

"I have all this thread to weave, but I cannot work the loom," said the girl.

"Ah, if you invite the old woman with the big hips to your wedding with the prince, I will weave your cloth for you," the woman offered.

"I will be glad for you to come to the wedding if you will do this work for me," said the girl. "I shall honour you for as long as I live."

"Very well. Stay in your room until evening, and tell the queen that her cloth will be ready tomorrow."

Once more, the work was done and the queen was pleased with the cloth. But this time, the girl found herself with the task of sewing the cloth into shirts for the prince. The girl was now in deep despair. She was so close to marrying the prince, but she had no skill whatsoever with the needle. As she sat and cried a third old woman, with a big red nose, appeared in her room. The girl explained her plight.

"Ah, if you invite the old woman with the red nose to your wedding with the prince, I will sew your shirts for you," the woman offered.

"I will be glad for you to come to the wedding if you will do this work for me," said the girl. "I shall honour

you for as long as I live."

"Very well. Stay in your room until evening, and tell the queen that the shirts will be ready tomorrow."

So again the work was done, the queen was pleased, and the girl found that preparations for the wedding were being made.

When the wedding came, it was the most lavish feast anyone could remember. The girl's old mother was invited, and the queen kept talking to her about how her daughter would enjoy herself spinning, weaving, and sewing after the honeymoon. Just as she was talking about this, the footman approached the high table and announced another guest. "The princess's aunt, Old Woman Big-foot, has arrived." The girl blushed, but the prince seemed to happy for her to come in. "Tell her that she is welcome, and find a place for her," said the prince.

When someone asked the old woman why her feet were so big, she explained that it was from standing all day working at the spinning wheel.

"Why, my dear," said the prince. "I shall never let you stand all day spinning."

Soon the second old woman arrived at the feast. When she was asked why her hips were so great, she said it came from sitting all day at the loom.

"Why my dear," said the prince. "I shall never let you sit all day weaving."

Finally the third old woman took her place. She explained that her nose had grown big and red from bending down sewing, so that the blood ran always to her nose.

"Why, my dear," said the prince. "I shall never let you sit all day sewing."

So it came about that the lazy beauty never had to spin, or weave, or sew again, and she lived happily in her laziness at the prince's court.

Paddy O'Kelly and the Weasel

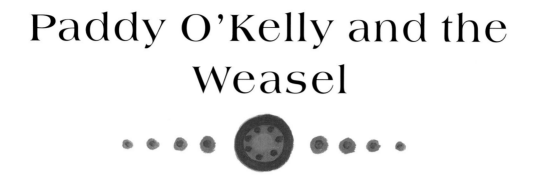

There was once a man called Paddy O'Kelly, and he lived in County Galway. Paddy had an old donkey that he wanted to sell, so he got up early one morning and began the journey to market. He hoped one day to be able to buy a horse, though he knew he would not get enough money for the donkey to buy himself a fine steed that day.

Paddy had gone a few miles when it started to rain, so he decided to shelter in a large house. No one seemed to be around, so he went into a room with a fire blazing in the grate. After a while he saw a big weasel come into the room and put something yellow on the grate; then the creature ran away. Soon afterwards, the weasel reappeared, went to the grate, and put down another yellow object. Paddy O'Kelly could see now that these yellow objects were gold coins, and he watched as the weasel came back and forth, every time leaving a guinea on the grate.

When the weasel seemed to stop bringing the coins, Paddy got up, scooped them into his pocket, and went on his way.

But he had not gone far when the weasel ran up to him, screeching and jumping up at him. Paddy tried to beat her off with a stick, but she clung on until some passing men let loose their dog, which chased her away. In the end, she disappeared down a hole in the ground.

Paddy sold his donkey at the market, and used some of the weasel's gold to buy himself a fine horse. He was returning home the way he had come when the weasel popped up out of her hole and attacked the horse. The steed bolted, and ended up nearly drowning in a nearby ditch, until two men passing by helped him pull the beast out. Paddy was exhausted when he got home, so he tethered the horse in the cow shed and went straight to bed.

Next morning, when he went to feed the horse, he saw the weasel running out of the cow shed. The creature had blood on her fur, and Paddy feared the worst. Sure enough, when he got to the shed he found not only his horse, but two cows and two calves dead on the floor.

Paddy called his dog and gave chase, and soon they were catching up the weasel. Suddenly, the creature ran inside a small hovel by the side of the road, closely followed by the dog, which started barking. When Paddy pushed open the door, there was no weasel to be seen, but an old woman sat on a chair in the corner.

"Did you see a weasel coming in, at all?" asked Paddy.

"I did not," said the old woman.

But the dog's instinct was to carry on the hunt, and he leapt at the old woman's throat, making her screech with a noise just like the weasel's cry. Paddy O'Kelly saw that woman and weasel were one and the same.

"Call off your dog and I'll make you rich!" said the woman.

The old woman explained that long ago she had committed a great crime. Her sin would be forgiven if Paddy took twenty pounds to the church to pay for a hundred and sixty masses to be said for her. She told Paddy that if he dug beneath a bush in a nearby field, he would find a pot filled with gold. He could pay for the masses with the money, and use what was left over to buy the big old house where first he saw the weasel.

"Do not be afraid if you see a big black dog coming out of the money pot," she warned. "He is a son of mine and will do you no harm. Soon I will die, and when I die, please do one thing more for me. Light a fire in this hut and burn it and my body together."

Straight away Paddy went to the bush, dug a hole, and found the pot of gold. As he lifted the lid from the pot, a black dog jumped out, and Paddy remembered the old woman's warning.

When he had the money, Paddy replaced his dead cows and horse, and also bought a flock of sheep. He called on the priest to arrange masses to be said for the old woman. And he went to see the man who owned the house where he had first seen the weasel. The owner warned Paddy that the house was haunted, but Paddy insisted on buying it, and stayed in the house all night, until a little man appeared.

The little man, whose name was Donal, made friends with

Paddy. They drank together and Donal played the bagpipes. Donal soon revealed that he was the son of the old woman, and told Paddy that he would be a good friend to him, so long as Paddy told no one else who he was.

Then Donal said, "Tonight I am visiting the Fortress of the Fairies of Connacht. Will you come with me? You shall ride there on a horse provided by me."

Paddy agreed, and at midnight, the two flew through the air on broomsticks that Donal brought with him. When they arrived, the fairy who seemed to be the leader said, "Tonight we are going to visit the high king and queen of the fairies." They seemed eager for Donal and Paddy to go with them, so off they all went.

When they arrived at the hill where the high king and queen of the fairies lived, the hillside opened up for them, and they walked inside. When all the fairies were assembled there, the king explained why they were all gathered together. "Tonight we are to play a great hurling match against the fairies of Munster. The Munster fairy folk always have two mortals to help them, so we would like you to come with us." They set off to the place where they were to play, and the fairies of

Munster were already gathered before them. And so, to the accompaniment of bagpipe music, they began their game.

Paddy saw that the Munster fairies were gaining the upper hand, so he helped the little people of Connacht, turning one of the opponents' human helpers on his back. Once this had happened, the two sides started to fight, and before long the Connacht side were the winners. The disappointed Munster fairies turned themselves into flying beetles and began to eat up all the leaves from the trees and bushes. This went on until the countryside looked quite bare, when thousands of doves flew up and devoured the beetles.

Meanwhile the Connacht fairies returned to their hill, and their chief gave Paddy a purse of gold for his help. Donal took him back home, and he was back in his bed before his wife had noticed that he had gone.

A month went past and Paddy settled down to enjoy his riches, when Donal came to Paddy and told him that his mother was dead. Paddy went to her hut and set fire to it with her body inside, just as she had asked. Once it was burned to the ground, Donal gave Paddy another purse of gold, saying, "This is a purse that will never be empty in your lifetime. I am going away now, but whenever you take money from this purse, remember me and the weasel."

Then Donal was gone, and Paddy and his wife lived long and wealthy, and left much money and a farm to their children. They all did as Donal had asked, and whenever they spent some of his mother's gold, they spared a thought for him and the weasel who had led Paddy to his wealth, when he had gone to sell his old donkey long ago.

The Dream of Owen O'Mulready

Owen O'Mulready was a happy man. He lived with his wife Margaret in a pleasant little house with a large garden. They had enough space to grow all the vegetables they needed, and Owen's master was kind and paid him good wages. Owen had everything he wanted out of his life – except for one thing. Owen had never had a dream. He was fascinated by the tales people told him of their dreams, and he very much wanted to have a dream of his own.

One day, Owen was digging his potatoes when his master came up and started to talk to Owen, as he often did. They began to talk about dreams, and Owen admitted that he had never had a dream, and that he would dearly like to have one.

"I can tell you how to make yourself have a dream," said Owen's master. "Before bedtime tonight, clear the fire from your hearth and make your bed in the fireplace. Sleep there tonight, and surely you will soon have a dream that you will remember for a long while, mark my words."

Owen said he would do this, and when evening came, he

cleared away the fire and made his bed in the hearth, just as his master had told him. When Margaret saw him doing this, she thought her husband had gone mad. But when he explained what his master had said, she let him do what he wanted, for she knew how badly Owen wanted his dream.

So Owen got into his hearth-bed, and soon was asleep. He had not been sleeping for long when there was a loud knock at the door. Owen opened it and a stranger was there. "I have a letter from the master which must be taken to America."

"You've arrived late for such a message," replied Owen. But he accepted the message, put on his boots,

353

and off he went, striding towards the west.

He came to the foot of a mountain, where he met a young lad herding cows. The boy seemed to recognize him, even though Owen had not seen him before. "Where are you going in the middle of the night?" asked the boy.

"I have a letter from my master to take to America. Is this the right way?"

"Yes it is. Keep going westwards. But how will you travel across the water?"

"I will work that out in good time," said Owen. And on he went, until he came to the sea.

Owen found a crane standing on one foot by the shore.

"Good evening, Owen O'Mulready," said the crane, who, like the cow-boy, seemed to know Owen. "What are you doing here?"

Owen explained his business and said that he was puzzled about how to get over the water.

"Sit up on my back, and I will ferry you to the other side," said the crane.

"And what if you get tired before we arrive?" asked Owen.

The crane assured Owen that he would not get tired, and off they went.

They had not flown for long, when the crane started to tire. "Get off my back, Owen, for I begin to tire," said the bird.

"I can't get down now, I'll drown in the water," said Owen.

Owen began to panic, when he saw some men threshing above his head. He shouted to one of the threshers: "Thresher, reach down your flail so that I can hold on to it and give the bird a rest."

The man held down his flail and Owen clung on to it with all his strength. As soon as his weight was off the bird's back, the crane flew off with a mocking cry, leaving Owen hanging in the air.

"Bad luck to you!" Owen shouted at the bird as it vanished into the distance.

Owen's troubles were not over. The thresher began to shout

for his flail. "Let go of my flail, Owen O'Mulready. I cannot get on with my work." Owen protested, saying that he would fall into the sea and drown if he let go, but the man still shouted for his flail, and began to shake the other end, as if trying to make Owen slip off into the water.

Suddenly Owen saw a chance of rescue. A ship had appeared on the horizon, and Owen began to shout and wave with his free hand. Gradually the ship steered towards Owen and still the flail was shaking and Owen thought he might not be able to hang on long enough.

"Are we under you yet?" shouted one of the sailors on board the ship.

"Not quite," replied Owen. The ship came nearer, and the captain began to shout to Owen.

"Throw down one of your boots. If it lands on deck, we shall know we are under you."

Owen kicked one foot, and his boot fell towards the ship. But Owen did not see where it landed.

He was distracted by a terrible scream, and suddenly he heard his wife's voice shouting "Who is killing me? Owen, where can you be?"

"Is that you, Margaret?" asked Owen, not quite sure where he was, or how she had got there.

"Of course it's me," replied Margaret.

Margaret got out of bed and lit the candle. The bed was in a mess and soot was all over the sheets. At first, she could not see her husband, but found him, half-way up the chimney, climbing up and clinging on with his hands. He had on one boot, and Margaret saw that the other had come off and had hit her and woken her.

"So the master was right about your dream," said Margaret, smiling.

"Yes, he was right enough," said Owen.

And Owen O'Mulready never wanted to have another dream again.

The King and the Labourer

A labourer was digging a drain when the king came up to him and began to speak: "Are you busy at your work?"

"I am, your majesty"

"Have you a daughter?"

"I have one daughter and she is twelve years old."

"I shall ask you one question," said the king.

"I am no good at solving questions," said the labourer.

"I shall ask anyway," replied the king. "How long will it take me to travel around the world? Have your answer ready by twelve o'clock tomorrow."

The labourer wracked his brains, but he could think of no way to answer the question. When he got home, his daughter saw that he looked troubled. She asked her father what was the matter, and he told her about the king's question.

"That is not so difficult," she said. "Tell the king that if he sits on the sun or the moon it will take him twenty-four hours."

At twelve o'clock the next day, the king arrived.

"Have you the answer to my question?"

"If you sit on the moon or the sun, your majesty, it will take twenty-four hours."

The king was impressed with the labourer's answer, but sensed that he had not thought it up for himself. The man said that his daughter had told him what to say.

"Here is another question," said the king. "What is the distance between the earth and the sky?"

The labourer could not imagine how anyone could know the answer. So again, he asked his daughter, and she told her father what to do. "Take two pins and wait for the king. When he asks you what you are doing, tell him that you are going to measure the distance from the earth to the sky, but that he must buy you a long enough line, so that you can

make the measurement.

When the king arrived at twelve the next day, the man did as his daughter had suggested.

"That is a good answer," smiled the king. "I do not think that you thought of it by yourself." Again, the man admitted that his daughter had thought of the answer.

"I am impressed with your daughter," said the king. "She must come to my palace to work. If you allow it, I shall be a good friend to you."

So the labourer's daughter went to the royal palace and worked in the kitchens. She worked hard, the king was pleased

with her work, and the girl grew into a tall and beautiful young woman. But because she came from a poor family, the other servants looked down on her and teased her. When the king heard of this, he made her father a knight.

The girl could not believe the king's generosity, but it soon became clear that the king loved the girl and eventually the two were married. Afterwards, the king took his wife to one side and told her that he had something important to say.

"The queen must never speak against the king in any judgement," he warned. "If you do, you must leave the palace."

"It would not be right for me to disagree with you," said the girl. "But if you ever have cause to send me away, please grant me three armfuls of whatever I choose."

"I agree to that," said the king.

And so the king and queen began a happy married life. They soon had a son, which made them even happier, and the labourer still could not believe his luck in being made a knight. One day one of the king's tenants came to the king to complain to him. He had a mare that had foaled, but the foal was always following his neighbour's old white horse, and the man thought that his neighbour was trying to steal the foal. The neighbour, for his part, insisted that the foal was his.

"This is how to solve the question," said the king. "Put the two horses and the foal together near a gap in the wall. Then lead out each horse in turn and see which the foal follows. Whichever horse it follows, her owner shall have the foal."

The king's order was carried out, and the foal followed the old white horse.

 When the queen heard what had happened, she went to the wronged owner and told him what to do. "I must not speak against the king's judgement," she said. "But go out and plant some boiled peas near where the king passes. When he asks you if you think they will grow, you can say: 'They're as likely to grow as that old white horse should give birth to a foal.'"

The man did what the queen suggested, and the king saw that he had been wronged. But he also guessed that such a clever ruse had begun with his wife. "Come here, wife," he said. "You are to leave the palace today, for you have given judgement against me."

"It is true that I did so, and I see that I must go," said the queen. "But grant me the three armfuls that I asked for."

The king was angry with her, but there was no going back on his word, so he indicated that she could take what she wanted. His anger turned to astonishment when she picked up

both him and his royal throne and carried him outside the
door. "That is my first armful," she said. Next, she took the
young prince in her arms, carried him outside, and placed him
in the king's lap. "That is my second." Finally, she gathered up
an armful of all the royal charters and placed them with the
prince. "And that is my third. I am happy to leave if these go
with me."

The king saw that there was no parting with a woman of
such wit. "Oh, dearest of women, stay with me!" he said. They
went back into the palace together, and the king ordered that
the foal should be returned to its rightful owner.

The Black Lad
MacCrimmon

There was once a young man called the Black Lad MacCrimmon. He was the youngest of three brothers and he was the most down-trodden of the three. His elder brothers were always favoured by their father, and were always given more food, and allowed more enjoyment, than the Black Lad. The Black Lad, on the other hand, was always given the hardest jobs to do when the four were working together.

The father and the elder brothers were all great pipers, and they had a fine set of pipes that they liked to play. The Black Lad would have liked to have played the pipes too, but he was never allowed. Always the brothers took up too much time with their playing to give the young lad a chance.

In those days, people said that the greatest musicians of all were the fairy folk. The Black Lad hoped that one day he would meet one of the little people and they would teach him to master the pipes.

The day came that the lad's father and his two brothers were getting ready to go to the fair. The Black Lad wanted to go too, but they would not take him. So the lad stayed at home, and when they were gone, he decided to take up the chanter from the set of pipes and see if he could play a tune.

After a while of practising, the lad began to pick out a tune on the chanter. He was starting to enjoy himself, and was so absorbed in what he was doing that he did not notice that someone was watching him and listening.

Suddenly a voice spoke in his ear: "You are doing well with your music, lad." It was none other than the Banshee from the castle.

"Which would you prefer," continued the Banshee. "Skill without success or success without skill?"

365

The lad replied that what he wanted most of all was skill, it did not matter about success. The Banshee smiled, as if she approved of the answer, and pulled a long hair from her head. This she wound around the reed of the chanter. Then she turned to the Black Lad MacCrimmon. "Now put your fingers on the holes of the chanter, and I will place my fingers over yours. I will guide you. When I lift one of my fingers, you lift yours that is beneath it. Think of a tune that you would like to play, and I will help you play. And my skill will rub off on you."

So the lad began to play, guided by the Banshee as she had told him. Soon he was playing with great skill, and he could master any tune that he thought of.

"Indeed you are the King of the Pipers," said the Banshee. "There has been none better before you, and none better shall come after." And with this blessing, the Banshee went on her way back to the castle.

The Black Lad carried on playing when she had left, and he could play all the tunes that he tried. When his father and

brothers returned, they could
hear him playing as they came
along the road, but by the time
they entered the house, the lad
had put away the pipes, and was
acting as if nothing at all had
happened.

None of them mentioned that
they had heard music when they
came in, but the lad's father took
down the pipes, and played as
usual. Then he handed them to
his first son, who played and passed them to the second son.
But instead of putting the pipes away after his second son had
played, old MacCrimmon handed the pipes to his youngest
son. "Now take the pipes, for no longer shall you spend all day
doing the hardest of the work and eating the meanest of the
food."

When the lad played, they heard that he was far better than
any of them. "There is no longer any point in our playing,"
said the father to the two eldest sons. "The lad is truly King of
the Pipers." And the lad's brothers knew that what their father
said was true.

Making a Wife

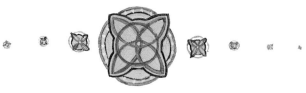

In the village of New Abbey lived a man called Alexander Harg, and he was newly married. His wife was a fine-looking young woman, and some people thought that if the fairies got hold of her, they would kidnap her, so great was her beauty.

A little while after his marriage, Alexander was out on the shore fishing with his net. Nearby were two old boats, left stranded on the rocks. He did not go too near for he had heard stories of little people being heard around them.

Sure enough, before long, Alexander heard a noise coming from one of the boats as if people were using hammers and chisels in there. Then a ghostly voice spoke up from the other old boat: "What are you doing in there?"

"Making a wife for Alexander Harg," came the reply.

Alexander, astounded and terrified by what he had heard, thought of nothing but running back home to see if his wife was safe. He burst through the door, locked it behind him, and took his young wife in his arms. Then he went round closing all the windows and making sure that no one could get in.

At midnight there came a loud banging at the door. The wife got up to open it. "Do not open the door," whispered Alexander. "There are strange things afoot this night."

So they sat together quietly, and after a while the knocking stopped. But just as they were relaxing again, the animals began to make terrifying blood-curdling noises. The pair of them stayed indoors, and did not open the door until morning.

When they did so, they found a statue, carved in oak, in the shape and likeness of Alexander's wife. The good man made a bonfire and burned the effigy, and hoped never to hear the ghostly voices again.

The Missing Kettle

There was a woman who lived on the island of Sanntraigh, and she had only a kettle to hang over the fire to boil her water and cook her food. Every day one of the fairy folk would come to take the kettle. She would slip into the house quietly without saying a word, and grab hold of the kettle handle.

Each time this happened, the kettle handle made a clanking noise and the woman looked up and recited this rhyme:

> A smith is able to make
>
> Cold iron hot with coal.
>
> The due of a kettle is bones,
>
> And to bring it back again whole.

Then the fairy would fly away with the kettle and the woman would not see it again until later in the day, when the fairy brought it back, filled with flesh and bones.

There came at last a day when the woman had to leave home and go on the ferry across to the mainland. She turned to her husband, who was making a rope of heather to keep the thatch on the roof. "Will you say the rhyme that I say when the fairy comes for the kettle?" Her husband said that he would recite the rhyme just as she did, and went back to his work.

After the woman had left to catch the boat, the fairy arrived as usual, and the husband saw her come to the door. When he saw her he started to feel afraid, for unlike his wife he had had no contact with the little people. "If I lock the cottage door," he reasoned to himself, "she will go away and leave the kettle, and it will be just as if she had never come." So the husband locked the door and did not open it when the fairy tried to come in.

But instead of going away, the fairy flew up to the hole in the roof where the smoke from the fire escaped, and before the husband knew what was happening, the creature had made the kettle jump right up and out of the

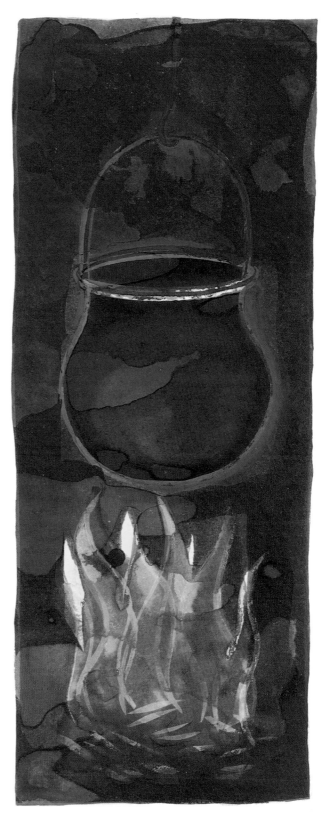

hole. The fairy made away with the kettle before he knew what to do.

When his wife returned that evening, there was no kettle to be seen.

"What have you done with my kettle?" asked the woman.

"I've done nothing with it," said the husband. "But I took fright when the fairy came, closed the door to her, she took the kettle through the roof, and now it is gone."

"You pathetic wretch! Can't you even mind the kettle when I go out for the day?"

The husband tried to tell his wife that the fairy might return the kettle the next day, but the woman would hear nothing of it. Off she went straight away to the knoll where the fairies lived, to see if she could get back the kettle herself.

It was quite dark when she reached the fairies' knoll. The hillside opened to her and when she went in she saw only an old fairy sitting in the corner. The woman supposed that the others were out at their nightly mischief. Soon she found her kettle, and noticed that it still contained the remains of the food the little people had cooked in it.

She picked up the kettle and ran back down the lane, when she heard the sound of dogs chasing her. The old fairy must have let them loose. Thinking quickly, she took out some of the food from the kettle, threw it to the dogs, and hurried on.

This slowed down the dogs, and when they began to catch her up again, she threw down more food. Finally, when she got near her own gate, she poured out the rest of the food, hoping that the dogs would not come into her own house. Then she ran inside and closed the door.

Every day after that the woman watched for the fairy coming to take her kettle. But the little creature never came again.

The Saint and God's Creatures

Long ago, at the time when the first Christians were building their churches in Wales, there lived a young lad called Baglan. He worked for an old holy man, who was struck by the boy's kindness, and his eagerness to serve God.

One day it was cold and the holy man wanted a fire in his room. So he asked Baglan to move some hot coals to make a fire and to his surprise, the boy carried in some red-hot coals in the fabric of his cloak. When the boy had set the coals in the fire, not a bit of his cloak was burned or even singed.

The old holy man knew a miracle when he saw one. "You are meant to do great works for God," said the holy man. "The time is passed when you should stay here serving me." And the old man produced a crook with a shining brass handle and offered it to the lad. "Take this crook, and set off on a journey. The crook will lead your steps to a place where you must build a church. Look out for a tree which bears three different kinds of fruit. Then you will know that you have come to the right spot."

So the young man took the crook and walked southwards a long way. In time Baglan came to a tree. Around the roots of the tree a family of pigs were grubbing for food. In the tree's trunk had nested a colony of bees. And in the branches of the tree was a nest where a pair of crows were feeding their young.

Baglan sensed that this must be the right place. But the tree grew on sloping land, which did not seem good for building. So the young man looked around until he found a nearby area which was flat, and there he began to build his church.

He worked hard on the first day, digging the foundations, and building the first walls, and he slept well after his labours. But in the morning he was dismayed to see that the walls had all fallen down and water was seeping into the foundation

trenches. So the next day, he worked still harder, and raised the walls stronger and higher than before. But when Baglan awoke the next morning, again the walls had been flattened. He tried once more, putting still greater effort into making his building strong. But again the walls were laid low, and Baglan began to despair of ever finishing his church.

Baglan kneeled down to pray, and then he sat down to think. Perhaps he was not building in exactly the right place. So he moved his site nearer the tree, for the holy man had told him to build where he found the tree with three fruits. Straight

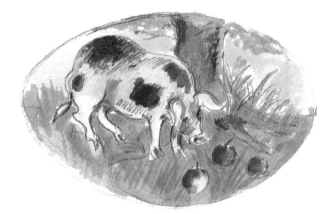

away things began to go better. The pigs, rooting with their snouts, helped him dig out the new foundations. The bees gave him honey. Even the crows offered him crusts of bread that they had scavenged. And this time, Baglan's work was lasting.

So he built and built until his walls surrounded the old tree, leaving windows for the pigs and bees, and a hole in the roof for the birds to fly in and out. As a result, his church looked

rather unusual, but he knew that it was right.

The young man kneeled down and prayed to God in thanks. And when he finished his prayer, he saw that all the animals – the pigs, and the bees, and the crows – had also fallen still and silent, as if they too, were thanking God that the work was completed.

After that, Baglan was always kind to the animals, and taught others to show kindness to them also. His crook may have been a holy relic that guided him to the tree, but even it could be used to scratch the back of the great boar.

Jamie Freel

Jamie Freel's mother was a widow, and they had little money to spare. But Jamie was one of the most hard-working lads in his village, and had a strong pair of arms, so they usually had enough to eat. Every Saturday when Jamie came home, he gave his mother all his wages, and thanked her sincerely when she returned half a penny so that he could buy his tobacco.

A short distance from where Jamie and his mother lived was an old ruined castle. The local people said that this was where the little people lived, and Jamie knew that this was true. He himself had seen them, usually at Halloween, when all the windows of the old ruin lit up, and he could hear their music inside the thick stone walls.

The more he listened to the fairy revels, the more fascinated Jamie became. So the next time Halloween came round, he decided to go to the castle, peer through the window, and see what was going on at close quarters.

When the night came, Jamie took up his cap and called to his mother, "I'm just away up to the castle, to see what is going on there tonight."

"Oh Jamie! You don't want to be risking your skin going there," said his mother. "You are all the sons I have got and I don't want to lose you to the little people."

"Have no fear, mother," he called out, making for the castle.

When Jamie looked through one of the castle windows, little people began to notice him, and he was surprised to hear them calling him by name. "Welcome, Jamie Freel, welcome! Come in and join our revels!" they called. And another of their number cried, "We're off to Dublin tonight to steal a young lady. Will you come along with us?"

Jamie liked the sound of this adventure, and was soon flying

through the air at alarming speed with the fairy host. Each town they passed, one of the little people called out its name, and soon the fairy was calling "Dublin!" and they were coming to land in a grand square in the centre of the city. Before long the fairies had kidnapped a young woman and carried her all the way back home.

Now Jamie was a good-natured lad, and the more he thought about this scheme, the more he was anxious for the feelings of the young lady. So when they were near home, he turned to one of the leaders and said, "You have all had a turn at carrying the lady, please let me carry her now." So it was Jamie who was carrying the girl when they arrived home, and he quickly put her down at his mother's door.

When it became clear that Jamie was going to keep the young woman for himself, the fairies grew spiteful. "Is that all the thanks we get for taking you to Dublin?" they screeched. And they tried turning the girl into all sorts of different shapes

– a black dog, a bar of iron, a wool sack – but still Jamie kept hold of her. In the end, when she had regained her own shape, one of the little folk threw something at the girl.

"There's for your treachery," screamed the creature. "Now she will neither speak nor hear." Then the fairy folk flew off to their castle and left Jamie and his mother staring at the poor girl.

At first, Jamie's mother could little think how they would look after a Dublin girl who could neither speak nor hear. But they managed, as they always had done before, and soon the girl herself was helping the widow with the cooking and housework. She even helped outside, feeding the pig and the fowls, while Jamie worked away mending his fishing nets.

After a year the three had settled down together, although sometimes the girl looked sad and Jamie and his mother guessed that she was thinking of her people and her comfortable home.

When Halloween came again, Jamie decided he would

go and see the fairies once more. His mother tried to stop him, but he was stubborn, and soon he was off across the fields towards the castle.

He crept up to a window and took care not to be seen this time. Soon he heard the fairies talking about what had happened a year before. The fairy who had made the girl deaf and dumb spoke up: "Little does Jamie Freel know that a few drops of this liquid would make her better again."

Now Jamie knew what to do. He burst into the castle and stole the liquid while the little people were still welcoming him. Then he ran home and gave the girl the liquid before anyone could stop him.

The girl was happier now she could talk again, and Jamie and she decided they would go to Dublin to find her parents. After a long and arduous journey they arrived at the girl's family home. But when they knocked at the door, no one recognised her. Her parents insisted that their only daughter had died over a year ago and that they had buried her. Even when she showed them her ring, they would not believe it, accusing her of being someone who had stolen the ring and was pretending to be their daughter.

Jamie and the girl looked at each other. They realised that they would have to tell the people the story of the fairies. It was Jamie who told the story of the flight to Dublin, how the young lady was stolen, and how she had been made deaf and dumb. When he had finished, the old man and woman saw that they had been deceived and that this indeed was their daughter. They showered the girl with kisses – and embraced Jamie, too.

When the time came for Jamie to return home, the girl wanted to go too, for the pair had become inseparable. The girl's parents realised that the two should be married, and sent for Jamie's mother to come to Dublin for the grand ceremony. Afterwards they were all happy, and Jamie felt that all his hard work had been richly rewarded.

Why the Manx Cat Has No Tail

In ancient times Noah was collecting together two of every animal to put in his ark. But the she-cat refused to go in before she had caught a mouse. After all, she thought, there might be no mice where she was going, and she was mad for meat.

So while all the other animals were lining up two by two, she was nowhere to be seen.

"Well," said Noah. "There will be no she-cat, and that is all there is to it."

All the other beasts were aboard, and Noah began to close the door, when up ran the she-cat. She made a great leap and squeezed through, but the closing door sliced her tail clean off.

No one bothered to mend the tail, so to this day, the cats of Man go tail-less.

But the she-cat thought it was worth it for the mouse.